**Tiger**sprung

Ulrich **Lehmann**

The MIT Press ▪ Cambridge, Massachusetts ▪ London, England

# **Tiger**sprung

Fashion in Modernity

This book was set in Frutiger by Graphic Composition.

Printed and bound in the United States of America.

Library of Congress Cataloging-in-Publication Data

Lehmann, Ulrich.

    Tigersprung : fashion in modernity / Ulrich Lehmann.

      p. cm.

    Includes bibliographical references and index.

    ISBN 0-262-12231-6 (hc. : alk. paper)

     1. Costume—History. 2. Costume—Psychological aspects. 3. Fashion—Psychological aspects.

    4. Modernism (Aesthetics)   I. Title.


GT580 .L44 2000

391—dc21

00-032901

meinen **Eltern**

meinen **Schwestern**

*Die Bildung hängt an seinem Leib wie ein Kleid an einer Modellpuppe.*
*Bestenfalls sind solche Gelehrte Probiermamsellen der Fortschrittsmode.*

**Karl Kraus**

Contents

# Introduction

This is a text on philosophical ideas in sartorial fashion. It is also a text on complementary ideas in the arts and society in the second half of the nineteenth century and the first quarter of the twentieth. The parameters that determine the aesthetic expression of these ideas, and that are also reflected in it, can be grouped under the term *modernité*.[1] Yet *modernité* not only defines the pictorial and verbal expressions that have shaped the past 150 years; more specifically it stands for the stylistic qualities of what is modern. It incorporates the idea that an artist decidedly embraces all the manifestations of modern life and reflects them in his or her art, without seeking refuge in the language of the classical. On the contrary, for the artist in modernity, beauty lies expressively in the contemporary and no recourse to the ancient ideal of sublime beauty is permitted. Fashion is the supreme expression of that contemporary spirit. It changes constantly and remains necessarily incomplete; it is transitory, mobile, and fragmentary. This quality ties it in with the pace and rhythm of modern life.

The hallmarks of *la modernité* found their most immediate reflection in *la mode*.[2] The artists who realized this concept began to explore sartorial fashion in or-

**1.**

Félicien Rops, *Modernité,* ca. 1883. Pencil and white chalk on paper, 20.7 × 15.2 cm.
Collection Babut du Marès, Namur.

*"But life, modern life, MODERNITÉ, where is it? And here it is, around the corner, everywhere, in the drawing
room, in the street, the real modern life that cries, laughs, entertains, and kills itself, is put on display under
the sun of gold plates and rags, in its joy and sorrow, with its nervous and strained physiognomy that does
not resemble any other."—From a letter by Rops, March 1878.*

der to arrive at a pictorial or metaphoric vocabulary that they would use to describe, analyze, and criticize contemporary society. The emergence of the aesthetic *modernité* therefore closely relates to the progress of *mode*—as a commodity, but also as an art form in its own right.

The stage for this original interplay between aesthetic concept and sartorial expression is Parisian society from the late 1840s to the late 1920s. In it the tolerance of the ephemeral (as fashion is always perceived), together with the emergence of the fashion industry proper, created a climate in which a discussion of clothes that went beyond the mere appreciation of their representational value flourished. The view of sartorial fashion as the pacesetter and indicator of stylistic developments within the nineteenth and early twentieth century seemed possible only in Paris. The economic circumstances that created an affluent bourgeois class with its conspicuous consumption, and the political requirements that made consumption the guarantee of social stability, provided the backdrop for the rise of haute couture. This craft, which soon developed into an industry, married the portable character of the sartorial commodity with the exclusivity of the work of art. It became the paradigm for a society dependent on both industrial production and aestheticized diversion.

There exist a number of excellent studies on diverse aspects of *modernité,* most notably in France, where investigations into the stylistic qualities of modern life traditionally have informed academic discourse. Yet numerous other writers have also contributed psychological, sociological, and philosophical analyses to this field.[3] The present text does not attempt to explain the various concepts of modernity, let alone embark on a "postmodernist" critique of them. It focuses on selected stylistics of modernity, for which I employ the Baudelairean coinage of *modernité.*

Studies on sartorial fashion are also very numerous indeed. Especially since the 1980s, an extensive body of writing has been devoted to clothes and their cultural value, accompanying the works by costume historians and an array of monographs on fashion designers and stylists.[4] Missing, however, are substantial investigations into the meaning of fashion that go beyond notions in the sociology or psychology of dress. Anybody interested in clothing on an "intellectual" level is offered a profusion of studies on why people wear, or have worn, certain shapes or styles. Alternatively, one can read studies on what the choice of a garment says about the mental makeup or sexual proclivity of an individual; likewise there are many texts on, for example, the emergence of subcultures that are assimilated into the sartorial mainstream. But an abstract analysis of fashion, on par with attempts to construct a philosophy of art, of music, or of literature, remains largely absent.

Obviously, one can argue that after exploring the philosophies of the "fine arts," including architecture, and their subsequent tentative application to some of the crafts (e.g., interior design), academics inevitably would turn to fashion, because they are always searching for new areas whose investigation might win them distinction. Also, the rash of fashion writing and theorizing in the 1980s and 1990s could be attributed vaguely to fin de siècle spirit; in the late nineteenth century, such spirit led to decorative excesses that proclaimed the favoring of form and appearance over content, glossing over cultural and societal anxieties much as fashion (regarded so often as an insubstantial surface) is said to do.

Since such explanations necessarily go to the heart of the present book, and since I am adamant that I will not be caught self-analyzing it at the start, the reader is left to make up her or his mind. Should the work, after being read, be dismissed as facile and "fashionable," I can always defuse critique by pretending that the topic, after all, demands such a treatment.

What follows is not a complete redressing of inadequacies in earlier philosophical analyses of the sartorial. *Tigersprung* rather attempts to trace a philosophy of fashion, as understood by a number of singularly sensible individuals who developed— independently, but having recourse to each other—the hermeneutical templates for such a philosophy. The study begins in 1840 with Charles Baudelaire and Stéphane Mallarmé, continues with Georg Simmel, and arrives, a century later, at Walter Benjamin, Louis Aragon, and André Breton.[5] This choice of authors and their selected studies, essays, and poetry clearly suggests an attempt to read sartorial fashion comprehensively as a paradigm of modern culture. A feature of this book is therefore the parallel concepts of *mode* and *modernité*. It is not only the etymological root—the Latin *modus*—that betrays the close relation between these two phenomena; the parallel chronological development of their inherent ideas, aesthetic expressions, and historical interpretations also shows that *la modernité* and *la mode* are indeed sisters in spirit and appearance.

The first chapter deals with the origin of *modernité* in the midst of the nineteenth century. For Charles Baudelaire, its most famous advocate, the birth of modernity is conceivable only through a deep understanding of fashion. His subsequent discussion classes the concept of a transitory fashion with a developing artistic avant-garde.

His ideas are taken up by another great "modernist," Stéphane Mallarmé, discussed in chapter 2. In 1874 he wrote and edited a fashion journal titled *La Dernière Mode* as the supreme example of a poetic and commercial *Gesamtkunstwerk,* in the spirit of both *mode* and *modernité.* That he chose to conceal himself with female pseudonyms in his endeavor adds even more complexity to the elegance and conviction of his writing.

This symbolist spirit of the late nineteenth century is followed by the German philosopher-turned-sociologist Georg Simmel. His four essayistic variations on fashion became infused with a radical spirit of modernity, subordinating its stylistic qualities to the new political and social configuration of the turn of the century and after. The conflicts of modernity that Marx had observed as a contemporary of Baudelaire began to coin substantial analyses of modern life. This inquiry into fashion's rationale is the core of the third chapter.

Chapter 4 treats Simmel's "heir" in regarding fashion as the obvious determinant of modernity, Walter Benjamin. My reading of his unfinished *Passagenarbeit* as a philosophical work in progress on sartorial fashion may seem an uncommon, even frivolous, addition to the numerous studies on Benjamin and his *Arcades Project,* studies written under various theoretical premises mainly in Germany and the United States. Yet Benjamin's writing is clearly a sourcebook of modernity, describing nineteenth-century Paris with the aesthetic and political hindsight of the late 1920s and '30s. The sheer number of quotations on and references to clothes and accessories in the *Arcades Project* is proof of Benjamin's infatuation with both the transitory and the paradigmatic quality of fashion. In his diverse writings between 1929 and 1940 the stylistic qualities of modern, metropolitan life are fused with a radical *modernité* that possesses revolutionary potential.

Chapter 5, on dada, surrealism, and fashion, aims to consider these philosophies in their artistic aspects as well as in their theoretical extension. It views the sartorial commodity as object of a modern mythology, imbued with a mysterious yet radical spirit, and provides examples to illustrate some of the hermeneutical tenets of fashion that are offered in the first four chapters of the book.

The title *Tigersprung* (the tiger's leap) originates in Benjamin's very last writings. Through fashion's ferocious leap, Benjamin brought together various splintered parts of modernity to form a new concept of history, a political ideal, and an aesthetic credo. One late fragment in his "Über den Begriff der Geschichte" ("Theses on the Philosophy of History") singled out fashion as the metaphor for the construction of history, for the definition of a special historical moment:

■

*History is object of a structure whose site is not homogeneous and empty time but one filled by now-time [Jetztzeit]. For Robespierre the Rome of antiquity was thus charged with now-time and blasted from the continuum of history. The French Revolution regarded itself as Rome reincarnate. It quoted ancient Rome as fashion quotes a past attire. Fashion has the scent of the modern wherever it stirs in the thicket of what has been. It is the tiger's leap into the past. Yet this leap occurs in an arena commanded by the ruling class. The very same leap in the open air of history is the dialectical one, which Marx has understood as the revolution.*[6]

■

Hidden in the depths of this enigmatic quotation are four separate reflections on fashion:

*1. In quoting from past clothing styles, fashion is able to break the historical continuum and to become both transitory and transhistorical.*

*2. Fashion is irreverent in its quotations. Its superficial appearance creates a strange independence from recognizable contents—and from this, its potential for hermeneutics ensues.*

*3. The (tiger's) leap is regarded by Benjamin as dialectical, following the philosophical tradition of Hegel, Engels, Marx, and Lukács. Through the quotation, fashion fuses the thesis (the eternal or classical ideal) with its antithesis (the openly contemporary). The apparent opposition between the eternal and the ephemeral is rendered obsolete by the leap that needs the past to continue the contemporary. Correspondingly, the transhistorical describes the position of fashion as detached both from the eternal, that is, the aesthetic, ideal and the continuous progression of history. Through the* Tigersprung *fashion is able to jump from the contemporary to the ancient and back without resting solely in one temporal or aesthetic configuration.[7] This generates the novel view on historical development. If coupled with the dialectical image, the tiger's leap "in the open air of history" marks a convergence that is revolutionary in essence.*

*4. Fashion is its most evocative in an imagined, "dated" condition. The "clothes of five years ago" (as Benjamin postulates vis-à-vis surrealism; see section 5.2)—that is, the expression of a past that has just ceased to be fashionable—are the ones fueling the imagination and phantasmagoria necessary for Benjamin's individual historiography.*

The third meditation within the fragment, which is integral to the Benjaminian tiger's leap, provides one key to the book as a whole: fashion is regarded not merely as the transitory and commodified result of craftsmanship but as a social force—a stylistic revolution sharing the same cultural features with a political one. The eminent Marxist historian Eric Hobsbawn comes to a similar conclusion in his series of studies on modern history: "Why brilliant fashion-designers, a notoriously non-analytic breed, sometimes succeed in anticipating the shape of things to come better than professional predictors, is one of the most obscure questions in history; and, for the historian of culture, one of the most central. It is certainly crucial to anyone who wants to understand the importance of the age of cataclysms on the world of high culture, the elite arts, and, above all, the avantgarde."[8]

The following pages stress a second point, the transhistorical character of sartorial fashion: it always appears as the most immediate present, affecting the future with its constant changes, yet it always quotes from the past. Its creators in haute couture "anticipate the things to come" so well because they do not anticipate at all—they merely create the perfect expression of the contemporary spirit, which, ironically, man-

**2.**
Max Ernst, *Man and Nude Woman,* ca. 1929. Collage on paper, 14.3 × 11.2 cm.
Private collection, Paris.

ifests itself in clothes whose design is drawn from a past sourcebook. They are able to recognize such expressions before they are generally realized, because of the absolute proximity of their works to the human body and its emotive responses. Clothes are closer to the spirit than intellectual contemplation or analysis is; and in the hand of a truly progressive designer, they can operate on an equally fundamental level. Therefore, they provide a veritable embodiment of a cultural concept, whose brief existence is itself a sign of fashion's growing dominance—it appears first reflected in a new dress or suit of a particular season, before it is disseminated in the media.

One could argue, for instance, that the apparently random cultural borrowing and quotation of "postmodernism" have been anticipated in the sartorial citation of couturiers such as Paul Poiret, Elsa Schiaparelli, or Yves Saint Laurent long before Jean-François Lyotard began to write his postulates. Similarly, the "deconstruction" of modern culture, especially literature, could be said to have been somewhat anticipated by Cristóbal Balenciaga's semi-fitted suits, his pronounced darts and seams of the 1950s and his use of patterns to indicate the cut of the fabric, thus displaying the underlying construction and not the "look" as the raison d'être of the garment.[9]

The characteristics of high fashion were established at the origin of modernity, the latter half of the nineteenth century. Subsequent sartorial avant-gardes are always *passéiste*. That is the third main point of this text: fashion has to mark absolute novelty yet has already died when it appears in the physical world (Simmel in particular emphasizes this idea). In order to become the new, fashion always cites the old—not simply the ancient or classical, but their reflection within its own sartorial past.

Since the time of Baudelaire, the artistic avant-garde has thrived on this concept. The *modernité* it incorporates is, by definition, ephemeral and eternal at the same time. In its urge to be radically new, it has to be conscious of what came before. Fashion is the perfect vehicle for fusing novel aesthetics with an underlying recourse to the past. But—and this qualification is crucial—it is only the truly modern artist who uses this device deliberately. His or her art becomes self-referential, ironically conscious of the quotation from the past. Essentially, *la modernité* equals *la mode,* because it was sartorial fashion that made modernity aware of its constant urge and necessity to quote from itself. Research into modernity generally neglects this idea and favors the ideal of progressive development within the avant-garde. By the same token, some proclaim modernity as "finished," having been succeeded by a "postmodern condition." As Benjamin shows, *Moderne,* in its necessary relation with *Mode,* has no certainty of progress; it is made up, through quotation, of autonomous fragmented periods that may relate independently to each other. As in fashion, this constant change and renewal continues modernity and thus renders unnecessary the qualifying term "postmodern."[10]

Although I do not aim to venture into a metacritical position, since the actual discussion and interpretation of primary sources is a sufficiently large task, a brief remark on the methodology of this book may be useful. Neither a retelling of modernity's inventory nor a deconstructivist entry into a post-Hegelian condition, *Tigersprung* refers back to the dialectical tradition. Thus it will not simply follow the succession of modernist styles or theories, nor will it shy away from exploring "old-fashioned" dialectical oppositions.

In the following pages, I show that fashion opens up a novel way of looking at modernity that can be explored from a number of artistic, sociological, philosophical, and historical perspectives. To keep the argument coherent and relatively concise, I have drawn on a limited frame of cultural references—one that can be criticized for adhering perhaps too obviously to the canon of modernism. From Baudelaire and Proust to Benjamin and Breton, the writers and visual artists cited here have been discussed numerous times. Yet precisely because their aesthetic experiences appear to be well known, examining the surprising impact of sartorial fashion on these artists within modernity suggests a substantially different way of looking at *mode* and *modernité.* While providing a complete study of neither modernity nor fashion, I present ideas and expressions that wear their elegant and ephemeral associations on their sleeves, yet always retain paradigmatic value up them.

My thanks go to those who helped and supported me throughout the completion of this book. Roger Conover, Alice Falk, Matthew Abbate, and Ori Kometani at the MIT Press for making its publication possible; Professor Dawn Ades for supervising its first incarnation as a dissertation at the University of Essex and for continuing her support;

Dr. Valerie Steele for her generous encouragement; Beatrice, Honey, Jessica, Matthias, Richard, and Uli for asking questions and then listening patiently to unfermented ramblings; Nico for painstakingly reading the text and making invaluable suggestions; the staff at the Lipperheid'sche Kostümbibliothek, especially Frau Dr. Rasche (Berlin); the British Library, the Courtauld Institute of Art, and the National Art Library (London); the Fashion Institute of Technology (New York); the Bibliothèque des Arts Décoratifs, the Palais Galliéra, and the Bibliothèque Nationale (Paris); Hans-Ulrich Müller-Schwefe (Frankfurt a.M.) for important editorial advice; Dr. Rüdiger Kramme (Universität Bielefeld), Professor Hans Mayer and Gertrud Rückert (Tübingen), Christoph Gödde at the Theodor W. Adorno-Archiv (Frankfurt a.M.), and Dr. W. Schultze, Humboldt-Universität (Berlin), for answering my queries; and the Kent Institute of Art & Design in Rochester (Great Britain), especially Professor Peter Robertson and Brian Bell, for research leave and academic advice.

Most of all I thank my sisters and my parents; to them this book is dedicated.

Wherever possible, I have used and indicated existing sources in English of the quoted passages. However, many of the texts—especially by Mallarmé and Benjamin—have not been translated yet, and in such cases the renderings are my own. Also, I have slightly modified a few of the existing translations, when (rarely) I perceived them to be factually wrong or when they seemed not to reflect the sartorial metaphors employed in the author's argument. Poetry, including poems in prose, are retained in the original throughout—translations are provided at the beginning of the respective endnotes.

The pictures accompanying the text are rarely intended to work as direct illustration; rather they provide associative visual parallels to some of the points raised. I have chosen to combine them with quotes intended to make such connections apparent.

**1**

# Baudelaire, Gautier, and the Origins of Fashion in Modernity

*Toute la modernité est fournie par lecteur.*
*Le chapeau—etc.*


Stéphane Mallarmé, Le "Livre" (ca. 1876)[1]


# ■ 1.1 Fashion Written I

To write about fashion, to discuss its impact and importance, always means to transform the fleeting and transitory into the statue-like and permanent, if only through black letters on a white sheet of paper. Fashion as a topic remains embroiled and disputed because of its alleged lack of substance—in artistic as well as metaphysical terms.[2] The profound and eternal are considered worthy of intellectual analysis; what is transient and fugitive will nearly always be equated consciously or unconsciously with the facile and futile. Yet herein lies fashion's most absorbing fascination: it challenges us to transpose transitoriness, also the hallmark of modernity, into a medium of high regard, while maintaining its distinct characteristics; to theorize and analyze, yet not to petrify.

Following the motto above, *la modernité*—and for Stéphane Mallarmé, as we will notice also in his journal, implicitly *la mode*—is understood differently by each reader. One is left with an individual interpretation, with an individual reading of its poetic expression. Any analysis of modernity therefore will remain incomplete and dispersed into a multitude of fragments—explanations from artists, historians, economists, philosophers, and so on. But the opposite condition also is inherent in the dialectics of modernity as well as of fashion. Admittedly, the amount and the diversity of fragmented details seem to prevent any overall impression, yet only the assembly of many particles can indicate the style and appearance of this theoretical, or poetic, figure. The more skilled the historian, the poet, or indeed the couturier is, the more obvious, meaningful, and beautiful its appearance will be. To arrive at a valid interpretation of both modernity and fashion, one must present the fragment while keeping an eye on the overall design.

In attempting to underline modernity's impact, one must evaluate quotations from the past—quotes that refer sometimes to the "eternal" yet more often to antiquity, to humanist values that implicitly transcend time and outlast changes in interpretation. In a similar vein, fashion is granted substantiality when related to a past as an eternalized ideal. But such references to the past only reveal a misunderstanding of the nature of modernity.

This chapter presents elements in the origin of the term *modernité* and explains its original dependence on sartorial fashion. It highlights the problematic effort to argue for fashion's profundity and demonstrates its significance for hermeneutics—starting, ironically, with its critical negation.

## ■ 1.2 *Mode et modernité*

### 1.2.1 Charles Baudelaire, the Originator

One of the first and most profound analyses of *modernité* is Charles Baudelaire's famous essay, *Le Peintre de la vie moderne,* originally conceived between 1859 and 1861 as an interpretation of the work of the draftsman Constantin Guys. Fashion not only constituted the actual inspiration for the greatest part of Guys's drawings but, more important, stimulated and guided Baudelaire's analysis; in due course it became the paradigm for modernity itself.

The idea that fashion had profound influence on Baudelaire has rarely been discussed in detail.[3] Yet though the sartorial is integral for understanding the confluence of Baudelaire's view of both modern art and modern life with Guys's drawings, fashion appears in retrospective interpretations only when it was regarded as surpassing mere flippancy, as going beyond the facade of fashion illustrations that would inspire not only Baudelaire's interpretation of Guys but also his formulation of aesthetics proper.

Among these interpretations, that by art critic Gustave Geffroy deserves particular attention because of Geffroy's collection of Guys's work, his intimate knowledge of nineteenth-century literature, and, most of all, his interest in fashion; the latter two characteristics were generated through his friendship with Stéphane Mallarmé, as we will see later on. Geffroy sets Guys in marked contrast to Baudelaire:

*He does not eschew any part of fashion; on the contrary, he depicts with scrupulous care every aspect of clothing he sees; but these are always depicted on a large scale, similar to the way in which the ancients depicted drapery and the old masters have depicted the garb of their age. Also, one never feels compelled to read these images as "fashion illustrations," first because the dress here accompanies the face, it keeps to its place and emanates a strong and calm harmony; second, because the face is animated by such a particular and vigorous feeling for life that it is really the only thing one immediately sees, and it requires a conscious effort to perceive anything else. Only then one looks at the dress, or rather at a clothed body presented in its shape and posture with all the flexibility and warmth of life; one looks thus at the face, body, and dress together; one looks at a human being.[4]*

The critic fails to realize that fashion is not meant to remain calm and composed; it did not serve simply as adornment or backdrop for the mostly schematized, in Guys's case figures. Face, body, and clothing—not "costume"—create the human being; yet it is precisely sartorial fashion that establishes the depicted as a *social* being, as a woman

**3.**

Max Ernst, *Baudelaire Comes Home Late*. Pen and india ink on paper. Published in *Littérature,* no. 8 (1923). Previously in the collection of André Breton.

or man who is set within progressing time. Guys's work has the merit of underscoring a social connotation while preserving the persistent aesthetic value of fashion, even within the most particular sartorial expression at the time of the artist's observation.

Yet this very aspect, neglected by Geffroy, rendered Guys's work a potent symbol for Baudelaire's fundamental aspiration in discussing modernity: to discover eternal beauty within the most fugitive expressions. What limits Geffroy's interpretation (and that of others) is his negation of fashion's transitory potential to crystallize constant change in one short moment. Through it the poet discovers the elemental dialectics that determine modernity: the coexistence of the ephemeral and the sublime, the fugitive and the profound. Geffroy attempts to omit the first component in order to highlight the second, which he considers infinitely more suitable as an artistic subject.

But for Baudelaire the original inspiration for his analysis was precisely the ephemeral and abased *gravures de modes.* He writes:

■

*I have before me a series of fashion plates dating from the Revolution and finishing more or less with the Consulate. These costumes, which seem laughable to many thoughtless people—people who are grave without true gravity—have a double natured charm, one both artistic and historical. They are often very beautiful and drawn with wit; but what to me is every bit as important, and what I am happy to find in all, or almost all of them, is the moral and aesthetic feeling of their time. The idea of beauty which man creates for himself imprints itself on his whole attire, crumples or stiffens the dress, rounds off or squares his gesture, and in the long run even ends the subtle penetrating of the very features of his face. Man ends by looking like his ideal self. These engravings can be translated either into beauty or ugliness; in one direction they become caricatures, in the other, antiques statues.*[5]

■

The engravings Baudelaire chose so carefully for literary inspiration were designed by Pierre de La Mésangère, an "erstwhile teacher of philosophy and literature" at the beginning of the nineteenth century.[6] He not only drew the sophisticated illustrations but, more important, added elaborate analyses of the sartorial in his *Journal des Dames et des Modes.*[7] Baudelaire confesses in a letter that he used the magazine "not just for the images, but for the text"![8] Thus it immediately becomes clear that although the aesthete greatly appreciates the sensual character of clothes, it is their written form that supplies epistemological significance. Expressed through the plates is the notion that fashion possesses dual characteristics; its impact is aesthetic as well as historical. Relying on the mediation of illustration and written critique, Baudelaire starts by establishing fashion as an art form in itself and as a timely reminder of the past, a past that is far from gone: it lives on through the clothes and is revived in the details of sartorial styles created anew each season.[9] Fashion not only is transitory but, as will be emphasized by Walter Benjamin later, is also immanent in the *transhistorical.*

At first, however, fashion does incorporate the idea of the eternal for Baudelaire; once it is created as beautiful, the body it clothes becomes a statue. Thus again it seems that to elevate fashion, to give it substance, one must establish a relation to antiquity. In itself, sartorial fashion stands, almost by definition, for the absolutely new—for permanent novelty and constant, insatiable change. Accordingly, for Benjamin fashion is revolutionary, detached from the continuous progression of history and the rather static concept of eternal beauty, as we will see. Since this characteristic of fashion appears self-evident, it was necessary to accentuate its opposite so that the dialectics of fashion might become clear. Therefore Baudelaire begins with his famous demand "to extract from fashion whatever element it may contain of poetry within history, to distill the eternal from the transitory."[10]

This aim will remain preeminent in the quest for modernity. And thus we see why *la mode et la modernité* are inextricably linked. Each needs to seek out the poetic and eternal element, the expression of permanence—not to lend it artistic or historical gravity, but to explain its metaphysical impact. Without the sublime in fashion's dialectical aesthetics, the ephemeral as its opposite and predecessor cannot exist; without the connotation of antiquity, modernity loses its raison d'être—its adversary and point of friction, which is also its stimulant. Note that this is not simple set of oppositions but a hermeneutical apparatus in constant flux. The modern does not regard the past as a defeated enemy. But even so, it subverts the static view of an eternal arsenal of values so often propagated by classical historiography.

Fashion and modernity, as the expressions of elementary progress, need the past as (re)source and point of reference, only to plunder and transform it with an insatiable appetite for advance. Without a fixed base against which to distinguish themselves, their haste appears without direction. Thus the quest for the modern reexamines, with a profound sense of self-directed irony, its own societal and poetic fabric again and again in order to find an element of the eternal (perhaps sublime), against which to set its inherently fugitive and ephemeral characteristics. The "eternal" marks the past—but merely one fragment of it, and not the concept of the ancients (*anciens*) itself, as we will learn (see especially the beginning of chapter 3). There is no fundamental preference for the modern over the old, only an instantaneous liking—or the liking of an instant—that is significant for the moment but all too ready to make way for new expressions. If such transitoriness appears to weaken the aesthetic significance of *modernité,* one must not forget that this concept is by its very nature not static but transitory, a figure to be regarded from as many viewpoints as possible.

The artist within modernity, as Baudelaire represented Guys, is confronted with the task of pausing and tracing sublime beauty within the speed of modern life. His aim is not to separate but to *dégager,* that is, to release and redeem, as he would otherwise fall back on the time-defying attitude of longing for a distant past—an attitude well known to Baudelaire and his fellow artists. Whereas most of the Romantic poets had met the emerging industrialization and commercialization of their societies with an imploring glance back at an idealized past, the artists in the mid–nineteenth century turned the inevitable to their advantage. They took up the challenge to offer a poetic antidote while simultaneously mirroring modern society. Two men especially (who previously both had ascribed themselves to the Romantic cause) inquired into modernity—most successfully through a written analysis of fashion: Baudelaire and his friend and fellow poet Théophile Gautier. And the two have been credited, in different ways, with the coinage of *modernité* as a neologism for the aesthetic and metaphysical principle behind modern life.

**1.2.2** Théophile Gautier, the Contemporary

Late in 1863, when Baudelaire's *Le Peintre* finally began to appear on the pages of *Le Figaro* (the first studies for the essay had been composed as early as 1859),[11] the sec-ond volume of the new French dictionary, compiled by Émile Littré, was finally pub-lished in Paris. The entries for *mode* and *modernité* read:

▪

**2. MODE** *(mo-d'),* s.f.//**1°** *Manière, fantasie. . . .* **2°** *Usage passager qui dépend du goût du caprice. . . .* **4°** *Modes, au pluriel, signifie les ajustements, les parures à la mode; mais dans cette acception, il ne se dit qu'en parlant de ce qui sert à l'habille-ment des dames. . . .*

**†MODERNITÉ** *(mo-dèr-ni-té),* s.f. *Néologisme. Qualité de ce qui est moderne. D'un côté, la modernité la plus extrême, de l'autre, l'amour austère de l'antique. TH. GAUTIER, Moniteur univ. 8 juill. 1867.*[12]

▪

The entry for *modernité* is a later addition, included from the second edition (1869) on-ward. Yet the lack of insight into the ambiguous character of modernity is already evi-dent in the definition of *mode,* which fails to treat fashion as signifier. For Littré the modern is but a capricious contrast to the past, as he sets "the most extreme moder-nity" against "the austere love for antiquity." In an earlier entry on *le moderne,* he traces back the meaning to a fundamental argument—to *"[l]a querelle des anciens et des modernes* [the dispute between ancients and moderns], a dispute that originated in the seventeenth century over the question whether the ancients or the moderns could claim superiority in spiritual matters."[13] The lexicographer made no attempt at a synthesis, and the *querelle* was carried into the nineteenth century. Modernity was not perceived as a dual character, let alone as the dialectical figure it assume in later decades, but simply as the latter part of a juxtaposition of old and new (of thesis and antithesis, if you will).

Littré took the last line of his entry from a text by Gautier, expressing a notion of *modernité* decidedly different from that of Baudelaire. Gautier is credited with the first documented usage of this neologism in its proper, stylistically apt sense. Tellingly, it is found in the official mouthpiece of Louis Napoleon's Second Empire, *Le Moniteur Universel*.[14] Its feuilleton contained a book review written by Gautier on a work about the Danish sculptor Bertel Thorvaldsen: "M. Eugène Plon has come to describe life and work in a magnificent opus that rests close to us on the table where we are writing this article. Thus on one side we have the most extreme modernity; on the other an austere love of antiquity. Here, the spirit fired by the hand racing across the paper; there the marble, hard and cold, hammered out by a powerful mallet."[15] Not fashion illustrations but the reproductions of marble statues inspired this reflection on modernity, in which journalism serves as the antithesis to classical sculpture. The fleeting glance at the work of art prompts the text, rapidly turned out by the reviewer. He does not pause to reflect but merely delivers the product as expediently and profitably as possible. Modernity here appears as nothing but the expression of literary commodities as part of the social life in the late 1860s; the past, as a reassuring contrast, maintains its immovable status, sublimely beautiful and eternally virtuous.

Yet Littré is not quite thorough in his etymological research. In fact, the first published use of *modernité* by Gautier occurred in the review of a fashionable work of art. In it, not surprisingly, sartorial fashion embodies the newly found modernity. Gautier describes in his *Salon de 1852* the work of Édouard Dubufe, a painter very much *en vogue* during the Second Empire:

*Therefore one is wrong to affect a certain revulsion or at least a certain disdain for purely contemporary expressions. For our part, we think that there are new effects and unexpected aspects in the intelligent and faithful representation of what we call modernity* [modernité]. *Thus when it comes to portraits one has to shake off the slavery of the old masters. . . . More than anybody else the portraitist can provide an idea of his epoch and make his painting bear an exact date. . . . The three portraits exhibited by him [Dubufe] . . . express with spiritual negligence the affectations of an idle dilettantism; his quick sketches of the high life are surprising in the nonchalance*

**4.**

Untitled photograph from the early 1860s. Daugerreotype.

*"I love clothes as I love books, to touch them, to play with them."—Gabrielle Chanel.*

*of the attitudes they portray. Above all, they are moderns, modern in their poses, in their intentions, in their clothes and accessories.*[16]

∎

Here, Gautier considers a variant of the *querelle*. For him modern art has to deal with modern life, with its trends and appearances as well as with its spirit. Yet this artistic rendition should not remain on the surface, as does Dubufe's with its plain representation of fashionable frocks; it should discover new effects and aspects through an "intelligent" investigation into modernity. In fashion, this entails using clothes as an abstract indicator of a contemporary aesthetic tendency, not just as an illustration of the latest modish style.

Both of Gautier's uses of *la modernité* point to a mutual configuration of commercial viability and recognition of contemporary style. For the reign of Louis Napoleon this combination proves significant. His government relied heavily on the contrast of a past as a static and historic fact—not to be questioned, let alone set in relation with the transitory present—with the facile life of conspicuous consumption. The reputation of the Second Empire was based on his uncle's politics and military exploits, displayed as grandiose, powerful, and, above all, belonging to a distant era. As its fugitive and harmless opposite, modernity was acceptable, even welcomed. Displayed as modern antithesis to the world of classic virtues—perversely associated with both Napoleon I's reign and that of his nephew—it was meant to generate production and consumption, particularly of luxury goods, and thus to offer a world of novelties and distractions. And any possible criticism of this state could be easily qualified or deflated by referring to the elevated condition of antiquity, whose civic virtues were, after all, fundamental to the idealized society governed by the present emperor.

The contemporary world was justifiably regarded as a marketplace,[17] and literary production was by no means an exception to the rule, as Baudelaire had realized early. He was much more critical than Gautier when it came to comprehending the implications of *modernité*. His "Du chic et du poncif" (1846) implicitly analyzes the difference between a modernity misunderstood and its actual paradigmatic quality: "The chic, a dreadful and bizarre word of modern fabrication[,] . . . is the abuse of memory; moreover it is the memory of the hand rather than an intellectual one"[18]—and the memory of the feebly racing hand observed by Gautier, at that. The vagary, the change of stylistics without substance—that is, without any awareness of the past—is simply chic, whereas the creation of style based on an idea (or a remembrance) of underlying aesthetics requires extraordinary efforts.

"To create a *poncif,* that's genius. / I need to create a *poncif.*"[19] It appears as no accident that the *poncif*—the artist's trademark, as employed with a touch of irony by Baudelaire—in French also denotes a pattern: in this case, a pattern that could be seen emerging in the different interpretations of *mode et modernité* by the poet and by the lexicographer. When Littré defined fashion after Gautier, he described it as "passing taste" or "caprice"; only its plural refers to the sartorial, and then exclusively to female clothing. Its singularity, in the literal sense of the word, is negated. Fashion is *du chic;* yet it obviously cannot create a *poncif,* the structural, and thus implicitly substantial, cultural pattern. Baudelaire, in contrast, reflects on the metaphysical *poncif* within changing fashion, which has to be traced and abstracted without losing any of its beauty and aesthetic appeal.

Yet behind the *poncif* also stood distinctly material reasoning. The proximity of fashion and modernity could be seen as nothing but the plain reflection of market strategies. In the late 1930s Benjamin would judge Baudelaire's (poetic) pattern: "Baudelaire was perhaps the first to conceive of an originality appropriate to the market, which was at the time just for that reason more original than any other."[20] The line between the positive adaptation of novelties as fashion's raison d'être and mere adherence to the latest commodity is very thin indeed. Thus Benjamin concludes, "the milieu of the market . . . determined a mode of production and of living very different from that of earlier poets. It was necessary for Baudelaire to claim the dignity of a poet in a society no longer capable of conferring dignity."[21] The danger that the fugitive and ephemeral character of the poetic object will lead to superficial and short-lived art appears immanent. Gautier mistakes the acceptance by his friend Baudelaire of fashion as paradigmatic for aesthetics and social existence in modernity for a facile adherence to all fashions symbolized by commercial vagaries. Though his doubts with regard to *les modes* were justified by the growing dominance of the market, the conclusion Gautier reaches, as expressed in his work for *Le Moniteur Universel,* had the opposite effect of that he intended. In his opposition to fashion, he left the avant-garde and became retrospective and dependent on the benevolence of the official Second Empire—which, ironically, needed the fashion industry to ensure its political and material continuation.

Before his conversion to the static and the status quo, fashion had offered Gautier possibilities that he regarded much as Baudelaire did. Moreover, fashion had promised the capacity to bridge the dichotomy between the moderns and the ancients. Gautier's early study of sartorial fashion, titled *De la mode* (1858), begins by looking at contemporary sculptors, painters, and their inopportune quest for the ideals of antiquity:

▪

*Already the nude is but a convention; the suit constitutes the visible form of man. . . . The modern dressing hinders them, so they say, from producing masterworks; listening to them it seems the fault of the black suits, overcoats, and crinolines that they are no Titians, van Dycks, or Velázquezes. Yet these great men once painted their contemporaries in clothing like ours, which is, although elegant, often ungraceful or bizarre. Is our clothing really as ugly as one makes it out to be? Does it not carry significance, sadly ill understood by artists who are filled only with notions of antiquity?*[22]

▪

In particular the crinoline, already on its triumphant advance to dominate high fashion in the Second Empire, becomes imbued with an almost sublime beauty.

▪

*That mass of rich fabrics makes a sort of pedestal for bust and head, the only important body parts, now that nudity is no longer acceptable.—If I am permitted a mythological approach to such a modern question, we could say that the woman in her ball gown conforms to the ancient Olympian etiquette.*[23]

▪

Gautier accepts the paradigmatic value of fashion in contemporary aesthetics and appreciates the existence of a *poncif*. Yet he still struggles—and this difficulty partly accounts for his later one-dimensional view of modernity—to realize the ambiguous and transitory characteristics that would render superfluous these willfully established contrasts and oppositions. Transposing an article of clothing or an accessory into the realm of the mythological, as Gautier does in *De la mode,* in hopes of maintaining the distance between fashion and reality is a curious compromise,[24] since combining transitoriness and the mythological only serves to diminish fashion's original impact and distinction.

Toward the end of *De la mode,* Gautier comes agonizingly close to fully recognizing fashion's significance. As it was, his last remark fits neatly between Baudelaire's *Salon(s)* of 1845/1846 and the perception of *modernité* and *mode* within the essay *Le Peintre de la vie moderne* some fifteen years later. Among contemporary artists, Gautier notes, "antiquity hinders their understanding of the present. They have a preconceived ideal of beauty; for them the modern ideal is a closed book."[25] In order to understand why it took Gautier almost a decade to convert this "modern ideal" to a concept of *modernité* (limited though it appears), one has to look back briefly on the word's etymology. Although Littré gave 1867 as the date for the first documented use of *modernité,* Honoré de Balzac had already employed it in 1823.[26] And a decade later, in his diary of May 1833, Chateaubriand described a journey from Paris to Prague and bemoaned the tiresome procedure that spoils his appreciation of the countryside: "The vulgarity, the modernity of the customs and the passport are in contrast to the storm, the Gothic portal, the sound of horns, and the noise of the torrent."[27] Here, modernity is equated not only with vagary but also with vulgarity. The medieval and not yet reified nature, obviously Romantic in their combination, contrast favorably with the excesses of modern times.

"Modernity" in the English language, however, appears more differentiated in meaning in its first documented use. Horace Walpole, in a letter of 1782, comments on the recent scandal that surrounded the falsifications (*Rowley Poems,* 1777) by the adolescent poet Thomas Chatterton: "I have scarce seen a person who is not persuaded, that the fashion of the poem was Chatterton's own, though he might have found some old stuff to work upon, which very likely was the case; but now that the poems have been so much examined, nobody (that has an ear) can get over the modernity of the modulation, and the recent cast of the ideas."[28] For Walpole, modernity, not surprisingly already appearing here in proximity to fashion, denotes for the first time stylistics and possesses an aesthetic quality. The fact that he observed it within poetry which has been fashioned to appear as old and written in a distant, medieval past, proves almost prophetic for the transcending quality ascribed to modernity more than a century later.

### 1.2.3 The Feminine Article

Back in France *la mode* had had to overcome the same adverse connotations of futility as *la modernité;* and remarkably enough, although the word *mode* had first entered the French language in 1380, it took until the mid–nineteenth century, the time of change within cultural and aesthetic parameters and the date of Baudelaire's first *Salon,* before it became established in conversation and literature as predominantly denoting sartorial style.

Mode derives from the Latin *modus,* meaning "manner" or "style." Its masculine form expresses above all rules of change and anticipation of cycles (e.g., "mode of living"). It governs the way in which an action or historic progress develops.[29] Although we have seen that a plural form exists to describe clothes, the *feminization* of the word in the singular (ca. 1845) was required to designate the aesthetics of fashion (and subsequently its industry and commerce). *La mode* temporarily subverted the rules of change, a will- and skillful easing of parameters. An erratic challenge to the fixed and substantiated "mode" of behavior emerged,[30] which in turn asked for poetic imagination: an imagination that not only gave meaning to the female form, as we will observe in the work of Mallarmé, but managed to venture beyond it. This movement beyond has remained a hallmark of truly great fashion up to this day.

From the general perception of varying styles, *la mode* came to focus exclusively on fashion—and thus on sartorial *objectification*. This focus in turn contains *in nuce* the division of subject and object that would prove so significant for modernity: the subject-related, male mode of behavior dominating aesthetic perceptions in Romanticism is superseded by the object-related, female *la mode,* which symbolizes as much a changed society enamored with progress and consumption as it does modern stylistic qualities.[31] The developing division of subject and object throughout the eighteenth and nineteenth century progressed until the object separated from, and dominated over, the subject—culminating in the Marxist definition of alienation. The philosophical tradition that regarded only the single—and heroic—subject as the place for cognition of the objective breaks down under the profusion of objectifications. Midway through the nineteenth century, the object as commodity increasingly came to designate the basis for aesthetic as well as social expressions.[32] The feminine article in *la mode* is but one symbol of this change. Yet its impact is more than just ironic. Women's fashion—that is, the objectification of the female—would flourish within the establishment of an unqualified form of capitalist and patriarchal society, out to dominate the female sex. The emphasis is on equating *la mode* with the ephemeral and the futile, which may be strong but is ultimately unimportant—as the woman does not really dominate anything but the consumption of an artificial reality of luxuries and vagaries.

On the surface, however, the tone of expressions also switched from fundamental and humanist to ephemeral and reified. And poetic imagination was challenged to establish a "beauté relative" beside the "beauté universelle"—to paraphrase Perrault's seventeenth-century distinction.

It fell to Baudelaire to develop from *la mode* an expression for the immediate, the unpredictable, and the charm of constant change. Yet in doing so, he anticipates the danger of its becoming a mere byword for ephemeral evanescence. He aims to underscore its distinct character, its capacity to transcend natural law as well as time, which would find its culmination in his analysis of *la modernité*.

■

*Fashion should thus be considered as a symptom of the taste for the ideal which floats on the surface of all the crude, terrestrial and loathsome bric-à-brac that the natural life accumulates in the human brain: as a sublime deformation of Nature, or rather as a permanent and repeated attempt at her reformation. And so it has been sensibly pointed out (though the reason has not been discovered) that every fashion is charming, relatively speaking, each one being a new and more or less happy effort*

*in the direction of Beauty, some kind of approximation to an ideal for which the rest-*
*less human mind feels a constant, titillating hunger. . . . If therefore the aphorism*
*"All fashions are charming" upsets you as being too absolute, say, if you prefer, "All*
*were once justifiably charming." You can be sure of being right.*[33]

*[F]or it is much easier to decide outright that everything about the clothing of an age*
*is absolutely ugly than to devote oneself to the task of distilling from it the mysteri-*
*ous beauty that it might contain, however slight or minimal that element may be. By*
*"modernité" I mean the ephemeral, the fugitive, the contingent, the half of art*
*whose other half is the eternal and the immutable.*[34]

▪

This definition, too, would appear to establish modernity as part of the contrasting pair of "the modern" and "the ancient": the "sublime deformation" marking an ambiguous go-between. Sublimity yes, but also a deformation—that is, reification—of the natural. Thus one encounters the two elements of modernity that have to be singled out in order to explain its aesthetic coinage in conjunction with fashion: (1) the ontological rupture between human and nature and (2) a corresponding rupture between subject and object through growing reification. Although there are many definitions of what constitutes modernity proper and a multitude of approaches to it (sociological, economic, etc.), I focus on these two aspects in order to concentrate the argument and create a thematic coherence.

Baudelaire writes about fashion in clothing (and, significantly, in makeup) as diametrically opposite to the natural state, that is, the undressed body, as well as assimilating the antinatural, the deformation or, some would argue, improvement of nature. This opposition will flow easily, as we will see in chapter 5, into fashion as the principal metaphor of the supernatural and surreal. The ontological gap that opens between the subject, in control of his Being and confident about his relationship with nature, and the sartorial object, which particularly throughout modernity enforces its reifying and deforming lawfulness on man, creates what Simmel calls "the concept and tragedy of culture." In this "tragedy" of a commodified culture, fashion implements the domination of an aesthetic concept (sometimes a trend or style suffices) over life and aesthetic experience proper. Fashion literally dresses the cognitive subject for a objectified existence, and the two strands of modernity are interwoven in the constant change of clothing, as it directly influences the body of the subject on a very intimate level.[35]

For Baudelaire, neither modernity nor fashion possesses descriptive function. Therefore the fluctuation of their expressions *does not belong to the present,* and no contrast in value to the past is established. If there is a *beauté universelle* (and Baudelaire is too much part of his time to cast off this concept completely), it can be found in the most ephemeral of expressions—and with only a shift in viewpoint and the observant eye of dandy or flâneur, the transitory beauty reveals itself as a new approximation toward the artist's incessant quest for an ideal. Thus modernity has acquired a (fluctuating) gestalt of its own, and the age-old *querelle* as well as the static concept of historiography have both reached their limits.[36]

Apart from *la mode* as its etymological basis, *la modernité* obviously relates to *le moderne,* which derives from the late Latin word *modernus. Modernus* in turn came from the earlier *modo,* and both words carry, besides their original connotation of time, also a sense of (stylistic) quality. In time, *modo* changed its meaning from "only," "at first," "also," and "just" to "now"; *modernus* came to express not only that something is "new" but also that it is "actual." Something that had just been set in an exclusively temporal contrast to its past was suddenly established within a *historical* construct.[37] Much later, yet still in the wake of this fundamental shift, the descriptive component of time, the male *moderne* in its then-established contrast to the ancient, would be bestowed with transitory fluctuating characteristics—the female *modernité*—which nevertheless left her admirers (poets as well as historians) with the problem of how to distinguish the rather vague outlines of this new conception.

Fashion and modernity obviously depend on the instantaneous, yet the poetic task from Baudelaire to Mallarmé and beyond has been to connect them with eternity—so that they might become "mobile images of an immobile eternity," in the words of Henri Lefebvre.[38] This connection is highly ambiguous. If modernity loses its descriptive function—that is, its position as contrast or antithesis to antiquity or the eternal—it also leaves the framework of established parameters. Thus to stress its impact, another (metaphysical) level would have to be added—"the lofty spiritual significance of the *toilette*,"[39] as Baudelaire puts it. To begin with, the poet extracts the self-contained quality of the present: "The pleasure which we derive from the representation of the present is due not only to the beauty with which it can be invested, but also to its essential quality of being present."[40] Yet this sense of the instantaneous appears only in "representations," that is, in documents that would potentially become historical. An abstract idea may well mirror the transitory, but its manifestations proper are in danger of being awarded to the past.

The possibility that the transitory quality of the present—what modernity is—would become dated is forestalled by the open attribution of modernity to antiquity: not as an opposition that admits defeat but as objectifications of a fugitive quality that would be as valued as the ideals of antiquity—one distant day or within the next instant. And here the perceptions of fashion in *Le Peintre* resonate with those previously formulated by Gautier in *De la mode:*

■

*The draperies of Rubens or Veronese will in no way teach you how to depict* moire antique, satin à la reine *or any other fabric of modern manufacture, which we see supported and hung over crinolines or starched muslin petticoat. In texture and weave these are quite different from the fabrics of ancient Venice or those worn at the court of Catherine [the Great]. Furthermore the cut of skirt and bodice is by no means similar; the pleats are arranged according to a new system. Finally the gesture and the bearing of the woman of today give to her dress a life and a special character which are not those of the woman of the past. In short, for any modernity to be worthy to become one day antiquity, it is necessary for the mysterious beauty which human life accidentally puts into it to be distilled from it.*[41]

■

But why relate fashion and modernity to antique ideals at all? If modernity is meant to signify the contemporary and transitory, why have recourse to the ancient sublime? The answer can be found in Baudelaire's respective interpretations of female and male fashion—and to some extent in Gautier's as well.

Consider first female clothing. Woman's dress is a mystery ("beauté mystérieuse"); it is mythologically trimmed. So that the poetic within fashion as well as within the female can be stressed, its social significance becomes almost completely abstracted. Many decades later, in the second book of Proust's *Recherche* (which fictionally begins in the early 1880s), young Marcel artificially elevates "les jeunes filles," "like those painters who, seeking to match the grandeurs of antiquity in modern life, give to a woman cutting her toe-nail the nobility of the *Spinario,* or, like Rubens make goddesses out of women they know to people some mythological scene."[42] Visual and metaphysical beauty ("relative" and "universelle") easily meets the challenge of regarding society and historiography in static terms. Woman's apparel may establish a distinct feeling of the present by its seasonal changes. Or it may relate to the past by quoting from it. Or it may also work toward its designation as a novel antiquity. Most important, however, these styles are made to attract, please, and fascinate.

The crinoline in its hypertrophic impracticality is the most potent symbol of the superficial consumer society of the Second Empire. It occurs in Baudelaire's interpretation of modernity—"the modern manufacture, which, we see supported and hung over crinolines"—as well as in Gautier's essay *De la mode*—"that mass of rich fabrics makes a sort of pedestal." Neither mentions its political connotation as the grandiose impediment to woman's movement or its abstruse metaphor of the female as a supreme objectification of conspicuous consumption. For Baudelaire the crinoline was nothing but the most recent sartorial creation, thus by definition charming and beautiful. Gautier went even further; not only did he avoid any connection between sociopolitical conditions and the crinoline, but in his text fashion literally broke from the confines of the real world and became exempt from social reality.

The years 1858 to 1861, so productive for Gautier's and Baudelaire's aesthetic experience, were also the flowering period of the Haussmannization of Paris; the demolition of the medieval city to make way for large boulevards and new houses for the growing middle classes. On the surface designed to address overcrowding and unhygienic conditions in the old inner city, these measures also represented the grandeur and pretensions of Louis Napoleon; in addition, they attempted to prevent a repetition of the 1848 Revolution by destroying the narrow urban structure that had allowed the construction of barricades and created social solidarity within the respective *quartiers.*

Alexandre Weill, a contemporary critic of Baron Haussmann's project, wrote in 1860: "From the viewpoint of both hygiene and artistry nothing is more ghastly than the interiors of the new houses along the Boulevard Sébastopol. All these crinoline mansions are in disguise and wear round hats on their heads. But it is their interior that has to be called dishonest."[43] The "crinoline facade" of the political (and architectural) system concealed dishonesty and the neglect of social problems inside. Yet these particular interiors, as Gautier described with unwitting irony, were destroyed not by a passion for social justice but by the most recent sartorial expression of this rampant capitalism:

▪

*A quite serious objection is the incompatibility of the crinoline with modern architecture and interior design. When the women were wearing dresses with panniers, the drawing rooms were vast, there were large double doors, the chairs spread their arms, the coaches easily admitted the circumference of skirts; the theater boxes did not resemble the drawers of a sideboard. Well then! One just has to build bigger drawing rooms, change the shape of the furniture and coaches and demolish the theaters! No bother at all!*[44]

▪

He advocates that the social order yield to female caprice. This paragraph says perhaps as much about the transitory power of fashion as does any serious and profound analysis. What rank must the sartorial expression occupy, if it first pretended to mirror and then to dictate urban development!?

### 1.2.4 The Masculine Mode

The second area of concern within the interpretation of fashion is devoted to male clothing. The patronizing ease with which Gautier glossed over the social connotations of female fashion is absent from his remarks on male apparel. Instead of mock destruction, we find fake statues erected with pretentiousness: "Are not the vent of the tailcoat and the creases of the trousers firm, noble, and pure like the folds of a chlamys or a toga? Does the [male] body not exist under its prosaic vestments like a statue under its drapery?" Such musings prompt the repeated (and rhetorical) question about male clothing: "Has it not its significance, sadly ill understood?"[45] This question echoes the one Baudelaire had posed a dozen years earlier in his first thoughts toward a spirit of modernity; also in the *Salon de 1846,* the poet asks about the *habit noir.* "[H]as not this much-abused suit its own beauty and its native charm?"[46] Yet once again, the contemporary suit is charming not simply because a parallel can be drawn to antiquity. Its metaphysical or at least poetic impact lies in its ability to adopt stylistic changes—the lifeblood of fashion—while maintaining a curiously uncompromising refusal to change its overall conception.

(Morning) coat, trousers, and—even as early as 1846—the *gilet,* all cut from one piece of fabric, stood for a continuing tradition that had begun some decades earlier with the French Revolution. Honoré de Balzac had claimed that "the Revolution was also a question of fashion, a debate between silk and the *drap.*"[47] It was a debate between fine stockings and elaborately decorated riding coats and a new sobriety expressed by an almost invariable costume, made uniformly of wool in somber colors,[48] that paraphrased the new bourgeois virtues of decency and frugality and was deemed an appropriate antidote to absolutist excesses. Consider once again Balzac on revolution, this time decidedly less enthusiastic about the new found sartorial equality: "The Revolution brought a time of crisis for attire, as well as for the civil and political order. . . . Finally, the French became all equal in their rights, and also in their garments, and the difference in fabrics or cut of the suits no longer distinguished social positions. But then how could one recognize anyone in the midst of this uniformity?"[49] In its general acclaim, this particular sartorial signification lies at the basis of Baudelaire's "beauté universelle," which necessarily was modified by the "beauté relative" of (often minute) stylistic alteration that appeared anew each season.

In the black suit Baudelaire would find the ultimate expression of fashion's poetic transhistoricalness. As early as 1846 he declares:

**5.**
Count Giuseppe Primoli, *Edgar Degas Leaving a Public Toilet,* 1889. Gelatin silver print,
21 × 20 cm. Fondazione Primoli, Rome.

*Before trying to distinguish the epic side of modern life, and before bringing ex-*
*amples to prove that our age is no less fertile in sublime themes than ancient ones,*
*we may assert that since all centuries and all peoples have had their own form of*
*beauty, so inevitably we have ours. That is in the order of things.*

*All forms of beauty, like all possible phenomena, contain an element of the*
*eternal and an element of the transitory—of the absolute and of the particular. Ab-*
*solute and eternal beauty does not exist, or rather it is only an abstraction skimmed*
*from the general surface of different beauties. The particular element in each mani-*
*festation comes from the emotions: and just as we have our own particular emo-*
*tions, so we have our own beauty.*[50]

The passion of the male poet is directed toward the woman. Thus his perception of female fashion is objectified—he adores her dress and figure, finds it mystify-
ing or openly erotic. In contrast, his view of male apparel is much more abstracted and
elevated. Although a strong element of the auto- (or homo)erotic pervades the dandy's
view of his own costume—and all artists who deal with fashion are habitual dandies—
the poetic attitude of the subject takes clear precedence over the material and visual.
In order to dress modernly, that is, in tune with the contemporary, man has to possess
modern attitudes, to embrace the present, to subject himself to a sense of *modernité.*
"As for the suit, the outer husk of the modern hero[,] . . . the studios and the world at
large are still full of people who would like to poeticise Antony with a Greek cloak and
a parti-coloured vesture."[51] Why this strange poetic license to disguise oneself for distinction?[52] For some artists, taking recourse to the past obviously appeared to be their
only weapon against the growing industrialization of society. But this escapist and apolitical attitude is not Baudelaire's:

*But all the same, has not this much-abused suit its own beauty and its native charm?*
*Is it not the necessary suit for our suffering age, which wears the symbol of a perpet-*
*ual mourning even upon its thin black shoulders? Note, too, that the black suit and*
*the frock coat not only possess their political beauty, which is the expression of an*

*universal equality, but also their poetic beauty, which is an expression of the public soul;—an immense cortege of undertaker's mutes [croque-morts], political mutes, mutes in love, bourgeois mutes. We are each of us celebrating some funeral.*

*A uniform livery of affliction bears witness to equality; and as for the eccentrics, whose use of violent and contrasting colours easily betray them to the eye, to-day they are satisfied with slight nuances in design and in cut, much more than in colour. Look at those grimacing creases which play like serpents around mortified flesh—have they not their own mysterious grace?*[53]

∎

The transitory in male fashion assumes political significance. The black suit and the morning coat, although they possess the potential to represent democratic equality, echo nothing but uniform disillusion with this morally corrupt monarchy. When Gautier had described the Parisians in 1837 as "veritable assemblies of *croque-morts*,"[54] his characterization held more gentle mockery and nothing of the criticism (albeit veiled) with which Baudelaire would implicate the bourgeoisie and its government of ignorance and injustice.

## ∎ 1.3 *Cravate rouge* and *blouse bleue*

Baudelaire's early aesthetic criticism falls into a time of political divisions and widespread calls for social reform. After the collapse of Napoleonic France, the Restoration (1814–1830) attempted to sustain monarchic principles within the framework of a constitutional monarchy; its hallmark was census suffrage, based on *charte constitutionelle* and *acte additionelle* (two chambers partly responsible for the budget, ministers answerable to the chamber for their actions, etc.). The growing influence of the ultraroyalists forced Charles X in July 1830 to abolish freedom of the press and change the electoral law. In the resulting July Revolution the clash between the bourgeoisie and the working class over instituting a constitutional monarchy or republican state was decided in favor of the monarchy with the "election" of the bourgeois king Louis-Philippe (of Orléans). The progressing industrialization and development of a capitalist economy in France led to the emergence of a proletariat as well as early socialist theories (formulated by Fourier, Blanqui, and Proudhon). The growing division in nineteenth-century society was displayed in the rebellion of the silk weavers in Lyons (1831 and 1834) and the Blanquist revolt of 1835. The politics of "Enrichissez-vous," a rallying cry for economic growth to maintain the bourgeois support for the monarchy, could not appease the social unrest; and when bad harvests between 1845 and 1847, contributed further to the economic depression, the protesters demanded the reform of the electoral law. Their demands went unheeded, and the February Revolution followed in 1848.

Unlike Gautier, Baudelaire was prepared to widen and adapt his critique, as their different approaches to fashion and modernity make clear. He considered fashion, apart from its aesthetic ideals, to be a social phenomenon, with potential to challenge established perceptions of historical reality. Baudelaire's views of both *la mode* and *la modernité* were far from static, and his uncompromising attitude toward aesthetics was reflected in his new interpretation of the present. But one cannot therefore assume that his political view was similarly progressive. At the time of the revolt by the weavers, who after all were the artisans who for centuries had provided the backbone for the artistic distinction of Parisian couture, the young Baudelaire wrote to his brother: "As a Parisian I am filled with indignation at the way they treated Louis-Philippe's name day in Lyons. Some small lampions here and there, and that was it. . . . All the young men wore a red cravat, a sign more of their foolishness than of their political persuasion."[55]

The scorn Baudelaire poured over the red cravat of his young contemporaries, as a socialist sign and sartorial accessory, is curious, as he himself was in the habit of *épater le bourgeois* through his apparel—including the maligned blood-colored necktie. Eugène Marsan, who had labored over a decade to assemble his "Manual for the Man of Elegance," evoked in 1923 the young Baudelaire: "He wore his black suit 'cornet-flared,' that is to say cut away at the nape, almost gaping, with an attention to detail that has been often imitated since and that looks like a mistake to those who are not in the know. . . . The pair of trousers in the same black was strapped over irreproachable patent leather boots. He insisted on finesse and pristine whiteness in his loose, unstarched shirt [*sans empois*]. But attention: he also sported a blood-red cravat and pink gloves."[56] During his time of conspicuous dandyism, friends such as Nadar, Asselineau, and of course Gautier would observe Baudelaire leaving his lodgings at the Quai de Béthune or in the historic Hôtel Pimodan, wearing a black morning coat with tails cut on the bias, a white shirt of the finest linen with extremely low-cut collars, a blood- or fire-red cravat (depending on his mood), and a top hat and mauve gloves that were molded to his hands.[57] Le Vavasseur, who had asked Baudelaire early for a contribution to a collection of verses and who had upon the poet's withdrawal agreed that "his precious (poetic) fabric had nothing in common with our cotton threads," judged his sartorial style as "Byron dressed by Brummell."[58] And his friend Champfleury elaborated on the significance behind Baudelaire's fashion:

■

*One has to take care not to mistake the blue shirt for an indication of socialism around 1845 to 1847. For Baudelaire it marked a new form of dandyism. It is important to note that below that shirt he wore black strapped trousers (the fashion among writers from that time: Balzac, etc.) and that the bottom of these* pantalons de chambre *embraced elegant shoes* à la Molière *that Baudelaire habitually showed off. . . . Thus no socialism really. A dislike of democracy became especially apparent in Baudelaire. . . . Also characteristic for Baudelaire during that time: with a shaven head and scarves of vibrant colors he crossed the river[;] . . . a frock coat sported in the Faubourg St. Germain, but also in shirtsleeves. Literary discussions, yet never socialist.*[59]

■

Is the revolutionary attitude thus a dandified pretense interspersed with sartorial quotes from literary history? Was the five-day bloody uprising of the weavers considered a mere inconvenience that required the replacement of silk with cotton for the fashion of 1834?[60] Was the bourgeois need for observed restraint already so distinct that political problems were simply objectified into fashion? According to one witness in Max von Boehn's history of nineteenth-century fashion, "political assassinations became so frequent during the 1830s that one began to design special 'assassination attires' for such eventful days."[61]

The eminence of black—Baudelaire's "deuil perpétuel"—appears here as nothing other than the sartorial reaction to yet another desperate protest against social injustice. But the *habit noir*—with its "beauté et son charme indigène, cet habit tant victimé"—has an important metaphor of ambiguity and transitoriness up its black sleeve: it may be a bourgeois fashion, but it can just as easily be bohemian. The stockbroker might combine it with a white shirtfront and pearl-gray cravat on his way to the Place de la Bourse, but the artist can subvert the same costume by wearing it with open linen in the cafés of the Left Bank while discussing revolutions, although not necessarily political ones. The "democratic equality" that Baudelaire dreamed for the black suit had also an ironic, even subversive connotation. The fact that the men of an entire "middle class" (an undistinguished one at that) wore black left much room for confusion and made it necessary to closely observe details—in sartorial as well as poetic or literary expression. The difference between industrialist and dandy, bourgeois and bohemian, was less distinct than the origins of modernity seem to require. The early objectifications were ambiguous because *both* "parties"—modern merchant as well as modern artist—embraced the progressive spirit of the times and turned it to their respective advantage.[62]

Apart from the revolutionary *cravate rouge* that Baudelaire, despite his earlier ridicule, would sport around his neck, or the strapped trouser of Romanticism or indeed the laborer's *blouse bleue* he chose to flash on the boulevards, the common determinant of his sartorial style remained the black suit. Looking at the portraits of the poet, painted between 1843 and 1844 by Émile Deroy or taken two decades later by the photographer Charles Neyt in Brussels,[63] one can observe how the transhistorical in male fashion operates. Baudelaire created a seamless passage from the Romantic mode of the bohemian artist to the purist fashion of modern man. However, even if the color of the suit is the same, the cut and perhaps also the fabric differ. The "beauté relative" qualifies any connection with the past, and the detailing may betray the smallest of "revolutions" in terms of style.

For the poet, the underlying attitude is that of the dandy, and thus one of duality: he displays on the one hand aversion to loud and open rebellion, on the other an even greater disgust at conformity. Baudelaire did not think predominantly in political

**6.**
Émile Deroy, *Portrait of Baudelaire* (detail),
1843/1844. Oil on canvas, 40 × 35 cm.
Musée National du Château, Versailles.

**7.**
Charles Neyt, *Charles Baudelaire,* 1864.
Modern print. Archive of the Suhrkamp
Verlag, Frankfurt a.M.

terms. His interest lay in contemporary society and its reifications. The poet could not cast off his ideal of beauty; and his quest to trace it within modern expression led him not to question the system as such but only to loathe its vulgarity. Therefore, when Baudelaire wrote in May 1845 so favorably about the bourgeois and even dedicated his *Salon of 1846* to them,[64] the bow to the "protagonists of modernity" was less ironic than one might suspect.

Such nods of course did not prevent him two years later from being among the first to inscribe himself on the list for Auguste Blanqui's left-wing Société républicaine centrale,[65] or to praise Pierre Joseph Proudhon's anarchist "banque d'échange" in the paper *La Tribune Nationale* as a "very desirable institution, where we see a distinct increase of representation and a generalization of the warehouse system."[66] Despite his often-expressed regret that Proudhon "never was and never will be a Dandy, even on paper"[67]—"dandy" being Baudelaire's term for aesthetic congeniality in combined sartorial and written form—the poet's views on politics and to a greater extent economics were influenced during the revolution of 1848 by the libertarian thinker. Yet as we have seen in his interpretation of fashion, the poet does not hanker after a new system; the status quo offered enough latitude. His concern is with change in an always transitory viewpoint; and if such changes apparent on the surface coincide with systemic alterations, with new social, albeit not necessarily political, demands, all the better. In Baudelaire the aesthete and artist had to take precedence over the political being. A certain conservative skepticism appeared justifiable to him, if the social framework, which he regarded as necessary to his criticism, seemed in danger of being overthrown.

However, in *La Tribune Nationale* Baudelaire gave fiery "advice to the workers": "We are not prepared to push the present back into the past. The Republic[an government] has done nothing for us, and we cannot respond but to gain the social renewal that is our right and legitimate demand through political revolution."[68] The transitory act of revolution—which by the winter of 1848 had been suppressed by the bourgeoisie, military, and Napoleon III, all defenders of the status quo—can also be regarded as a supreme expression of modernity. In *Mon cœur mis à nu* he would remember his agitation:

■

*Mon ivresse en 1848.*

*De quelle nature était cette ivresse?*

*Goût de la vengeance. Plaisir* naturel *de la démolition.*

*Ivresse littéraire; souvenirs de lectures.*[69]

■

A remembrance of the past revolution, which he had read about, prompts the poet's participation in the present one; the political struggle mutates to an aesthetic citation. Much as writers on the playing field of fashion have always enthusiastically responded to the idea of proclaiming a "revolution" each time a stylistic innovation is created or recycled, so those describing modernity often required some titillation and provocation for it not to fall back onto the past. In this light Baudelaire's declaration sounds almost cynical: "Production has to be organized; consumption does not have to be disorganized."[70] The "Enrichissez-vous" of the Second Empire would be juxtaposed with an individualized "Enivrez-vous":[71] the only way out of these implacable times seemed drunken consumption.

## ■ 1.4 What Price Revolution?

For the artist of modern life, the revolution was not a political struggle, let alone a class conflict *avant la lettre,* but the consequence of a necessary renewal. As society became increasingly abstracted and objectified, Baudelaire realized that he would be unable to prevent the parallel loss of intellectual gravity. His solution was to imbue the object, especially the sartorial one, with poetic and ontological meaning. And his description of the encounter of fashion and modernity best exemplifies this idea. The subject-related *modus,* or *le mode,* had fallen behind *la mode* as the paradigm of modern times; therefore the latter required an elevation to sheer poetry, possibly ontology. Or, if appropriate, it should be revolutionized—instead of one great political revolution, it would under go a profusion of little stylistic ones. If social reality was to invade with a genuine revolution of its own, it would have to be reified—according to disposition either by *cravate rouge* or *blouse bleue*—and its aims qualified as attacks on the social status quo and not the political structure.

This structure was analyzed by Karl Marx in two essays that frame the time of Baudelaire's hermeneutics of *modernité* in starkly different terms. One was philosophical, the "Contribution to the Critique of Hegel's Philosophy of Law" (1843); the other one was historio-political, *The Eighteenth Brumaire of Louis Napoleon* (1852). In his "Contribution" Marx explains:

■

*The abstraction of the* state as such *belongs only to modern times, because the abstraction of private life only belongs to modern times. The abstraction of the* political *state is a modern product. . . . Man is the actual principle of the state—but unfree man. It is thus the democracy of unfreedom—estrangement carried to completion. The abstract reflected antithesis belongs only to the modern world. The Middle Ages are the period of actual dualism; modern times, one of abstract dualism.*[72]

■

Here, the division between intellectual subject and material object experienced its critical climax. The "abstract dualism" that signifies the reification of private life and the political system as a whole initiates modernity. All expressions of bourgeois capitalist society mirror the complete exteriority of the human spirit and subsequent materialism.[73]

The reign of Louis-Philippe, the challenge of the 1848 revolution, and especially the Second Empire are all manifestations of a quest for the modern. Albeit under different auspices, they share a belief in the material object. Even when recognized as the nemesis of the subject, it is simultaneously regarded as the subject's savior. The same holds for Baudelaire's and Guys's (and perhaps also Gautier's early) interpretation of fashion and its potential. Although it is the transitory and feeble depiction of a society characterized in the same way, fashion also directs that society: it manifests a constant urge toward the new and unashamed ephemerality, coupled with a selective recourse to antiquity in order to demonstrate its aspiration to become the sublime and eternal.

Marx's essays of the 1840s and 1850s on the abstraction and dualism in modern society thus represent the politicized parallel to Baudelaire's theses on the aesthetic abstraction and ambiguity of *mode et modernité;* in the late 1930s both would be transferred, as we will see in chapter 4, into Benjamin's epistemological framework.

## ■ 1.5 The First Tiger's Leap

Writing (between 1851 and 1852) on the February Revolution and the coming to power of Louis Napoleon, Marx contrasts the one-dimensional perception of history, similar to the simplistic enthusiasm that looked on fashion as being merely the charming arbiter of the new that had become typical of the Second Empire, with the revolutionary spirit of 1789: "Consideration of this world-historical necromancy reveals at once a salient difference. Camille Desmoulins, Danton, Robespierre, Saint-Just, Napoleon, the heroes as well as the parties and the masses of the old French Revolution, performed the task of their time in Roman costume and with Roman phrases, the task of unchaining and setting up modern *bourgeois society.*"[74] The recourse to the past is regarded as instrumental to the formation of modernity, of modern times, in the same way that (visual) quotes from the ancient account for the charm and potential of fashion. The origin of a bourgeois modern society lies in the adaptation of democratic ideals from antiquity. Yet in 1850, the situation had changed; to reach back to the past then meant to veil the division in contemporary society, to reconcile the Parisian bourgeois with consumerism and facile politics. A qualitative change within the perception of modern times was to be implemented, but its political realization would have to wait another two decades,[75] while Baudelaire's pamphlet to the workers died away almost unheard and remained a solitary voice of realpolitik in the work of the poet. One could argue, with Marx, that the concept of modernity lends more than just a helping hand to this retardation and charade—that fashion and modernity are but a parody of the possible yet failed revolution, realizing on the facade what has been wasted within.

What Baudelaire's, and later Mallarmé's, writings on fashion signify, however, is the appreciation of the modern as a challenge to historicity, to the established historical and also social fabric that pretends to clothe intellectual life. They overturn the idea that the present is just the last in a long list of temporal entities that follow neatly one after the other. Fashion's constant quotation of the past, drawing not only on stylistics but also, since fashion is a social phenomenon, on ideas that shape society, breaks up the historical continuum and gives modernity, since both are here inextricably linked, its time-transcending (transitory + transhistorical) potential. A number of artists and theoreticians would realize that potential in the course of the following decades. Benjamin, as perhaps the most original among them, freed the revolutionary potential within the challenge to historicity and threw a bridge from Baudelaire to the Marx of the early 1850s. Almost a century later in Paris, as we saw in the introduction, Benjamin echoed Marx's observation on Roman dress within French revolution(s):

History is object of a structure whose site is not homogeneous and empty time but one filled by now-time [Jetztzeit]. For Robespierre the Rome of antiquity was thus charged with now-time and blasted from the continuum of history. The French Revolution regarded itself as Rome reincarnate. It quoted ancient Rome as fashion quotes a past attire. Fashion has the scent of the modern wherever it stirs in the thicket of what has been. It is the tiger's leap into the past. Yet this leap occurs in an arena commanded by the ruling class. The very same leap in the open air of history is the dialectical one, which Marx has understood as the revolution.[76]

The idea that a revolution—the transitory in history per se—quotes from the past much as fashion does applies Marx's political thought to aesthetics. The objectification and abstraction of society are connected with its latest expression. Suddenly a temporal entity from the past is—for example, through a stylistic quote—isolated in its impact (a genuinely materialist virtue) and thrown into the now. The historian takes a great leap to find the instantaneous and immediate in what has long gone.[77] Within the spirit of modernity, each historic fact is potentially quotable. The July and February revolutions of 1830 and 1848 were also attempts to revive the "original" of 1789. For some, the ideals of antique Rome were redressed and served as genuine virtues of the French Revolution; for others, as can be observed in the Empire fashion after 1800, Roman civic ideals were just filled with charm and contemporary beauty.

Although Benjamin's quote features the interpretation of Baudelaire and the nineteenth century, it belongs to the twentieth and will thus be discussed later. For the time being, it suffices to see the tiger's leap as describing a potential that in this form could be realized neither by Baudelaire nor by Mallarmé, to whose perception of modernity—perhaps apolitical but certainly paradigmatic—we now return.

## ■ 1.6 Quote within a Quote

The modernist quotation from antiquity is not simply a deferential copy, as for example can be seen in the sculptures of Thorvaldsen, whose reproductions Gautier had admired. Fashion as the most complete expression of *modernité* speaks of the irreverent, ironic, and even the tactless. It is capable of turning the ancient into the very modern because its citations always have to remain incomplete. The chemises of the Empire were as far removed from the classical, that is, Greco-Roman style, as would be the pleated dresses designed by Mariano Fortuny a century later.

Yet both designs strongly claimed the past as their source of inspiration, which each attempts to follow faithfully. In the extreme, classical sculpture, perceived as the antithesis to modernity by Gautier, becomes not superseded by reverential plastic works but replaced by fashion. In an essay of 1859—significantly a study of Gautier—Baudelaire complains, "the wind of this century has gone mad; the barometer of modern reason shows that a storm is brewing. Have we not recently seen an illustrious and well-accredited writer . . . exclaim in his hatred for all things beautiful: A good tailor is worth more than three classical sculptors!"[78] The exclamation did indeed come from an illustrious source. The historian Jules Michelet characterized the rectification—and reification—of nature, society, and artistic production in particular in an uncompromisingly positivist manner. In his book *L'Amour* (published the previous year) he praised fashion's potential: "For one tailor who understands, copies and improves upon nature, I would give three classic sculptors."[79] The suit or dress represents the object; but since any sartorial fashion is as close as possible to the body, the subject thus manages to reclaim him- or herself, at least partially, from some of the commodification that had become so dominant. That Baudelaire characterizes the book by Michelet as "disgusting"[80] demonstrates their dichotomous attitudes toward the character of the modern. For the positivist advocate of *modernité,* the adornment surpasses nature and transitory fashion *replaces* the eternal and the sublime; for the poet, such adornment is merely one part of fashion's dialectics. Modernity for him is not a successive improvement to the style of the *anciens;* instead, it incorporates and reflects that older style in its most ephemeral expressions. Michelet, whose lectures on "social renewal and revolution" at the Collège de France had been suspended for the first time in January 1848—a time when, just a few streets away, one could observe Baudelaire promenading with his blue worker's shirt under his black suit and coat[81]—regarded *modernité* as pertinent for the present in its manners, modes, and aesthetic experience, but not as subverting the relation of past and present or to historicity as such.

At times "social renewal," in both men's and women's clothes, is capable of expressing the metaphysical in fashion's potential: man's apparel through the persistence of the *habit noir,* which transcends time and style with its abstracted and invariable appearance; woman's dresses through their beauty, which compelled the artist to elevate them to a mythological, even mystic, status. Thus Baudelaire writes: "Women who have exaggerated the fashion to the extent of perverting its charm and totally destroying its aims, are ostentatiously sweeping the floor with their trains and the fringes of their shawls; they come and go, pass and repass, opening an astonished eye like animals, giving an impression of total blindness, but missing nothing."[82] While the man is separated by his socially coined rationale from the clothes he wears, the woman who is in constant movement ("pass and repass") finds herself bound to passing fashion. As a rule, man's sense of style and distinction comes from the nuance(s) with which he individually appropriates the static male dress code, while woman's individuality becomes immediately apparent in the particular clothes she wears at any given moment, whether they are absolutely à la mode or dated and old-fashioned. Interiority and exteriority (*le mode* and *la mode*) played off against each other in this society, and the uniformity of the masculine provided the backdrop for the sartorial excesses of the feminine.

Yet clothes are only the surface; their impact increases if they are shifted, lifted, or undone so that the female form appears underneath the fabric. For Baudelaire such exposure not only provides an erotic fascination, it also reveals the other side of modern times. For his Romantic counterpart Gautier, fashion and modernity instead conceal human nature and emphasize the ontological rupture, although this is no longer a certain cause for complaint. At the very beginning of his essay *De la mode* Gautier states, "In the modern age clothing has become man's second skin, from which he will under no pretext separate himself and which belongs to him like an animal's coat; so that nowadays the real form of the body has been quite forgotten."[83] The human figure had become a total abstraction and submitted itself to constant change of appearance—a fact that has to be accepted by the modernist.

This fact is even more integral to understanding the woman and her fashion: "Where is the man who, in the street, at the theatre, or in the park, has not in the most disinterested of ways enjoyed a skillfully composed toilette, and has not taken away with him a picture of it which is inseparable from the beauty of her to whom it belonged, making thus of the two things—the woman and her dress—an invisible unity?"[84] As objectifications, the sartorial and the female appear as one. But within the dialectics of modernity, there has to be an antithesis to the abstracted sartorial surface. Baudelaire had to leave the Parisian streets to find it. In 1841 the twenty-one-year-old poet embarked on a journey to Mauritius and the Bourbon Islands. In his prose poem "La Belle Dorothée," his persistent memory concentrated on one image from that time in particular.

■

*Every now and then the sea-breeze lifts a corner of her flowing skirt, showing a flash of her superbly shaped leg; while her foot, worthy of one of those marble goddesses who stand in our European museums, plants its impeccable imprint in the fine sand.*[85]

■

Once more, the feminine form is idolized and antiquity evoked; Baudelaire compares the innocent and untamed beauty favorably with classic statues because of her original purity. Then he employs the same, almost fetishistic, regard to translate this very image to the Parisian boulevard. There, however, ancient beauty finds its equivalent, in

**8.**

Édouard Manet, *Baudelaire's Lover,* ca. 1862. Oil on canvas, 90 × 113 cm. Museum of Fine Arts, Budapest.

terms of sublimity, and antithesis, in terms of modernity, within the fashionable woman on the sidewalk: "She advances towards us, glides, dances, or moves about with her burden of embroidered petticoats, which play the part at once of pedestal [see Gautier!] and balancing rod; her eyes flash out from under her hat, like a portrait in its frame. She is the perfect image of the savagery that lurks in the midst of civilisation."[86] The hem of the skirt, by that time had become a crinoline, elevates and supports modern woman. Her savagery becomes spiritual, no longer an expression of the rampantly physical. The footsteps "in the fine sand" are now audibly echoed on the pavement of the city. But when they sound too loud, rash, and vulgar, the poet is taken aback; true *modernité* is a subtle virtue appreciated by few. Those who are interested only in the fashionable aspect neglect its transcendent and transhistorical qualities, as he observes in the superficial attitude of the Parisian "courtesan in her prime," who is "proud at once of her youth and the luxury into which she puts all her soul and all her genius, as she . . . points a toe whose over-ornate shoe would be enough to betray her for what she is, if the somewhat unnecessary extravagance of her whole toilette had not done so already."[87]

For a grave contrast—that is, an image of modernity that embodies its metaphysical aspect—the poet continues with the same evocation of a lifting of the skirt and the revelation of the leg underneath. Yet this time the fashion, as befits modernity, is unostentatious, subtle, and somber but remains full of dramatic potential—it can only be black. Benjamin, in his 1939 essays on Baudelaire, would later claim that the poetic incident that Baudelaire describes symbolizes "the figure of *Chock,* indeed of catastrophe,"[88] the moment in one's existence where the fleetingness (and futility) of Being materializes in an encounter removed from ordinary temporal perception.

∎

*À UNE PASSANTE*

*La rue assourdissante autour de moi hurlait.*
*Longue, mince, en grand deuil, douleur majestueuse,*
*Une femme passa, d'une main fastueuse*
*Soulevant, balançant le feston et l'ourlet;*

*Agile et noble, avec sa jambe de statue.*
*Moi, je buvais, crispé comme un extravagant,*
*Dans son œil, ciel livide où germe l'ouragan,*
*Le douceur qui fascine et le plaisir qui tue.*

*Un éclair . . . puis la nuit!—Fugitive beauté*
*Dont le regard m'a fait soudainement renaître,*
*Ne te verrai-je plus que dans l'éternité?*

*Ailleurs, bien loin d'ici! trop tard! Jamais peut-être!*
*Car j'ignore où tu fuis, tu ne sais où je vais,*
*O toi que j'eusse aimée, ô toi qui le savais!*[89]

■

These lines written in 1860 poetically contain each element paradigmatic for both *modernité* and fashion that Baudelaire had formulated up to this point. The literary rapprochement via metaphor within the prose poems of *Le Spleen de Paris* and the critical approach through various parts in *Le Peintre de la vie moderne,* culminate in this sonnet to re-create the original encounter between the artist and his modern muse— which not only for mythological but also for erotic and etymological reasons had to be female.

The setting is not the beach or a salon; the flâneur meets the apparition of modernity in the urban space. Her figure is abstracted, clad in pure and simple black. Her fashion expresses "grand deuil," a noble paraphrase of the "deuil perpétuel" appropriate as the visual catharsis of perplexing and implacable times. In her sorrow she appears "majestic," that is, sublime, as part of the *côté épique* of modern society. She passes the poet; and only after her figure has become instant history, is he able to recall this transitory moment. In passing she gathers her skirt, yet not just any skirt. The hem, which once again appears "to swing," is described in detail, as a particular expression of contemporary fashion; the nuance is important, as it makes the clothes the element of the transhistorical, of *modernité,* in contrast to her leg, which in its statuesque beauty constitutes the element of the eternal, of *antiquité.*

**9.**
Anders Zorn, *The Widow*, 1883. Watercolor on paper, 54.6 × 32.2 cm.
Zornsamlingarna, Mora.

Through the poet's remembrance, modernity is thus able to fulfill his claim and become antiquity, while he follows his own advice ("Enivrez-vous!") and becomes intoxicated from the "softness" and "pleasure" she gives him for that brief standstill in time. Her beauty has to be "fugitive," because it could only thus become an "image mobile de l'immobile éternité." The ephemeral finally becomes eternal; only in his unfulfilled desire can the poet hope to have rendered this image as a dark and passing memento mori of modernity.

Although Baudelaire might have seen this apparition once in the flesh, her visual image had already been prefigured and imprinted on his cortex from the time he had begun to collect the works of the painter of modern life, Constantin Guys. In December 1859 he had written to his friend and publisher Poulet-Malassis, "Despite my troubles, and despite your shortage [of material support], I have bought and ordered superb drawings from Guys."[90] A great number of these artworks show bourgeois women who lift the hem of their dresses to take a careful step forward. Given the extreme volume of the crinoline, this sight must have been ubiquitous on Parisian streets from the 1850s onward. Guys depicted this precarious and delicate moment again and again, as it allowed him to display his touch in rendering folds; it also added an element of the mysterious and the erotic to his portrayals.[91]

One drawing in particular offers the visual equivalent of the "Passante":[92] Guys sketched a young woman, dressed in black, who reveals her white shoe, stocking, and *volants* while progressing diagonally past the beholder. The grace and mobility captured in this gesture perfectly illustrate the stylistic quality of what is modern. The dark and stiff sheets of fabric, as the crinolines were mostly underwoven with horsehair, make up an abstract plane, while the gathering of the textile conveys a fleeting character, a sense of the immediate and instantaneous. The woman, "soulevant, balançant le feston et l'ourlet," fuses the static and the mobile, standstill and movement—once again the dialectics of modernity. In describing Guys's depiction of the women passing in the streets, Geffroy evoked Baudelaire's critique of nearly a half century before:

■

*That other bourgeois woman crosses the street, in somber dress and coat, her profile framed by a huge hood, her slight hands holding the skirts; the bottom of the foot*

**10.**

Constantin Guys, *Woman Lifting Her Skirt,* 1850s. Ink and wash on paper. Previously in the collection of Gustave Geffroy.

*"In heaving clothes, in the color of mother-of-pearl, she dances even when she walks."—Charles Baudelaire.*

*progresses with caution to sense the cobblestones. . . . Yet another woman, sporting
a hat and shawl, her face emerging from underneath the black ribbons, appears ingenious and full of mystery. She is a splendid, veritable statue draped in a shawl, bedecked by a hood, surrounded by her peers in similar attire, a magnificent group of
women* comme il faut, *in the fashion of 1860. . . .*

*[T]hose women of the past who have found their historians and their poets
are transformed into eternal characters, as lasting as libraries and museums. They are
prefigured in the memory of future man; they reign and will reign quite unlike their
governance when they were alive.*[93]

∎

Again, the woman and her clothes are transposed into a classic art form. Yet her statue-
like impact, although already awarded to the past, is equally imprinted on the "memory of future man." Fashion, as Benjamin would point out, happily takes the tiger's
leap.

## ∎ 1.7 A Passing Fashion

Baudelaire collected Guys's images with a passion, and the drawing of the woman who
lifts her skirt would become not only the visualization of his concept of *modernité* but
also its carrier through time, passing on the concept to other poets—poets who would
also regard the proximity of fashion and modernity, expressed in the drawings, as crucial to their respective aesthetic experience.

In 1928 a remembrance of this continuing tradition within modernity appeared. Its author described a visit he had paid one December afternoon of 1897 to an
eminent poet, whose pupil he once had been. In his tutor's collection of artworks, next
to works by Manet and Whistler, one image in particular caught his eye: "He had an
extraordinary Guys: a woman dressed in a very bourgeois attire, lifting the bottom of
her skirt to reveal her leg and a laced-up boot; it came to him from Baudelaire via de
Banville."[94] Considering that pedigree, it is fascinating to speculate about what particular drawing it was and how and when it arrived in the poet's drawing room. However,

**11.**
Constantin Guys, untitled drawing, 1850s. Ink and wash on paper. Private collection.

the quality of *instantané*—the instantaneous "snapshot," as the photographer Nadar characterized Guys's figures—makes it futile to date or title individual drawings. Detailing in the fashion, such as the bodice above the voluminous crinoline, may allow a fairly precise determination of the point in time at which the depicted scene was meant to have taken place; yet as Baudelaire described in "L'Art mnémonique," Guys sketched from memory and not from a model.[95] The quality of the scenes does not depend on time, although their fascination depends on the impression of one distinct moment. Its depiction in art adds to fashion the historicizing quality of the sublime and eternal, as the artifact (in this case the drawing) gains its impact only from becoming part of historicity—that is, of course, if the art is influential and lasting enough. The pose of the female passerby gathering her dress became increasingly transitory with every step Baudelaire took in his criticism and poetry to arrive at "À une passante"; and although it would inevitably lose its contemporaneity, the expression was still admired over the years.

Théodore de Banville kept Guys's drawing after Baudelaire's death in 1867 and thus symbolically accepted his role as advocate of modernity. His own muse, whom he met in the park rather than at the corner of the street, continued to be the same as the one in Guys's imagination, and that of Baudelaire, who had written on Banville's congenial ideal:

■

*Finally, you ask whether even the most lyrical poet would ever descend from his ethereal realm, whether he never senses the flow of the life surrounding him . . . ? But surely! the poet knows how to descend into life; but rest assured if he agrees to do so, it is not without a goal and profit that he shall gain from his travel. . . .*

*Even in idealized poetry the muse may mix with the living, without breaking with tradition. First of all she shall pick up a new toilette. A well-worn modern finery will add an exquisite grace, a new ironic tone (a* piquant *as some might call it) to the beauty of the goddess. . . . The immortal Venus might well, when she wants to pay Paris a visit, descend from her pedestal in the grove of the Luxembourg.[96]*

■

Modernity also allows the muse to dress in an appropriate, that is, the latest, fashion to visit Parisian society and its artists. When Banville left the drawing of the modernist muse to the poet whom he regarded as his "heir," he also passed on an idea.[97] And in his writing on fashion, the new owner of Guys's drawing describes the "goddess," who once descended into the Jardin de Luxembourg, as now crossing the city to reach the Tuileries and begin her treasure hunt for the fashionable and modern. Her costume is given, as befits fashion journalism as the modern form of publication, in the most elaborate detail: "A gray felt hat adorned by gray feathers and a bronze-colored ribbon ending in alternating gold and silver tassels. Facing the open air, this attire might not shine, as it really requires footlights. But Diana in the Tuileries herself, who is all goddess! cannot obtain it and thus has to descend from her pedestal to go . . . to one of the renowned tailors or couturières and the huntress becomes *sportswoman;* it is the almost indispensable style for a hunting outfit today."[98]

In the year 1874, the goddess, or indeed the statue, has left her pedestal behind. Perhaps she descends because the crinoline, which had so far—according to Gautier and Baudelaire—itself served as a pedestal, has gone completely out of fashion. By now she possesses the sense of irony to discard any pretense to the classical, sublime, and eternal, and she attaches herself entirely to the ephemeral and commands her hunting costume from the best dressmaker. The muse of Guys, Baudelaire, Gautier, and the others requires elevation no more. She has become absolutely modern; she has progressed from the charming to the paradigmatic (to the pragmatic even?). However, the same essential task for the modern artist remained: to seek out the dialectical within modernity just as his or her "hunting ground" had turned from the predominantly artistic, the realm of drawing, criticism, and poetry, to the modernist, the realm of fashion journalism and fashion illustration.

According to the epigraph at the beginning of this chapter, modernity needs to be furnished by each reader. Therefore fashion would now acquire a distinct artistic, hermeneutic significance of its own. To modify the modern in order to maintain the "côté épique" became the new challenge.

**12.**

Paul Helleu, *In the Park of Versailles: Mme Helleu Seated Next to a Sculpture,* ca. 1897.
Drypoint on laid paper, 31.9 × 26.3 cm. Lumley Cazalet Ltd., London.

*The image of "Diana" and her latest fashion.*

**2**

# Mallarmé and the Elegance of Fashion in Modernity

*André Courrèges:* "Et des mariages de coton avec des tissus
plume synthétiques peuvent faire que le plume vous protège
des changements climatiques de l'extérieur.
Le coton vous garde votre qualité intrinsèque de chaleur intérieure.
Ces mariages-là vous font sentir très à l'aise!"
*Jean-Pierre Barou:* "De ça Mallarmé, qui s'occupait aussi de mode,
ne parlait pas!" (Rires.)
*André Courrèges:* "Mais Mallarmé vivait avec son époque.
Moi, je vis avec une machine à laver!"

*Interview (1983)*[1]

# ■ 2.1 *Mode et modernité:* Stéphane Mallarmé, the Modernist

The poet who came to acquire Guys's illustration of a woman in her black dress from
Baudelaire via Banville was, as one might have guessed, Stéphane Mallarmé.

Baudelaire provided a hermeneutical structure for *mode et modernité*. He established an interpretive discourse around fashion and its principle of constant change
as characteristic of modern social existence. Through these hermeneutics Mallarmé could now focus on the pure aesthetic quality of modernity and on his inquiry
into the adornment and elegance that accompanied this newly "found" pace of life.
Baudelaire had aimed at establishing a dialectical relation (not his terminology, of
course) between *modernité* and *eternité*. Visual art and literature were meant to represent fashion as a potent, modern subject matter, which, coupled with the sensual
appreciation of clothing by the aesthete, dandy, *tigresse,* or flâneur, generates an

acceptance of the contemporary and present as one side within the aesthetic experience of modern man and woman. The other was to be marked by the sublime serving as point of recourse and of friction for modernity, which anticipated the objectifying and commodifying of both sublimity and antiquity. Mallarmé, in contrast, eschews eternity; for him the instantaneous is sufficient without the need for an antithesis. The present is valuable *as* present, a quality that surpasses Baudelaire's view as extolled in *Le Peintre;*[2] it is absolutely unique and has to be mediated as such.

The abstraction postulated by Marx, and bemoaned by many nineteenth-century artists rooted in Romanticism as fatal distance from nature, is embraced by Mallarmé because it affords him a concentration on pure form and a focus on the (fashionable) commodity that would separate it from the capitalist realm so that it could become a poetic object proper. The modern mythology that would form about such isolation and elevation would later be debated by the surrealists and Benjamin.

Mallarmé interweaves these two strands of *modernité*—the ontological rupture and reification—by choosing what appears to be the most fugitive and ephemeral range of objects possible. Fashion was the absolute abstraction of nature and at the same time the mysterious carrier of instantaneous beauty. Therefore clothes and accessories discussed in the apparently minor and facile medium of fashion journalism provided the poet with a "mythological enclosure" in which the modernist investigation into the structure of language and, implicitly, aesthetics, could take place.[3]

Yet his relationship with fashion appears also as the most straightforward among the artists and poets examined in this book, because it was rendered as a commercial enterprise. As we know from the writings of Balzac, Barbey d'Aurevilly, Gautier, and others, throughout the nineteenth century many writers contributed to fashion magazines; but Mallarmé is the first to regard fashion as an area imbued with all characteristics necessary to discuss *la mode* as the stylistic nucleus of the wider implications of cultural (as well as social, economic, and political) *modernité.* Also, these writings enabled him to create a complete and truly modern *poncif* that is very much in the Baudelairean vein of "du génie"—and not merely for material reasons, although he obviously wanted to see his project succeed in a capitalist economy, but equally for aesthetic ones.

**13.**
Jacques-Henri Lartigue, *Along the Bois de Boulogne,* ca. 1911. Glass negative,
9 × 12 cm. Association des Amis de Jacques-Henri Lartigue, Paris.

*An early equivalent of* une passante *in the twentieth century. The perfect quote within a modern representation of a contemporary fashion.*

From the folds of his fashion journalism Mallarmé arises as the great formalist, as a writer who endlessly and intricately designs his poetic fabric, who weaves hitherto forgotten or obscure words into it, embroiders it with metaphors or comparisons from which the actual object is absent, and borders it in the most perfect formal mode possible.[4] All this endeavor was not simply intellectual, it but also concerned with appearances: the look, the "figure" of a piece of writing (see "le chapeau") tended to outweigh its contents. Albert Thibaudet in the first complete study of Mallarmé's style speaks of the "rejection of the subject"; this rejection is then semantically extended to the syntax and rhythm of *La Dernière Mode*.[5] This structural operation obviously befits modernity's "rupture" but at the same time already points toward pieces like *Un Coup de dés* or the so-called *Livre:* modern formalist experiments in which the factual subject matter is minimized almost to nonexistence on the vast expanses of the white book pages.

Side by side with these intricacies in his symbolist and later modernist poetry rest petite pleasures like the "Éventails" (for women of the haute bourgeoisie as well as his family), "Dons de fruits glacés," or "Les Loisirs de la poste." The banality of these occasional poems may be almost stupefying, yet their ephemeral and facile sovereignty, together with their formal beauty, easily reconciles the reader to them. Moreover, the lack of content was programmatic: when the world was seen as more and more abstracted, then abstraction itself became the aesthetic and metaphysical focus. The changing sociopolitical façade of the nineteenth century required Marx's analyses while Baudelaire and others occupied themselves with the alterations *inside* this world—yet both shared the inquisitive look into the philosophical reasoning behind the rapid change. Mallarmé accepted this conditioning of society, which had become less conspicuous after 1870, and demonstrated—with hidden irony—its facile nature to the bourgeoisie by celebrating what is always present and presented, that is, what is close in temporal as well as physical terms: *la mode.*[6]

There is a temptation within modernity—not confined to Mallarmé's journalism, of course—to flee the realm of the artistic and became occupied exclusively with all things ephemeral. One is drawn toward the quest for social and cultural expressions that are in the closest contact with the present, coupled with the "heroic ability"

**14.**
Édouard Manet, *Portrait of Stéphane Mallarmé,* 1876. Oil on canvas, 27 × 36 cm.
Musée d'Orsay, Paris.

to forget that this immediacy will soon become its own past.[7] Mallarmé might have thought that editing and contributing to a supremely fugitive, and ultimately short-lived, fashion magazine represented the most ephemeral gesture possible for a poet. *La Dernière Mode* is indeed an intricately constructed work of art whose appearance resembles a beautiful dress that flows past the beholder (or rather the reader). Only the sudden nostalgia for its perfume makes one venture beyond the fabric into the folds and pleats of the work[8]—a nostalgia alien to his contemporary readership and thus exclusive to a retrospective review, which for its part finds it hard to communicate the sensuality that was conveyed by the written fashion at that time.

## ■ 2.2 The Goddess

Mallarmé is credited with the saying that "fashion is the goddess of appearance."[9] By the time he began to contemplate his project of publishing a magazine entirely devoted to this demanding goddess, she had already descended from her pedestal into the modern city. Not that this descent would disqualify her as a poetic subject. On the contrary, as the past symbol of the sublime within the ephemeral and fugitive, she could now be observed entirely and literally en passant! In the beginning, the goddess as the fashionable muse inspired Baudelaire to his dictum that "by *modernité* I mean the ephemeral, the fugitive, the contingent, the half of art whose other half is the eternal and the immutable."[10] This definition of modernity followed the logical/ironical progression offered by the title "Le Beau, la mode et le bonheur" ("Beauty, Fashion, and Happiness"), given at the very beginning of Baudelaire's essay on Guys. Three years after this seminal publication, Mallarmé wrote to a friend about his intention to publish on his part a "glorification of beauty"—a project that would eventually turn into *La Dernière Mode:* "I am in the process of laying down the foundations of a book on beauty. My soul moves among the Eternal, experiencing many thrills, if one can mention the immutable in those words."[11] Again, beauty is aligned with the eternal and immutable. Yet for its expression in modernity, another notion is necessary: it also has to be the most contemporary, the most immediate beauty possible. And, following Baudelaire, the beauty has to be entirely disinterested, not judged by norms of utility or commercial practice. The previous year, Mallarmé's friend Paul Verlaine paraphrased Baudelaire in the same manner already infused with decadence: "Of course, the real aim of poetry is Beauty, Beauty alone, pure Beauty, without any addition of Usefulness, Truthfulness, or Righteousness."[12] Using this concept of beauty, Verlaine gave fashion's erratic and irreverent behavior, as well as its function as a beautiful facade, a priori absolution.

In an undated manuscript, Mallarmé would juxtapose the Baudelairean "le Beau, la mode et le bonheur" with the objectified and pragmatic conflict of "le Beau et l'utile." The aesthetic (and epic) part of life, which Baudelaire had regarded as the appropriate antidote to excesses of industrialization, would remain for Mallarmé the necessary counterbalance to continuing objectification. For him, the ambiguous, even dialectical character of modernity is thus a combination of both concepts—concluding, as one expects, in fashion.

▪

*In Beauty and Usefulness one must introduce a degree of Truthfulness. Beauty can just become some sort of forsaken ornament. Usefulness on its own, if the purpose is mediocre, can express only inelegance. To shape in true fashion demands a certain oblivion from the artisan as to what the use of the object will be; that is what counts— the application of the idea as a totally modern expression of truth. This transformation of the gift of creativity does not come without flaws or failure; yet what marvel, in the achievement, can exist in that umbrella, that black suit, that "cut."*[13]

▪

The suit, the umbrella, a top hat or ball gown—all these may serve as supreme examples of the subjective being transposed into the object, and thus as epistemological elements of modernity. Yet such is the emphasis on immediacy that Baudelaire's modernity appears in immanent danger of becoming mere modernism. Would it not require the transitory, the transhistorical character, ready to transport one back and forth between past and present?

Mallarmé found an early expression for transitoriness as well. In some quatrains, collectively titled "Photographies," the poet momentarily transfixed the dress styles worn by his friend and lover, the occasional high-class *vendeuse* Méry Laurent:[14]

**15.**
Édouard Manet, *Autumn,* 1882. Oil on canvas, 73 × 51 cm. Musée des Beaux-Arts, Nancy.

*"Manet is trying to get for [Mallarmé] from the editor-in-chief of a new magazine* L'Art et la Mode *the commission for reviewing books; yet Mallarmé is more interested in other news that Manet has for him; 'I will make "Autumn" after Méry Laurent. I went to talk to her about it yesterday. She has had a pelisse made. What a pelisse, my friend, in vibrant brown lined with antique gold fabric. It is stunning. I left Méry Laurent saying: "When you have grown tired of wearing the pelisse, will you please leave it to me?" She promised me, and it will create a sensational background for all the things I dream of doing.' . . . This extravagant coat marks the start of Méry Laurent's life of luxury and elegance."—Henri Mondor.*

■

*II*
*Blanche japonaise narquoise*
*Je me taille dès mon lever*
*Pour robe un morceau bleu turquoise*
*Du ciel à quoi je fais rêver.*

*III*
*Folle robe d'une péri*
*Et dedans plus*
*Pour les changer en soi Méry*
*De nos chimères se décore.*

. . . . . . . . . . . . . . . . . . . .

.

*V*
*Très fidèle à mes amitiés*
*Dans un bleu reflet qui s'argente*
*Sous un, si vous en doutiez!*
*Que ma robe seule est changeante.*

. . . . . . . . . . . . . . . . . . . . . . . . . . .

*VII*
*Je ne sais pourquoi je vêts*
*Ma robe de clair de lune*
*Moi qui, déesse, pouvais*
*Si bien me passer d'aucune.*[15]

■

The goddess, who left her pedestal to command new (blue) dresses or a hunting out-fit, now asks to be documented—if not on a frieze for eternity, then at least in a photo for a society column, displaying each of her latest items of apparel.

Yet this is but appearance, significant as that is for dressmaker and wearer alike; the poet on his part aimed at renewing aesthetic experience. The crux for poetry—and literature in general—remained, as Lessing had observed a century before, that writing describes the object only in temporal succession: one view, one situation after the other. By contrast, visual art is able to realize the object in a "fruitfully chosen moment," within the spatial coexistence of figures and colors.[16] The "photographs" of Laurent may capture her body and clothes in one particular instant, yet the blue dress that envelopes her constantly changes its look: from turquoise-blue fabric reminiscent of the sky, via silken folds that glisten and gleam to evoke mythic creatures, to a silvery blue, subtle but strong like the mutual admiration and love affair that binds her to the poet. Mallarmé faced the limitation of written description not by successively picturing the same situation from different angles but by contemplating Laurent's figure in a single view—a view, however, that repeatedly returns to her apparel as he adds yet another of the diverse aspects that will in the end complete her poetic character. Obviously, facial expressions or gestures could also be observed in different ways according to momentary impression, but such descriptions would be less significant. The poet intends to describe the most important aspect of Laurent's character to him—her love and friendship: an immutable fact. But to convey a visual impression of how his friend appears before his eyes, the fugitive and ephemeral must become fundamental. Fashion—as in Baudelaire's "Passante"—left an impression of outward beauty on the beholder that could change but could also support inner sentiments and provide an attractive counterbalance to the psyche. Even within the speed of modern times, poetry might rest assured "que [l]a robe seule est changeante," while it was still preserving the innermost feelings.[17]

Accordingly, *La Dernière Mode* would not become a document of social changes or studies in character. Its existence would be too short to accomplish such a goal in any case. But within the brief months of autumn and winter 1874/1875, the magazine described innovative changes in styles and apparel that superseded each other.[18] Mallarmé did not question the circumstances in which his writing was produced and distributed (which is not necessarily the same as accepting them). But he did engage in the flow of impressions that fashion created. And these creations provided an elegant outlet for the artist's imagination in modernity; they would eventually become its mirror.

Throughout the nineteenth century art lost its institutional ties to church, court, and state. The principles of the Enlightenment added to this trend a questioning of the established order and substituted "natural" reasoning for the transcendental *ordo*—which had hitherto provided art with both topoi and justification. Thus the separation of artistic genres declined.[19] At the same time modernity would request that art choose and define its respective tasks again and again. One Romantic position—occupied by Schlegel, whose aesthetics Baudelaire adapts in his "L'Art philosophique," as we have seen—maintains that the subjective within language and theory should become inseparable components of artistic practice. Yet the static character of these components would impede the artist's ability to express the transitoriness of modern life. Mallarmé, in circumnavigating this dilemma by adding a distinct exterior character, a visual and fugitive quality to his poetry, had a twofold aim. Ultimately, the formalism of the *Livre* (from the early 1870s) would lead to the pictorial radicalism of *Un Coup de dés* (published 1897). In a parallel action, his subjective quest for the visual was transformed into an exclusive concern with objectified appearance in *La Dernière Mode,* which presents the other, more impressionable (perhaps even "impressionist") option.

## ■ 2.3 The La(te)st Fashion

Baudelaire's *poncif,* the marketable commodity that the artist had to produce in order to succeed in modern culture, appears to be alien to a more introspective character. Thus one might suspect at first that *La Dernière Mode* was merely a sarcastic response to the refusal by the *Parnasse Contemporain* (essentially a decision by Anatole France) to publish Mallarmé's famous "Faune" during the early 1870s.

"[Q]uite despairing of this awful tyrannical book that I have to produce, I have . . . tried to write and edit on my own . . . a magazine la Dernière Mode," Mallarmé later confessed to Verlaine.[20] At the moment in which the poet's demand for complete artistic integrity failed in the commercial world, he willfully decides to play by its rules. Instead of critique or cynicism (Baudelaire's way), he openly commits himself to contemporary society and its expectations; nobody could claim that as a *poncif,* a

**16.**

Edmond Morin, cover page of *La Dernière Mode,* no. 1 (6 September 1874).
Lithograph, 20 × 13 cm.

fashion magazine was not commercially viable. Yet *La Dernière Mode* led from its very beginning an ambiguous life of its own. Although Mallarmé conceived the journal as an enterprise, once he began to live out the assumed roles of editor-in-chief, staff writer, interior designer, and so forth on paper, the "poet" in him grew more and more distinct and very much infused his chronicles and description of apparel.

*Modernité* and the rhetoric of fashion are equally dialectical. Within them the eternal is combined with or opposed by the self-ironical attitude that attaches to the ephemeral. Mallarmé's original idea was to follow Baudelaire into the inquiry of sublime beauty. It was only a vital sense of the instantaneous and ironic, which he also observed in his predecessor, that made him accept the turn from criticism to (fashion) journalism. But whereas Baudelaire sported the cold irony of the cynical dandy, Mallarmé's irony (although at times dandyesque) was generous and warm. In *La Dernière Mode* he did not strive for the absolute manifestation of *la mode;* its "côté épique," but for the self-referential and openly futile; its "côté contemporaine." Yet for the enterprise to fully succeed, he had to apply care and skill in poetic expression. Roland Barthes comments in his *Système de la mode,* "If it were a matter of a dialectic of the serious and the frivolous, i.e., if the frivolity of Fashion were *immediately* taken as absolutely serious, we would then have one of the most elevated forms of the literary experience: i.e., the very movement of the Mallarméan dialectic apropos Fashion itself (Mallarmé's *La dernière mode*)."[21] The "excessively serious" and the "excessively futile" make up the rhetoric of sartorial fashion,[22] yet excess was alien to the avid readers of nineteenth-century fashion journals, and most certainly to the contributors as well. This journal's potential to provide the "most elevated form of the literary experience" is far from exaggerated—Mallarmé realized the complexity of the project, in which fashion's reflexive and representative functions meet, from the very beginning.

In 1867, however, he still dreamed about his book on beauty. He writes to his friend the decadent poet Villiers de l'Isle-Adam: "I have yet to achieve the perfect definition and the dream inside of two books, both novel and eternal, one of them all absolute 'Beauty.'"[23] Here, the dialectics are paraphrased by the "eternal" and the "novel" (i.e., the "transitory" of Baudelaire); yet the element of novelty remains in itself futile *and* serious. The claim to "absolute beauty" refers once again to its latest, instantaneous expression, which is recognized according to the hallmarks of the classical and sublime. Beauty can be found in almost any expression of modern life; any artisan (especially the tailor of black suits, as we have seen) is capable of producing beauty and—by definition—creating art, as all these objects are potentially artistic if they truthfully represent their inherent ideas. What results is Mallarmé's credo to compose "a compendium that intends to study fashion as art."[24] Fashion as art—Gabrielle Chanel would surely object. Yet the scene is not set in the twentieth century, when fashion and its business have become common property and a mass of publications disseminate the latest styles within days of their first appearance. Toward the end of the 1860s, fashion was still designed and produced within a closed-off social framework. The couturières and couturiers remained more or less anonymous to the middle-class public at large. Of course, the goddess, like the mundane Parisian woman, would have known where to turn in order to obtain a certain cut, a certain workmanship; but the names of tailors and dressmakers still had an aura, were still traded as well-kept secrets. Then, in 1858 one dressmaker decided to display his *poncif* with as much pomp and circumstance as possible. Charles Frederick Worth opened his first *maison* in that year and quickly became the first household name among the artisans who hitherto had striven to maintain a certain anonymity to guard their reputation. Couturiers and couturières such as Robert Pingat (an independent house from 1864), Jacques Doucet (finally established as a couture business proper in 1871), and the Callot Sœurs (from 1895) followed suit.

France from 1848 to 1870 was curiously torn between the ancient and the modern, as it suffered a sociopolitical equivalent to the conflict introduced by the concept of modernity. On the one hand ruled the emperor Louis Napoleon, who held up the absolutist principles of Bonapartism and Caesarism; on the other there were growing demands, which had already been declared in earlier revolutions, for "necessary liberties," voiced by the parliamentary opposition under the historian and subsequent president Adolphe Thiers (later replaced by Émile Ollivier). Concessions such as freedom of the press and the accountability of individual ministers led to the *Empire libéral,* safeguarded by 83 percent public approval in the plebiscite of 1869.

This combination of the old regime and new democratic tendencies became mirrored in the French bourgeoisie. In a given *hôtel particulier* one might find the pretensions of old families and old customs; in a palais next to them, the nouveaux riches who gained and lost their reputations on the stock market. This uneasy coexistence of tradition and contemporariness, epitomized in Proust's *Recherche* by the relationship between the Guermantes and Verdurins, also characterized the readership of Mallarmé's journal. A publication like his had to possess a distinctly aristocratic air (Mallarmé's literary conscience demanded that much); but since the subscribers came from the middle class and not the nobility, he had to tailor his writing carefully to avoid estranging them with too many luxurious images or metaphors. As we will see, his "Correspondance avec les Abonnées" would solve this potential dilemma ingeniously.

Although the Franco-Prussian War of 1870/1871 exposed the desperation of the absolutist regime, the society of the Third Republic was not fundamentally different from the one before the war. The monarchists/Bonapartists still held the parliamentary majority and, most important, the economy carried on as before. Once again, the resulting revolt against social injustice, born out of frustration that yet another possibility for fundamental change had been wasted, was based partly on historical reminiscence. The Parisian Commune of 1871 was spearheaded not necessarily by the workers' organizations but by urban craftsmen, artisans, and members of the educated middle class. However, as a symbol for the heroic failure of an idea the Commune gave rise to powerful labor organizations and syndicalism. During that time Mallarmé continued, albeit much less actively, the modernist tradition of Baudelaire and sympathized with the radical *Comité central* and the Blanquistes. He himself subscribed to a number of anarchist publications,[25] and one can only wonder what impact this morning reading must have had when, after a day's teaching at the *lycée,* he returned home to write and edit his fashion magazine.

In November 1871 Mallarmé moved to the rue de Moscou in Paris; there his plan to publish a magazine devoted to his goddess surfaced once more (partly because of his and his family's strained finances). He wrote to his friend, the poet José-Maria de Heredia:

**17.**
Jean Béraud, *Pont de l'Europe,* 1870s. Oil on canvas, 48 × 73.5 cm. Private collection,
United States.

■

*Recently, I have been all over Paris, to try to collect subscriptions to help me start this beautiful and luxurious review that occupies all my thoughts: L'Art décoratif, published every month, Paris, 1872. The unlikely pretext for this letter is the following one: Only one man can design the frontispiece: Claudius Popelin. He has been perfectly charming toward me and has accepted. All is agreed, so do not ask anything of him. But being so endeared to him, could you perhaps mention all this in your next letter? Soon. "You have heard that I am publishing a journal: and that he was designing the cover for it: the more, the better, etc." . . . But what on earth are you doing so far from Paris? Some wonderful new poems, I bet. Just come back soon to read them out to us.*[26]

■

The project was about to take shape; already Mallarmé envisaged literary contributions by his poet-friends; already he chose the lithography of the frontispiece in order to attract the maximum number of prospective readers.[27]

The concept and form of the planned L'Art Décoratif originated from another luxurious publication to which Mallarmé had earlier contributed. In 1865 the Parisian journal L'Artiste published a second contribution by Mallarmé (the first had been in 1862), titled "Symphonie littéraire."[28] In it, guided by the "modern muse of impotence," he paid homage to the three poets he admired most: Baudelaire, Gautier, and Banville. This homage, however, in its retrospective tone also had the air of an adieu. In July of the same year, L'Artiste, edited by the erstwhile dandy Arsène Houssaye, featured for the first time a column, "L'Art et la mode" by a mysterious Comtesse d'Orr. This (golden?!) Comtesse (who might be regarded as the female equivalent of one the most famous of all nineteenth-century dandies, the Comte d'Orsay) would continue to write regularly on the combination of the eternal and the ephemeral, and from the very beginning her tone appears in tune with the most literary of written fashion. It anticipates a fixation on the topic that was seen subsequently in La Dernière Mode: "If I wanted fashion in all its bizarre caprices, there would be much to say and contradict. . . . It is impossible to dream more diverse and more ravishing outfits, the show is enchanting. . . . Eternal beauty as a small and charming literary miniature . . . was present in the midst of all these scents."29 Who might have concealed his or her poetic license behind this pseudonym? In his memoirs, Houssaye was not prepared to lift her mask, although he does allude to the identity of the "goddess" whom Mallarmé rendered "Diana in the Tuileries." In 1865, the very same year in which Mallarmé and the "Comtesse" first wrote essays for his magazine, "when she [Diana] was only seventeen, she dared to change fashion, at the opera, at the races, everywhere, by dressing in Directoire fashion: no hoops, no padding, nothing but a dress molded to her shape. This is worthy of a price from the Académie des Beaux-Arts."30 It was quite an achievement indeed, considering the sartorial demands of 1865 and its textile excesses. Even the most adventurous arbiter of taste had better be a nubile teenager to carry off the transparent chemise of 1800.

In 1885, when Houssaye looks back on the time when a sartorial style could easily be equated with an artistic innovation, the present appears shallow and insubstantial in comparison. He sighs pessimistically:

∎

*Unfortunately fashion has returned to illusionary fashions and the* suivez-moi jeune homme *[colorful long ribbons, attached to a light hat, which fall down the back of the wearer]. It always comes to this.*

*Among Egyptians and among Greeks the art of dressing was an art. Among the French, it is often a caricature of beauty. Cleopatra and Aspasia dressed like goddesses. Our great ladies and courtesans dress, here and there, like madwomen.*31

∎

This very time that his contemporary Baudelaire judged as "mad," when the "barometer of reason showed a storm brewing," is retrospectively perceived as a classical period, its fashion equated with statue-like beauty, while present clothing is regarded as superficial, even vulgar. As Baudelaire did in opposing Michelet, Houssaye would elevate fashion to art only in remembrance. Still, one wonders whether he had readily sympathized between 1865 and 1874 with the Comtesse and Mallarmé, who had both proposed to study "la mode comme un art."

The flow and counterflow between the paradigmatic value of fashion and artworks left their mark on Mallarmé. Yet his plan to produce a magazine similar to

Houssaye's could not be realized. The poet had to wait another two years until his neighbor in the rue de Moscou, the publisher Charles Wendelen, asked him to add a descriptive text to the hitherto exclusively visual series of engravings titled *La Dernière Mode*. Wendelen had, together with his wife, previously published fashionable magazines such as *La Saison* and *Les Modes de la Saison*. In the new enterprise, his role would be limited to coordinating print and distribution, while his wife would advise Mallarmé on the practical problems concerning fashion in Paris—that is, the location of shops, prices, and the distribution of goods.[32]

In December, "le Directeur Marasquin" (a character representative of Wendelen's role) gave a summary of the first six issues published during summer and autumn of 1874: "None of the first six issues of our second year (the first was without text), which established our publication in material and intellectual luxury, is lacking anything, not even success."[33] Although the claim to material success was a touch exaggerated, what the second series aspired to immediately becomes clear: luxury in both appearance and contents. Wendelen employed two illustrators to create the engravings for his previously rather unsuccessful publication,[34] and as Mallarmé had already let down Popelin (as well as de Heredia) by abandoning *L'Art Décoratif*, another illustrator had to be found who could make the new project distinctive. Once again, Banville would serve as an intermediary. In 1868 he had collaborated with the artist Edmond Morin on *Sonnets et Eaux-Fortes*, a book that, as the title declares, paired sonnets and etchings; it was suggested by publisher Alphonse Lemerre.[35] Through his friends Banville and Lemerre, Mallarmé was able to secure Morin's talent, which was often employed to illustrate literary texts.[36] As a thank-you, he rushed a copy of the first issue of his journal to the Lemerres: "I leave dazed, exhausted, the cover of my journal already printed and hundreds of letters written. Soon, you, or rather Madame Lemerre, will receive this folly-cle."[37]

The "folly" of the luxurious cover was thus created; the next task was to compose an equally sophisticated content. First Mallarmé would call on a number of his friends to embellish the journal with literary contributions; that alone would distinguish the magazine from other publications on the market. Yet he also had to ensure that the regular columns—as continuity was essential to keep subscribers—mirrored

**18.**

Edmond Morin, title page of *La Dernière Mode,* no. 1 (6 September 1874).

Lithograph, 20 × 13 cm.

the exclusivity and high standards of his project. For the authors of his literary reviews "Nouvelles et Vers," Mallarmé drew on connections made during the past twenty years: Banville as the modernist link to the original inquiry into fashion and art by Baudelaire; François Coppée, Sully Prudhomme, and Catulle Mendès from the previously acrimonious Parnassiens; Léon Cladel, the realist writer, as the Blanquist connection to politics; as well as Émile Zola, whom Mallarmé, despite their fundamentally different aesthetics, recognized as a novel force in literature. Alas, Zola's contribution would never be used, because the magazine folded. Mallarmé wrote to him in November 1874, on occasion of the premiere of Zola's comedy *Les Héritiers Rabourdin* (which would be favorably reviewed in *La Dernière Mode*): "The press has proved yet again to be completely ignorant. What! a vulgar print: yet is it not appreciated by the most refined taste? I for my part will admire a painted or drawn poster as much as a fresco or an apotheosis, I do not find any aspect of art inferior to another; I enjoy all aspects equally."[38] If one takes Mallarmé's declaration at face value, it is curious that he would leave the high ground of the *Parnasse Contemporain* only for an equally elevated expression of contemporary life—haute couture. The commodity is equated with the artwork, so much is true; but it is a very exclusive commodity indeed. Mallarmé's professed interest in mirroring real life (and perhaps politics as well) did not actually progress beyond the occasional sympathetic utterance. The manifestation of beauty within his "mythological enclosure" would always take precedence, in both aesthetic and intellectual taste, over the reality that could be seen on the Parisian streets around him.[39]

## ◼ 2.4 Fashion Written II–IV

### 2.4.1 The Epic and the Epicene

In order both to distinguish and to combine the serious and the futile, the eternal aspect and the transitory in his writing on fashion, Mallarmé commits himself to gentle schizophrenia. Copying the roles of the mysterious Comtesse d'Orr, of his goddess Diana, and of the Baudelairean dandy, Mallarmé split himself into a number of poetic personae, all of whom he concealed under female pseudonyms. Thus *La Dernière Mode* came to comprise the following columns, each written by a highly individualized yet fictional character:

*1. The articles on "La Mode," which regularly opened each issue and which contained philosophical reflections on fashion, "created by a woman of the world who also happens to be a distinguished writer: Mme [Marguerite] de Ponty."*[40]

*2. The "Gazette de la fashion," which from the fifth issue onward featured a look at the commercial side of Parisian fashion as well as "all the weekly recommendations, luxurious and practical. It lies with you, Mesdames, to have absolute confidence in this foreign-sounding pseudonym of a well-known Parisian: Miss Satin."*[41]

*3. The "Chroniques de Paris" by Ix., an ambiguous character and immediate descendant of the Baudelairean "l'homme des foules"*[42]*—the flâneur with an observant eye for fashionable passantes. A woman-about town, she would eventually come closest to the factual association of art and fashion.*

*4. A number of supporting "domestic" characters: a chef, an interior designer, "une dame créole," Zizi (the "bonne mulâtre de Surate"), Olympe, plus some others, whose contributions Mallarmé adopted from various sources.*

*5. Finally, "les Abonnées," who, with dependable regularity, gave the cues for Mallarmé's explanations and elaborations. They were rewarded with an additional service by "[t]he Parisian expert who makes all the acquisitions for La Dernière Mode, Madame Charles, [who] puts herself entirely at your disposal."*[43]

From the outset the characters of each were as clearly defined as figures on a stage, in order to cover as many facets of fashion's rhetoric as possible. From sublime analysis by de Ponty to gossipy accounts by Miss Satin, from metaphysical speculation about the immutability of fashion, again by Ponty, to considerations of its paradigmatic role within the secluded female world by Ix., the dialectics of modernity and fashion were debated in imaginary dialogues between the pseudonyms and readers and among the different columnists themselves. In their rhetorical and stylistic refinement, these fictional debates can bear comparison with their historical model, the Platonic dialogues.

When the Italian poet Luigi Gualdo received the first issue of *La Dernière Mode,* he enthused to fellow Parnassien François Coppée:

•

*I have received a letter from Mallarmé that may yet prove to be his best work—written on a paper prospectus for the fabled fashion journal. I have also received an issue of the journal where I have recognized under the pseudonym of XX [sic] the same Mallarmé, and where I have found the first chapter of your novel, hidden underneath a fashion drawing!! What kind of journal is this?*

*I will reply to Mallarmé within the next days and I have written to Bourget [the poet and dandy Paul Bourget, always in tune with the fashionable] of whom I have not read anything yet.*[44]

•

Another letter, some months later, shows Gualdo still confused about the writing of the journal, yet much more certain of its impact and importance: "I have but one issue of the fashion journal. Is the entire text by the Master, or have the Mallarmisms made such progress that all the editors write like him?"[45] The pseudonyms were not meant to conceal the real author entirely. Mallarmé corresponded openly under the letterhead of *La Dernière Mode.* The stylistic coinage of "Mallarmism" united the various roles, and the poet did not go so far as to assume different prose styles for each fictional columnist. Such a method, amounting to nothing more than "pastiches et melanges," would hardly distinguish the rhetorical quality of written fashion.

Yet if the male artist makes almost no attempt to hide his poetic identity, will not the writing appear alien if subsequently credited to a woman? Can one expect an empathy from Mallarmé that would transgress gender? To be sure, Mallarmé greatly enjoyed the role-playing that the pseudonyms made possible. As we have seen, his occasional poems on postal addresses, festivities, or fans rested calmly beside his modernist intricacies. The deliberate unimportance of these topics allowed the poet to relax, while an ironic attitude qualified the cautious banalities. Assuming in his writing a female identity became for Mallarmé less a transgression of gender than a way of occupying the *social* status of a woman. *La Dernière Mode* permitted the poet to indulge in all things futile, facile, and domestic, without having to fear any social, or artistic, sanctions for his less than sublime—that is, nonmasculine—behavior. In the intimate setting of eight folio pages, Mallarmé reveled in the chance to give advice to his "chères abonnées" on education (professional interest here), on entertainment, or—the ultimate in positioning himself in the place of a woman in society—on buying or even designing dresses and accessories.[46]

The gowns and hats depicted in *La Dernière Mode* were created beforehand. Although Morin was perfectly capable of rendering a stage costume into a fashion illustration, he was most certainly not responsible for designing apparel novel to the sophisticated readership of the magazine. For sartorial luxuries, the previous expertise of the Wendelens might have come into play, yet Mallarmé's aesthetics required other, more congenial sources. The lithographs of issue 6 thus carried for the first time the caption "Créées [sic] par Madame de Ponty"—the writer ventures to become a couturier![47] Here the reformation of nature in high fashion aligns itself with the abstraction of language to create an unsurpassed semantic and sartorial formalism under the guise of self-effacing commercial prose. The *modernités* of Baudelaire and Gautier come to bear on fashion together.

Innovative clothing in the early 1870s was not created in studios to be presented on a catwalk; the designers or *faiseuses* developed their ideas on and in accordance with the wishes of their female clientele. The only way to see these new creations was to attend exclusive balls or receptions or to peek into the boxes at the opera, or into the enclosure at Longchamps. Once admired, the dresses vanished—more often than not, after their first appearance—into the recesses of their owners' wardrobes. Fashion was not yet attached to the name of its designer but to the status (and style) of its wearer. But, most significantly, the creations were also admired as artworks in themselves. Marguerite de Ponty emphasizes the dichotomy between the dress that flows and moves with the woman's body and the gown as an entity independent from its wearer:

■

*First and unique article:*

*Whereas we have been using traditional materials for the making of ball gowns that seem to envelop us like rising, fanciful mist made up of all whiteness, the*

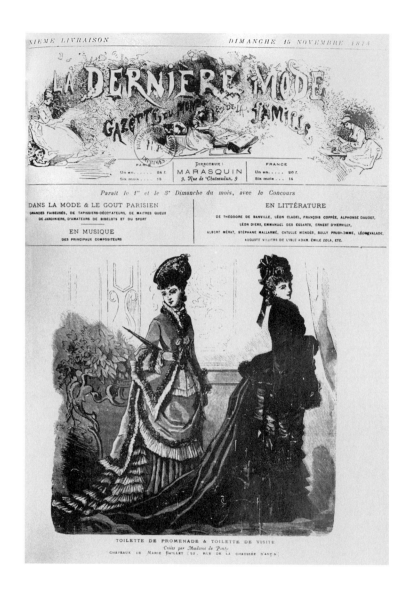

**19.**
Edmond Morin, cover page of *La Dernière Mode,* no. 6 (15 November 1874).
Lithograph, 20 × 13 cm.

*gown itself, bodice and skirt, molds the figure more than ever before: delicious and clever contrast between what is left vague and what is shown distinctively.*[48]

∎

This opposition was carried out on a textual level by the diverse voices of Ponty and Miss Satin or, more generally speaking, by dichotomous comment on and poetic evocation of dressing.

Sartorial notes at grand occasions were recorded by Mallarmé's circle of female friends and quickly dispatched to the "editorial office" in the rue de Moscou. In November 1874, the Comtesse de Callias (Nina de Villard) wrote:

∎

*My dear Stéphane,*

*If there is a problem in my using the name of your journal to gain seats at the [theater] Italiens, please tell me so without any hesitation; I have other ways if this one should be impractical. I will try and describe to you the toilette of Rousseil in "L'Idole":*

*A long train of grosgrain faille in* pain brûlé *[dark brown] lined with pale taffetas, the front of the skirt a thousand pale flounces held tight to the body by large ribbons set on the bias representing enormous flowers in burned orange, the sleeveless* gilet *in the same brown as the train displayed pale shirtsleeves—It all seems a bit extravagant, doesn't it? Yet it is superb and I would urge you to copy the gown for your fashion illustration.*[49]

∎

Leading actresses on the Parisian stage were traditionally at the cutting edge of fashion, as were great courtesans, and many couturiers would have one particular protégée (e.g., La Réjane for Jacques Doucet) whom they adorned with their most daring creations, willfully ignorant of the requirements of the actual play. Thus Ix. took the advice of her "correspondent" and faithfully reproduced Mme de Villard's description in her "Chronique de Paris."[50] In addition to depending on the eyes of various female spectators, Mallarmé also relied on Méry Laurent's mnemotechnique (cf. "Photographies") and her ability to supply him with the latest sartorial trends through her own professional knowledge as former buyer for a fashion house.

**20.**
Édouard Manet, *Nina de Villard,* 1873–1874. Gouache and graphite on woodblock, 9.9 × 7.3 × 2.4 cm. Musée d'Orsay, Paris.

Yet above all, he took it on himself to tailor the perfect apparel for his "goddess," so intricate that they would become the visual equivalents of his literary work. In the fourth issue of *La Dernière Mode,* the fashion that had hitherto been circumscribed and analyzed for its metaphysical contents is now detailed; invented by a fictional persona, it now enters the real contemporary world:

■

*Autumn has begun and so has the journal itself with this season: the last two issues have done very well . . . in showing the more or less dazzling changes of the latest Fashion. The journal is designed to give, to even the most cursory of its readers, an account of Parisian society in all its pleasures and obligations everywhere, at social gatherings or in the intimacy of their homes. Parties: what parties? of course, since it is an excuse for dressing up. . . . Will there be gala dresses? No, hunting outfits; and so that they can be even more appreciated they will be shown against the background of a green park to trigger your imagination, not in a drawing room or on a street corner. Two sketches: the first recorded at one of our most prestigious dressmakers, as the outfit was leaving under the name of an illustrious lady for a rendezvous with a princely, dare I say royal, hunt. [The description of an outfit follows.]*[51]

■

In antithesis to this fashion, probably created for a "quasi-royal" occasion, Mallarmé places an imaginary design:

■

*Shall we compare the garment that we have created in our imagination to an authentic one? . . . [The description of the second outfit follows.] Which one would you chose, my ladies, while you still can and the great hunts have not started yet? The first of these outfits has the advantage, being as simple and practical as the other, of having been designed for a contemporary beauty; while the latter has not been worn by anybody yet.*[52]

■

The question of exclusivity is for the poet entirely rhetorical. Only the clothes of his imagination could ever hope to satisfy his quest for modern beauty, sartorially as well as literally. Mallarmé invents fashion as he invents his own syntax. But his ideals were

**21.**

Gustave Caillebotte, *Study of a Couple under an Umbrella,* 1877. Oil on canvas, 46 × 32 cm. Private collection.

*Whereas he clearly worked out the male apparel in his sketch, Caillebotte left the definition of the female day dress to the last minute, to incorporate into the final picture—titled* Rue de Paris; Rainy Weather— *any changes in fashion that would occur while his painting was in progress.*

not destined to be realized if they remained poetic. In suggesting a possible hunting costume (*chasse* suggests also the vigorous pursuit of an idea), Mallarmé deliberately rouses a desire dormant in the women who leafed through his journal at teatime—a desire unlikely to be realized and thus comparable to the post meridiem, lustful dream of his "Faune." In *La Dernière Mode* conspicuous consumption, the sublimation of a female sexuality that was socially restricted and often had to be repressed, found a gentle and generous expression.

Because the clothes designed by Mme de Ponty could not be copied, even if the most skillful of couturières should scrupulously follow her/his description, the textile resembled the textual. The image of the beautiful clothes is meant to remain immaterial, like the comparatives missing from Mallarmé's verses or the blank spaces between the lines of his late formalist poetry. "Clothing is language [*langage*], fashion creates and dreams within this language, but fashion also supplies a language about clothing," Michel Butor later echoed.[53] Here the dialectics in fashion, especially in Mallarmé's pairing of *mode et modernité,* surface again. Fashion is an unspoken dream within language (a language that will receive a systematic structuralist analysis in sections 2.5 and 5.4); in reality clothes appear often brash and vulgar, much more rarely subtle and eloquent. The form of the hunting costume is imaginary, while the "background" that the readers had to conjure up constitutes a real, social anathema to the poetry in written fashion.

On a textual level, the paragraph on the *costume de chasse* ends with a mythic evocation of Diana and her descent from the pedestal in the Tuileries to order new clothes and become a Parisian *sportswoman*. It is an oneiric image contained within the language of fashion and shared with the readers under the pretext of describing autumn novelties. However, commercial reality demanded also that Ponty (a.k.a. Mallarmé) supply the "abonnées" with proof of the exquisite style that prevailed in the journal and create an intimacy between ladies of fashion who shared the same exclusive taste in clothes. Admittedly, any couturier could have occupied this role professionally, but Mallarmé did not intend to change into a mere artisan (despite his high appraisal of the tailor of *habits noirs*); he wanted to be taken seriously in his endeavor to offer a truly modern voice in literature. The veiled figure of the modern poet who stands behind *La Dernière Mode* permits indulgence in all things "unmanly," yet the knowledge of his true authorship, shared by the artistic community, prevents a decline in his artistic, or social, status.

Here as in his politics, Mallarmé kept himself far from rigorous commitment.[54] He enjoyed assuming the role of a passive, soft, and subservient figure—in part because this displayed an empathy with the expected behavior of the female in nineteenth-century public life. Yet he did not realize, or he repressed knowledge of, the sexual and social ramifications of such a fictional change in gender-specific behavior. His is not the servitude of a Leopold von Sacher-Masoch, who ostentatiously subverted contemporary social and sexual norms by assuming the literary persona of a man joyously submitting himself to the will of women (and passively living this role in many variations throughout his life).[55]

Mallarmé's empathy with a woman's psyche has a particular precedent in Jules Barbey d'Aurevilly, who, some three decades before *La Dernière Mode,* wrote his column for fashion magazines. But whereas Mallarmé had a weakness for domesticity within the female character, Barbey d'Aurevilly put himself in the position of women (of his own social stratum, naturally) because they devoted their lives to elegance and refinement. Instead of wishing, like Mallarmé, to compose a "Gazette du Monde et de la Famille," he began to constitute fashion and its paradigmatic value for the *Moniteur de la Mode* and *Le Constitutionnel.* His concept of beauty, in dialectical relation to the elegant, was spelled out as early as 1843: "Therefore between real beauty and elegance lies a vast difference; thus again elegance is beauty on a small scale, beauty in miniature. But all beware! beauty in miniature is like a realm gone to seeds. Both have a short life span."[56] Beauty was juxtaposed to its modern component, elegance—a "kingdom ruled by the female sex." To appear elegantly dressed was far from being fashionable, yet elegance could be achieved without beauty—even despite it. Modernity increasingly required reaction, not composure. It left less and less time to cultivate the beautiful. Whereas Baudelaire discovered beauty in the appearance of clothes, Mallarmé would describe it in the *spirit* of dressing, in the ephemeral and facile quality of the la(te)st fashion.

Barbey d'Aurevilly published his lines on elegance under the female pseudonym of Maximilienne de Syrène, in remembrance of the woman he had "silently adored" in his youth. Her particular style and grace, which he once evoked in a fragment of prose,[57] was the sensual basis for his almost complete empathy with a woman's judgment of her clothes. "Elegance is the small sex of beauty," he claimed.[58] Elegance—the smaller *and* fairer sex?—appears as contemporary and modern. Not for Barbey d'Aurevilly the normative character of eternal beauty, which forced one into restrained boredom. The speed of life was reflected in the twists and turns that fashion traces.

■

*Among ourselves, one is wrapped up in the most ceremonious words with an extravagant attire as with a black uniform worn for too long, and we do find very impertinent this so-called tolerance that refers to an attire as extravagant; for, in the end, what could be more charming, more sacred, more triumphant in the field of fashion than extravagance, as it remains in the light of truthfulness? Within a society like ours, on the verge of profound boredom, it is for extravagance in all its forms that one has to take up arms!*[59]

■

He was truly a model for the young Baudelaire, who at that time followed the same sartorial caprice to stay "in the light of truthfulness," to dress in an ostentatious and colorful manner.

However, while he subsequently turned to purism, Barbey d'Aurevilly himself could never sympathize with the exclusive rigor of the black suit. In 1861 the fifty-three-year-old was described as still sporting colorful, and thus by implication effeminate, attire: "He wears white gloves, trimmed with black, rose-tinted or in *mi-partie;* his cuffs are heavily starched, almost to the point of patent leather; his tight trousers are strapped and in a white, red, black, and green tartan check; sometimes in zebra patterns, sometimes like the skin of a snake or like a tiger's coat."[60] His was a constant and vain tiger's leap;[61] it would never be satisfied with the ubiquitous black worn by his male contemporaries from Baudelaire to Mallarmé and beyond. Although he foreshadowed their refined rhetoric on fashion, his style was more impatient and much more cynical than it was ironic. In April 1846, while Baudelaire at the Louvre busied himself composing the second "Salon" in which his thoughts on fashion (and the importance of the *habit noir*) would first surface,[62] Barbey d'Aurevilly left the museum to find among female shoppers a less than sublime but metropolitan modernity: "While the exhibition at the Louvre brings together the amateurs of painting, attentively judging the works submitted to their examination, an exhibition of a different kind has the happy privilege to reunite a crowd that, although less numerous, is in its entirety no less composed of admirers; we should say admiresses, since it addresses women only. We are speaking here of the exhibition of shawls offered by the beautiful stores along the Chaussée-d'Antin."[63] In the conflict between the eternal and transitory beauty of fashion, Maximilienne de Syrène knew to which side (s)he would defect. Fashion is too futile perhaps, yet surely too serious, to be constantly qualified through aesthetic reflection on the sublime. This dichotomy had first to be realized polemically by Barbey d'Aurevilly and theoretically by Baudelaire before it could appear as the self-evident but nevertheless ambiguous basis for the writings of Ponty, Ix., and the other avatars of Mallarmé.

The Parisian women of the nineteenth century claimed the *journaux de modes* for their own. Excluded from contributing to any of the political—that is, "serious"— press, they were forced to focus their interest, hopes, and passions on the pages of fashion magazines. Although most of the owners, and the majority of editors, were men, the contributors to this insular world were expected to be feminine—if not in sex, then at least in attitude, sensitivity, and pseudonym. Within the columns of these journals, a successful style of writing was expected to contain a certain *poncif,* but its overall tone should resemble intimate, polite chat. The female subscribers were expected to appreciate refined and at times frivolous compliments, but to analyze, even favorably, the facility of fashion was felt to be out of place. The futility of female bourgeois existence could be gently ridiculed, but a writer should never cut out the ground from under the delicate feet of her *abonnées.* Thus the aspiring female pseudonyms of Barbey d'Aurevilly and Mallarmé enjoyed only a brief life. About the former, Jacques Boulenger would write in his book on elegance under Louis-Philippe: "He wrote society columns for the *Moniteur de la Mode* under the pseudonym of Maximilienne de

Syrène, 'perfumed impertinence for the dullest minds and most beautiful figures of the century.' It was for this 'repertory of idle nothings' that he proposed, in April 1843, to describe the life of George Brummell. But the editors found their contributor too 'literary,' and soon Mlle de Syrène fell out with them!"[64] The "impertinence" in her tone suggests that Mlle de Syrène was still unmarried, as seems appropriate for a fictional symbol of youthful adoration, while Mme de Ponty's more reflective tone seems to indicate that she cared for a husband and family. Yet Maximilienne composed her columns, albeit sporadically, over a period of nineteen months, while Marguerite's career as *monitrice de la mode* lasted but six.

The "success" of *La Dernière Mode,* so proudly announced in issue 6, never materialized.[65] On two more occasions Ponty and the others composed their columns, then the end of the journal came. In mid-January 1875, Mallarmé made a desperate appeal to the publisher Wendelen to keep his project going. Judging by the response to this lost letter, the poet's shady suggestion jangled the nerves of the erstwhile benevolent "directeur Marasquin":

■

*Willard absolutely forbids me to play any part in the transaction that you have proposed, because of fears of fraudulent bankruptcy, as I have told you again and again; it would impeach my word, given not only to Madame de Locmaria but also to other people, if any fraudulent intent were to be suspected.*

*I do not mind people saying I have been unsuccessful in my business ventures, but I want to keep intact my reputation as an honest man. As I told you yesterday, as soon as the new position I am hoping to create for myself gets stronger, I swear to pay you back, as I intend to pay off Monsieur Morin and all my other creditors.*[66]

■

The society lady Baronne de Locmaria subsequently acquired the rights for *La Dernière Mode* from Wendelen, but she managed to publish only one further issue. Without the intricate relations between the different voices of "Mallarmism" and without the literary contributions from distinguished writers, the journal lost its appeal and raison d'être. The flesh-and-blood contributors had been warned immediately by Mallarmé about the changed character of *La Dernière Mode*. Thus toward the end of January, he wrote to Coppée:

■

*A quick word.*

*I have been robbed of all the work that I produced during several months at the fashion journal, for which you have been kind enough to allow me the publication of your work.*

*At the moment I am not sure into which hands this paper has fallen, it looks like there might be some vague attempts of blackmail being made, etc.*

*Could you therefore refuse at all cost your collaboration with any unknown person who would ask favors of you, similar to those that you had granted me.*[67]

■

Identical letters were sent to Zola, Albert Mérat, and also Alphonse Lemerre. But it would be a last effort to protect his delicate creation. A few days later the Mallarméan enterprise to impose an intimate rhetoric of art and fashion on a commercial world came to its untimely end.

### 2.4.2 *Mode et fiction—modification*

In September 1874, Philippe Burty, a journalist and friend, praised *La Dernière Mode* as the early realization of Mallarmé's belief in the formal significance of the word, its structural independence as a hallmark of a reified modernity. Later this notion would find a parallel expression in the much more austere and fragmentary *Livre*. Burty enthuses: "I have just received your second issue. It is perfect. You have invented the word in the netting of three lines."[68]

Just like an article of clothing, "the word" can be invented, inverted, and reformed if it is perceived as an abstract entity in itself and not just a particle within verbal expression. Although most of the words used in everyday communication have become coded through their social or literal significance, they do acquire independence if taken out of their normative context. In order to create such an independent

**22.**

Edgar Degas, *Mallarmé and Renoir,* 1895. Gelatin silver print. Bibliothèque Littéraire Jacques Doucet, Paris.

*Aging modernists in black suits. "What will appear soon as the oldest, had appeared first as the most modern."—André Gide.*

expression, the writer either can strip down the word to its etymological or structural basis or can "displace" or "dress" it by having it take on an unusual or alien connotation. Within Mallarmé's œuvre poetic coherence demanded that the reader encounter both techniques combined: for obvious reasons the language of *La Dernière Mode* was mainly concerned with "dressing up the word," while the transposition of Mallarmé's style onto the pages of a fashion magazine ("le mallarmisme") was itself a grandiose displacement.

In the second to last issue of the magazine, the "Conseils sur l'Éducation"—in which Mme de Ponty advised mothers on questions of intellectual training—states that "language cannot be discovered by accident, it is composed just like a marvelously intricate piece of embroidery or lace: not single thread of an idea is lost, this thread keeps appearing and disappearing, twined with another. Everything is combined to form a pattern—complex, simple, or ideal—retaining memory; it is not the instinct for harmony that, grown-up or young, one carries within oneself."[69] The word's ultimate aim—whether in its spoken or written form—is to create a beautiful design, like the intricate pattern in a piece of lace. Much as one thread dis- and reappears over and over again in the fabric, a modal entity or, more generally speaking, a poetic potential is never lost but is temporarily concealed by another thread, only to reappear in the very next moment. This holds true for the textile basis of fashion as well as for its sartorial superstructure. Within modernity fashion is the agent willfully preserving the past, enabling a thought or aesthetic concept to reappear at any given, and sometimes inopportune, moment.

Yet in Mallarmé it is less the conceptual than the haptic, sensitive, and, above all, sensual that distinguishes the word. Valéry relates this capacity to the character of the modern:

▪

*Amongst the moderns, none but this poet had dared to make this sharp division between the power of the word [parole] and the ease of comprehension. . . . No one else dared to represent the mystery of all things by the mystery of language. . . .*

*These sensuous properties of language [langage] also stand in a remarkable relation with memory. . . . The instinct for the mnemotechnical value of form appears very strong and very assured in Mallarmé, whose verses are so easy to remember.*[70]

∎

The "mnemotechnical value" can be defined as the art of generating memory through appropriate exercises or, as Freud would later put it, as *Erinnerungsarbeit.* Developing the audience's capacity to remember is of obvious importance for the artist wishing to ensure that his or her works make a lasting impression on the mind of the reader or beholder. It is of greater importance, however, in the creation of these works. In order to eternalize verses or pictures it is necessary, as we have seen, to establish a functional relationship between antiquity and modernity, between past and present. And from Baudelaire via Mallarmé and Valéry to Proust,[71] this emphasis on remembrance is inseparable from the sartorial. The rapidity with which the impressions of nineteenth-century progress successively forced themselves on the artist were countered by using its most contemporary expression, fashion, to refer back to the past and create a standstill (as Benjamin notes) that appears far from conservative or retrospective; instead, in its transhistorical potential it becomes a genuine paradigm of modernity.

The thread that continually surfaces from the depths of the woven textile also reappears, as Benjamin observes, in Proust. The mnemotechnical value of fashion accounts for its capacity to create its own *durée* and is of the greatest importance for the writer who put Henri Bergson's theory into the most poetic of forms. The way in which the quest for ever more intricate (and intimate) remembrance determines the life of his hero renders Proust's *Recherche* the ultimate attempt to fuse past with present. The protagonist Marcel does not intend to remain in the past, yet it is this past that provides him with a reason for present existence. The past is evoked through detailed description of *la mode:* the mode of manners, of habits, and, most of all, of sartorial fashion. During the very last months of his life Proust still wrote letters to certain duchesses requesting detailed description of gowns that they had worn on particular occasions—an even less mediated method than Mallarmé's reliance on the Comtesse de Callias. The author then matched the account with his own memory and brought the past through an article of clothing into his own present. In contrast to the *mémoire volontaire,* the purposeful evocation of facts long gone, stands the *mémoire involontaire,* which envelops the writer in the poetic fabric of the past. Benjamin describes Proust's *Recherche:* "[H]ere, the main role for the remembering author is occupied not by his experience, but by the weaving of his memory, by a Penelope work of remembrance. Or should one rather speak of a Penelope work of forgetting?"[72] The metaphor is well chosen, as one would expect. What could be more fitting than the garment woven in and with the memory Penelope kept of her husband Ulysses? All of her remembrance was woven into it, and so was the experience of the two decades she had spent separated from her husband. Finally, both were fused into the present through the simple gesture of Ulysses putting on her *Erinnerungsarbeit* and wearing it as a constant reminder of the transient state of things. (One would hope that Penelope's memory was accurate enough that the garment fit.) "When the Romans described a text as a fabric, then none is finer and more densely woven than Marcel Proust's," continues Benjamin.[73] The intricate and dense pattern woven by the author in his narrative cycle, in which the yarn of certain motifs reappears in the surface of the poetic fabric that had been employed as its weft from the very beginning, shows that Proust already found *le temps perdu* before he had lost it.

To embroider the text also means to render it more artificial. At the same time, the multitude of *fils de l'idée*—here, the Mallarmism is particularly intricate—allows hitherto concealed meanings to surface between the words. As the writing itself is concerned with fashion, its structure—the thread—must be evocative of the past. Thus, the denser the poetic fabric, the more intricate the relation between the modern and the ancient, the ephemeral and the eternal. Marguerite de Ponty concludes her article for the first issue in summer 1874:

■

*Could it be that Fashion is now emerging from art exhibitions? Already, one has seen with astonishment, yet not without some satisfaction, a portrait, even several, in which young and modern faces can be seen over those old-fashioned, long-waisted figures of past centuries. One is curious to find out by the beginning of September, if this resurrection will last for more than one season! For now, dazzled by all these iri-*

*descent, sparkling colors in opal shades, we could not see without difficulty things as vague as the Future.*[74]

■

Whereas Baudelaire chastised painters of the Salon because they were not prepared to establish a relation to contemporary aesthetics, that is, with modernity, Ponty drove this idea more than two decades later to the point of absurdity. In *Le Peintre* Baudelaire distinguished fashion as the modernist counterbalance to classical, academic painting; Mallarmé exposed contemporary expression—that is, the present (and future) fashion—as founded on the typical art of the Salon, which couples the ancient costume with "jeunes et modernes visages." The irreverent, yet politely trimmed irony did not stop at its own intellectual heritage; it also provided a highly appropriate means to keep a distance not only from his own writings, as the pseudonyms would ensure, but also from dominant artistic tradition.

By eschewing the moral and critical "high ground" of the fine arts and by focusing on manners and *modes,* Mallarmé enters a modern realm of insubstantial distractions. The seemingly futile and facile character in discussing female fashion provided him with an intimate interior, equivalent to the "rêve intérieur" that he mentioned to Villiers de l'Isle-Adam, in which the poet's critical eye could wonder and touch on any subject, as long as he dressed it with decadent intricacies that might well conceal tangible critique. Mallarmé steps into this interior voluntarily and with a profound sense of irony. He can come and go as he pleases, since unlike journalists who are writing commercial prose, but also distant from the pretence of literary critics, he seems unburdened by professional constraints. Mallarmé revels in the ambiguous; any social critique that might lie beneath his stylistic judgment is as difficult to specify as the adopted sex of the writer(s) in his fashion publication.

Before the century came to an end, Remy de Gourmont would evaluate the impact of the *Journal de Modes* and its author. In "Stéphane Mallarmé and the Idea of Decadence" he writes:

■

*Mallarmé was the prince in this ironical and almost injurious realm—as it would have been if the word had been understood and used in its true sense. . . .*

*Mallarmé's work is the most marvellous pretext for reverie which has yet been offered to man who is weary of so many heavy and useless affirmations: a poetry full of doubts, of changing nuances and ambiguous scents, perhaps the only one that will be able, hence forward, to give us pleasure.*[75]

■

Eight years earlier Gourmont had exhumed the sky-blue covers of *La Dernière Mode* in all their significance: "It is about women, about rags, that the most precious and curious words have been written (and these words are of a very high professional standard). . . . These pale blue pages proved . . . in the course of their brief existence that armed with style and panache one could leave one's mark, be it in a boring recipe, the description of a dress in all its technical details, or even in the editing of a publicity piece or an advertisement."[76]

Yet the poet's writing was not simply a mark or *griffe,* nor was it the *poncif* that Baudelaire had demanded of the artist desiring to succeed in bourgeois society. The syntax and choice of words become remarkable not because they occurred in the context of a fashion magazine, but because they were seamlessly integrated and singularly suited to the subject matter. The words ("faits modals") do not simply describe sartorial fashion, they can be said to *constitute fashion,* to act as its signifiers—without, and this is important, descending into fashion-conscious speech or becoming fashionable as novelties.

Each issue of the magazine had to be composed within a period of ten days to allow time for typesetting and printing. In autumn 1874, Mallarmé began his fourth year as teacher at the lycée Fontanas (later Condorcet—a highly reputed school that Proust would attend). One of the pupils in his English class complained later: "He was very distant and inattentive, absorbed in unknown works. He did not care about his class; all the time he wrote for his fashion journal!"[77] Yet the rapid turnaround demanded by this type of commercial publication did not pressure its author; curiously enough, it allowed him to relax. The speed of production corresponded with the quick changes that the journal's subject matter demanded. Modernity constantly asked one to revalue one's position, and the lack of time as well as the limited space that was left for criticism between the illustrations and recipes provided a welcome excuse not to linger too long on one particular topic. With a quick change of pseudonym Mallarmé crossed over to the next theme and explored another opportunity within the rather "injurious realm"—this time, through the poetic description of a gown.[78]

Mallarmé composed his verses with the utmost care and precision, and his modernist experiments often remained fragmentary or in a transitory state because his quest for purity made constant reworking and abstraction necessary.[79] The "Vers de circonstance" provided occasional distraction; yet only the combination of topoi and style within *La Dernière Mode* offered a regular, if short-lived, forum for "la crème de l'esprit fouetée d'une main rapide" that Gautier had considered to be the basis of *modernité.* However, Gautier had also suggested that contemporary writing should be commercially viable, and Mallarmé subverts in a willful and ironic manner the expectations of the market. When *La Dernière Mode* first appeared in September 1874, the column on fashion had no actual subject at hand. During the summer months wealthy Parisians fled the city, and no fashion was created or displayed in studios or salons. At that very moment the first article by Mme de Ponty appeared, titled "La Mode—Bijoux." In it Mallarmé takes up his long-cultivated project to publish the "treatise on precious stones," which he had mentioned as early as 1867 in his correspondence with Villiers de l'Isle-Adam.[80] In modernity, the artistic rendering of a subject becomes its own raison d'être. For the modern poet, the decoration, whether jewelry, embroidery, or—in textual terms—metaphor, was as significant as the contents. If these contents were to describe and discuss decorative objects, the metaphor had to compete with them in exquisiteness and refinement.[81]

This article gives a first indication of the method Mallarmé would employ: his theories were tailored specifically for an imaginary readership by an alter ego who possesses all the knowledge and literary experience of the poet, yet chooses not to elaborate but merely hints at underlying aesthetics. The modernist preference to present instead of theorizing not only catered to prospective subscribers but was a reflection of the ephemeral and transitory: the loss of a firm epistemological basis elevated movement to maxim. This is not to say that the guiding principle of an ideal (eternal/ sublime) beauty has to be discarded. In the article on "les bijoux," the jewels' mineral permanence was ironically subjected to fashion:

■

*Today, not having yet all the elements at hand to begin the description of an outfit, we shall talk about the means to perfect it: Jewelry. A paradox? no: is there not in jewelry a notion of permanence, and should one not talk about it in a Fashion magazine, seeing as one has to wait for fashion styles between the months of July and September. . . . Decoration! this word says it all: and I would advise a Lady who is hesitant as to whom to entrust with the design of a coveted piece of Jewelry, to go to the architect who has built her house, rather than the illustrious dressmaker who made her ball gown.*[82]

■

The advice to employ a (male) architect rather than a female dressmaker for the creation of a piece of jewelry is not to be taken simply as an example of a patronizing or patriarchal attitude that Mallarmé might have sported underneath his feminine guise. As a modernist he knew that in decoration restraint was all-important: the impeccably cut *habit noir,* the geometrically cut stone facade of an urban villa, and the well-weighted cut of a jewel are all expressions of the same purist aesthetics. Accordingly, the design of the precious stone should be judged in terms of the relation of mass, simplicity, and cut and not by its decorative value alone,[83] as presumably a *faiseuse* or *modiste* would, since she would be concerned with the relationship between garment and accessory and not with the object in its own right.

If this advice appears to indicate a preference for the intellectual foundation over the decorative and sensual, or for static fabrications over flowing fabrics, then that preference is certainly due to the sexual ambiguity of Ponty and the other contributors. Although feminine in appearance they, or rather the poet behind them, had of course an education typical of the nineteenth-century man and thus the corresponding socialization, with all its prejudices and clichéd attitudes. That bias becomes clear in the first column by Ix. Like the column "La Mode," the "Chronique de Paris" did not have any actual society news in the first issue and thus the tone became unintentionally "metaphysical"; Ix. begins by writing, "A chronicle: without a past? we are here with only the unknown future."[84] Yet is knowledge of the future of any interest to the fashionable readership, except perhaps the dates of forthcoming entertainment and publications? Is it reasonable to expect a precise prediction of what will be worn in the next season? Does any fashion magazine actually speculate about future style, or does it not rather display its advantage in knowledge of the present that owes all to insider information supplied by the dressmakers?

Fashion relies on the past to evoke its future only in retrospect; it exists in a transitory state comparable to the daily life of the female member of the haute bourgeoisie, who spends her day unconcerned about temporal constraints. Ix. declares, "Only the lady in her isolation from politics and morose concerns has the necessary leisure to free herself, her apparel completed, to cater to the need to adorn the soul as well."[85] The first duty is to choose the dress, the second to dress the soul. Both acts evoke the ancient within the modern, one through sartorial quotation and the other through poetic impression(ism):

■

*A book is closed very quickly, so boring; one lets the gaze wander in this cloud of impressions that one has conjured up readily to interpose, like ancient gods, modern woman in the mundane adventures of her Self. . . . Has not the external world has a profound influence on our deepest instincts? it provokes and refines them.*

*One learns everything on the spot, even beauty; how to hold one's head; one has to learn it from someone; that is to say, from everyone, like the manner in which to wear a dress. Shall we escape this world? we are part of it; so back to nature? one travels through it at full steam, in its external reality, with its landscapes, its places, to get somewhere else: a modern image of its insufficiency for us! For if the pleasures we know within our four walls were to relinquish their season's lead for open-air games, long rambles through the woods, or regattas on the river, where we are keen to rest our eyes in an oblivion created by the vast and naked horizon, would we not find therefore a novel perception able to appreciate the paradox of intricate and complex outfits that the ocean has embroidered at the bottom with its froth?*[86]

■

In this remarkable passage lx. not only displays the fashionable ennui of a dandy, she prefers the ironic fatality of the decadent poet as well. Every profound impression in life, everything beautiful, is but a repetition—embodied especially in the style of a gown. But where can one escape to find genuine expression? Even the volatile speed of modern life, which enables the most rapid distractions, cannot—and does not intend to—alter the perception created by the proximity of *mode et modernité*. Every phenomenon is judged according to the rules of contemporary commodified society. The horizon at the sea resort might offer a brief repose, yet in the very next instant it is transformed again into the sartorial: a fabric, sky-blue as the cover of Mallarmé's magazine and subjected to the rule of fashion. When Baudelaire in 1860 elevated a woman's dress and the embroidered festoon that adorned it to a paradigm of modernity, he could not have possibly foreseen that this perception would progress, some dozen years later, to regarding even the sky and sea underneath as nothing but the same sartorial expression: the vast horizon as an ingenious piece of apparel, embroidered by the ocean's foam.

### 2.4.3 *Vocabulaire vestimentaire*

The vocabulary of *La Dernière Mode* is characterized by the undefinable, transitory, and immaterial. Words such as "vapor," "clouds," "perfume," or "dream" recur in conjunction with both the female and her clothing, interposing them in surrounding space. The instantaneous creation of a shape or form is all the object requires for its poetic rendition; in passing from the present, the form is akin to the short life span of fashion and the changing shape of modernity. The voids soon destined to be left by these creations are no negatives: for Mallarmé they constitute a necessary antithesis to the material. The still vastness of the ocean contrasts with the traveling fashionable crowd; the white space on the book pages makes possible the associative reading of poetry.

      The nontangible also creates the allure of the woman and her gown. She remains distant, aestheticized, and thus essentially asexual. Although her figure and

**23.**
Unknown photographer, folio page of an evening gown in the Worth Archives,
May 1903–January 1904. Photographic print, 6 × 10 cm. Museum of the Costume and
Fashion Research Centre, Bath.

maybe even her mind are observed, only the sartorial ideal capable of defining her remains. As the modernist observes, the impact of the garment always lies in its abolishing eternal values, ideals. Accordingly, Ix. singles out in her first "Chronique" the "gown of vaporous fabrics creased in impatience."[87] So too Miss Satin poetically evokes an ideal gown, captured in its transitory state and realized in the fashion for autumn and winter 1874/1875, without forgetting a little commercial interjection: "We have all dreamed this gown without knowing it. M. Worth, alone, knew how to design apparel as fugitive as our thoughts."[88] The dress is not dreamed up as a novelty; its impact derives from its preexistence in our collective imagination. The designer only has to realize the attire, which is as fugitive as the thoughts of the female clientele, whom Ix. isolated from reality and confined to the salon and its "rêve intérieur." The female bourgeois is pure recipient; her appearance and existence is determined by the male—in the figure of her husband and provider as well as of her couturier. While his head is troubled with the rational in modernity, that is, political and economic progress, her head is—literally, as the vocabulary of the fashion magazine suggests—"in the clouds," concerned only with representations of her futile dreams.

Marguerite de Ponty would of course (ad)dress the social position of her "own sex" sartorially: "To this charming paradox of the male suit and the insignia of official status that are dressed again, one day, by beauty and noblesse, we oppose the ancient costume of essential femininity, white and vaporous, which she wears for a wedding. Can there be a greater contrast?"[89] The duality of the ancient and the modern is reflected in the customary habiliments of man and woman. Yet the invariable male *habit noir* occupies the contemporary position, that is, modern sartorial control; the female wedding dress represents instead the eternal beauty of antiquity—compare "[l]a robe blanchie en l'ivoire fermé," worn by Mallarmé's Hérodiade[90]—even if her appearance is subjected to much more change than is the man's suit. While change in society might on the surface belong to *la mode,* its fundamentals are regulated by *le mode.* Does Mallarmé's choice of pseudonyms thus signify an intellectual and aesthetic alteration, in contrast to Barbey d'Aurevilly's more sensual and sexual one? Is the constant discussion of the latest fashion by Miss Satin and others an attempt to show only the warp within the poetic fabric and to figure a domination of the present over the past (by implication still more substantial)?

In one of his earliest poems Mallarmé already suggested a preference for vaporous, flowing garments and thus of feminine aesthetics over the restricting purism of the black suit, which symbolized the social positioning of the male. A sonnet titled "Contre un poëte parisien" appeared 1862 in the *Journal des Baigneurs* (published in the sea resort of Dieppe, where much later in Ix.'s column the fashionable world would reach its limit):

■

*Souvent la vision du Poëte me frappe:*
*Ange à cuirasse fauve—il a pour volupté*
*L'éclair du glaive, ou, blanc songeur, il a la chape,*
*La mitre byzantine et le bâton sculpté.*

*Dante, au laurier amer, dans un linceul se drape,*
*Un linceul fait de nuit et de sérénité:*
*Anacréon, tout nu, rit et baise une grappe*
*Sans songer que la vigne a des feuilles, l'été.*

*Pailletés d'astres, fous d'azur, les grands bohèmes,*
*Dans les éclairs vermeils de leur gai tambourin,*
*Passent, fantasquement coiffés de romarin.*

*Mais j'aime peu voir, Muse, ô reine des poëmes,*
*Dont la toison nimbée a l'air d'un ostensoir,*
*Un poëte qui polke avec un habit noir.*[91]

■

Various vestimentary codes comprise this early attempt at a poetic manifesto. The white cape of the dreamer, "Dante's shroud," or the glittering garments of the great bohemians still represent for Mallarmé a noble past, an antiquity of sublime ideals; and therefore he criticizes the contemporary clothes of the Parisian poet (here, Emmanuel Des Essarts—a most benevolent "victim," who treasured this sonnet until his death). In pursuing a social life the poet leaves the necessary seclusion of art behind and must betray his obligations toward his muse. Remnants of Romanticism stir in Mallarmé this objection to modernist vulgarities and lead him to regard contemporary fashion as a vagary and not as the basis for new stylistics. But in due course—in fact, before he even moved to Paris—Mallarmé clothed himself in the black redingote and matching trousers that would guide him through modernity. The restricting purism of *le drap* or *l'habit noir,* however, left a deeply rooted desire for the flowing, immaterial, and immediate. Mallarmé, in his by then habitual dark wool suit, gives way to it in his "rêve intérieur": describing the intimate female world of beautifully designed frivolities, and at the same time feeling deep into the interior of language, of words and syllables—into the elaborate pleats and folds of the text.

## ■ 2.5 Mallarmé and His Subscribers: Corresponding Ideals

Although the poet decides to poetically account for his ambiguity, in both stylistics and gender positions, he nevertheless seeks affirmation. In addition to exchanging letters with fellow artists and authors, Mallarmé corresponds with the readership of *La Dernière Mode* to further elaborate his objective and to reassure himself and his addressees of their shared aesthetic experience. For artistic questions he naturally relies on the Parnassiens and other friends. But how congenial could his dilettante "très chères abonnées" possibly be? In creating so many pseudonymous authors in the magazine, Mallarmé elegantly sidesteps a possible incoherence in attitude and appearance. So why not ensure that the recipients of his contemplations also match his aesthetic ideal? In his imagination, a concourse of feminine beauties, all of social, metaphysical, and sartorial distinction, leafed through the pages of *La Dernière Mode* every fortnight. Thus he ventured to create them a priori instead of actually waiting for any of their letters.[92]

The correspondence of issue 2 begins with an apology to Mme la Marquise M. de L—— that the French postal service did not handle the magazine with the care it deserved—an ironic hint at a certain delicacy and unworldliness, or an attempt to forestall further complaints? Like the rest of his writing, Mallarmé's advice on dressing was based on abolition; the abolition of both semantic and sartorial accessories and decoration. One starts with the contemporary profusion of details only to abstract it subsequently, perhaps in an "architectural" fashion.

■

*Mme DE C. L——, FROM NEVERS: Please do not fret, Madame, about the richness of our dresses; it is always possible to suppress certain ornaments in complex apparel; while it is often very difficult to add them, when the apparel is too simplistic.*[93]

■

In the journal, correspondents from the nobility dominate, and the impression of exclusivity the "marquises" and "baronnes" create must—surely?!—be put down to their greater sophistication and thus readiness to put pen to paper. A large order of garments and accessories was dispatched toward the end of October to the Russian court, and the "editorial staff" (Mme Mallarmé or Constance Wendelen) must have considered it quite a challenge to spend the royal dispensation—even if it would turn out to be nothing but another of Mallarmé's *féeries,* a small commercial "prose de circonstance" that provided the poet with an opportunity to compose a vestimentary code for an unknown, perhaps imaginary, but certainly idealized woman.

■

*Mme LA PRINCESSE K——, FROM SAINT PETERSBURG: We have received the sum that you, Princess, dispatched to us; the boxes will be shipped on the 29th of this month, containing a day dress in* cheviotte gisèle *[Scottish lamb's wool with relief embroidery in muslin], another very simple one in Persian light wool with jet-black trimming, a* toilette de visite *in slate-gray velvet and satin with decorative waves of feathers, another in rose-colored cashmere under strips of white gauze trimmed with smooth silk; also a ball gown in blue* poult-de-soie *[thick and flexible taffeta, its selvage having perpendicular edges] with tulle effect in brilliant white and garlands in rose-colored flowers. The three girl's outfits are very simple, since at fifteen one is still a child: a wool dress in navy, a dress in black velvet with a belt in rose-tinted satin, and a white gown in Chambéry gauze, embroidered with blue knotting. We have supplied also matching headgear and veils for these various dresses and outfits.*[94]

•

It is intriguing to speculate on what, if any, the specifications of the princess were. It seems as if the first dress in lamb's wool matches the lithography in the previous issue. Or had the noble client ordered sight unseen, simply sending off some measurements for all the clothes to be designed especially for her?

Although Mme Wendelen claimed in a letter toward the end of September that there were already a number of subscribers in England and Paris,[95] the pretended or real exclusivity of the journal might itself have caused its demise. Ponty uses the correspondence in the first issue (just one baroness among the addressees) almost entirely to elaborate on financial matters, the journal's contents, and forthcoming topics. In the second number, however, only one part is devoted to commenting on the magazine itself; the rest already was occupied with sartorial advice. Since *La Dernière Mode* did not announce forthcoming issues or topics on its pages, the letters page had to serve from the beginning as a space for self-promotion. Yet to retain its air of distinction, such publicizing had to be as veiled as possible. Thus the correspondence chose to reply to a fictional but never prosaic readership. From issue 3 onward, the number of addressees from the ranks of nobility and from outside France—Britain, Italy, Spain, Poland, even Germany (alas, there was no postal agreement so soon after the Franco-Prussian War, as Mallarmé regrets)[96]—swelled steadily and the tone of the editorial staff from *La Dernière Mode* grew more and more intimate and personal. In the last published issue, Ponty stressed "that our information does not come simply from great dressmakers, as has been stated at various points in the magazine, but also from the *haut monde.*"[97]

Such a claim, perhaps based on the correspondence of a certain comtesse (in this case the Comtesse de Callias, not the Comtesse d'Orr . . .), may have enhanced rather than restricted the appeal of the journal, as bourgeois women longed to copy the style of the upper class. But its price set *La Dernière Mode* beyond the means of most of the *juste milieu,*[98] rendering it almost as exclusive as the titles of the correspondents suggested. Wendelen's hopes for its circulation are not documented, yet in

September he dispatched a mere "hundred copies" of the second issue to the provinces.[99] Therefore we can assume that in the beginning no more than three hundred copies were printed, since fewer than half the correspondents came from the city of Paris itself. To be sure, Parisians might have preferred to communicate orally rather than by letter with an editor who was said to frequent their circle(s) anyway. Or perhaps the disparity in numbers reflected an attempt to make the distribution of his magazine appear wider than it actually was. Mme Wendelen's claim of an expanding readership after Mallarmé edited the first number might have been true, especially since she paid back a fifth of his original investment;[100] undoubtedly, some of the women who read the magazine must have subscribed and written letters. Since these apparently were not inspiring enough to tickle the poet's literary senses, he chose instead to answer letters that were never written. Even when his dialogue with the "très chères abonnées" at times departed from the Platonic ideal and tended toward the feeble and "vaporous clouds" to which he liked to raise (or confine) the writing of *La Dernière Mode,* it always remained full of charm: "Lydie . . . from Brussels: Yes dear child, you will look ravishing at your first ball. The white will not make you too pale, and the tulle effect that you inquired about, in our last *Courrier de Modes* devoted to social occasions, will envelop you in a moving cloud of transparent vapor."[101]

When Ponty chose to answer a complaint that reached the magazine in December 1874 criticizing its omission of the latest sartorial trends—the most heinous sin for any fashion publication, especially one bearing the title *La Dernière Mode*—she put this critique in quotation marks, suggesting that it came from one of the "abonnées." Yet its tone is seamlessly integrated into the poetic fabric that had already enveloped the seemingly diverse contributors: "Unbelievable! from underneath the canopy formed by fabrics from all centuries (those worn by Queen Semiramis or those fabricated by the genius of Worth or Pingat) fashion lifts the curtain! suddenly shows itself to us metamorphosed, new, forward-looking; and that is the very moment when you choose to present the traditions that govern children's wear for three-month-old babies up to eleven-year-olds."[102] The style of this indignant complaint, which aligns fabrics of Queen Semiramis with creations of Parisian couturiers and which uses the Mallarmism of metamorphosis in fashion, indeed suggests that it originates from *inside* the magazine. And if the omission of novelties like *fanchon-fileuse* (a delicate, triangular handkerchief worn on the head) or "the large stand-up collar" cast doubts on the journal's expertise and was responsible—as this column was featured in the last issue published—for its demise, then one could almost believe in a poetic attempt at suicide that by mere chance succeeded. Significantly, Mallarmé also used the critique as a pretext to formulate his credo for the proper writing on fashion: "No! for a compendium that intends to view fashion as art [thus following the mysterious comtesse and her articles in 1865], it does not suffice to say 'this is what is worn'; one has to state 'this is the reasoning behind it.'"[103] Since fashion appears to be infinitely self-referential, with each detail quoting or referring back to the past, the basis of its fascination is as veiled as it is important. Only a poetic inquiry into its multitude of meanings could hope to achieve intimacy with and insight into this realm. That multitude finds its analogy in the Mallarméan folds of the text—that is, the modal composition based on "pli selon pli" (fold upon fold).[104] The writer as designer, who creates and clothes—in his role as Mme de Ponty—high society women in folds of wool or chiffon, and who conceals—as Mallarmé the symbolist poet—the word within the folds (the textile voids) of the text, was singularly well equipped for an inquiry into fashion's paradigmatic value.

Although Mallarmé aims at creating abstract aesthetics, the object of his interpretation is the sartorial. Thus, for the folds to appear, cloth had first to be woven from the temporality of the *fil(s)*. The warp thread, which would later become so important in the Proustian creation of *durée,* is taken quite literally by Mallarmé. And the poetic fabric it would determine remains an element of the transhistorical potential—a recurring interplay of thread(s) as the basis of fashion's metamorphoses, creating the future while remaining rooted in "ancient attitudes." But this thread was also significant for the intimate and interior interpretation of fashion and finery.

∎

*Like two threads, one of silk or even wool and the other of gold, crossing each other and then entwining, we perceive the changes and the evolution of fashion during the social season. There has not been any noticeable change in the last fortnight; nothing has become manifest in the ball gowns. . . . The outfits at these special occa-*

**24.**
Edgar Degas, study for the painting *Mme Camus at the Piano,* 1869. Black chalk and pastel
on brown paper, 43.5 × 32.5 cm. Collection E. G. Bührle, Zurich.

*sions constitute a fantasy in themselves, sometimes a risky endeavor, bold and futur-*
*istic; this comes to light through ancient habits. Yes, do look, and you can see, in be-*
*tween the satins, some evidence of the secrets that already are being revealed under*
*the gauze, under the tulle or lace.* [105]

■

Fashion appears here almost as the *evaporation* of temporality. For the poet it marks a
fantastic and irrational state that he longs to explore. But it also retains a strong social
component, as the female subscribers are restricted to a "floating world," one of conspicuous consumption. The constant, if strictly seasonal, change in haute couture kept
women in suspension—in the case of a new Worth or Pingat creation, perhaps even in
suspense. While men were expected to have a sense of epistemological tradition and
historiography, women were geared only toward immediacy, the eternally new. That
"new" is not necessarily a prediction of the future, since fashion is never conceived beforehand solely as a static concept but instead reacts to and speculates about stylistics.
Its shapes and forms never surprise us entirely, as everything has already existed in
some other appearance. The female is thus held in the present, condemned to view the
past merely as sourcebook; the coming of yet another facile change alters the surface
of things but, alas, never the rules.

    In Ix.'s first column, one chic reader—perhaps more imaginary than ironic—
complains: "Books, theater, and simulacra achieved in color or in marble [cf. the
*modernité* of Gautier and Baudelaire]: it is always Art; but what about life, immediate,
cherished, and manifold, ours with its profound nothingness [*les riens sérieux*], does it
not enter into your consideration at all?" [106] The reader asks that her life with all its serious trifles be integrated into a fashionable discourse that already interprets art and its
simulacra. Her fatalism accepts the world to which a bourgeois woman was confined
as a fact; her only concern is subjectivity, since only through it she would be able to
consider herself with any profundity. Mallarmé, or rather Ix., swirls around this moral
question, implicit in the "riens sérieux" (as well as in the aforementioned "aventures
banales de soi"), in a cloud of perfume and chiffon. His/her reply elevates the social life
inside the "salon attesting to your glory"—a salon that also, one might argue, houses
a gender-specific defeat—making it an assemblage of all that is significant in the pres-

ent age, indeed in modernity. After fusing the glittering jewels, flowing fabrics, ornaments, and "thousand secrets" overheard in the interior into one *littérature particulière*, Ix. concludes by stating: "Nothing is to be eschewed in the existence of an age; everything in there belongs to everything else."[107] In *La Dernière Mode* social life itself becomes fiction. In her existence in society the bourgeois female appeared "before a unanimous fold," as Mallarmé with inadvertent criticism qualifies the complacent and facile glamor of the woman and her fan—and here he did not exempt his own family.[108]

The skillful juxtaposition of details in one dress creates a contemporary look for women, and the reputation of Charles Frederick Worth was based partly on his ability, as one who had been apprenticed to a printer of fabrics, to combine diverse patterns. The visual and verbal instant, "le pli modal"[109]—the modal fold that prompts one word/definition to refer to another word/meaning—was literally responsible for the interdependence of writing and topic. Each description of an object at a reception or in a ballroom ideally was related in appearance to the style of another—"pli selon pli"—and furthermore self-referentially pointed to its own significance. Mallarmé thus designs a

▪

*[d]ress for the end of September 1874. Outer skirt in dark red grosgrain faille, decorated on the bottom of the train with three small flounces set in large folds with satin piping on each side of the front: the fourth flounce, much higher up, is gathered and supports a very small tier cut on the bias. The* tablier *[front panel] is formed by a flounce with one large tripartite fold; and the visible support lining, on both sides of the panel, is hemmed by small gathered pieces of fabric and three long and narrow folds repeated thrice: on top of it all, a very large endive-shaped arrangement. A* cashmere polonaise *in the same hue. . . . Sleeves with lapels where the flounce in faille is equipped with a triple fold and fixed, in its middle, with a small strip of the same grosgrain. Laced-up back.*[110]

▪

Read for "fold," (self-)reference and repetition of metaphor; for "tablier," narrative; for "flounces," (levels of) subtext—and the ephemeral description of an outfit turns into a structuralist reading of poetic composition.

Thus the relationship between writing, topoi, and meaning becomes transparent. Clothes, especially female gowns, raise folds—thus they form a material analogy with the interdependence of words and meaning that Mallarmé raised as the artistic problem he aims to explore.[111] The fabric that had been tailored for these clothes is made from weft and warp thread, which either run underneath each other or surface—analogous to (a remembrance of) the past within the poetic manifestation of modernity. The different folds of the text, constituted of the thread imbued with temporality and housing reflexive voids, would combine to display an intricate, intimate, and above all modern world in which fashion aspired to fuse all its signifiers to an ultimate "word."[112]

The limitation of written expressions, the problem raised by Lessing, disappears within fashion's transitoriness. The visual representation of a garment is not superior to the written one, because the clothing in *La Dernière Mode* is never situated in one particular moment in time. Away from the whirl of contemporary fashion, these garments are elevated by their "author" to an abstract value. This touch of hubris in denying his readership the latest sartorial information would cost the entrepreneur Mallarmé dearly. The concerns of the poet, however, lay elsewhere. The significance of both *fil(s)* and *pli* allowed written fashion to lose its temporal, although not historical, aspects. Furthermore, the use of words such as *vaporeux* and *nuage* renders the topoi immaterial, as we have seen. And when Mallarmé ventures into metaphysics ("vers l'idée"), his accounts of dresses or gowns always left them intangible, as they were fashioned into irreverent and imagined objects of the "rêve intérieur." Even the close description of the lithographs managed to eschew the material and deal rather with aesthetic experience; matters of temporal succession would not affect the representation. The transitoriness and impermanence paradigmatic to fashion elevate its written form, as well as its dream potential, above any painterly account: "What a miraculous vision, a picture one dreams about rather than painting it: for its beauty suggests certain impressions analogous to those of the poet, profound or fugitive."[113] Ironically, this erasure of temporality occurred in the pages of a journal entirely devoted to the latest in fashion, that is, to the instantaneous and the present. But precisely because Mallarmé never forgets his artistic aspiration or lowers himself to record the emerging industry of haute couture, the representation of fashion in his magazine now floats unconstrained by any specific time and place.

In interpreting the sartorial Mallarmé stood in contrast to his predecessor Baudelaire. He did not stop only to observe and be mesmerized by the embroidery on a dress, although for Baudelaire such observation had also been a modernist mnemotechnical exercise and not merely description. Mallarmé looks for the idea behind the sartorial decoration, elaborating it stylistically and perhaps even metaphysically: "Today [more than a dozen years after Baudelaire's 'Passante'], it is a matter of picking up the background color of a dress with an embroidery of silk and gold without neglecting the delicious and sparkling details, which are the finishing touch put there by taste."[114] Contrary to this promise not to neglect the sartorial detail, the temporal requirement—the need to give an account of what was worn during this precise time in autumn and winter 1874/1875—was ignored, leading to the downfall of the Mallarmist forum for fashion in the real and commercial world.

In retrospect, Verlaine enthused about *La Dernière Mode* and its author:

∎

*How curious and interesting to the extreme, should I add? are the articles handled by such a great artist who concerned himself with nothing less than the life he wanted, competently understood and sophisticatedly decreed clothing, jewelry, furnishings, even columns on theaters and menus. Recommendations for a few intelligent and lucky readers! . . .*

*[F]or one can discover in this exquisite poet a deep and knowledgeable philosopher, very advanced in his painstaking and focused quest for those who are able to see clearly.*[115]

∎

Verlaine paraphrases here a remembrance written to a correspondent by Mallarmé who, even late in his life, would continue to dream about the sophisticated charade that had been his fashion journal: "I . . . tried to write up by myself clothing, jewelry, furnishings, even columns on theaters and dinner menus, a journal La Dernière Mode, whose eight or ten issues still, when I undress them from their dust, help me to dream for a long time."[116]

**25.**

James Abbot McNeill Whistler, *Portrait of Mallarmé,* 1892. Lithograph on laid paper, 9.5 × 7 cm. Musée départemental Stéphane Mallarmé, Vulanies-sur-Seine.

# ■ **2.6** *La Dernière Mode* in Retrospect: "Après nous le délice?!"

Leafing through the pages of his *journal des modes,* did Mallarmé inhale the perfumed air of utmost refinement, of life's "côté épique," which the magazine continued to spread; or was the scent just the dust of nostalgia? Did he imagine his "goddess" and a romantic ideal of beauty or, more mundanely, literary intimacies with females of high society? Did he merely mutter regrets about a potentially lucrative opportunity that had been missed, or did he rue the frustrated attempt to find a forum to enact a latent ambiguous sexuality, the tendency to mentally cross-dress, much as Barbey d'Aurevilly had done? Did Mallarmé dream about becoming one with his female readership, or was *La Dernière Mode* just the hyperbolic expression of a masculine desire to enter unnoticed the boudoir of a woman and observe her dressing and undressing?[117]

We can only speculate about the answers to these questions. However, the magazine's capacity to make its author not merely remember but *dream* about his writing would appeal much later to the surrealists, who regarded the literary and visual representations of the nineteenth century as a sourcebook for the social and sexual unconscious concealed by time. The garments and accessories of the past half century in particular, in their transhistorical immediacy, reflected for the artists of the 1920s and 1930s an *(haute) bourgeois* taste that still determined the normative character of their own society. Only that age imparted to this fashion a mysterious, irrational, and imaginary character—which, in the case of *La Dernière Mode,* had of course been immanent from the beginning.

In 1933 the surrealist magazine *Minotaure* published "La Dernière Mode de Stéphane Mallarmé," in which Henry Charpentier accounts for a fascination that went beyond mere historical interest.[118] The author, a poet and prolific chronicler of Mallarmé,[119] was a frequent contributor to *La Nouvelle Revue française;* he was only at the margins of the surrealist movement, while *Minotaure* itself was arguably not the most progressive of magazines. But Charpentier's review appeared in the same issue as Tristan Tzara's seminal text on the surrealist and dadaist perception of fashion—"D'un certain automatisme du goût" ("On a Certain Automatism of Taste")—indicating that there was a tendency prevalent at the time to regard garments and accessories as prime examples of the concept of "la beauté CONVULSIVE," the energy inherent in each object that enabled it to redefine its own historical or aesthetic significance.

The article by Charpentier framed on the first page a blown-up detail from a black-and-white engraving by Pecqueur that illustrated issue 4 of *La Dernière Mode*.[120] The way in which the woman's profile and her coiffure, an enormous mass of dark hair decorated by large pearls that almost resemble eyeballs, is cut out and enlarged in the middle of a text invites comparison with the collage-novellas (e.g., *La Femme 100 têtes*) created by Max Ernst toward the end of the 1920s. Ernst unearthed nineteenth-century engravings and woodcuts, stripped them of their inconspicuous contexts, and modified or rearranged them to tell tales of terror, mystery, and imagination. Although many of the collages originated from journals on popular science, Ernst's fascination with the putatively innocent interior of the bourgeois world shows in the repeated use of illustrations from family publications, mail-order catalogues, and fashionable magazines.[121] Besides the woman's profile, two other illustrations reprinted from *La Dernière Mode* appear in a similar mode, left unaltered but alienated from their context. A strange patina conjures the fashion lithographs from the mid-1870s into surreal conversation pieces, while the depiction of children's clothing evoked, in more ways than one, the spirit of *Alice in Wonderland*.[122]

Charpentier's review of Mallarmé's fashion writing begins by describing the "declining year of 1874," when one could find "on the pedestal tables of slightly somber salons, behind the rising facades of the Quartier Monceau and the Champs-Élysées, where, over the windows draped by lace curtains as in a Manet painting, travels a pale light of the autumnal city: La Dernière Mode."[123] His evocation of the atmosphere of restrained splendor and artful references in which the magazine was conceived and read becomes imbued with the air of a decaying era; it was sophisticated yet condemned to fall prey to ever-progressing modernity and modernization.

After listing some of the "contributors" to the magazine, Charpentier elaborates on the man and the reasoning behind them: "M. Mallarmé was a bourgeois Parisian. His officious grandfather, finance minister during the Directoire, had been cruel to the Desmoiselles de Verdun, and it seems that all his descendants were con-

**26.**

F. Pecquer, illustration for *La Dernière Mode,* no. 4 (October 1874).
Wood engraving on paper.

**27.**
Trichon and F. Pecquer, illustration for
*La Dernière Mode,* no. 3 (October 1874).
Wood engraving on paper.

**28.**
Unknown artist, illustration in *Littérature,*
n.s., no. 17 (December 1920).

*The surrealists ironically quote an advertisement for
children's clothing, suggesting that underneath
the bourgeois surface lurks prostitution, where "the
clients favor" underage girls—and not just their
dresses.*

cerned to erase from memory, through exquisite gallantry, the spilled blood and mowed-down heads of the young women, who had been seduced too easily by the handsome emperor."[124]

Thus the reader not only was provided with a Freudian sideswipe about the poet's forefathers but also encountered at least some of the ironically charged political fervor that distinguished many of the dadaists and surrealists. Although Mallarmé is judged a bourgeois, he is "first and foremost a poet"; more significantly, he is a self-defined "man of regular dreams": "This regularity was one of the ready gifts of his spirit. I often see him before me, deep in his chair, enveloped in smoke and dreaming indefinitely about some object on which his eye would come to rest."[125] This habit was, of course, congenial to the surrealists—except that they preferred the café or the group meeting for their collective imagination about objects. Yet their most inspired dreams would prove to be those which had come to them in the seclusion of their own four walls. To dream about an object meant to fixate on it with intensity and profound penetration. It also meant to return to this object day after day, until one discovered its essential qualities that otherwise one's own indifference and routine behavior would prevent one from perceiving. Following in the tradition of both Baudelaire and Mallarmé, of flâneur and *rêveur d'intérieur,* Charpentier states: "Among the passersby, wandering in the mist, the dreaming poet is in reality the only authentic, lucid surveyor."[126]

The transitory nature of the object, especially an article of clothing, renders it for most passersby unrecognizable; only the dreaming poet or the Baudelairean *homme des foules* is capable of realizing its potential for the imagination. Like the flâneur who became transfixed by the symbolically laden "feston et l'ourlet," Mallarmé was able to observe a sartorial intricacy until "the complete possession of the object transforms it for him first of all into the words that express it."[127] Once the poetic fabric that Mallarmé created had raised the "folds of the text" in his dream of the garment and its subsequent transformation, he would contemplate whether it existed in spiritual unison or dissonance with the realm in which everything was interdependent with the other. "This is when it will create that mobile and singular world of thought and of sensations, which do not cease to increase and spread around their indifferent pretext: the silk of time's balsam, ephemeral glassware, or a dazzling console."[128]

This metaphysical world did not require sublime poetics. It required expressly the latest, most facile, and transient of objects. And, as Charpentier suggests, these were necessary not simply for reasons of social grace or commerce: "A woman's attire or a decorative *étagère* would also perfectly suffice for his imagination. This would help him thus to unite, without attending in the least to his most noble faculty, a courteous, cheerful, and a touch frivolous interest, which he presented as the most correct of fauns to the ladies of polite Parisian society, with his incessant need to evoke poetry in all matter hidden."[129] The negative connotation given to "frivolity" in Mallarmé's topoi can be credited to the ambivalence that the surrealists (and other artists in France in the 1930s) displayed toward a bourgeois audience: an open and politically charged disgust on one side, a fascination with its artificiality and its obsession with "les riens sérieux" on the other. The adherence of the "most correct of all fauns" to this world was motivated politically only on a secondary level; it originated primarily in a refusal to participate in the vulgarity of modern life. This was in itself a decadent, almost schizophrenic attitude, yet not as uncommon as one might think.[130] In particular, the artists who sought to be uncompromisingly modern in their writing often isolated themselves from its social consequences. They detested the rampant consumerism, industrial progress, and political activities in France after 1830, because they feared the removal of a socially adequate base for their art. Thus their first reaction, manifest to some degree in Barbey d'Aurevilly, Baudelaire, Gautier, and Mallarmé, had been isolation, decadence, elitism, and dandyesque attitudes.[131]

For the author of *La Dernière Mode* the crowd in the street did not offer fascination comparable to that of the social gathering in a salon; yet even there, he—like Proust—remained in his chosen role as the distanced and sophisticated spectator. On Mallarmé's disregard of public acclaim and opinion Valéry writes:

∎

*I think you will appreciate the full nobility of his refusal. But some people would like to see in this the insular tendency of a mind that wants to get away from the most common opinions. They will perhaps speak of "schizophrenia," a strange*

*name invented to designate the malady of isolating oneself from one's fellow men—*
*for we are living in an age where everything demands, imposes, works towards the*
*uniformity of the individual, as it does with cities, names, clothes. . . . But on what*
*did Mallarmé, in his separation, his lucidity, the firmness of his believes, find his*
*resolution?*[132]

∎

Both Valéry and Charpentier in 1933 characterize Mallarmé's writing as "lucid," especially his poetic interpretation of the sartorial. Like the woman in her salon who endeavors to "dress her soul," Mallarmé is characterized by an air of soft sophistication,
of refinement that withdrew from the harshness of the outside world. Guided by a
particular modern "goddess," the "muse moderne de l'impuissance," he subsides into
the folds or pleats of a garment and into self-reflexivity until he comes to regard himself as "a purely passive soul that is nothing but a woman's still."[133] This description
would again raise the question of his latent transgendered role in *La Dernière Mode,*
were it not for Valéry's explanation that Mallarmé's passivity was due to an exclusively
aesthetic sensibility: "he displayed an infinite softness, which emanated from the most
absolute of spirits."[134]

The constant "interior dream(s)" and the self-mirroring and concentration on
one's own personal and artistic refinement obviously invite comparison with Proust's
*Recherche,* where modernity appears within the most sophisticated of settings, much
like the transient world in Mallarmé's fashion journal. Whether the quest or *recherche*
was directed mainly toward *mot, mode,* or *modernité,* it had to remain appropriate to
the topoi—sartorial fashion as the most significant among them; in textual terms, this
meant being fragmented. True, the lack of marketability and financial miscalculation
cut short the existence of *La Dernière Mode,*[135] and Proust's death prevented further
work on the proofs of the last books of *La Recherche.* But the secluded, self-referential
air in both creations would have made them seem incomplete in any case. Valéry's characterization of Mallarmé's poetry could therefore also apply to Proust's prose as well:
"But this man as much as commanded us to infer a whole system of thought relating to poetry, a system evolved, tested and continually renewed *as an essentially infinite work,* of which any realised or realisable works were only fragments, sketches,

preparatory studies."[136] If *La Dernière Mode* is a fragmented yet integral part of Mallarmé search for "the word" and his modernist endeavor to find the ultimate poetic expression, then its short life only prompts speculation about the subsequent and perhaps ultimate form of Mallarmé's writing on fashion. Perhaps his final work, *Le "Livre,"* would have included meditations on sartorial beauty, but perhaps Mallarmé's fashion writing depended on the confines of a commercial enterprise to flourish.

On a mundane level, however, the end of the journal did not mean the disappearance of the name Mallarmé from fashion journalism. In May 1896 Geneviève Mallarmé, the thirty-one-year-old daughter of the poet, who once appeared coquettishly hiding behind the "unanimous fold" of her fan, would write in a letter to her papa: "Yesterday I brought Mme de Broutelles the first installment of my calendar. . . . Please do not tell me off for all the crossing out, but I was madly working on all the entries until six o'clock this morning, and all other mornings; but I am happy with the result since I have nearly three months' worth of facts and transcripts."[137] Her calendar was simply a contemporary version of Ix.'s "Chronique de Paris" and "Journal de Quinzaine." It had to be compiled, as in 1874, every fortnight. Mallarmé's daughter remembered from the tender age of seven that her father "came back to Paris in the autumn that followed the Commune and then settled in the rue de Moscou. At that time, he wrote his fashion journal all on his own."[138] Already then his purist taste and his skill as an reporter of the "profound nothingness" appeared to have shaped her own aesthetic experience. Now she sought the advice of the erstwhile chronicler for her own column, which appeared in the Parisian *La Mode Pratique* over a couple of years. One of the very last letters by Geneviève to her father, written in 1898, shows that she shares his interest in the observation and interpretation of fashion: "We work, arrange, and prepare things in view of the summer departure. I slave away, as street urchins would say, at the interminable calendar. . . . I have met Madame Laurent in half-mourning, black dress, gray hat; as well as the harem, dazzling in sequins, feathers, and light dresses—Auntie thus resembled a maid."[139] The century was reaching its end, and with it passed an era of *modernité* that had begun more than forty years earlier with the passion that the Baudelairean flâneur felt toward ephemeral and passing fashion. The look of the *passante* was toward the end once more transferred to

**29.**

Edmond Morin, cover page of *La Dernière Mode,* no. 7 (December 1874).
Lithograph, 20 × 13 cm.

Méry Laurent (no longer in "deuil perpétuel" nor "grand deuil," but "demi-deuil"), who had once been the youthful inspiration, enveloped in her shining blue gown, of Mallarmé's poem "Photographies," as well as the sophisticated advisor to *La Dernière Mode*. Her style, albeit still remarkable, has now become dated, plain, and dark; in contrast, her female companions and relatives, dressed in shiny new clothes, walked by without distinction, refinement, or class—in short, without any sensibility of fashion's true potential.

The positivist innocence in the equation of *mode et modernité* was gone forever. The progress of the modern world would continue to be reflected in sartorial fashion; but Baudelaire's original perception that modern life moves with or around man, depending on whether he sees himself as an artist or a dandy, as well as the belief that this perception merited aesthetic assessment in itself, could not be maintained in any simple form. Though Mallarmé might have realized that *modernité* as the condition of the modern was in reality a cover for an increasingly troubled social condition, he displayed no interest in exposing that condition. His aim was to find a creative balance and arrive at a modern aesthetic experience. That he chose to make sartorial fashion the basis for his brief but significant approach toward this experience is an irony very much befitting the self-referential mode of modernity.

**3**

# Simmel and the Rationale of Fashion in Modernity

*Diese Abstraktheit der Mode, in ihrem tiefsten Wesen begründet und als "Realitätsfremdheit"*
*ein gewisses* ästhetisches *Cachet dem Modernen selbst auf ganz außerästhetischen Gebieten*
*verleihend, entwickelt sich auch in einem historischen Ausdruck.*

*Georg Simmel (1911)*[1]

Once it had dawned on even the most aesthetically inclined character that, rather than being characterized simply as a positivist and progressive force, modernity incorporated the social reality of modern times, inquiries into its epistemological cohesion began to arise. Having found that Baudelaire's prose and poetry described the original metaphysics of *modernité,* and Mallarmé's writing reflected its aesthetics, I turn now to aspects of modernity's rationale. And having restricted the inquiry to sartorial fashion as modernity's purest expression, I must distinguish between sociological and political interpretations of *Mode und Moderne.*[2] The sociological account is epitomized in four essays by Simmel, and their close parallel reading makes up the body of this chapter; the political view is developed in chapter 4 through an interpretation of Benjamin's *Arcades Project.* In order to understand both concepts, it is important to bear in mind that post-Mallarméan *modernité* had already acquired a substantial history of its own, which subsequent interpreters could consciously reflect.

## ■ **3.1** *Mode und Moderne:* Georg Simmel, the Philosopher

Georg Simmel (1858–1918), whose interpretation of fashion and its philosophy as well as its sociology provide the basis for this chapter, is not exclusively an interpreter of modernity. Yet, in his observations, he focused on the modern urban life around him. Simmel is distinguished further by his being the first profound analyst of fashion—the first academic to attempt an expressive and concise interpretation of the subject. And he was the first to do so in the context of a modernity that is aware of its own past. His genuine interest in *Mode* and *Moderne* was coupled with the insights of an academically trained mind.

Jürgen Habermas has allocated to Simmel the role of a "child of the fin de siècle"—that is, in the negative sense, a child of his time who remains unable to transcend "fashionable" confines. At first, this does not appear to diminish Simmel's influence and significance for Habermas:

■

*[He] still stood on the other side of the chasm that would open up between Rodin and Barlach, between Segantini and Kandinsky, between Lask and Lukács, Cassirer and Heidegger. He writes on fashion differently from Benjamin.* Yet he was the one to establish the relationship between fashion and modernity, *he influenced Lukács down to the choice of his titles, he inspired Benjamin to observations on the over-flow of stimuli, the density of contact, and the acceleration of movement in the metropolitan space of experience, and he changed the mode of perception, the themes and style of writing of a whole generation of intellectuals.*[3]

■

Later in this chapter it will become clear that Habermas, influenced by the tradition of the Frankfurt School, qualifies his positive assessment by omitting Simmel from his study of modern aesthetics, the *Philosophical Discourse of Modernity.* That book was based on a series of lectures delivered between 1983 and 1984—after Habermas had published his afterword to a collection of Simmel's essays in which the critical appraisal quoted above is found. It is precisely the ephemeral and commercial character of this afterword that contributes to Habermas's somewhat offhand yet significant character-

**30.**

Unknown photographer, portrait of Georg Simmel, ca. 1900. Modern print. Archive of the Suhrkamp Verlag, Frankfurt a.M.

*Summer suit in cool wool, waistcoat in off-white wool gabardine, white cotton shirt with detachable collar and cuffs, assorted silk tie. The perfect relaxed outfit for the intellectual-about-town.*

ization: Simmel indeed establishes the relation between *Mode* and *Moderne*—sartorial fashion and modernity.

Simmel wanted his philosophy to reflect transitory existence. He was part academic dandy, part sensitive *homme des foules*. Like Baudelaire he strove to maintain a sophisticated distance, yet was compelled to observe modern society around him. Because he emphasized the structure of urban social groups in his writing, sociologists tend to claim him very much for their own. The recent interest in Simmel's writing in Germany, and indeed the early opinion of the Chicago School and its successors that he was the first to establish "formal sociology," appears to relegate studies on Simmel firmly to the field of sociology.[4] Yet one could argue that despite his formative influence on early sociology, Simmel's continuing fascination with the stylistics of modern times—with *modernité*—in fact transcends boundaries within academia.[5] Unlike the poets Baudelaire and Mallarmé, however, Simmel had to describe and analyze rather than evoke. Thus his observations appear "established"; but at the core of his writing there always remained a fascination with the fleeting immediacy of life.

Simmel's philosophical roots lie within Kantian thought,[6] and he was influenced by the developing neo-Kantianism in southwestern Germany (extolled by Cohn, Rickert, Lask) at the turn of the century that focused on cultural expressions—their justification and their relative values. At the beginning of the twentieth century Simmel arrives at a *Lebensphilosophie* (philosophy of life) that attempts to encompass and explain social and aesthetic manifestations by appealing to an absolute yet transient principle. This idea about life as a process paralleled Henri Bergson's *élan vital*, which was strongly echoed in the German culture of the late 1900s.

In his writing, Simmel potently realizes modernity's social reality as fragmented, coherent only in its absolutely dispersed incoherence. Society as a whole is regarded as *Gewebe* (fabric), and the relations within social interactions are observed in detail, as if the sociologist/philosopher is venturing into the folds to find the connections between different methodological embroideries or threads. Close in spirit to approaching life with a Mallarméan aesthetics—the German "symbolist" poet Stefan George became, like the sculptor Auguste Rodin, a friend of Simmel's—yet imbued with an insatiable curiosity about reality, he begins to look on fashion as the most immediate manifestation of modern life. For him sartorial fragments come to represent societal appearance as a whole.

In his first analysis of the subject of fashion, dating from 1895, Simmel shows a pragmatism that drew both on Herbert Spencer's social evolutionism and on Kantian epistemology; the resulting ideas were sketched in "On the Psychology of Fashion."[7] In this essay, the Kantian heritage accounts for Simmel's philosophical focus on the subject-object relation. Simmel asks where cognition is founded, in the objects of cognition or in the cognitive subject. Or, to apply the question to fashion: can cognition said to be founded in the clothes we choose to wear, or is it in the human mind that chooses them? In this essay, cognition and self-awareness are regarded as the creative achievement of the subject, aided by guidelines extracted from the conglomerate of experience. The aesthetic perception thus appears determined by a modern sense of beauty, equivalent to Baudelaire's *beau relatif.*

A decade later Simmel's thoughts on dressing, now set forth under the appropriate title *Philosophie der Mode* (*Philosophy of Fashion*),[8] were still occupied with the subject-object problematic; but here he transferred them to another sphere to establish the dualistic relationship of *subjective and objective culture.* Although this work can be seen as specifying the duality of empiricism and rationalism—whose conflict Kant had originally attempted to mediate by establishing their interdependence—it also shows the increasing tendency, by Simmel and others, to analyze the material abstraction of life itself. Again influenced by neo-Kantianism, which would prepare the ground for phenomenological thought, Simmel singles out terms such as "value" and "culture" and establishes their existence outside natural causality. He also explores the independent rank of "atheoretical" works as references for his studies. This methodology is reflected in his own preference for formulating ideas in the literary essay and the feuilleton, a preference that aligns his writing with works on fashion by authors from Balzac and Gautier to Barbey d'Aurevilly and Mallarmé. Furthermore, Simmel employs a modernist critique of historic reason that would leave its mark on the later materialist studies by Ernst Bloch and Benjamin.[9]

These notions and tendencies also shape Simmel's concept that different "worlds" within our daily existence, such as religion, philosophy, science, and the arts,

**31.**
Lesser Ury, *Café with Seated Gentleman,* 1889. Ink and wash on paper, 20 × 16.2 cm.
Private collection.

**32.**
Lesser Ury, *Café Bauer*, 1906. Oil on canvas, 59 × 38 cm. Private collection.

*Two paintings of men in top hats, sitting in Berlin coffeehouses, show how little male fashion altered over the course of almost two decades. Yet although the shape and color seem to remain the same, the cut and the nuances have changed considerably. The same is true of Simmel's essays on fashion before and after the turn of the century.*

relate back to different modes of organization within our mind, each of which arranges the totality of the material that constitutes the existence of the worlds according to an individual plan. Each of these worlds follows a complete and sovereign logic that does not relate back to any of the others. Each has equal value; each possesses its own truth as well as its own errors. Thus the philosopher steps back, like Baudelaire's dandified observer, in an attempt to gain a total view. Yet that glance at the world from a distance is not refuted by close-ups; each view has its own authority. Accordingly, individual existence is regarded as determined by a number of these worlds, but by none of them exclusively. It follows for Simmel that society is formed by the constant attempt of its members to unify homogeneous segments from all these heterogeneous worlds or circles, an attempt that causes the social conflicts that provide the background of our existence.

At this point formal sociologists stepped in, claiming that Simmel had established a quasi-geometric order of society in which certain groups or circles overlap, as in set theory, forming intersections where social interactions are exposed. As useful as this interpretation might be in explaining the workings of sociology, especially during its infancy at the turn of the century, when the discipline was defining itself, I am more interested in explaining Simmel's essential understanding of fashion; my own argument focuses on the philosophical origin and coinage of the elements within his *Lebensphilosophie.*

Simmel maintains that by not contesting the conflicts between heterogeneous worlds, either in life or in philosophical reflection, but instead coordinating them as elemental possibilities, our minds gain in intellectual ability and creative potential. The synthesis that Hegel had sought in the realm of the objective therefore cannot be found—a reflection that corresponds with the objectification of modern life postulated by Marx. Rather, this synthesis exists in movement between antithetical poles and finally is enacted within the cognition of the reflective subject. Characteristic of the perception of modernity and of Simmel's thought was the effort to maintain dualities, by relating them through analogies and seeking a "third sphere" that did not entail their abolition. Problematic configurations are not there to be solved; their significance rests in their appearance, in the act of experiencing them. Therefore Simmel's profound interest in the subject of fashion appears to be logical, since fashion's fundamental ambiguity and transitoriness seem to deny any preconceived and invariable solution and invite a system of coexistence that values each mode of expression.

The transitory and ephemeral contain another notion that became of primary importance to Simmel's progression toward a philosophy of life. His later writings revolve around the idea that life is always limited to subjective forms that reflect themselves. The consciousness of how these self-reflected forms limit our interpretation of reality functions as a survival strategy against the organic "limitation" of death. The constant reassessment of these forms, adding to possible interpretations promotes the human desire to live. In Simmel's view, death does not come from outside. Life carries death knowingly within itself and is thus forced toward fundamental reflection; the more a person is individual and self-reflective, the more dies with him—the more he is "capable of dying."

Simmel proposes an analogy to this idea in a 1911 revision of his 1905 essay on fashion, now simply titled "Die Mode."[10] In it, he incorporates a passage on the unchanged character of mourning and how its "democratic" blackness has been maintained as a symbol over centuries. Juxtaposing this notion to the principle of the ever-changing sartorial fashion, he concludes that *fashion carries death within itself.* As soon as it manages to determine the totality of a group's appearance—which must be its ultimate aim—fashion will, because of the logical contradiction inherent in its characteristics, die.[11] And the more subjective and individualized a style of clothing is, the more quickly it will perish.

Both fashion and modernity exist within dual sets of limits of time and life span, formed on a material level by increasing reification through the capitalist mode of production and created on a vital level as an individual *durée* (perhaps imaginative, as in Proust) that is independent from reality. Simmel's perception of modern culture thus moves between the negative pole of Marx's abstracted and objectified world, in which time and life span are regarded as commodities, and its positive opposite, the Bergsonian identity of time and self.

# ■ 3.2 Simmel's Methodology

### 3.2.1 Mode to Measure

It is significant indeed that Georg Simmel was the first to use a sartorial metaphor to exemplify modernity's fragmented reality, which his philosophy of life would subsequently seek to explain. In his *Philosophie des Geldes* (*Philosophy of Money,* 1900; 2d ed., 1907), he wrote on the division of subject and object in modern society:

■

*The radical opposition between subject and object has been reconciled in theory by making the object part of the subject's perception. Similarly the opposition between subject and object does not evolve in practice as long as the object is produced by a single subject or for a single subject. Since the division of labour destroys custom production . . . the subjective aura of the product also disappears in relation to the consumer because the commodity is now produced independently of him. It becomes an objective entity which the consumer approaches externally and whose specific existence and quality is autonomous of him. The difference, for instance, between the modern clothing store, geared towards the utmost specialisation, and the work of the tailor whom one used to invite into one's home sharply emphasises the growing objectivity of the economic cosmos, its supra-individual independence in relation to the consuming subject with whom it was originally closely identified. . . . It is obvious how much this objectifies the whole character of transaction and how subjectivity is destroyed and transformed into cool reserve and anonymous objectivity once so many intermediate stages are introduced between the producer and the one who accepts his product that they lose sight of each other.*[12]

■

Although this analysis appears at first to be economic, the last sentence underscores the growing imbalance between subjective and objective culture, which Simmel would continue to analyze in "The Terminology and Tragedy of Culture" (1911).[13] The increasingly sophisticated contents of culture become paradoxical, insofar as they have supposedly been created by the subject for the subject, yet in their intermediate state they are objectified and abstracted from the sociocultural conventions that led to their emergence: they begin to follow an immanent logic of evolution and drift away from their original purpose. Simmel concludes that the fetish character that Marx assigned to the economic object in the age of commodities was only a specifically modified case of the general fate awaiting all contents of culture.

In a felicitous analogy to the creation of the object within the subject, the clothes made to measure for the individual become superseded in modernity by off-the-peg suits and dresses, essentially independent from the subject. As reifications, these clothes acquire a dynamic of their own, unconcerned with the actual wishes of the subject who might one day wear them. The alienation that Marx observed in the relation of laborer and product becomes extended to the relation between sartorial commodity and its consumer.

This theoretical construct appears at first not to be entirely applicable to fashion because recourse to sociological factors is preferred in explaining the evolution of clothing. Yet because of the spread of wealth and diffusion of customs, changes in garments within modernity became much less accountable to clearly defined social conventions and much more relevant to aesthetic reflection. Similarly, in the course of his writings Simmel moves from formal sociology to taking a more metaphysical view. This shift makes the general conflict and the proclaimed "tragedy" within culture a perfect fit for a philosophy of fashion. "[F]ashion . . . becomes less dependent upon the individual," declares Simmel in 1907, "and the individual becomes less dependent on fashion. Their contents develop like separate evolutionary worlds."[14] Because fashion evolved in modernity according to individual, willful, and perhaps irrational ideas, it now can acquire significance as a means of *cognition*. By ascribing a particular evolution to fashion, Simmel hopes to counter the anti-individual dominance of prêt-à-porter clothing and return to a subjective made-to-measure practice. Relying on the cognitive tendency to create new categories and classification from the individual's social environment, he achieves a creative correspondence between the erstwhile estranged subject and object.

His fellow sociologist Max Weber elaborates on the historic and cognitive importance of fashion in an essay of 1906 about the logic governing cultural studies.[15]

Weber begins by referring to an earlier remark by the neo-Kantian philosopher Heinrich Rickert, who stated that while the refusal of a crown constitutes a historic event, it is completely insignificant which particular clothes the emperor wears at that moment. He responds that it was indeed of no significance for historic causality that a particular tailor produced certain clothes for the king; yet as a cognitive means for the *constitution* of fashion, these very clothes would be of the greatest significance: "The coats of the king are, in this case, to be considered as instances of a *class*-concept, which is being elaborated as an heuristic instrument—the rejection of the Kaiser's crown, on the other hand, with which they are compared, is to be viewed as a concrete *link* in an historical situation as real *effect* and *cause* in a specific real series of changes. These are absolutely fundamental logical distinctions and they will always remain so."[16] The act of refusing the crown can easily be categorized under the norms of historicism; clothes, however, require a new classification outside the realm of cause and effect. In the formation of modernity, fashion in this way escapes submission to traditional and historicized perceptions, since its transitory character defies any classification. And because fashion is deemed too insignificant to be included in historical analyses, it avoids standstill and at the same time fulfills Simmel's demand that creative achievement be the basis of cognition. Constantly changing yet unaffected by the rigidly positivist progression of changes within historicism, fashion thus can parallel any irreverent movement of *modernité*.

### 3.2.2 Fashion, the Fragment, and the Whole

Simmel's first essay on fashion is imbued with the spirit of the fin de siècle. "On the Psychology of Fashion" was published in 1895 in the Viennese weekly *Die Zeit*.[17] At first it appears similar to one of Mme de Ponty's *chapeaux* on "La Mode," minus the poetry; but beyond its evocative prose, it indicated what the next decade would bring in the analysis of sartorial fashion.

In October 1904 the *International Quarterly* in New York published an extensive contribution by Simmel, simply titled "Fashion."[18] This version was based on a long

**33.**
Kurt Schwitters, *Mz 180—Figurine,* 1921. Collage on paper, 17.3 × 19.2 cm.
Marlborough International Fine Art, London.

essay that would appear in book form in Germany under the title *Philosophie der Mode* (*Philosophy of Fashion*). It was eleventh in a 1905–1906 series, Moderne Zeitfragen (Contemporary Issues in Modernity), that was published in Berlin by Pan Verlag. The series started off with *Strafrechtsreform* (Penal Reform) by Simmel's fellow sociologist Ferdinand Tönnies, who is regarded as having exerted considerable influence on Simmel's formal concepts of sociology.[19] Other contributions included writings by advocates of the women's movement, such as Ellen Keh and Helene Stöcker; the series ended with a book by Eduard Bernstein, *Parlamentarismus und Sozialdemokratie* (*Parliamentarism and Social Democracy*). This last title could be seen as fairly programmatic, since the political and social ideas expressed within the Zeitfragen series tied in with a tendency toward liberalism that was prevalent in mainstream social democracy at the time.

Six years later, in 1911, Simmel included the essay "Die Mode" in a volume with the "irritatingly complicitous" title *Philosophische Kultur* (*Philosophical Culture*);[20] it began part 2 of the book, which was headed "Zur philosophischen Psychologie." One can therefore regard Simmel's last complete writing on the subject of clothing as reflecting the confluence of a psychology of fashion (1895) with its philosophy (1905); in much the same pattern, Simmel had first envisaged his work on the monetary system as dealing with the psychology of money, only to change direction after 1897 to analyze the philosophy of money in the book of that title.[21]

While Simmel's early works were still shaped by the "insight of a psychologist," as his pupil Karl Joël puts it, he later developed a philosophical relativism in order to detect "the *reasoning* behind all style."[22] In contrast to Adorno, Joël sees in Simmel much more than the mere chronicler of aesthetic experience that he appears to be in focusing on fashion. "Things that might satisfy the interests of the aesthete," concludes Joël, "were for this forerunner of all modernity but a signal, a gearstick to shift into high speed."[23] Here, the combination of high-speed travel and modernity conjures up the image created by Mallarmé's alter ego Ix., described in chapter 2: s/he had characterized the late-nineteenth-century *beau monde* as racing through the modern world in search of reason in the sophisticated yet meaningless sphere of "les sens riens"— only to end up at a sea resort where the ocean, instead of offering repose to the eye, was again reminiscent of the apparently implacable dominance of fashion within modernity that hurried change along progressively.[24]

Influenced in his perceptions by the intricacies of fin de siècle aesthetics, Simmel nevertheless turns to basics in the methodological approach of his first study on fashion: "The physiological basis of our being that indicates the alternation between tranquillity and movement, between receptivity and activity, thus contains the character of our intellectual and spiritual [*geistigen*] development."[25] This dualism, rooted in Aristotelian philosophy, essentially determines Simmel's subsequently postulated dualism of interiority and exteriority, subjective and objective culture, the stable and the fluctuating, the sublime and the ephemeral, *eternité* and *fugitivité*. And such a notion is later rendered more poignant in "Fashion," where he states: "We recognize two antagonistic forces, tendencies, or characteristics, either of which, if left unaffected, would approach infinity; and it is by the mutual limitation of the two forces that the characteristics of the individual and public mind result."[26] Here he found already the dualism of subject and object within the "tragedy of culture," which is itself later transformed into more general terms in the 1905 essay on fashion: "The way in which we are given to perceive vital expressions prompts us to experience a multiplicity of forces at each point of our existence, in such a way that each of them essentially transcends its actual expression. The infinite characters of these vital expressions collide with each other and are transformed into pure tension and yearning."[27] The potent, albeit fragmented, objectification and abstraction in modern life so influence individuals that they either attempt to strengthen the subjective—ironically often via aesthetic contemplation of an object—or gladly subjugate themselves to the objective dominance of externals. In modernity, there was no question as to which of the two would become the most influential; thus Simmel's second and third essay on fashion both state that "Man has ever had a dualistic nature. This fact, however, has had but little effect on the uniformity of his conduct, and this uniformity is usually the result of a number of elements. An action that results from less than a majority of fundamental forces would appear barren and empty."[28] Simmel appears essentially to have put into sociological terms Baudelaire's aesthetic dictum, equally constructed around human duality: "the eternal part of beauty will be veiled and expressed if not by fashion, at least by the particular temperament of the artist. The duality of art is a fatal consequence of the duality of man."[29]

In 1911 Simmel elaborates on the notion that the tension inherent in the mutual limitation of elements (or "worlds") which normally would result in uniformity, is fundamentally more potent than visual appearances suggest—as exemplified in clothing. Life thereby gains an influx of inexhaustible possibilities—necessary for human survival, as we have seen—that complement its fragmentary reality.[30] This idea refers back to the very concept of modernity, since the fragment is its component but also its metaphor. In a posthumously published diary entry Simmel mused: "The world and life as a whole, in the way we recognize, live, and accept it, is a fragment; yet the single detail of fate or achievement often appears well-rounded in itself, harmonious and unbroken. Only the whole is a piece; the piece can be a whole."[31] It was not only Baudelaire who stressed how important even the smallest fragment of fashion would become for understanding modernity as a whole (as, e.g., in his appeal to painters to realize how aesthetic and "poetic" the modern bourgeois becomes if depicted in his "cravats and patent leather boots").[32] Although it appears absurd at first to contemplate the metaphysical significance in foot- or neckwear, Simmel's investigation of subjective and objective culture renders fashion a suitable metaphor for the fragmented abstraction of modern social reality. Without it, the subsequent dadaist and surrealist observation of the bourgeois reflecting (on) himself, whether in the shiny surface of his patent leather shoes or while choosing his tie in front of the mirror, certainly would not have been understood in the same potent manner—even with the help of psychoanalytical theories. In attempting to understand social development through modernity, one has to first understand fragmentation. "Social evolution takes the form of a spontaneous disintegration," as Tönnies had observed already in 1895.[33] And nowhere was that breakup more immediate than in the rapid changes of sartorial fashion, which were instantaneous reflections of social status.

Each of the socio-aesthetic fragments has the power to form, writes Simmel, "within the history of our species, the way in which the tendency toward continuity, unity, and equality becomes fused with the tendency toward change, specialization, and the singular."[34] In society, the first side manifests itself in *imitation*—that is, the

**34.**
Unknown photographer, *Skirt Turns into Trousers, Auteuil,* 1910. Private collection, Munich.

adherence to preconceived social, political, or indeed aesthetic ideals. Simmel describes the inclination toward *imitatio* as "psychological heredity," a carryover from the life of the group to individual life.[35]

To best understand why imitation within modernity plays such an important role in Simmel's theory, we should view it as a way of quoting from the past. Not only is imitation crucial, in the Baudelairean sense, to grasp fashion, but discussion of it also starts Simmel's inquiry into the modern. Moreover, imitation and its opposite, invention, form the basis of the famous *querelle* mentioned in chapter 1—the original debate between ancient and modern aesthetic ideals. A brief excursus into the origin of that quarrel thus seems appropriate.

## ■ 3.3 Imitation and Differentiation

### 3.3.1 *La querelle des anciens et des modernes*

The birth of modernity is also founded in its independent sociocultural properties distinct from those of the classical and ancient, the unchangeable ideals that determined the idea of beauty as much as the concept of progress within historicism.

In the *querelle* between the ancients and moderns, modernity found, from the seventeenth century on, its most eloquent advocates among those who regarded the dispute not merely as a question of new versus old stylistics but as the by-product of a quest for an entirely original artistic and historical distinction that could be perpetually redefined without losing its character. At the root of the *querelle* lies a transformation from the *classical* perception to the *historical*. In the realm of aesthetics, ethics, or the arts, cultural expression was no longer measured against an absolute definition of the perfectly beautiful but was judged in relative terms. Antique or contemporary artworks were seen not as independent of time, exemplifying the ideal of classical notions of beauty, but as products of their respective epochs. Each had to be regarded in relation to its cultural context.

An early advocate of a modern *beau relatif,* Jean Desmarets de Saint-Sorlin, in 1670 established with his *Comparaison de la langue et de la poësie Françoise, avec la Grecque et la Latine* the first critical account of the *querelle.*[36] This text is the forerunner of the more comprehensive *Parallèle des anciens et des modernes* by Charles Perrault (1688) in at least one important respect: its emphasis on the duality of *imitatio* and *inventio.* Desmarets wrote that there was no reason to dispute the argument put forward by the *anciens* that antiquity had already reached an unsurpassable degree of perfection. Nature, as well as man, was already perfected from the moment of creation. Therefore it had always been possible to imitate this perfection. However, the greater task for any artist lay in *inventing* images for which nature had not provided a model.[37]

Perrault built on this concept in the "Dialogues" of his *Parallèle* (published in three revised editions between 1688 and 1696): the mimetic ideal was no longer self-evident; art was not understood as analogous to nature but became independent, abstracting what nature had traced out. The *anciens* might have accepted natural forms without reflecting on them; now the moderns *analyzed* the natural process. They invented devices and machines that, in employing the laws of nature, rationalized and abstracted processes so that they could cope with a novel problem or situation.

The machine that Perrault celebrates as the prime example for his postulate was one for fabricating silk stockings. In a single process this machine created a product that the hands of even the most skilled workman would have to labor for many hours to create. Perrault marvels:

*How many little springs draw the silk fibers toward them, then let them go and take them up again & pull through such-and-such a stitch in an inexplicable fashion, & all this while the laborer who operates the machine understands nothing, knows nothing, nor even thinks about it; so that one can make a comparison with the most extraordinary machine that God has created—I am talking about man in whom a thousand operations happen every day so that he can feed himself & keep himself alive without any knowledge on his part, nor any understanding or even thought of what is happening.*[38]

∎

This particular *inventio* is highly significant. White silk stockings were absolutely de rigueur for any member of the upper classes in seventeenth-century society, in whose number academics like Perrault obviously belonged. Given the conditions in Paris at that time, a considerable number of these rather delicate accessories were required if one was to pride oneself on maintaining an impeccable appearance throughout the day. Thus men like Perrault naturally admired the efficiency of this machine. Yet the workman operating it "understands nothing" of the device. The process so important for modernity—the alienation of the laborer from his product, which Marx and Engels would identify most conspicuously in the spinning mills of nineteenth-century Leeds or Manchester—can already be seen in the weaving of fabrics in France toward the end of the seventeenth century.[39]

From the very beginning, the self-determination of *la modernité* appears closely joined to and sharply distinguished from *la mode*. The relative beauty advocated as contrast to the absolute and sublime is not a positive concept from the outset; its character is developed in relation to fashion. The *beau relatif* originally appears as willful, arbitrary, and something that could not be subsumed under the established norms of the eternally beautiful—although characteristics from the latter were needed for it to create a distinct beauty of its own. Thus in Perrault's *Parallèle* the justification for modern beauty was most closely linked to the "extraordinary approval" of sartorial fashion. An abstract "subite révolution des modes" vehemently called for a reliance on cultural parameters and removed beauty from the normative influence of the eternal and natural.[40] Although "modes" in the plural—here as in other texts on matters of taste or fashion—negatively connotes the random and frequent successions of *la mode,* Perrault realizes how revolutionary such increasingly intense *inventio* is; he concludes that just like every other cultural expression, the written word in antiquity, too, had been prone to fashion's influence: "This applies to all that depends on taste & extravagant imagination, & while eloquence is one of these, it pleases in two or three different ways, sometimes dressed *à la Greque,* & in the fashion of Demosthenes, of

Thucydides & of Plato, or dressed *à la Romaine* & in the fashion of Cicero and Titus Livius."[41] In this context, his choice of terms in describing the "dressing" of literature is far from arbitrary. *Imitatio,* the mimesis of natural forms on which classical art was based, is being superseded by invention; and fashion offers its most futile and most sophisticated coinages alike.

When a powerful fashion industry established itself in France during the second half of the nineteenth century, fashion gradually became accepted as a cultural phenomenon, as the writings of Gautier, Baudelaire, and others make clear. Ironically, at that time the stylistic *inventio,* the frequent emergence of new forms particular to modern times, came to be replaced by a focus on *imitatio,* intended to assess the place of fashion in the social structure of modernity.

### 3.3.2 *Imitor ergo sum*

The charm of imitation is to be found in its ability to make expedient and meaningful action possible, while at the same time requiring no great personal and creative application. "We might define it as the child of thought and thoughtlessness,"[42] notes Simmel. His interpretation of the term "imitation" is very likely to have originated from his early review of Gabriel Tarde's *Les Lois de l'imitation* (*The Laws of Imitation*), published in 1890.[43] Simmel accepts Tarde's definition which stressed the manner in which something is passed from the group to the individual, but challenges the absolutist principle that imitation has only one aspect; he sees a counterbalance, the "charm of contradiction" that would later result in the dualism of imitation and differentiation—most potently realized within fashion.[44] On this very topic Tarde still had remarked that "imitation as part of the current of fashion is nothing but a rather weak stream running alongside the grand flow of customs."[45]

For the French sociologist, forms within society were objectified and clear-cut entities, especially if perceived as "extra-logiques." Simmel, and Tönnies with him, followed Tarde in viewing society as a scientific entity *in itself*. He emphasized the relationship between the whole and the fragment, the general and the individual, thereby creating an analogy between social relations and logical ones, in order to stress the methodological importance of sociology, which was still a young science in need of academic gravitas and self-assurance.

Imitation assures the individual that he or she need not stand alone in taking action; by following a path already chosen by others, he or she is relieved from the difficulties of self-definition. Simmel adds, perhaps reflecting on himself, that imitation "grants us in practice a curious comfort, which it also allows us on a theoretical level, once we have managed to arrange a singular fact under a general heading."[46] Imitation also connects the present with tradition and lends gravitas to "implacable times" when each person increasingly felt (at) a subjective loss. In contrast to *imitatio* as the unthinking reference to a past object, the subject requires *inventio* to define what is indisputably modern. The historical view of moderns in the *querelle* needs to be distinguished from what Simmel early in 1895 regards as a paradox: because the individual perceives his own existence as continuous, he tends to regard history, despite the discontinuity of diverse and unrelated events, as equally continuous.[47] For Simmel, perceptions of both history and temporal progression can be avoided only by reason, by considering the teleological.[48] In the *Philosophy of Fashion,* Simmel concludes: "Teleological man is the antipode to imitative man."[49]

The Kantian definition of the teleological that shaped Simmel's own maintains that the world has to be regarded as *purposive.* An individual realizes its purpose and acts accordingly can decide subjectively, determining things without having to imitate his or her environment. Reading Kant through Simmel, we can see that such an individual can also make aesthetic reflections on an object a priori, without having to define it first. Thus in defining a form as purposive, whether using pragmatic or aesthetic categories in coming to that decision, one can rely on a completely subjective judgment.[50] The dispute between teleology and causality that Simmel observes within human actions is settled by maintaining that the final consequence already comes into effect psychologically before "it is clothed [!] in objective visibleness."[51] Therefore teleology does not affect the rigor of causal connections. Simmel also notes that the "vital conditions of fashion as a universal phenomenon in the history of our race are circumscribed by these conceptions."[52] If one assumes that the idea of the teleological, as distinct from the imitative, exists in one's psyche before it is objectified—not so much as a pragmatic purpose to be fulfilled as an aesthetic experience that is desired—and if one further assumes that the subsequent aesthetic judgment of this objectification is also anticipated before the object proper is defined, then one might have an answer to the age-old question of how fashion comes into being.

A style of clothing owes its origin to teleology; its distribution in society functions through imitation. Aesthetic purposiveness makes the original designers of haute couture, in contrast to mere stylists, suddenly decide as a group on certain sartorial features (influenced, no doubt, by material conditions or a shared preference for a particular quotation from past fashion). No natural causality forces them to agree, and if questioned, to a one would deny having prior contact with their colleagues; each would maintain that the particular style of clothing was entirely his or her own idea. In modern fashion, *inventio* appears no longer as an individual act, or at least is not readily recognizable as such, but as a collective effort. Yet this collective claims to be unaware of its own existence.[53]


### 3.3.3 Difference and Reference

Against imitation, seen as the search for harmony within the constant change brought about by modernity's speed, Simmel opposed differentiation, the desire to change social reality, which he saw as an act that also demands harmony. Because the design of clothes or accessories has to be based on quotation, even the most distinctive and distinguished follower of fashion will inevitably imitate others. In order to retain the original aspect of *inventio* and difference within modernity, Tarde establishes a further distinction in his *Laws of Imitation* between "the imitation of an own and ancient model and the imitation of a foreign and novel model."[54] He describes ages when the first form had dominated, as in ancient Rome, and others when the second form had shaped life; the latter qualified as "the most radical and most revolutionary."[55] Yet the division is ambiguous, for antiquity exists in its dialectical opposition as an integral part of modernity and vice versa. "Every old master has had his own modernity," as Baudelaire put it.[56]

**35.**
Unknown photographer, Charles and Marie-Louise de Noailles at the Bal de Matières
in costumes made from paper, card, and cellophane, 1929. Private collection.

*A fashion imagined—conventional evening wear designed from virtually nothing.*

Tarde was obviously aware of the problematic—not so much in aesthetics as in sociology: "One always refers back to old morals if one introduces political novelties or change." Thus he further subdivides his categorization to arrive at modernity's very own coinage of *imitatio:* "The times when the principal motto is 'everything new is beautiful' are essentially exteriorized[,] . . . and the times when the sole maxim is 'everything antique is good' live entirely introspective lives."[57] It seems curious that the self-reflective subject, confining itself to the *vie intérieure,* is despite his or her sensitivity and intellect unable to shape modernity. Only contact with the exterior, the reification and abstraction in modern life, provides guidelines for modernity's definition a posteriori. Modernity's *inventio* is thus the *inventing of a classification for the object,* which may imitate a previously unexperienced external influence on the group. The person who invents—that is, wears a new form of clothing that stylistically quotes from an as yet unrecognized, forgotten, or neglected external force—succeeds in differentiation. In contrast, imitation proper—that is, adapting a sartorial style that is followed everywhere—is but a self-imposed restriction. It originates from the interior of the subject and negates the objective forces in the modern environment.

Tarde's distinction between exteriority and interiority, between apparent invention and imitation, is also the divide between different strata in society. Modernity as embodied through fashion is created, as architect Adolf Loos would observe later, in and for the ruling classes of the city. Therefore the vital differentiation within crowded urban spaces, said Simmel, "is achieved even more forcefully through the fact that fashion is always class-based. The fashion of an upper stratum differs from the one of a lower and is abandoned at the very moment the latter begins to adopt it."[58] The upper class could, together with the luxury industry that provided its sartorial distinction, appear as "exterior," since it operated outside the social mainstream. As the antithesis to imitation enacted on society's lower levels, a process that would always sound the death knell for a particular fashion, the invention of the upper echelon, was ascribed a teleological nature by Simmel. Yet its "purpose" that prefigured and governed certain apparel or habiliments—white tie and tailcoat or the long ball gown—was essentially defined by long-standing tradition, which fashion would tentatively modify (thus the tuxedo became an alternative to white-tie dress from 1886 onward). Mallarmé,

**36.**
George Grosz, illustration for his essay "Impressions from Paris," 1924–1925. Ink on paper.

costumed as Ix., would of course have concluded sniffily that this purposive aspect within the style of the upper class was nothing but "les riens sérieux."

Simmel sought to form an aesthetic judgment of an object on a metaphysical level and to define the origin and development of fashion on a material one. However, he largely eschewed considering the significance of economic factors in the formation of fashion. (He left that task to his colleague and contemporary Werner Sombart.)[59] This deliberate omission allowed Simmel to situate his analysis of fashion in the interpersonal sphere. Through its strong element of distinction, fashion formed an enclosed habitat where the philosophical ground and subsequent flowering of social expressions could be studied in detail. By removing fashion from the social mainstream, Simmel could abandon almost completely the moral stance that had prevailed in most of the academic discussion on fashion up to that point. When differentiation, or *inventio,* or the teleological lead to fashion's formation, while the imitation in the middle of society in turn regularly deals a deathblow to it, then exclusive and seemingly snobbish attitudes become unavoidable.

Not surprisingly, Simmel incurred the criticism of many of his contemporaries, including some who readily acknowledged their debt to him. In *History and Class Consciousness* Lukács dismissively characterized Simmel as "the apologist of fashion."[60] A recent essay attempts to defuse this criticism by ascribing an "objective irony" to Simmel's essays on fashion and seeing in them antagonisms that continue to battle, cloaked under the outward form of cooperation: "The value of Simmelian formulations is contained in the nuances, which are overlooked no less by Lukács than by those who, like Talcott Parsons, aim to reconstruct systems out of Simmel's nonsystematic formalism."[61] This claim, however, appears too apologetic, since relativism, albeit concealed behind irony, sidesteps direct critique instead of countering it. Simmel's work does not require relativism; in rendering the dualism inherent in fashion analogous to the dialectical perception of modernity (thereby reuniting Kant and Hegel, in a manner of speaking) he establishes a relationship between *Mode* and *Moderne* that is both original and theoretically firm.

## ■ **3.4** The Revolution in Fashion

The "subite révolution des modes" that the *modernes* claimed as significant merged in the nineteenth century with the Baudelairean notion that *la modernité* is fashioned through *la mode,* is determined by the effects of ever-changing styles. This permanent revolution defines great parts of the cultural parameters anew each season and thus ensures that beauty remains essentially relative.

In 1974 the French sociologist Pierre Bourdieu specified this notion of the revolutionary that is particular to fashion: "In fact, I think that a specific revolution, something that marks a 'turning point' [*qui fait date*] in a given field, is the synchronisation of an internal revolution and of something outside, in the wider world."[62] The external changes, the stylistic revolt against existing norms or normative aesthetics, could be fused with an internal revolution that was able to challenge historical causality.

The specific sartorial revolution to which Bourdieu refers is the clothing designed by André Courrèges, regarded as "Le Corbusier of fashion,"[63] who in the second half of the 1960s challenged established haute couture by using "high-tech" materials such as plastic and metal and by incorporating fashion for the emerging youth market (e.g., the miniskirt). That Bourdieu would cite Courrèges's example is significant, not only because of his status as a revolutionary and enfant terrible of fashion but, more important, because he epitomizes in his architectural approach— building his designs out of industrial materials or prefab components—the challenge that the modernist delivers with purist vigor against the sentimentality still embedded in traditional perception. This challenge issued by architects such as Henry van de Velde and Adolf Loos at the turn of the century corresponded to Simmel's positioning of fashion as a guiding principle of modern society between the poles of imitation and differentiation.[64]

Bourdieu's "révolution interne" can be taken quite literally; it is the analysis of fashion from the inside, from the interior of the salon or the dressmaker's studio or from between the folds of the text (as in *La Dernière Mode*). And on a sociological level one cannot get any closer to the inside of society than by examining its dress,[65] where the analyst attempts to find indications of a change in the present "l'univers englobant." This change is so complex and manifold that its origin proves hard to detect. Hence the attempt of social philosophers like Simmel or cultural philosophers like Benjamin to deduce modernity from its tiny fragments became such an important metaphor for modern culture itself.

When we look at the strong cognitive tendency in their philosophical systems, it becomes obvious why Simmel and Benjamin considered it important to explain the whole—in regard to society and also within epistemology. Siegfried Kracauer, Simmel's erstwhile pupil and a close friend of Benjamin, stated that for Simmel "the relation of singular entities . . . is . . . the fragment of a total world" and that he aspired "to encompass the world in its totality. To reach his goal he chooses two paths, the epistemological and the metaphysical. One leads him to a true realist denial of the absolute, to a renunciation of a personal understanding of totality and to a presentation of manifold typical worldviews. The other leads him to life's metaphysics and to a grandly designed attempt to understand the form of appearance out of its absolute principle."[66]

This description strongly echoes the duality inherent both in Simmel's socio-philosophical worldview and in the aesthetic or economic superstructure typical of modernity. On the one hand, Simmel realizes that an absolute principle, whether regarding beauty or thought, cannot be upheld. On the other hand, he makes a desperate attempt to counterbalance this complete fragmentation by searching for metaphysical reason in either aesthetic perception or a mode of existence.

## ■ 3.5 Class and Classification

Simmel's theoretical fabric ("das Gewebe"), as described by Kracauer, is not woven according to a fixed system of thought; neither can it be compared to the literary work of remembrance that Benjamin would find in Proust. Its essential purpose was to exist and through its existence give evidence of the interrelationship of all things.[67] Fashion is the red thread that runs through this fabric: "The insight into the spirit of fashion helps one understand its growing dominance in the age of civilization, an epoch that Simmel regards as continuing into the present."[68] According to Kracauer, Simmel felt that the beliefs that could lay a metaphysical foundation were missing from modern society. Since men and women no longer determined themselves from within, fashions (*Moden*) as a significant element of objective culture would dominate many of the actions and expressions within society.

Two points are important here. The first is that the word "fashions" is plural. Whenever Simmel initiated a discussion on fashion as a concept or paradigm, he gave the impression of covering all kinds of fashionable expressions—in manners, modes, and so on. From the etymological viewpoint this appears logical, as the German word *Mode,* used to describe a style of clothing, originated—like the French term—from the Latin *modus.* Although Simmel began by referring to different forms of behavior, attitudes, and so on, his texts always continued to exclusively employ the feminine singular *die Mode* and thus to center on sartorial fashion and the significant role of clothing for social existence.

For Simmel fashion is originally based on class. The distinction of one stratum from another can obviously be expressed in many ways—through modes of living, manners of speaking, and the like—none, however, is as effective and visually direct as the dress code. In Berlin society of the 1900s, such codification was very significant indeed. The high prices of homes in urban areas prevented members of academic circles from acquiring large houses; thus Simmel, his wife, and his son lived, as any normal middle-class family would, in a rented apartment.[69] Also, the German language did not reflect class distinction as clearly as the French or particularly English of the time did, though there were of course many accents and modes of speaking. Therefore, in order to reflect the refinement and to emphasize the exclusivity that the topic of fashion carried in itself, Simmel aims to set himself apart from the masses—that is, from the middle class, since the lower strata in fact posed no competition. For this maneuver a distinct way of dressing has to be adopted. The modern male intellectual thus favors English tailoring: bespoke suits in a cut that is appropriate for an urban environment. These suits were much more relaxed and less pompous and stiff than the apparel of the Prussian civil servant, who still wore a morning coat and thus felt compelled, in order to reach his desk without being ridiculed in the streets, to put on an overcoat (or invest in a cab) to literally cover his embarrassment, notwithstanding the summer heat he might have to endure. The Viennese architect Loos, an astute observer of sartorial signifiers and absurdities, writes on the sartorial life span of such a dress code: "It's a comical effect—which is precisely what has always caused the downfall of any piece of wearing apparel."[70]

In another essay published the same year, Loos elaborates on fashion in modernity, on what he ultimately considers the correct way of dressing: "Rather, it is a question of being dressed *in such a way that one stands out the least.*"[71] Such a standard implies wearing the right clothes for the right occasion: a top hat worn skating looks ridiculous, as would a red tailcoat at a grand ball. Yet this postulate cannot be maintained everywhere; what is appropriate in London's Hyde Park might well be considered extravagant in Beijing, Zanzibar, or even on Vienna's Stephansplatz. Thus, to be dressed correctly one should go unnoticed in what Loos called "the center of culture." For the Anglophile and modernist aesthete, that center had to be London, the place where contemporary male clothing was tailored.

Also in 1898, the poet Guillaume Apollinaire would provide a poetic and ironic account of one spiritual and aesthetic pilgrimage to the British capital for the sake of the sartorial—in this case, the bespoke suit. His poem "L'Émigrant de Landor Road" begins:

▪

*Le chapeau à la main il entra du pied droit*
*Chez un tailleur très chic et fournisseur du roi*
*Ce commerçant venait de couper quelque têtes*
*De mannequins vêtus comme il faut qu'on vête*[72]

▪

Yet there was not simply one particular road or sophisticated part of the city where well-dressed men convened; Loos has to modify his statement further.

▪

*Of course, it might certainly happen that during his wanderings the stroller would come upon surroundings with which he contrasted sharply. He would then have to change his coat as he passed from one street to another. This would not do. We may now formulate our precept in its most complete form. It goes like this: an article of*

**37.**

Photo of the coffered wood interior of the gentleman's outfitter Knize in Vienna, designed by Adolf Loos, 1902.

*Significantly, Loos's first modernist and purist interiors were realized for the famous Viennese company that tailored suits in the Savile Row style for a Continental clientele.*

*clothing is modern when the wearer stands out as little as possible at the centre of culture, on a specific occasion,* in the best society. *This is a very English axiom to which every fashionable intellectual would probably agree.*[73]

.

As could be seen in the attitudes of dandies from Balzac to Mallarmé, to be truly modern male fashion should be as purist, abstracted (cf. *le drap noir*), and inconspicuous as possible. And as Simmel's work suggested, Loos's postulate on fashion could hold only in the uppermost echelon of a society in which the sartorial was essentially determined within urban confines. "The urge to stand out grows in equal measure to the proximity in which people live together. Fashion is thus essentially an urban phenomenon,"[74] observed Kracauer. One has to assume that the interest Simmel displayed toward fashion was not entirely academic; it had application to himself as well. He himself would use his attire, that is, bespoke English tailoring, because it was distinct from the off-the-peg suits that began to appear on the streets of Berlin around him. And fellow economist and sociologist Sombart would comment accordingly on Simmel's difficulties in finding a professorship: "He is too distinguished."[75]

The need to be distinguished was not based simply on class or aesthetics, although Simmel went as far as to take up the fashion of the black *pardessus* from his friend, the poet Stefan George;[76] both were certainly aware of the Romantic tradition of the overcoat and the symbolist implications it had carried since the days of Gautier, Baudelaire, and Mallarmé. The need for distinction remains deeply embedded in modern urban society,[77] and fashion dominates *modernité* because it is essential to mutually excluding and approximating homogeneous spheres in a objectified heterogeneous society.

## ■ 3.6  Critical Theory versus Simmelian Analogy

Habermas's seminal statement—that it was Simmel who "establish[ed] the relationship between fashion and modernity"—appears to credit the philosopher-cum-sociologist with a profound insight into the paradigms of *modernité.* It suggests that Simmel follows Baudelaire and Mallarmé in making the connection between sartorial changes and an overall reassessment of the stylistics in modern life. However, Habermas does not follow through on the notion of an artistic and intellectual tradition that had made clothes a focus of its interpretation and investigation, though he does underscore Simmel's continuous influence on Benjamin. As the next chapter makes clear, this influence can be easily traced in the numerous quotations, both literary and scientific, that Benjamin assembled on the topic of sartorial fashion. Seen in this context, Simmel occupies a pivotal position between nineteenth-century attitudes toward *mode et modernité* and twentieth-century analyses of the sartorial commodity and the social impact of fashion.

What does Habermas make of Simmel's role at this pivot? Alas, not much. Apart from the acclaim noted above, he appears to deny that Simmel's philosophy had any impact on our perception of modernity proper. In part, he displays the habitual negligence of interpreters of modernity regarding fashion. However, the complete omission of Simmel's ideas from Habermas's *Philosophical Discourse of Modernity* (1985) is surprising indeed, especially because the study emphasizes the element of transitoriness and maintains that modernity remains unfinished, that its parameters continue to determine intellectual and social existence. These are characteristics that Simmel already had set forth in discussing fashion, as we have learned.

Habermas's first formal thoughts on the subject of the book came in a speech, delivered when he accepted the Adorno Prize in September 1980, titled "Modernity—An Incomplete Project." Here he focuses on an aesthetic reading of modernity. Habermas establishes a chain of reasoning, from Baudelaire to Benjamin and to dada and surrealism, which is distinguished by temporal perception: "The new time consciousness, which enters philosophy in the writings of Bergson, does more than express the experience of mobility in society, of acceleration in history, of discontinuity in everyday life. The new value placed on the transitory, the elusive and the ephemeral, the very celebration of dynamism, discloses a longing for an undefiled, immaculate and stable present."[78] The "new value" of the transitory and ephemeral ascribed to Bergson's philosophy is of course far from new; Baudelaire, Mallarmé, and others in the literary and aesthetic tradition looked at fashion in order to determine the eternal *within* ephemera. The "stable present" must appear as a version of the subject's desire to create an individual *durée* in order to oppose the transitoriness in modern culture. Yet in the very next sentence—curiously not part of the American translation—this modernity is described as a longing for true, metaphysical presence that can be used to describe a novel concept of both the temporal and the historic, that stands against the classical, against the sublime: "As a self-negating movement, modernity is the 'longing for a true presence.'"[79] It is the term "self-negating" that, rather than being a postmodernist ploy, reveals the tradition from which Habermas's particular conception of modernity originates. This tradition, which provides an important critique of Simmel, also accounts for one element in Benjamin's ambiguous challenge to historicism.

The persistent struggle to construct an identity between subject and object, between thought and reality, which Simmel condensed to the point that it became integral to the relationship between subjective and objective culture, was approached in a new way in Adorno's *Negative Dialectics.* Though that book was published in 1966, the approach was prepared much earlier, most crucially in the 1947 *Dialectics of Enlightenment,* which Adorno had co-written with Max Horkheimer. Reflecting on the heritage of the Frankfurt School, Habermas read Adorno's negative dialectics as "a continuous explanation of why we have to circle about within this *performative contradiction* [i.e., that the critique of ideology must demonstrate in its descriptions the very criticism it had to denounce beforehand], should indeed remain in it; and of why only the insistent, relentless unfolding of this paradox could open the prospect of that magically invoked 'remembrance of nature within the subject, in whose fulfilment the unacknowledged truth of all culture lies hidden.'"[80] Although Adorno's is a politically motivated questioning of reason and critique, the last sentence clearly implies an aesthetic orientation, and it appears—certainly methodologically—to be not too far from Simmel's perception of a cultural critique in which paradoxes are to be not solved but transformed into dualities or analogies that allow a dialectic structure to remain at their bases.

Within the German tradition of idealists such as Schiller and Schlegel and of the aesthetic perception of the Romantics lies "the artistic representation of wholeness [*Gesamtkunstwerk*] that explains the Frankfurt School's fascination for aesthetics which embody a nonalienated relationship between man and nature, subject and object, and reason and the senses."[81] Yet in the twentieth century the political impetus behind this notion became decidedly different, as capitalist abstraction had to be refuted in favor of socially justifiable principles within aesthetics. In the same vein as his discussion of Benjamin, Habermas notes the effort of subjective expression to maintain its status in the face of ever-increasing rationalization: "Only art, which has become autonomous in the face of demands for employment extrinsic to it, has taken up positions on behalf of the victims of bourgeois rationalisation. Bourgeois art has become the refuge for a satisfaction, even if only virtual, of those needs that have become, as it were, illegal in the material life-process of bourgeois society."[82] This is analogous to the "truly cultivated existence," ironically bourgeois in essence, to which Simmel referred when he maintained that all possible knowledge, creativity, refinement within a Being do not grant any real cultural identity, if these elements are simply additions to the pattern of values that is and will remain outside of an individual's personality. In that case a person is civilized—"besitzt Kultiviertheiten"—but not cultured—"ist nicht kultiviert." Culture is achieved only if significant cultural elements, originating from the supraindividual, develop in the soul longings and urges that are already present and internally traced out, thereby completing the subject and his or her act of cognition. Simmel concludes that "here finally the conditionality of culture emerges, through which it presents a solution to the subject-object equation."[83]

The ultimate aim of Benjamin, Adorno, Horkheimer, and others was to attack the intellectual, ideological, and ultimately realpolitik maneuvers that conspired to establish a leveling and totalitarian principle in culture. Yet such opposition originated in the battle against the oppressively rational tendency in modernism, prepared within the folds of Simmel's philosophical fabric. Benjamin's subsequent interpretation of fashion as the "tiger's leap" thus would have no basis without Simmel's writing.

## ■ 3.7 The Second Tiger's Leap

In one of his lectures on Kant from 1904, Simmel spoke of the perception of time and how it is generated in the memory of the subject. The past is the "curiously qualified consciousness," which, in contrast to the new, has to maintain something from earlier impressions. "Just like the future—which we create by endowing the present in our fantasy with that particular past brand of consciousness—the past is in no way real."[84]

Objectively speaking, even the present itself is not real; reality lies only within a particular *point* in time. Any temporal extension must be subjective, generated through memory. Once different temporal stages become established, the relation between them emerges by an "action of the soul," defined as "reproduction." On this specific relation of past and present, Simmel writes: "The temporal relationship between the past, which is objectively nonexistent and merely remembered and the present is created only by—to put it in modern terms—*experiencing it;* that is, it takes on the form of my experience, which spreads over the real and, via remembrance, also over what is no longer real."[85] Reading Kant, Simmel thus defines the concept of "time" as unreal: only in experience is the subject able to distinguish any temporal succession. This definition of course corresponds with Baudelaire's attempt to explain the temporal entity that he himself aesthetically "experienced" and that he considered most influential to artistic creation proper, namely the present, as nondefinable or transitory. When Simmel coyly remarks that "experiencing" was an essentially *modern* term, he affirms Baudelaire's famous dictum on the contrast between the immediate (the point in modern time) and the eternal (which denies the temporal): "La modernité, c'est le transitoire, le fugitif, le contingent, la moitié de l'art, dont l'autre moitié est l'éternel et l'immuable" (By "modernity" I mean the ephemeral, the fugitive, the contingent, the half of art whose other half is the eternal and the immutable).[86]

As we have seen, this reflection by Baudelaire originates in his discussion of fashion. He demands that the painter of historical scenes clothe the figures in appropriate, that is, modern, habiliments and apparel. Thus the present, as the contemporary artwork, becomes both distinguished from and part of the past. Artistic remembrance of an event creates a temporal relation within the reproduction (as

**38.**

Émile Pingat, promenade costume, ca. 1888. Silk velvet with metallic silver thread embroidery. Modern studio photograph by Lynton Gardiner. Brooklyn Museum of Art, Anonymous gift in memory of Mrs. John Roebling.

*Here, the dressmaker Pingat—who, according to the Goncourt brothers, always talked about fashion as if he was offering something illegal and immoral—not only quotes a style from the eighteenth century but also changes sartorial gender. An embroidered male riding coat was enlarged and became, more than a hundred years later, the woman's jacket in daytime apparel. The quotation as sartorial remembrance is irreverent indeed.*

Simmel, following Kant, demands).[87] In introducing a transitoriness, a temporal relation contrasting with the eternal and absolute, which hitherto had been the sole measure in aesthetic perception, Baudelaire is able to distinguish further a *historical* view that would endow the work of art with a relative yet genuine beauty tied to the present and immediate.[88]

But Baudelaire also requires the dual character of fashion to maintain the principle of sublime beauty, which he regards as integral to a work of art. The clothes depicted by the artist's memory should appear modern and be classified as such (see Max Weber in section 3.2.1); the event proper, however, remains historical and ennobled. Eternal virtues are to be displayed in the picture or celebrated by the poet; and because fashion, even in its most contemporary form, quotes from the past, the modern clothes do not appear out of place in the reproduction of an event from antiquity. In fashion *quotation is sartorial remembrance*—as much able to create an intricate temporal relation as chart a metaphysical experience.

After Baudelaire, this theme was expressed in Benjamin's *Tigersprung* as an integral part of his "Theses on the Concept of History"; and Habermas in turn follows in *The Philosophical Discourse on Modernity* with a Benjaminian "dialectical image" of his own: "Eternal beauty reveals itself only in the mummery of time's costume."[89] Fashion, embodied by contemporary costume, reveals itself in an aesthetic and an extravagant mode, much as the dialectics of fashion are embodied in the early modernist creations of haute couture (by Émile Pingat, Mariano Fortuny, Paul Poiret, etc.), in which past cultures—for example, Roman clothing or Directoire dresses—flow in a transitory gestalt of silk and chiffon through to the present. Yet seen through the intellectual austerity of Habermas and Critical Theory, such a revelation is judged negatively as disguising the true value of art—and, ironically, it becomes a much more bourgeois perception than it was at the time of Baudelaire. For the "subjectively" writing theoreticians such as Tarde, Simmel, and Benjamin evidently there is no mummery; instead the dresses alternatively generate and epitomize *modernité*.

Baudelaire's postulate was taken up by Benjamin to address the paradoxical task "of obtaining standards of its own for the contingency of a modernity that has become simply transitory."[90] Whereas Baudelaire could satisfy himself by regarding the constellation of the transitory and the eternal as combined in the authenticity of a work of art, Benjamin attempts to relate the aesthetic experience to history. This relation becomes most important to Habermas as he begins his interpretation of modernity. Benjamin creates the term now-time (*Jetztzeit*), a transitory immediacy that is interspersed with "splinters" from a completed time, which he described as "messianic"—that is, as the possible solution to the problem inherent in the normative gestalt of history. Habermas points out that the most potent realization of now-time is "helped by a motif of mimicry that has become tenuous, as it were, and that now was to be ferreted out in the appearances of fashion."[91]

However, irreverence toward the past is best achieved by quotation as imitation rather than by mimicry, since the constant change in fashion cannot be satisfied simply by a historically accurate copy. The clothes have to "invent" the old, not mimic it. Habermas focuses on Benjamin's observation that "[t]he French Revolution regarded itself as Rome reincarnated. It quoted ancient Rome as fashion quotes a past attire. Fashion has the scent for the modern wherever it stirs in the thicket of what has been. It is the tiger's leap into the past. Yet this leap occurs in an arena commanded by the ruling class. The very same leap in the open air of history is the dialectical one, which Marx has understood as the revolution."[92] A "révolution interne" and the social challenge from outside arrive at the same time because fashion incorporates the abstract character of modernity, allowing it to subvert a hitherto exclusively historical perception. As Simmel had written some twenty years before Benjamin, "Fashion's potential for abstraction, which is founded in its very being, lends a certain aesthetic style to modernity itself, even in nonaesthetic areas; because of fashion's 'estrangement from reality'; this potential is also developed within a historical expression."[93] Fashion's potential for abstraction, its indifference toward objectification—ironic, because it itself accounts for the constant production of new commodities—enables us not simply to make retail sales but to make value judgments about history. The terror of reification, which Marx had seen to be the reason for the subject's uncertainty and loss of control of the object—"all that is solid melts into air"[94]—is transferred from ethics to aesthetics, becoming in the process transitoriness and immediacy.

By embracing the instantaneous as the label of aesthetic experience in modernity, Benjamin interprets the reification of ethical and moral problems positively, as a necessity that is not merely a necessary evil. With the tiger's leap, the political critique of modernity jumps back (with Marx, ambiguously) to Baudelaire's original aesthetic coinage of *modernité*. Simmel correspondingly explains the "modern indifference" toward the spiritual and ultimately humanist requirements of the subject because these requirements "conflict with the absolute unobjectiveness in the development of fashion and also are in conflict with the aesthetic appeal of fashion that exists by virtue of its distance from the substantial and material meaning of objects."[95] Here Simmel does not bemoan the demise of the subject under the taxing control of commodities; brought to bear instead on the subjective interpretation of modernity, the commodities, especially the sartorial one that dresses the subject, in turn are imbued with metaphysical value, thus handing back dominance to the acting subject in a fragmented modern culture.

There remains at the core of the *Tigersprung* an attack on the linear norms of historical progress. Through this challenge to historicism, Benjamin hopes to counter his own fear that modernity, rooted in the economics of bourgeois capitalism, might employ fashion to accustom itself to any shock of the new launched by the artistic avant-garde throughout its formative years at the beginning of the twentieth century.

Briefly slipping on Benjamin's interpretive mantle, his friend Adorno finds that "fashion is the permanent confession by art, to the effect that art does not measure up to the ideal that has been put before it."[96] One cannot neatly separate fashion from art, the so-called ephemeral from the sublime, as the bourgeois *Kunstreligion* would prefer. Adorno states that the artist, the aesthetic subject, had within the avant-garde polemically separated him- or herself from society. In modernity, art communicated through fashion with an "objective spirit"—however falsified or corrupted it might appear. Art cannot maintain the arbitrary and unconscious character that earlier theories ascribed to it. It is completely manipulated yet independent of demand—though since the discussion is situated within capitalism, demand has to enter the equation at some point. Adorno stresses that because the manipulation of the consumer in the age of monopolies has become the prototype for the prevailing social relations of production,

**39.**
August Macke, *The Fashion Boutique,* 1913. Oil on canvas, 50.8 × 61 cm. Westfälisches Landesmuseum für Kunst und Kulturgeschichte, Münster.

fashion itself represents a socially and culturally objective power. He refers to Hegel, who maintained in his *Lectures on Aesthetics* that it is art's task to incorporate what is essentially alien to it.[97] Yet because art has become confused over the probability of such an incorporation, fashion throws its decorated hat into the ring and aspires itself to incorporate this alienation, reification, or codification of objectified culture. Thus Adorno argues that if art wants to prevent its own sellout it has to resist fashion, while at the same time including or accepting fashion into its fold in order to avoid turning a blind eye to the prime movers of social and cultural existence, such as progress and competition. Adorno credits—not surprisingly—Baudelaire's "Painter of modern life," Constantin Guys, with first reflecting that the true modern artist is the one who maintains his own powers in losing himself to ephemera. He follows both Marx and Simmel in observing:

■

*In the age where the subjective spirit becomes even more powerless in the face of social objectivity, fashion announces the surplus of the latter within the subjective spirit, painfully alienated from it, but a corrective to the illusion that the subjective spirit is pure Being-in-itself. Against those who despise it, fashion's most powerful response is that it participates in the apt, historically saturated, individual movement. . . . Via fashion art sleeps with something that it renounces normally and from this it draws the strength that otherwise must atrophy under the renunciation on which art is predicated. Art, as illusion, is the dress for an invisible body. Thus fashion is dress as the absolute.*[98]

■

What Adorno sees as essentially negative—namely, that fashion's absolutism in view of sartorial codification does away with the ambiguities in culture that are necessary to prevent totalitarianism—has to be read simultaneously as an affirmation of its value for cognition. As Simmel's *Philosophy of Money* postulates, the subject-object division is reconciled by relocating the spirit of the latter into the former; and both Benjamin and Adorno—despite all the latter's criticism about the vagueness of Simmel's "philosophy of life"—do accept this claim. Fashion serves for all three as a historical corrective and, even more important, as a philosophical idea (although to varying degrees). It seamlessly integrates the object into the individual subject. Fashion directs the sartorial but also goes beyond it. Thus contrary to the usual evaluation of cultural objects, it appears that art merely "dresses" society or history with claims of absolute understanding, while fashion in its incompleteness represents underlying principles in modernity.[99]

# ■ 3.8 Elements of Fashion

### 3.8.1 The Stranger

Simmel always maintained the philosophical significance of fashion; nevertheless, he continued to underpin it with sociological observations: "Social forms, clothing, aesthetic judgment, the whole style of human expression, are constantly transformed by fashion, in such a way, however, that fashion—i.e. the latest fashion—in all these things affects only the upper classes."[100] Social evolution, as Simmel observed, demands that as soon as the lower classes begin to adopt a particular fashion and thus destroy both the distinction between classes and the coherence of each respective class, the upper echelons discard their old clothes and put on new styles in order to retain the differentiation—"thus the game goes merrily on."[101]

While Simmel carries the structural concept in Tarde's *Imitation* into twentieth-century urban modernity, where exterior and interior become refined in order to fit a dress code that would allow for differentiation inside fixed class barriers that were increasingly diffuse, he also drew on Herbert Spencer's earlier *Principles of Sociology,* which initiated sociological coinage proper with terms such as "imitation" and "distinction." In 1882 Spencer wrote:

■

*Everywhere and always the tendency of the inferior to assert himself has been in antagonism with the restraints imposed on him; and a prevalent way of asserting himself has been to adopt costumes and appliances and customs like those of his superior. . . . [H]abitually the tendency has been to multiply the precedents for imitation and so to establish for wider classes the freedom to live and dress in ways like those of the narrower classes. Especially has this happened as fast as rank and wealth have ceased to be coincident—as fast, that is, as industrialism has produced men rich enough to compete in style of living with those above them in rank.*[102]

■

Modernity hastened this process because fashion, embracing the externals of life, was most ready to respond to the call of money. Modernity also led to the dependence of fashion (and luxury goods in general) on the capitalist mode of production. Sombart considers several reasons why luxury items were produced for bourgeois classes, outside the court and nobility, that began to consume conspicuously. One lies in the nature of the production process itself. The greater part of the raw materials are of foreign origin; therefore, time and money must be invested to import them. Their subsequent processing is in general more elaborate, time-consuming, and, in short, expensive: it requires a high degree of specialization and skill from the laborer. And the exclusive nature of this high-quality work exists only to distinguish it from the broad basis of production that capitalism had established. Another factor was the nature of the distribution and sale of these exclusive articles. The luxury trade was not only dependent on but also highly vulnerable to changes in fashion. Success required both capital to survive stagnation in the market and flexibility to adapt the production process to match changing demand.[103]

As befits the materialist age created by the growing separation between laborers and their product, fashion requires an element of alienation for its success. It has to appear not as something that develops organically but as an artificial creation. Its teleological origins always have to lie outside the culture, class, or social grouping that eventually adopts it. "Generally speaking, only the stranger seems able to produce an impression of respect, which leads us to imitate them," writes Tarde,[104] who characterized as "exteriorized" the tendencies in society that sustain fashion, as we have seen. Sombart finds that fashion brought in from outside, or initiated by a stranger, contains a strong element of rationality, since it is created away from the established order with which a subjective relationship might exist. For such fashion to be accepted, expedience dominates social or aesthetic considerations.[105] As Simmel observes in 1904, in a work written between those of Tarde and Sombart:

■

*There exists a wide-spread predilection for importing fashions from without, and such foreign fashions assume a greater value within the circle, simply because they did not originate there. . . . As a matter of fact the exotic origin of fashion seems strongly to favour the exclusiveness of the groups which adopt them. Because of their external origin these fashions create a special and significant form of socialization, which arises through mutual relations to a point without the circle. It sometimes appears as though social elements, just like the axes of vision, converge best at a point that is not too near. . . . Paris modes are frequently created with the sole intention of setting a fashion elsewhere.* [106]

■

Within modernity, fashion's evolutionary path thus becomes ever more unpredictable and erratic until the changes within the objectified world can no longer be reasonably assessed by the subject. Subsequent arguments dismissing fashion as whimsical and futile are likely to arise at this point: because the subject feels unable to account for the twist and turns in fashion, although its actual creation can be understood as a quotation from historical models or different cultural settings, he or she denies its influence, relegating it to the insignificant and belated.

The latter part of the above passage on estrangement or alienation in fashion is taken by Simmel from the first version of the *Philosophy of Money,* where it concludes a short analysis on the stranger within the monetary process. "Der Fremde" ("The Stranger") is also the title of an extended excursus within Simmel's *Soziologie* of 1908. [107] These studies indicate how personal experiences are at the base of Simmel's reflection and analysis. For him, the stranger is the "potential wanderer," arriving one day and staying the next without embodying anything but a transitory being. A curious relation between nearness and remoteness distinguishes the stranger: the original distance in his relationship with a group means that even when in physical proximity, he remains far away, while the element of strangeness arouses the curiosity of members in a group, thus establishing an approach to someone who is essentially distanced.

For Simmel, the liberal intellectual of Jewish origin who was denied his academic merits both by the Prussian establishment and by sections of society from which he would seek distance, the stranger is a significant character indeed; and he is furthermore the rationalized equivalent of Baudelaire's observant flâneur. Within both the stranger's "objectivity" (as one not involved in group relations) and his "abstract character" (those in a group can observe only the most general of qualities in a person coming from outside), Simmel finds on an individual level an analogy to modernity's socioeconomic tendency.[108]

What Sombart would make the main topic of his analysis was a starting point for Simmel: in the development from an enclosed zone of primary production to advanced capitalism, there entered, in addition to the already-occupied posts within the economic structure, a person who does not claim a place in this zone as such but expands it and connects it to others, without having any actual power of production himself. This becomes obvious within the capitalist monetary system. From the earliest cultures onward, money tokens always have been brought in from the outside, for their abstract value—as their practical use was necessarily unknown—as well as for their rarity. Here again, Simmel concludes by drawing an analogy to modernity's paradigm: "This calls to mind fashion, which is often particularly valued and powerful if it is imported."[109] The ambiguity within fashion is comparable to the ambivalent objectivity embodied in the figure of the stranger. It cannot be explained simply by distance or noninvolvement; it exists mainly because of the dialectical construct of nearness and remoteness.

∎

*Objectivity is by no means nonparticipation—as the latter exists beyond subjective or objective action anyway—but a positive and definite way of participating: similarly, objectivity in theoretical observation [and here Simmel, as distanced observer of society, repeats his own credo] is far from implying that the mind is a passive tabula rasa on which things imprint their qualities, but it signifies the full activity of the mind, working according to its own rules; only that the mind has erased accidental distortions and emphases whose individual and subjective differences would create entirely different images of the same object.*[110]

∎

In maintaining a distance, the stranger can observe and through that observation create individual aesthetics, or perhaps merely a style that sets him apart from the crowd. Loos states that the perfectly dressed man is he who remains inconspicuous in high society, but one has to add that he also potentially could become an arbiter of fashion, simply by remaining at a well-judged distance from any given group. Sartorially this is best expressed in the abstract and somber character of the *habit noir,* or, to choose a later feminine equivalent, of Gabrielle Chanel's original "little black dress."

Aesthetic individualism was more dominant in Paris than anywhere else. In his 1905 essay on fashion Simmel adds an afterthought to his observation on French couture: "In Paris itself, fashion displays both the greatest tension and reconciliation of its dualistic elements [i.e., imitation and differentiation]. Individualism, the accommodation of what is personally becoming, is much more fundamental than in Germany; however, at the same time a certain broad framework of a general style, of the latest fashion, is strictly maintained so that individual expression never falls into but always lifts itself from generality."[111] There are the two social tendencies that, combined, are prerequisites for the formation of fashion: the need for association on the one hand and the need for distinction on the other. When one of them is missing, fashion fails to appear. Most lower strata have few and seldom very specific fashions, and the style of clothing in so-called primitive cultures is much more stable than in cultures of Western Europe. Because they had more overtly ritualized social structures, the danger of mixing or effacing, which classes within Western societies combated by differentiation, was less immanent. Simmel writes that fashion helped different social groups maintain their respective coherence, as "people wearing the same kind of clothing behave more or less in the same way,"[112] a matter of primary importance for modern life with its individualism and fragmentation. The pace of change within fashion indicates how much our perception has become blunted and needs to be constantly stimulated. The more a society displays symptoms of overstrained nerves caused by persistent external stimuli—a condition popularly known in Simmel's time as "neurasthenia"—the more quickly fashion will have to mutate (see Tarde), as the progressing desensitization will make ever greater stimulation necessary to successfully differentiate among groups. Simmel postulates that while those in "primitive cultures" had feared strange appear-

**40.**

Unknown photographer, Redfern directs the fitting of a costume design, ca. 1907.

*The house of Redfern introduced English tailoring to Parisian women. The designer propagated the tailored female "costume," i.e., jacket and skirt made from the same cloth (much admired by Proust's fictional Odette de Grecy). Charles Poynter Redfern (son of the founder of the house, John Redfern) is presented in the photo like an artist, dressed in a painter's cloak and pointing a phallic painter's stick at the model's midriff; the gown itself is much less austere than usual.*

ances, the process of civilisation, made possible the removal of feelings of unease about novelties. Furthermore, in modern societies a particular connotation came into play: a person who wants and is able to follow fashion mostly sports *new* clothes. Because of its novelty, however, the dress or suit inflicts on us posture and attitude much more than an old one did. Eventually, the old clothes had become completely responsive to our individual gestures, giving way to each of them and often displaying, in the tiniest of idiosyncrasies, our ties. That we feel more "comfortable" in worn clothing than in new shows that the former had imposed on us its particular law of form, which through the long process of wearing was transferred onto our movements. Hence new attire grants its wearer what Simmel calls a "supraindividual regularity."[113] Its novelty exerts a prerogative over the wearer's individuality. As new clothes are put on, the materialist abstraction reaches the body itself—long after the a priori acceptance of this postulate has taken hold in the mind of the consumer.

As noted in chapter 1, the dialectical coinage in modern aesthetics was marked for Baudelaire by the divergence of the ephemeral and the sublime. For Simmel it was expressed in the dualism between homogeneous imitation and differentiation, between stability in value and constant change within social expressions; thus it was particular to the way in which fashion constitutes modernity. Simmel found that if one of the above "patterns" was absent, as in some cultivated societies at certain points in history, fashion could not develop. In the principality of Florence at the end of the fourteenth century there is said to have been in male attire hardly any fashion in its proper sense, because everybody endeavored to wear a style that was as individual as possible. As a consequence, the instinctive social cohesion without which there can be no fashion as such faltered: excessive individualist expression held sway. At the other extreme, Simmel described how the Venetian nobility decreed that it must wear nothing but black, in order to prevent the masses from realizing how small in number *i nobili* who governed them actually were. In this case fashion did not exist because the other constitutive element, the notion of distinction, had been deliberately removed. Nor did this public decree negate fashion alone. Complete equality in clothing—represented by the invariable black—symbolized the internal democracy of this noble body. Even inside the nobility, fashion was not allowed to gain a foothold, since it would immediately have functioned as a correlative for the formation of a separate group within the nobility itself.

Black clothing belongs to those sartorial expressions that appear to negate fashion. Yet through its concerted resistance to trends it gains the status of a supremely "objective" gesture, untouched by the temporal progression within changes in clothing. This status accounts for the fascination that the black suit—"this much-abused *habit,*" as Baudelaire put it in 1846[114]—has held for artists and aesthetes alike since the Burgundy and Spanish courts in the mid–fifteenth and eighteenth century. Purist restraint in clothing creates a uniform cover under which the most daring and revolutionary thoughts can germinate; and a subsequent flowering of ideas grows even more distinguished and remarkable against the dark plane of the melancholic *habit noir.* In regard to modern beauty, Baudelaire (rather ironically) claims that the dandy's head bears traces of "one of the most interesting characteristics of Beauty, of mystery, and last of all (let me admit the exact point to which I am a modern in my aesthetics) of Unhappiness."[115]

This "unhappiness," caused, for example, by the loss of a close friend or relative, is reflected in one particular kind of black clothing: that of mourning, which equally belongs to those sartorial expressions that negate fashion. Although notions of distinction, association, or equality can also be present in mourning, the symbolism of the black attire sets the mourner apart from the more colorful agitation of other people. Insofar as all mourners are in that condition the same, they constitute an ideal community in their differentiation from the rest of society. Yet since that community is not of a social nature, there exists only sartorial equality but no unity, and the potential for creating fashion is absent. For Simmel, "this underlines the *social* character of fashion."[116] Although the dark garments might offer notions of separation and connection, the absence of a social intention—which is not identical to mere custom—turns them into the visual opposite of fashion.

In Victorian England a curious predominance of mourning established itself. Many widowed women continued to wear black until they died or, more seldom, remarried, and their daughters until they became engaged; some women almost welcomed the death of even the remotest of kin, as it provided an opportunity to dress continually in black. Yet when the noncolor became ubiquitous, an "inappropriate" attention began to be paid to those originally pious and austere garments. Women showed a certain penchant for differentiation, and subtle changes began to shape the changing "fashion" of mourning, demanded by bourgeois women from their dressmakers.

∎

*"Which is the mother?" asked Lord Sevenoaks.*

*"The younger-looking of the two. Lobelia, her daughter, always wears such morbid looking hats, they make her look quite ten years older than she really is. Her mother always wears black—now she is losing her figure. She always pretends to be in mourning for someone, simply as an excuse for wearing black; she has been in black now for three seasons."*

*"In other words," said Lord Sevenoaks, "she has been losing her figure for three years."* [117]

∎

In the Victorian age, when sensuality appeared to be removed completely from the public mind, mourning was the ultimate and adequate excuse to renounce any indulgence in fashion without the fear of being accused of being unfashionable and backward-looking. Black was practical, economical, morally correct, and perhaps even "democratic." However, Victorian society imitated moral restraint and did not act for aesthetic reasons; the black tailcoat and the bulging dress of the bourgeois couple in London or Paris of the 1870s or 1880s had nothing in common with the dandy's *habit noir* and the tailored riding outfit of the *amazone*—except for its color.

### 3.8.2 Transitoriness

It was transitoriness that would prevent fashion from succumbing to the blackmail of bourgeois society at the end of the nineteenth century. In 1895 Simmel states: "The essence of fashion lies in the fact that it is always only a part of the group that practices it, while the great majority is still on its way to fashion. It never is but always becomes."[118] In one of his later essays, Simmel transfers this postulate into a meta-physical context. Writing on Bergson, he describes life as "a continuously flowing creation of the new, of what has not existed previously; it does not exhaust itself in the law of cause and effect, which only generates one thing from the same, but it is a truly creative force that cannot be calculated like a mechanism but has to be experienced."[119] The notion that the very character of fashion demands that it can be exercised at one time only by a portion of a given group is again singled out by Simmel: as soon as a creative example has been universally adopted, when apparel previously worn by a few becomes common sartorial parlance, one can no longer speak of fashion as a cultural parameter.

■

*The distinctiveness which in the early stages of a set fashion assures for it a certain distribution is destroyed as fashion spreads, and as this element wanes, the fashion is bound to die. By reason of the peculiar play between the tendency towards universal acceptance and the destruction of its very purpose to which this general adoption leads, fashion includes a peculiar attraction of limitation, the attraction of a simultaneous beginning and end, the charm of novelty coupled to that of transitoriness. The attraction of both poles of the phenomena meet in fashion, and show also here that they belong together unconditionally, although, or rather because, they are contradictory in their very nature. Fashion always occupies the dividing-line between the past and the future, and consequently conveys a stronger feeling of the present, at least while it is at its height, than most other phenomena. What we call the present is usually nothing more than a combination of a fragment of the past with a fragment of the future.*[120]

■

In 1905 Simmel appends a definition that echoes both Baudelaire and Mallarmé: "The question of fashion is not 'to be or not to be,' but it always stands on the watershed between past and future."[121] Thus Simmel connects the literary tradition of French modernism with Bergsonian thought;[122] he ascribes to Bergson the idea that each moment differs from the previous one by sheer virtue of coming later. Simmel reads *la durée* as Bergson's idea that it was only through constant change that things can survive. In a strictly unchangeable persistence, the beginning and the end of Being could not be distinguished; they coincide and thus do not last.[123] A transitory fusion of past into present, and vice versa, is required to lend meaning to life and to make possible creativity within it.

The late French philosopher Gilles Deleuze wrote in his study *Bergsonism:* "We have great difficulty in understanding a survival of the past in itself because we believe that the past is no longer, that it has ceased to be. We have thus confused Being with being-present. Nevertheless the present *is not;* rather, it is pure becoming, always outside itself. It *is* not, but it acts."[124] Transitoriness creates a state, as Deleuze proposes in an exaggerated definition, in which the present "was" in each and every moment, while the past "is" eternally and at all times. This claim echoes Baudelaire's aesthetically charged perception of past and present, as well as the indebtedness we feel toward the past, as demonstrated in the Benjaminian tiger's leap. And indeed Bergson uses the term "leap" to describe the act of putting oneself back into the past. In immemorial or ontological memory the leap proper can be made: a leap into being, into being-in-itself, into the being-in-itself of the past. In such recollection, ontology will be exchanged for psychology and we pass from the virtual into an actual state—much as we hear language prior to analyzing it, placing ourselves at once in the sensual perception of the sound before perceiving it psychologically. However, as Deleuze observes as well, the notion of a "leap" (he has in mind Kierkegaard's "leap" in history and ethics that attacks Hegel's concept of the nodal line) seems alien to Bergson's concern with continuity.[125] Benjamin, for his part, would pronounce judgment on the arbitrariness and endlessness that Bergson's notion of such continuity seemed to imply: "The *durée* from which death has been eliminated has the negative infinitude of an ornament. Tradition is excluded from it."[126] What seems appropriate in Proust (and Benjamin makes this connection in a footnote), namely that the atrophy of experience enables one to behold an immensely private world and in the end to find deliverance in oneself alone, must be criticized if it appears in the guise of ontology. Set against the veritable experience of *modernité* in Baudelaire's poetry, this critique is best expressed by Benjamin in a sartorial metaphor: "It [*la durée*] is the quintessence of a passing moment [*Erlebnis*] that struts about in the borrowed dress of experience. The spleen [as in Baudelaire's collection], in contrast, shows the passing moment in all its nakedness."[127]

When Benjamin evaluates the *durée* within a historical context, he argues like a materialist. Yet his criticism does not touch on Bergson's metaphysical rendition of Baudelaire's "le transitoire, le fugitif" within modernity; he accordingly accepts and in fact draws on the concurrent conception of Simmel, who arrived, although in more tentatively, at this very point via fashion. I say "tentatively" because Simmel never developed his interpretation of fashion's presence in the direction of metaphysics proper. The observation on the transitoriness of fashion, made en passant in the first essay, assumes a metaphysical air in the 1904 and 1905 versions; but it is put aside once more in favor of a sociological analysis in the 1911 essay. Thus at a time when the idea of a transient reality became more and more significant for Simmel, the spread of fashion through life was accelerating: "That fashion becomes incredibly dominant in present culture . . . only shows the concentration of a current psychological trait. Our internal rhythm demands a constant shortening of the periods in which the change of impressions takes place; or, to put it differently: the accentuation of the stimuli shifts increasingly from its substantial center to its beginning and end."[128] The rapidly consumed cigarette was replacing the longer-lasting cigar, the travel mania that Mallarmé had observed in the craze for the express train divided the year in several short periods with sharp accent placed on departure and arrival—all this led to a breathless interpretation of modernity that Kracauer emphasizes in Simmel's philosophy: "we have become oversensitive, we adore change, perhaps because we long to escape the void in our souls; but these characteristics and inclinations favor the formation of fashion, which, in order to remain in power, is to no small degree dependent on our ready capacity for change, our craving for the new."[129] This passion for change explains why fashion endows human beings with a much stronger feeling of the present than does any other social phenomenon. The notion that fashion carries its inherent death—its transitoriness—far from devaluing it, simply makes it more attractive. "Fashionable" is used as term of judgment only by people who intend to criticize an object for factual reasons; that is, when it is applied as a standard of utilitarian or material value. Novelties and new appearances would not be classified as fashion, thinks Simmel, if we believe in their logical origin and continuity.

However, within modernism many a fashion came to stay. Once established as paradigmatic for modernity, it indeed becomes an aesthetic, as well as sociological, topic in itself, which could be referred to or quoted. Thus Loos defines the truly modern: "Fashion progresses slowly, more slowly than is generally assumed. Objects that are truly modern, remain so for a long time. However, if one overhears an article of clothing talked about as having ceased to be modern after just one season, in other words, it has become conspicuous, then one can also declare that it never had been genuinely modern, but falsely posed as such."[130] Loos's definition is essentially that of a purist, drawing on the modernist perception of "utilitarian" aesthetic norms. *Modernité* for him was marked by expedience and (an almost Kantian) purposiveness. As indicated by the nineteenth-century *habit noir*, worn by the progressive artist and the immaculate dandy alike, modernism would begin to establish its own brand of the "classical" to balance the ephemeral. From Loos to Bauhaus, modernist architecture with its angular lines and clearly defined shapes exemplifies a *rappel à l'ordre* that lays the foundation for a normatively sublime and eternal spirit, against which a new set of discriminations can subsequently be launched.

That fashion as such can never be generally *en vogue* allows the individual to reassure himself or herself that the act of adopting an outfit still represents something particular and personal. At the same time he or she feels comforted by the fact that a set of people are striving for but not, as in the case of other social satisfactions, actually *doing* the same thing. A follower of fashion is regarded "with mingled feelings of approval and envy; we envy him as an individual, but approve of him as a member of a set or group."[131] This attitude marks a particular, rather conciliatory, nuance of envy. The elements of fashion are not denied to any one absolutely; a change in fortune might favor an individual who had previously envied the fashionable person. Simmel adds that this social behavior, this nuance of envy, arises because an observed object acquires value detached from the reality of who actually possesses it. An article of clothing thus becomes comparable to an exhibited work of art: it provides pleasure no matter who owns it. After the Second World War the haute couture industry sustained itself on this basic principle. Dresses and gowns on the catwalk become almost common property through extensive media coverage and advertising. The woman in the street can participate in an aesthetic choice by obtaining either a downgraded prêt-à-porter model or a bottle of perfume—both pale reflections of the original sartorial invention.

Fashion furnishes an ideal field for individuals with dependent natures, who yet self-consciously seek attention and exposure. It can enable even an insignificant person to become a representative of his or her class, an embodiment of a joint spirit. Fashion alone—as it, by definition, never establishes a norm to be fulfilled by everybody—characteristically provides a possibility of obedience to social rules while at the same time permitting the individual to stand apart.

In 1905 Simmel elaborates further on the interplay between differentiation and imitation particular to *modern* fashion. His use of the term "modern" anticipates Loos's definition in denoting both the contemporary and fashionable: "If modernity is an imitation of it [the mere negation of a social example], then deliberate unmodernity is its imitation under reversed premises, which nevertheless testifies to the power of social tendencies that render us dependent in some positive or negative manner."[132] A reaction against fashion can spring either from the refusal to make common cause with the mass or from the delicate sensibility of the individual who fears a loss of individuality if he or she succumbs to the forms, tastes, and customs of the general public. Such opposition is regarded by Simmel not as a sign of personal strength but as escapism. An individual who became aware of his or her readiness to adopt fashion would ideally remain self-reflective and realize the arbitrariness of the whole process, thus becoming able to differentiate it from mere obedience. There is no escaping fashion; and its negation, so much favored by academics, is no less fashionable than any outright adherence to its principles. Having ironically resigned himself to this very fact, Kant concludes, a century before Simmel: "But it is always better, nevertheless, to be a fool in fashion than a fool out of fashion."[133]

## ■ 3.9 *Fin(esse) de siècle*

Although Simmel's postulates on fashion acquire in retrospect an almost canonical air, they were (necessarily) very much of their time. They owe a great deal to the aesthetic atmosphere in Berlin around the turn of the century. A February 1903 diary entry by a distinguished *homme des lettres,* Harry Graf Kessler,[134] bears witness to both the proximity and the distance between Simmel and the artistic culture of the time:

■

*Spent morning at [Max] Liebermann together with Simmel and Vandevelde [Henry van de Velde]; discussed foundation of club. Both Liebermann and Simmel told me in almost the same words that it has to be used to rally round the few cultured people living among the barbarians. Mainly against official art, against the Siegesallee [the central axis in Berlin]. Positively: l'Art pour l'Art, or something like that. As a model, Liebermann has the London Athenaeum in mind. Before Simmel and Vandevelde arrived, L. put last touches to his Poloplayers. While doing so he spoke fervently again: "Painting is all rhythm. Hence it's nonsense, if one says that a painting is badly drawn but well painted. A painting can never be badly drawn and well painted. It's all one thing, as painting is rhythm, nothing but rhythm. If this line here is different, then this color has to differ, too." To Simmel he raged in a rather trite and vulgar manner against Wagner. He denied him everything; "even art." Klinger as well. He conceded him only a standing as an artist. "Y'know, there are artists an' bellboys. Well, Klinger isn't a bellboy." Simmel took on the task of finding a suitably formulation for the "l'art pour l'art" position in the membership application.—Today, as before, Liebermann returned to the idea that a frame had to close off the picture; a work of art should not encroach on the frame. It should, as Simmel put it, remain an island within life.[135] It appears to me that here is a fundamental discord in the perception of art. For L. and Simmel the renunciation to form life oneself. Essentially, art as a flight from life. Romanticism. But one could argue about this, i.e. whether the other [i.e., realism] actually could be put into practice.[136]*

■

Although Georg Simmel might have favored the cultivated atmosphere of the salon over debates in the studio, his connection with Kessler and van de Velde and his being entrusted with drawing up the programmatic statement for the artists' foundation show Simmel's standing within the leading artistic circles of his time. That standing suggests in turn that his philosophy of fashion has to be seen in relation to the aestheticism of Kessler (and the magazine *Pan*) as well as to the modernist endeavors of van de Velde—especially the reform dresses that he designed together with his wife from 1894 onward. Obviously, these considerations do not render Simmel part of a thriving avant-garde; but viewed in context of contemporary culture in Berlin at the turn of the century, the aptness of Simmel's perception of modernity becomes clear.

As was true of Count Kessler, the written word was Simmel's chosen form of artistic expression; thus both were greatly influenced in their formative phase by ideals of symbolism and fin de siècle literature. Simmel's friendship with Stefan George, Rainer Maria Rilke, and, of course, Auguste Rodin prepared this common aesthetic ground. Simmel's artistic preference, together with a corresponding Mallarméan *douceur* and a strong liking for the stylish interior, is evoked in the recollection of his son Hans. Toward the end of 1941 he described his father's collection of Japanese prints (of the late 1890s, and thus slightly later than the *Japonisme* of Whistler, Montesquiou, etc.) and his subsequent fascination with related artifacts from Japan: "He gradually acquired a drawer full of Japanese fabrics, a few figures in bronze and porcelain, a few pieces of netsuke [small, intricately carved ivory toggles], some dozen woodcuts, and at least half-a-hundred 'pots': earthenware from Japan and porcelain from China."[137] The purist beauty of the Japanese fabrics and pottery had been an important influence in late-nineteenth-century modernism; obviously Simmel, whose aesthetic experience incorporated distance and restraint as well as sensuality, found a perfect complementarity in Japanese ceramics. Hans remembers: "Sometimes, once or twice a year, we celebrated an 'orgy of color.' Father brought home a large bunch of roses, sometimes other brightly colored flowers. We then spread out some of the fabrics and placed a number of flower-filled 'pots' on top. Such a feast, in which apart from us three, only one or two of our closest friends were allowed to take part at times, lasted no more than two hours—then all was removed again."[138]

Such a feast was certainly not part of the Berlin bourgeois lifestyle, not even for the most aesthetically inclined character. This story again emphasizes the degree of Simmel's refinement, in both manners and taste, which bordered on stylization. It is thus tempting to read autobiographical content into a key passage from his *Philosophy of Fashion:*

■

*It is this very significance of fashion that is accepted by sophisticated and particular people who are using it as a kind of mask. They consider blind obedience to general norms in all things external as a very deliberate and desired means of preserving their personal feelings and their taste, which they are eager to keep only to themselves so that it is not displayed in appearances that are accessible to all. . . . Thus the soul triumphs over the given conditions of existence, which, at least in regard to its form, belongs to the highest and finest of triumphs: namely, that the enemy itself is transformed into a serf and that the very thing that appeared to violate the personality is voluntarily seized, because this leveling violation is transferred here to the externals of life in such a way that it provides a veil and protection for everything that is spiritual and now all the more liberated.*[139]

■

Like Baudelaire, who saw it embodied in the figures of the dandy and flâneur, Simmel found individual poetic freedom veiled by an extrovert adherence to the apparent futility of fashion. Yet not only did adherence to social norms conceal and protect the sensibility of the subject, it also shaped his perception of the environment. In discussing Baudelaire's *modernité,* Benjamin would take from Simmel the very notion of fashioning one's exterior to explain how the flâneur individualizes his aesthetic experience amid the urban crowds by using a textile concealment: "The mass was an agitated veil; through it Baudelaire saw Paris."[140]

Fashion allows the individual a particular distance that is considered proper by society. However extravagant a mode of expression or appearance might be, if it is fashion(able), the individual can feel protected against the embarrassment he or she ordinarily experiences being at the center of social attention. In equating fashion with "concerted action," Simmel maintains that both phenomena are characterized by an omission of shame. As a member of the crowd an individual will agree to things that would have aroused fear or loathing had they been suggested to be undertaken alone. One of the strangest sociopsychological traits in society exemplified by concerted action is the way in which fashion tolerates a breach of modesty that, if seen in only one individual, would be angrily repudiated.

The manner in which fashion abstracts and levels the personality within the mass would directly influence Kracauer's essay "Ornament in the Crowd," where Simmel's erstwhile pupil characterizes the massing of people as an aesthetic component within capitalist production and as fundamental to a modern urban culture organized along rationalist lines.[141] The hands in the factory chain gang, for instance, find their cultural analogy in the bare legs of American dance troupes like the Tiller Girls. Modern men and women could only perceive themselves as particles of the mass. Thus the diversions of popular culture, of which mass-produced fashion is itself an integral part, invariably had to consist of mass ornaments themselves.[142]

Simmel again employs an "objective," though veiled, irony to account for the crowd's eager acceptance of changing appearances and apparel: "Fashion also is only one of the forms by the aid of which men seek to save their inner freedom all the more completely by sacrificing externals to enslavement by the general public. Freedom and dependence also belong to those antagonistic pairs, whose ever renewed strife and endless mobility give to life much more piquancy and permit a much greater breadth and development, than a permanent, unchangeable balance of the two could give."[143] The same quantum of dependence and liberty can at one time help raise moral, intellectual, or aesthetic values to the highest level, while at another time, through a mere change in its distribution, it can bring about the exact opposite. One is left to conclude that the value of life would increase if all unavoidable dependence is transferred as much as possible to the externals of life, thus leaving room for internal progress and development. But fashion is not just a changing masquerade; it influences social and cultural thought, which is determined to an ever-growing degree by people's reaction to the external forces in modern life. In fashion, the antagonism between unifying imitation and individual demarcation is reflected in and transferred to its *form,* much as personal relations between individuals reflect elements that have nothing to do with

**41.**
Walter Ballhause, *Clothes Make the Man,* 1932. Photo from the series *A Day in the Life of the Unemployed Engine Fitter Karl Döhler.* Archive print, 24 × 33 cm. Rolf Ballhause, Plauen.

*A photographic example of new sobriety; the unemployed gazes at the unobtainable clothes in the shop window—a flâneur against his will.*

social obligations. Simmel observes that fashion is the objectified example of "the parallelism with which the relations between individuals are repeated in the correlation between the psychic elements of the individual itself."[144]

Consciously or not, the individual often establishes a mode of conduct or style for him- or herself that, through its rhythm of rise, sway, and decline becomes denoted as fashion. This is essentially personal fashion, a borderline case within the generality of social fashion. On the one hand it arises from the desire for individual distinction and thus is born out of the same impulse that forms social fashion. But in personal fashion the need for imitation, similarity, and blending in with the crowd is satisfied purely by the individual alone, through the concentration of individual consciousness on one form, content, or style of fashion, as well as through imitation of the self that takes the place of the more common imitation of others. "Indeed, we might say that we attain in this case an even more pronounced concentration, an even more intimate support of the individual contents of life by a central uniformity than we do where the fashion is common property," argues Simmel.[145] Is this to be understood as the veiled plea for dandyesque sophistication in Baudelaire's and Mallarmé's vein, which transfers ideals of the interior to the individual traits of exterior apparel?

## ■ 3.10 Fashion's Phantom

"We have seen that in fashion the different dimensions of life, so to speak, acquire a peculiar convergence, that fashion is a complex structure in which all leading antithetical tendencies of our soul are represented in one way or another."[146] This observation not only justifies Simmel's attempt for an in-depth philosophical analysis but also shows that on a sociological level, the total rhythm in which individuals or groups move has to significantly influence their relation to fashion. The various strata of society relate each in its own way to fashion simply because the kind of existence that each stratum regards as the most favorable evolves in a conservative or in a progressively changing form. Fashion operates on one level among the lower classes, which are less ready to move and which evolve much more slowly. And yet fashion operates in much the same way among the uppermost echelon of society, which is conservative, even archaic, because it fears any movement or change as such—not because change as such might be harmful to it, but simply because any modification of the status quo that maintains the upper class's rank must invariably appear suspect and dangerous. To put it sartorially: both cotton or calico workwear—for example, a coverall or an apron—reflect, in the same degree as the habit of dressing for dinner in black tie or evening gown, the least flexible attitude to fashion.

Simmel implies, as Weber does more strongly a few years later, that the class that accounted for the variability of life throughout history was the bourgeoisie. The pace of social and cultural development decisively changed, once the *tiers état* rose to significance after the French Revolution. From that point on, fashion, representing the variable and contrasting forms of life, appeared much broader and more agitated—seeming to coincide with rapid sociopolitical transformations. Irony fuels the interpretation that material dominance is craved by the crowd, if not politically then perhaps sartorially: "Man requires an ephemeral tyrant the moment he has rid himself of the absolute and permanent one. The frequent change of fashion represents a tremendous subjugation of the individual and in that respect forms one of the essential complements of the increased social and political freedom."[147] Revolutions, as Baudelaire and Barbey d'Aurevilly observed, became stylistic affairs rather than political revolts as the Second Empire progressed. Those classes and individuals striving for constant change find that their rapid development gives them a social advantage over others. They find in fashion a life-form that keeps pace with the movements in urban modernity. "In this context," wrote Simmel in his final essay on fashion, "one is required to point out simply the concurrence of a multitude of historical and sociopsychological instances in which the city, in contrast to more narrow milieus, becomes a fertile soil for fashion: the unfaithful rapidity in the change of impressions and relationships, the simultaneous leveling and concentration on individual elements, the massing of people in an urban environment, and, as a result, the vital reserve and distance."[148]

Within the urban capitalist process of production, there are commodities that cannot be "imitated," simply because their price does not allow their purchase by any but the highest stratum. When the commodity becomes available in a different medium, for example, a painting reproduced as a chromolithograph or photographic print, it naturally loses exclusivity. Other items, like the motorcar, for instance, remained in the Europe of Simmel's time a strictly limited luxury. Even when in the mid-1920s Francis Picabia and Le Corbusier praised the eternal beauty of the Hispano Suiza, and elevated the sports car to the Parthenon, it was the coveted exclusivity of the product and not its mass-produced industrial aesthetics that first drew their admiration.

In sartorial fashion, the facilitation of imports, the sophisticated mechanization of weaving techniques, and the industrialized process of pattern cutting and of manufacturing garments greatly accelerated the adoption and diffusion of trends from haute couture into outfits for the middle and lower classes. Yet distinguishing between the tailor-made and ready-to-wear continued to be of vital importance: although the clothes might appear the same at a cursory glance, the slightest scrutiny would easily deflate the pretension of the off-the-peg garment; only the substantial, the made to measure, would stand the test of time and retain its social prestige.

However, timeliness did become more important than time. The notion that an article of clothing has to convey eternal beauty lost its cachet. For Baudelaire fashion had to incorporate both the ephemeral *and* the sublime. Simmel thought that fashion, especially in regard to its own momentum in modernity, appears ephemeral only at first; once it acquires permanent value as a cultural variant, it loses its definition of *modisch* and becomes modern. The speed with which fashion changes has important bearing on its content. Above all, that speed reduces the costs and extravagances of fashion, as exemplified by the turn from the exaggerated bustles and *faux culs* of the 1870s and 1890s to a modernist concentration on line (notwithstanding that as a "defensive" reaction, the refinement and sumptuousness of the fabrics used in these simple cuts increased manifold). The more a commodity becomes subject to the rapid changes of fashion, the greater grows the demand for cheap products of its kind—apart from the most expensive end of the market, which continues to represent *inventio* on an extravagant scale. "Not only," writes Simmel, "because the larger and thus poorer mass of people still possess enough purchasing power to determine industrial production and insist on objects that at least bear the outward and inexact illusion of modernity. But also because even the upper echelons of society could not afford to adopt the rapid changes in fashion, forced on them through its pursuit by the lower classes, if the articles were not relatively cheap."[149]

In modernity a curious circle begins to spin: the more quickly fashion changes, the cheaper the articles have to become; and the cheaper they become, the more they entice consumers and force producers to speed up the change of these fashionable and short-lived articles. The predictable limit to what novelty (whether genuine or not) the designer and manufacturer could create within these rapid modes of production led the paragons of fashion increasingly to adopt details or entire styles from different sets of culture (e.g., Poiret's "Confucius" coat of 1905, or his "Sultana"-style dresses half a decade later) or from a different, that is, lower, class. This dynamic turns Simmel's theory of imitation literally on its head—as had already been apparent in the fashionable millinery of late eighteenth century France:

■

*It was about this time that the bonnets* à la révolte *made their appearance. At the beginning of May, 1775, the high price of flour had caused trouble, and bakers' shops were pillaged in Paris on the 3rd. The misfortunes of the people were made a pretext for a new fashion. There were also various hats ornamented with ribbons—like, for instance, the bonnet* à la laitière—*or with flowers. Bonnets, fetching some 50* livres, *were decorated with wreaths of roses and acacias, and so on. The bonnet* négligé à la reine *and the bonnet* à la paysanne *had great success.*[150]

■

The people soon forgot this example of a stylistic revolution when the real political revolt took place, and it caustically epitomizes the fate that has to befall all fashion: Marie-Antoinette's ignorance about the people's situation contributed to the malaise that would prompt the revolting public to sever from her body that part which formerly had been so gracefully adorned by the *bonnet à la révolte.* So too fashion's inevitable ignorance of the reality behind the positivist and continuous historical progress must account for its death: "The very fact that fashion calls attention to itself so forcefully, that it represents an instantaneous concentration of social consciousness onto a certain point, contains the seed of its death, its destiny to be replaced."[151] This particular characteristic of fashion was for Simmel, in contrast to Sombart, the reason why it remained essentially in contradiction to the development of modern economics.[152] The rapidity of development is important indeed for the actual articles of fashion because it denies them certain economic advantages. In well-established branches of modern Western industries, the speculative element gradually ceased to play an influential role. Movements in the market could be better monitored, requirements could be better foreseen, and production therefore could be regulated more accurately than before. This regulation led to an increased rationalization of the product, as the oscillation of supply and demand decreased. But "the oscillations between poles, which modern economics in many instances already know how to avoid, and are able to deduce entirely new economic structures and theories, these oscillations still hold sway in areas directly subject to fashion."[153] In *The Psychology of Money* Simmel concludes, as we have seen, that fashion thus follows its own evolutionary path, establishing a contrast to the reified and objectified world.

Yet he also ascribes to fashion the second Baudelairean dictum on *la mode et la modernité,* that is, the eternal value of fashion—not necessarily as an element of aesthetics but rather as part of a psychological process. In its dual relation with the combined characteristics of the ephemeral and the evanescent, fashion maintains this "peculiar quality, that every individual type to a certain extent makes its appearance as though it intends to live forever."[154] If one acquires an item that was meant to last only for a certain period of time, one would choose it according to the latest fashion and not that of one or two years ago. But it is obvious that the item's attractiveness will fade in time, just as the earlier item had lost its appeal. It will have to submit itself to criteria other than those establishing a contemporary style. "A dialectical-psychological process appears to takes place here," says Simmel; "there is indeed always a fashion, thus fashion as a generic term is immortal. This process is reflected in each of fashion's manifestations, although the very nature of each manifestation demands it *not* be immortal."[155] The fact that the change itself does not change endows each of the objects it affects with a psychological appearance of duration.

Baudelaire aimed to disengage the eternal from the transitory in both fashion and modernity, in order to bring it as close as possible to the work of art. Simmel regards fashion as determined by transitoriness and change. Any return to old forms and styles is dictated by economic constraints. Fashion is revived once distinction from and opposition to the latest vogue emerges again, if an earlier fashion has been partially forgotten. The Benjaminian connection between the revival of fashion and the "tiger's leap into the past" in order to burst open the continuum of history was not, or could not, be realized by Simmel, even though he underscored the tradition of perceiving fashion as dualist and concurrent to the dichotomous character on which the *Tigersprung* is partly based.

None of the expressions by which the human mind attempts to master the "material of existence" and adapt it to its purposes can be so general or neutral that its contents, indifferent to their own structure, would uniformly yield to it. Thus fashion could in the abstract absorb any chosen contents; any form of clothing, or art, for that matter, can become fashionable. And yet some forms appear to be disposed to become fashionable, while others resist it. Although obviously the sartorial is the ultimate playing field for fashion, some clothes or accessories yield more quickly to fashion's changes; others—the male tie, for example—remain comparatively stable, though as subspecies they may fall frequently in and out of fashion. Once an article of clothing acquires a moral value and becomes socially normative (as in the case of the tie), changes tend to occur much less frequently.

Following Baudelaire and Mallarmé, Simmel employed the term "classical" to determine aesthetic norms "comparatively far removed from fashion and alien to it."[156] Yet the classical as aesthetic principle can itself become a perpetual motif within the course of fashion, as seen in Paul Poiret's modernist adaption (1907) of the Directoire line of the 1800s, which in turn was based on antique styles of dress. Just as the external antagonism of life is transferred to the inner relations between individuals, so too the dualism represented by the "classical," or sublime, and the ephemeral in fashion becomes manifest in each sartorial item itself. At one time a particular aesthetic principle prevails in a garment, at another its opposite; yet more often, owing to modernity's transitory character, both poles coexist or are quoted in one design. The classical provides fashion with an "external fate," with something invariable and of eternal value. Yet when extreme forms inherent in its surface, which for Simmel was exemplified in the baroque,[157] fashion becomes merely a "historical expression of its material peculiarities": that is, the objectification of its transitory character. Baroque forms especially are visual examples of the "subjectification to an instantaneous impulse which fashion realizes as a form of social existence."[158] Confronted with unusual or bizarre shapes, a beholder's appreciation of an object soon fades and he or she longs, first from a purely physiological standpoint, for the change that fashion provides. Describing the baroque court of Louis XIV—where, according to the king's sister-in-law, the Palatinate Princess Liselotte,[159] men behaved and dressed like women and vice versa—Simmel emphasizes as "self-evident that such behaviour can be countenanced by fashion only because it is far removed from that never-absent substance of human relations to which the form of life must eventually return in some way, shape, or manner."[160] Fashion's capacity to abstract and to stylize turns here—significantly, in the context of effacing sexual roles—into an unnatural extreme.

The ambiguity in Simmel's analyses, partly caused by his leaning toward the literary analogy, renders one and the same phenomenon metaphysically substantial and intricate; but that ambiguity, if seen with the eyes of Simmel the sociologist, also turns it into a social malaise, an essentially negative expression. This methodological ambiguity (like its structuralist equivalent, the "Mallarméan dialectic" paraphrased by Barthes),[161] is covered by Simmel's "objective irony," which also reflects the fundamental principle that

▪

*Fashion is both too serious and too frivolous at the same time, and it is in this intentionally complementary interplay of excess that one finds a solution to a fundamental contradiction which constantly threatens to destroy its fragile prestige: in point of fact, Fashion cannot be literally serious, for that would be to oppose common sense (of which it is respectful on principle), which easily deems Fashion's activity idle; conversely, Fashion cannot be ironic and put its own being in question; a garment must remain, in its own language, both essential (it gives Fashion life) and accessory (common sense considers it thus).*[162]

▪

Simmel faces the same inconsistency. Because of fashion's inherent dialectics, he sees himself confronted by the need to render it part of a philosophical system, especially in regard to the very ambiguity it embodied. But he also displays, or feels compelled to display, a frequent reluctance intellectually to take fashion's formative character seriously, a tendency that results at times in contradiction or in outright negation of the epistemological potential of the topic.

Nevertheless, fashion's ambiguity matches Simmel's own methodological and stylistic approach, which moved, sometimes uneasily, between structural formalism and almost poetic evocation. This tendency surfaces again in the closing passage that appears uniformly in all four essays:

■

*The peculiarly piquant and suggestive attraction of fashion lies in the contrast between its extensive, all embracing distribution and its rapid and complete transitoriness [the right to be unfaithful to it];[163] and with the latter of these characteristics the apparent claim to permanent acceptance stands in contrast. Furthermore, fashion depends no less upon the narrow distinctions it draws for a given circle, the intimate connection of which it expresses in the terms of both cause and effect, than it does upon the decisiveness with which it separates the given circle from others. And, finally, fashion is based on adoption by a social set, which demands mutual imitation from its members and thereby releases the individual of all responsibility—ethical and aesthetic—as well as of the possibility of producing within these limits individual accentuation and original shading of the elements of fashion. Thus fashion is shown to be an objective characteristic grouping upon equal terms by social expediency of the antagonistic tendencies of life.[164]*

■

Concerned with the general character of change, yet deliberately excluding everything from the discussion but the sartorial fashion one dresses in, Simmel draws a bridge from economic and sociopolitical interpretations to a pre-phenomenological philosophy influenced by *la durée* and literary analogies. The complexity and diversity of these studies perhaps do not add up to a complete analysis, but Simmel must have expected that much from the very beginning. Of all the expressions in modernity, fashion's significance and charm were what could be rationalized least and what therefore—ironically—became the most typical. "It's what Max Weber called the 'routinization of charisma': how can the unique irruption which brings discontinuity into a universe be turned into a durable institution? How can the continuous be made out of the discontinuous?" asks Bourdieu in 1974.[165] But here he is referring neither to a methodological question nor to the formulation of a philosophical problem. What concerns the sociologist is the sustained, yet unsuccessful, effort to find a worthy successor to the institutional couture house of Chanel, after the death of Coco early in 1971—and thus the continuation of fashion's history, which is marked through its essential incoherence in rationale as well as appearance.

4

**Benjamin and the Revolution of** Fashion in Modernity

*Die Mode ist die ewige Wiederkehr des Neuen.*

*—Gibt es trotzdem gerade in der Mode Motive der Rettung?*


*Walter Benjamin, "Zentralpark" (1939/1940)*[1]


The various interpretations of fashion follow an immanent logic. First, Baudelaire, Gautier, and others established *la mode* at the birth of *la modernité.* Mallarmé brought this concept to its most fugitive and sophisticated conclusion: *La Dernière Mode,* the la(te)st fashion—a sartorial *Gesamtkunstwerk* conceived in the age of commodities. These original conceptualizations of fashion in modernity, both pictorial and literal, had to generate an analytical interest in its tendencies. Simmel was the first, some two decades after Mallarmé's magazine was published, to inquire into the possible rationale behind sartorial intricacies. In this chapter we will see how Walter Benjamin went one step beyond Simmel. Once fashion's rationale had been explained, its political potential had to be explored. In the tiger's leap, Benjamin applied that rationale, taking it in the obvious direction.

# ■ 4.1 The Object

The hallmark of modernity is the ever-growing objectification of society. Marx interpreted particular aspects of this tendency as *Entfremdung* (alienation), Simmel characterized it more neutrally as *Verdinglichung* (reification), and Weber as *Rationalizierung* (rationalization).

In order to explain the new sociocultural parameters in society, these theoreticians thus perceived the *object* as representative of the grander social structure, the cultural fragment as representative of the totality of the historical process. A Hegelian heritage leads scholars, especially German ones, to focus on the subject-object relation, now seen not as "man-nature" but as "man (subjective perception)–object (inorganic commodity)." One object in particular, because of its spatial and metaphysical proximity to the subject itself, came to express the intricate and varied aspects of modernity—that is, sartorial fashion, adorning and enveloping the human body and comprising a faceted multitude of garments and accessories.

Most significant for fashion is its ephemeral, transient, and futile character, which changes with every season. This insubstantiality with regard to linear historical progress, as well as fashion's marginal position in the cultural spectrum, appealed especially to those who considered the fragment particularly expressive for modern culture, representing *in nuce* (as well as *in novità*) the shape of modernity. Not least because of Simmel's influential view of the fragment, a number of men who had listened to his lectures as students continued to explore the inherent metaphysical value in the marginal and popular expressions of culture.

Walter Benjamin (1892–1940) closely followed Simmel in defining fashion as the ultimate metaphor for the varied views on modern life concentrating on its fragmentation and diversity. Based on his reading of Baudelaire and Proust, whose works he translated and analyzed, Benjamin looked back on the nineteenth century both as the birthplace and the childhood of modernity and as a "prehistory" that would influence contemporary historicism and a materialist/messianic interpretation of society.

**42.**
Unknown photographer, Walter Benjamin
(with Gert Wissing and Maria Speyer) in
Saint-Paul de Vence, May 1931.
Photographic print, 12 × 8 cm. Theodor W.
Adorno Archiv, Frankfurt a.M.

*"I glanced upon the creases in my white beach
trousers . . ."—Walter Benjamin recording his
sensations after smoking hashish in Marseilles,
September 1928.*

**43.**
Unknown photographer, Passage de
l'Opéra, late nineteenth century. Private
collection, Paris.

From 1927 up to his premature death in 1940, Benjamin assembled material for a study of the nineteenth century that was to decipher modernity's political, poetical, and philosophical potential from the visual and literary fragments he found in the streets and libraries of Paris, a city he proclaimed as the "capitale du XIXe siècle."[2] The assemblage of this material he provisionally titled *Passagenarbeit* (*Arcades Project*) after what he considered to be the architectural cradle of modern society. For him, the glass-roofed links between Parisian streets and boulevards maintained, in their often-dilapidated condition, the mystique of nineteenth-century life and the remembrance of the first age of consumerism.

In the tradition of Baudelaire, Mallarmé, Proust, and Simmel, Benjamin focused on sartorial fashion as the single metaphor capable of evoking the time he was trying to recapture for his work. The simple number of references to the word *Mode,* as well as the multiple connections and far-reaching conclusions drawn from them, renders fashion the central issue, somewhat obfuscated by epistemological excerpts, for his incomplete *chef d'œuvre*. Within the project, a great number of topoi are raised and elaborated on. Yet fashion is rarely mentioned, let alone interpreted.[3] One of the aims of this chapter is to assess fashion's significance for the *Arcades Project*. Benjamin's view of the relation *mode et modernité* is described in the context of studies of the subject both literary (Baudelaire and Proust) and theoretical (Marx and Simmel)—studies he quoted directly for his project or that coincide with his own approach to the sartorial.

## ■ 4.2 The Idea of Fashion

Reading through the French and German sources up to 1928 in order to trace out a philosophical tradition concerned with the sartorial, Benjamin remained frustrated by his search. In a letter to the poet Hugo von Hofmannsthal he bemoaned "the sparse material that thus far constitutes all efforts to describe and fathom fashion philosophically."[4]

Implicitly, Benjamin's task would be to come up with a more penetrating and inspirational study of the subject. Yet within an academic or "intellectual" context, the question always arises whether fashion is, in its "frivolity," not just one marginal element in the much larger fabric of life. Isn't it a phenomenon that merely manifests instead of occupying a cultural (let alone metaphysical) sphere and thus meriting philosophical speculation? Does Benjamin merely show the interest of someone who takes pleasure in reading between the lines (or folds) of a text, but not of a theorist who aims at a final assessment of culture or modernity as such?

The presumptions behind such questions, partly founded on a biased view of fashion's inherent insubstantiality and transitoriness, which accordingly appears to mark Benjamin's interest in fashion as nothing but indulgence, were refuted by an altogether unexpected source. In his last work, titled *Aesthetic Theory*, Theodor Adorno, much more inclined to follow the prosaic and substantial in his philosophical discourse, acknowledged his debt to Benjamin in battling for a perception of fashion as fundamental to aesthetics and politics alike.

■

*The usual tirades against fashion that equate the fugitive with the futile are not only allied with the ideology of inwardness and interiority, which has long since been exposed politically and aesthetically as an inability to externalize something and as a narrow-minded concern with the thusness of the individual. Despite its commercial manipulation fashion reaches deep into the works of art, not simply exploiting them. Inventions like Picasso's painting with light appear as transpositions of experiments in haute couture where the cloth for dresses is merely draped around the body and pinned together with needles for one night, instead of tailoring it in the usual sense. Fashion is one of the ways in which historical change affects the sensory apparatus and through it works of art—in minimal traits, often hidden from themselves.*[5]

■

Here, Adorno moved directly from the sartorial surface to sensual perception and historical progress. He thus followed both Simmel and Benjamin toward the same goal, fashion's metaphysics. Benjamin had postulated some forty years earlier that it was integral to modernity that contemporary fashion (i.e., a fashion aware of its heritage and tradition) came to play the counterpoint to apolitical and restricted forms of sensualism—precisely because it appeared to have originated from such an apolitical stance. Significantly, Adorno deduced a material insubstantiality from the fact that any haute couture creation is unique and remains singular (even if the same dress is at times measured for up to three clients) until the next collection. The pride that both those in ancillary industries (weavers, embroiderers, etc.) and the seamstresses take in producing, often right up to the *défilé,* perfect examples of their craftsmanship is negated because of the facile appearance of the design. The dialectical structure that lies in the perfect creation of sartorial fashion, namely that it was designed to last forever by those aware that it will "die" within six months (cf. Simmel), remained unrecognized by Adorno, since he does not consider the topic capable of carrying such profound meaning.

More apparent for Adorno is the Benjaminian notion that *die Mode* possesses the power to fashion a new look for history. It does so on a large scale, by reshaping the silhouette of historical structures, by altering the way one perceives the succession of past epochs and the relation of the present to them—thus time itself. On a smaller scale it also focuses on the sociohistorical accessories, on the nuances within the appearance of the past, that reveal and determine more than mere historicism ever would.

After having considered a possible structure for his project, Benjamin in 1928 felt confident about coming to terms with the amount of literature and research that would provide him with the foundation for his work on Paris in the nineteenth century. However, up to that point he had focused merely on topical interpretations and did not foresee the multitude of possible approaches. "I continue to think about the things you said to me concerning the *Paris Arcades* project when you were here," wrote Benjamin to Hofmannsthal, a poet and dramatist whom he greatly respected, not least because of his role in Berlin's cultural life (in conjunction with Count Kessler, Simmel, etc.). "What you said drew on your own plans and was supportive and lent precision to my thinking, while making what I should most emphasize ever clearer to me. I am currently looking into the sparse material that thus far constitutes all efforts to describe and fathom fashion philosophically: into the question of what this natural and totally irrational, temporal measure of the historical process is all about."[6]

The "irrational" aspect was later given a more complete analysis in Benjamin's "Central Park" fragments and in the equally fragmentary "Theses on the Philosophy of History" (both ca. 1938–1940), written in close conjunction with his study on Baudelaire, whose essay on the painter of modern life first sparked Benjamin's awareness of the paradigmatic value of fashion within modernity. Yet did he continue to regard fashion and its relation to historiography as the main topic of the *Arcades Project* after his first studies on the Parisian arcades were undertaken (1927–1929)?

The answer can be found in a conversation that would take place in 1939: Georges Bataille, part of the troika that led the Collège de Sociologie, had earlier that year approached Benjamin to give a talk on the ambitious project that was known to be consuming most of his time and energy. In autumn he finally caught up with the German immigrant and inquired what the topic of the promised lecture would be. Benjamin's reply was terse: "Fashion." The German philosopher Hans Mayer, who witnessed the exchange, maintains that this was a "coded" answer:[7] in fact, what Benjamin intended to talk about was the *Arcades Project* as a whole. His reply had been just one of the "understatements and mystifications he favoured so much."[8] Indeed, the choice of subject must have been hard to appreciate. To those aware of existing on the brink of a catastrophe and having an at least partial knowledge of the atrocities being committed in Mayer and Benjamin's native country,[9] as well as knowledge of their own precarious existence in the French capital, the idea of anyone presenting (to a largely politicized and progressive audience) a paper on a topic as "marginal" as fashion must have seemed impudent. For Benjamin, however, that was the subject foremost in his thoughts. It had guided him first through a labyrinth of visual and textual sources and subsequently directed him toward a materialist concept of history. By 1939, fashion had already changed from being just one element of nineteenth-century cultural history to the essence of the *Arcades Project*.

## ■ **4.3** Mode and Metaphor

**4.3.1** Skirting the Memory

From the outset Benjamin was concerned with what his project could evoke in the reader's mind. One highly symbolic passage is retained throughout the years that lay between his earliest notes of 1927/1928, containing observations and quotes for his first exposition on the "Pariser Passagen," and the later manuscript sheafs, assembled in his Parisian exile, which constitute the base from which the project would have grown: "What the child (and in much weaker recollection the man) discovers in the folds of an old fabric, into which he pressed himself while holding on to the mother's skirt—this has to be part of these pages." [10] We see here some of the connotations that fashion is able to carry, and that Benjamin's writing explores: the tactile and olfactory qualities of the fabric as well as the warmth and the intimate scent of the skirt, evoking not only the wearer but also her surroundings, as the much-worn textile takes on the odor of the room she moves in. These qualities universalize the metaphor, as the sensation has a collective, archetypal air about it—something every person has experienced at some point in his or her childhood. In designating the sex of the child in the phrase added in parentheses, Benjamin's adds a psychological dimension to the metaphor. Pressing one's face deep into the folds (and not just on the plain surface of the fabric) of a textile that clothes the female lower body has strong fetishistic connotations. Thus this act would determine to some degree the boy's sexual rite of passage. [11]

But above all, the passage is about remembrance—about "the remembrance of things past" to be precise, since Benjamin's project on the Parisian passages had also followed on his preoccupation with Proust's evocation of *le temps perdu,* the observation of nineteenth-century Paris that would also, despite their different premises, become Benjamin's subject matter. "When the Romans described a text as a fabric," as we have read already in Benjamin (see section 2.4.2 above), "then none is finer and more densely woven than Marcel Proust's." And he adds:

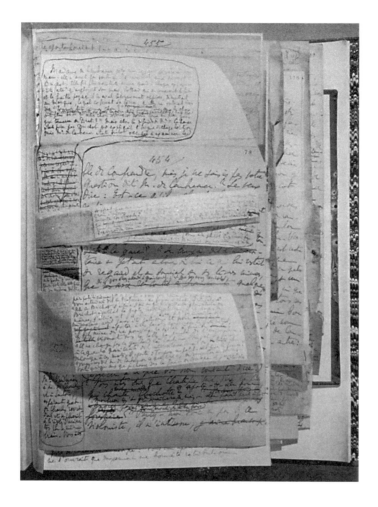

**44.**

Photo of a manuscript page from the *cahier* of Marcel Proust's *Sodome et Gomorrhe*.
Bibliothèque Nationale, Paris.

*"In the craft of weaving, Plato distinguishes the warp, the masculine element, and the weft, the feminine element. In the weaver's frame, the feminine and the masculine cross each other as the vertical and the horizontal."—Jean-Pierre Venant.*

■

*There is yet another sense in which remembrance issues a strict weaver's notation [diagram to plot weaving patterns]. Only the actus purus of remembering itself, not the character of the author, let alone the narrative, constitutes the unity of the text. Indeed, one could say that this intermittence is merely the reverse side of remembrance's continuum, the back pattern of a tapestry. This is what Proust meant, and this is how he must be understood, when he said that he would prefer to see his entire work printed in one volume in two columns, without any paragraphs at all.*[12]

■

Text becomes textile; the collected works of remembrance are ideally woven like a tapestry or fabric, similar both in epistemological structure and in textual appearance. Benjamin described the appearance this fabric was meant to lend to life: "*À la recherche du temps perdu* is the continuous attempt to charge an entire existence with the utmost presence of mind. Proust's method consists of realization [*Vergegenwärtigung*], not reflection." This *Vergegenwärtigung,* which in German stands for both realization and the act of bringing something into the present, was read as the dialectical image, a tiger's leap into historical awareness: "This dialectical penetration and realization [*Vergegenwärtigung*] of past correlations puts the truth in present action to the test. This means: it causes the explosive that is contained in the past (and whose symbol proper is *fashion*) to ignite. To approach the past in such a way means not to deal with it, as previously, in a historical but rather in a political manner, within political categories."[13]

The sartorial brings in its train the political, and an intricate pattern begins to take shape. Benjamin's analysis of nineteenth-century Paris and its arcades has to constitute an act of remembrance. For this notion, this textum, Proust's *Recherche* offers a complex notion for the weaver. Moreover, it represents in itself the aspiration to render text into a fabric, designing the pattern for a narrative silhouette defined by openly visible seams: *temps perdu* becomes *temps retrouvé.* However, the fabric forms an infinite number of pleats and folds in which the child's memory is embedded, and the meanings of the work remain hidden.[14] Benjamin used this model as more than a mere reference. He also developed from it, as becomes clear in the close relation between metaphors, a structure for a new approach to the philosophy of history. He finds in Proust's textum the constant realization of the past within the present, leading him to the concept of the "dialectical image" in which the explosive within history is ignited and subsequently blasts the very foundations of historicism.[15] As this explosive is fashion, it becomes apparent that fashion is the indispensable catalyst for both remembrance and a new political—that is, materialist—concept of history. Yet this model is not simply a structural abstract, it is also deeply and sensually woven into Proust's literary style, as Benjamin observed in his essay "The Image of Proust." Throughout his work on the *Passagenarbeit* Benjamin would move between the analytical and materialist approach to fashion taking it as an indicator of social relations, and the poetic one that regards fashion as a simulacrum for the human figure and his or her emotions.

Like his work on Baudelaire,[16] Benjamin's study on Proust developed initially from efforts to render the author into German. Parts of the *Recherche* had been translated by Benjamin, working closely with the Berlin author Franz Hessel, between November 1925 and December 1926.[17] The project began with *Sodome et Gomorrhe,* which Benjamin translated on his own (the manuscript has apparently been lost); then followed *À l'ombre des jeunes filles en fleurs* and *Le Côté de Guermantes,* which were published in 1927 and 1930, respectively. During that period Benjamin made frequent allusions to an essay he envisaged bearing the title "En traduisant Marcel Proust" ("To Translate Marcel Proust").[18] Early "arabesques" for this project were "spun" by Benjamin in February 1929,[19] at a time when he reached also the first conclusions for his project on the Parisian arcades. One of the notes for the Proust essay, which was published some four months later, read: "The hallmark of his creation which is hidden in the folds of his text (textum = fabric) is remembrance. To put it differently: before Proust no one had been able to prize open the secret drawer of 'atmosphere' and make what had been inside truly his own (so far only a scent had been pouring out from it)."[20] Benjamin's metaphor of the fold, which at first appeared to generate and determine the child's memory, and later that of the grown man, thus is revealed to have originated in his engagement with Proust's literary method. In "Neoclassicism in France," an essay published earlier that year, Benjamin altered and amended this metaphor to establish the connection between the Proustian use of fabric and gowns to evoke memories and the metaphysical value of the actual object—that is, the significance that fashion and elegance carry for the perception of past and present time. Musing about the gods in Jean Cocteau's version of *Orphée,* which had been staged in Berlin during the winter of 1928/1929, Benjamin concludes: "Perhaps these gods are very good at understanding the threshold between times. In Proust they thus trouble a scent with a whiff of their presence or break from a fold (and it is always the most recent vial, the cut of the latest fashion; it is always the most elegant, most ephemeral medium of these archaic workings)."[21]

Why the fascination with the metaphor of the fold? On the one hand it is obvious that Benjamin ascribed great stylistic value to metaphor—both for literary and, following Simmel's method, philosophical reasons. In a letter to Hofmannsthal he wrote: "I am currently paying close attention to Proust's use of metaphor. In an interesting controversy with Thibaudet about Flaubert's style, Proust declares metaphor to be the essence of style itself. I admire the way in which he updates the perhaps generalized tradition of the great poets to extract a metaphor from the nearest and most banal element, adapts it to today's situation, and as it were mobilizes a whole complex of worn-out circumstances in order to employ them for a more fundamental expression."[22] Within this context, and in a vein perhaps instrumental for understanding his *Arcades Project,* Benjamin continues to lament the "difficulty of finding a place for the publication for my ephemeral, although perhaps not at all superficial, considerations."[23] Here he sides clearly with the French author's sentiment. Benjamin employed the metaphor of the fold, especially in conjunction with Proust's writing, because it appears mundane and banal—and, more important, because the fold determines the object that is closest to the human body and can be metaphorically transposed into writing.

### 4.3.2 Back in the Fold

The skirt, or any other piece of clothing, for that matter, in which the child buries his face is inseparably tied to its wearer, even when it seems to have been discarded (see the surrealist use of clothing as simulacra for the human body in chapter 5). As Théophile Gautier observed in *De la mode:* "The garment of the modern age has become for man of a sort of skin, which he is not prepared to forsake under any pretext and which clings to him like an animal's hide, nowadays to the point that the real shape of the body has been quite forgotten."[24] The drapes, pleats, and folds move with man, but they are not an actual part of his body. They are capable of forming their own microcosm of meanings, psychological as well as sociological. The intriguing task for the writer is to take this microcosm and develop out of it, or transpose it into, the macrocosm of human material existence. From this relation between micro- and macrocosm stems the potency of the sartorial metaphor. It is perfectly tailored to express in itself the position individuals assume toward their contemporaries as well as to history; but the metaphor is far from being direct, as it still carries with it the notion of replacement or estrangement. Although clothing is *worn,* it *does not belong to* the wearer. In representative fashion like formal attire, it even remains essentially alien to its possessor. In determining the wearer's every move, granting self-confidence or hindering his or her physical or social progress, fashion inflicts its own system of legality. Such power is especially evident in the dress code of the nineteenth century, since it had been to the utmost degree subject to social rules and customs. Suits and dresses were meant essentially to denote membership to a certain social caste and were not intended to make the wearer feel protected, warm, or comfortable. With the growth of a prosperous bourgeois class it became more difficult to establish class distinctions, as money could now buy access to what had formerly been exclusive in the code. Thus fashion changed its degree of formal rigidity and estrangement for those men and women who were already well versed (by birthright and upbringing) in its expressions and could play the rules of garb to their own taste. To be truly fashionable meant to possess a barely detectable (at least to the outsider) yet nevertheless expressive sign of sartorial individuality, within the confines of a vesture determined by the socially de rigueur.

Through representation and displacement, fashion comes to symbolize a human being. Thus the nineteenth-century poet, or the writer looking retrospectively at that period, sees fashion as the ultimate metaphor. When modernity led to a changing of the social and economic parameters, it also changed the cultural outlook. Artists who were progressive and contemporary enough to accept this challenge started look-ing for a way to engage with these changes that would at the same time reflect ratio-nality—thus mirroring the positivism that was dominant in the nineteenth century due to the widespread belief in scientific and technological progress. Fashion, occupying the position of the eternally new, the constant pacesetter within rapidly progressing modernity, seemed from a positivist viewpoint a perfect agent. What fascinated the truly modern artist was fashion's mystique, its understanding of historical, even archaic expression, and—what Benjamin came to emphasize—its sense of the mythic, which offered a counterpoint to the threat of modern reification and rationalization, as well as providing a vehicle for aesthetic experience. The notion of the mythic became in turn the "other" in the ambiguity of modern existence, as observed by Bataille, Lacan, and others who regarded the subject as no longer in conflict with the object but in am-biguous rivalry with itself.[25]

More mundanely speaking, fashion is also an integral part of daily life—more so than any other form of applied art, let alone the "sublime" expressions of the fine arts. The great majority of us, at least of those who are not required wear a specific uni-form, deeply contemplate dressing almost every morning of our life, whereas thoughts that concern art or artifacts come to us much less frequently.

What had been considered as artistically marginal, sociologically banal, and metaphysically ephemeral became—not within a season, but within the formative pe-riod of modernity—valuable and virtuous for the painters of modern life, that is, for those who attempted to artistically probe the myths of modern society. The spirit of el-egance and contemporariness in fashion provided its original appeal for many artists, yet those who were able to see through the upper layer of clothing, beyond the outer pleats, realized, as Benjamin observed in Proust, that "it is always the most elegant, most ephemeral" that serves to indicate the archaic rules and perceptions that influ-ence society and culture alike.

Much as happened in the debate between *modernité* and *antiquité,* the dia-metric opposition of up-to-date elegance and archaic spirit would prove to be fashion's greatest challenge to both philosophical and historical thought. Encompassing every-thing that was at the height of its time, yet in the same moment leading us back into antiquity, fashion became for Walter Benjamin the one dialectical image, the "tiger's leap in the open air of history"; and ultimately, as he would observed in Marx, it also became a symbol of modernity's potential for not merely stylistic but fundamental change.[26]

It was not for this reason alone that Benjamin intended to analyze and discuss fashion at length in his unfinished work on nineteenth-century Paris. The sheer volume of notes and excerpts he assembled concerning the topic speaks for itself. First there is the manuscript sheaf composed of almost a hundred notes and quotations on *Mode*. Next to it, the references to clothes or fashion in general—but like Simmel, Benjamin is almost exclusively concerned with sartorial fashion—are more than just numerous. They can be singled out among the notes he used for his first exposition, as the very foundations of the project; they thus become both the chalk marks for the outline and the seams on the fabric from which Benjamin would design his project.[27]

## ■ 4.4 Construction; Work

The fragmented state of Benjamin's manuscripts, excerpts, and notes raises a number of questions. To begin with, how are we to designate the writing itself? Its German editor, who deciphered and sorted the manuscripts Benjamin had left behind, chose to name it *Passagen-Werk*. But a complete *Werk* (in the sense of opus) it is obviously not, so why the title? Benjamin himself had referred to it as being in a transient state, as a "project on the Parisian arcades" or, in short, the *Passagenprojekt* or *Passagenarbeit*. In ascribing to the manuscripts a finality by lending them the status of an complete work, the editor appears to derobe the project of its transitoriness—a quality within the structure itself that reflects the most important part of the contents, namely Benjamin's aim to analyze the ephemeral, the ambiguous within the history of Paris as the capital of the nineteenth century. The editor justifies his action by equating the fragments of the project with "the building materials for a house, of which the ground plan has just been sketched out, or excavations are just about to be completed. . . . Next to it one finds an accumulation of excerpts from which the walls would have been erected. Benjamin's own reflections would have served as the mortar, holding the building together."[28] Since Benjamin's undertaking bears the architectural construct of the arcade as its title, the comparison to house building seems appropriate. But it misrepresents the author's intentions. The *Arcades Project* (the English title maintains the incompleteness of the work) was not meant to be a "house." No excavation would have been dug to make the theoretical foundation (cast-) concrete and immovable, no walls would have been erected to keep out possible amendments or alterations, and the excerpts would not have served as a rough mixture to stick material (thoughts) together.

I do not intend a simple criticism of the way in which the enormous task of assembling the fragments was accomplished, nor do I mean to question the editor's authority. But his choices demonstrate the repeated tendency to favor the concrete, constructed, and thus by implication substantial over the ambiguous, transient, and ephemeral. A "fault" similar to the one censured in Adorno's criticism of Simmel is encountered again in discussing Benjamin's analysis of fashion; it appears as if the *Passagenarbeit* had to be "reconstructed" in order to make any interpretations and analyses worthwhile. Another commentator asked, "since the work was perhaps inherently destined to become its own ruin, is one not entitled to consider the ruin as the work?"[29] Here we have a building again, yet one that never was intended to be anything but crumbling and dilapidated, as the ambitious claim that Benjamin made in his "Theses on the Philosophy of History" and subsequently in the *Arcades Project*—namely, to fuse theology and historical materialism into a messianic historiography—could never have been fulfilled![30]

Within the historical continuum, a scientific or artistic product is appreciated only if considered stable and complete. Anything in a transient state has the suspect label of insubstantiality attached to it. Yet the changed modes of perception championed by modernity deliberately challenged this perception. The *Recherche* is of course "complete" insofar as the author was able to conclude the narrative (in *Le Temps retrouvé*); yet one can imagine how different the various proofs would have looked if Proust had lived to subject them to the same technique of constant addition that he had employed on all his manuscripts before 1922, when part 2 of *Sodome et*

*Gomorrhe* appeared. Proust's remembrance was never to be completed, since every detail spurred a whole string of subsequent memories. The narrator's final reflection on his remembrance of things past meant that the whole process had to become almost infinite and self-perpetuating. Proust's position within the French narrative tradition makes it impossible to call the *Recherche* (unlike that other modernist mainstay *Finnegans Wake*) a "work in progress." Yet the idea that some writing, even when published, derives part of its meaning and appeal, from remaining essentially incomplete and transient would become a feature of modernity.

After a Proustian fashion, although owing partly to different reasons, Benjamin's *Arcades Project* was meant to appear like a fabric—a fabric constantly in the making, woven from notes, materials, excerpts, and theoretical patterns, from which subsequent pieces on Baudelaire, fashion, revolution, history, and so forth were tailored. It was meant to remain a progressing assemblage of texts, and its fragmentary and ambiguous character, its discontinuity, was an inherent part of its potential. These *Passagen* are no "buildings"; this architectural metaphor merely establishes the surface. These *Passagen* are "passages" in the original French sense of *passer,* both "sujet nom d'être animé ou d'objet en mouvement" and "partie, fragment d'un texte."[31] Their significance appears complex and transient, shifting as the reader becomes a flâneur who saunters through them. Their transitoriness, the way in which an archaic, mythic quality becomes fused into the modern, is important for Benjamin's perception of the past, of *antiquité:* "*Rites de passage.* . . . These periods of transition have become increasingly hard to recognize and are experienced less and less. We have become lacking in threshold experience. Perhaps the only one that is left to us is the sensation of going to sleep. (But with it also the sensation of waking.)"[32] The rites of passage in modernity are not elaborated rituals in the anthropological sense, aimed, for example, at initiating an adolescent into the society of adults. They occur in a much more subtle, less recognizable way. One of the most significant *rites de passage vestimentaire* in the nineteenth century took place on the first special occasion on which a boy was allowed to discard his short pants or knee breeches in favor of the long trousers worn by grown men. This change of attire was the primary outer expression for the actual rite of passage in society, the boy's leaving home to go to a boarding school or *école*.

The emphasis Benjamin put on the sensation of going to sleep and subsequently awakening, as the only "threshold of experience" left to modern men and women, again refers to Proust's act of remembrance: "In the same way in which Proust begins his life story with waking, each representation of history has to start with waking; in fact, it should not be concerned with anything else. So this one [the *Arcades Project*] is about waking from the nineteenth century."[33] The historian has to be able not only to read a dream psychoanalytically but also to understand its literary transposition. In dreams as in fashion, the truth lies in the folds, not merely in appearance. He notes, "the exploitation of dream elements in waking is the canon for dialectics. It is exemplary for the thinker and imperative for the historian."[34] Dialectical historiography evolves from the transition between dream and waking, and the history, in this instance that of the nineteenth century, is one of collective memory (perhaps part of the collective unconscious) into which we sink while sleeping, only to travel forward through time to wake up and find ourselves confronted with the remembrance of these dream fragments. This is indeed what the young Marcel experiences at the very beginning of *La Recherche*. Waking in the middle of the night, still half asleep, he feels at first like a prehistoric man, equipped only with archaic sensations. Yet memories quickly "would come like a rope let down from heaven to draw me up out of the abyss of not-being, from which I could never have escaped myself: in a flash I would traverse centuries of civilization, and out of a blurred glimpse of oil-lamps, then of shirts with turned-down collars, would gradually piece together the original components of my ego."[35] The vague image of turned-down collars is an ambiguous memory. It could refer back to a period before the nineteenth century (throughout which high collars had been de rigueur or to the time when the protagonist had been a little child, too young to wear anything but soft shirts with *cols rabattus*. Yet the memory helps Marcel find himself and, as he remembers an ephemeral element from the past, helps establish his own presence within the course of history.[36]

Barthes would some decades later also evoke the symbolic dimension of clothes within a mythical dream and connect it with the transitory that we find ex-

**45.**
Unknown photographer, the young Marcel Proust with *col rabattu,* ca. 1880.
Bibliothèque Nationale, Paris.

*"Concerning [Proust's] mémoire involontaire: its images do not come uncalled; rather they are images that we had never seen, before we remembered them."—Walter Benjamin.*

pressed both in Benjamin's project and in fashion itself: "On the one hand, we could say that in its profane way the garment reflects the old mystical dream of the 'seamless' ['*sans couture*']: since the garment envelops the body, is not the miracle precisely that the body can enter it without leaving behind any trace of this passage?"[37] Clothing has an essence that is unrelated to the body it adorns. Clothes and accessories take on a symbolic value that requires abstract perception, omitting the human element. The sartorial is seen thus as object influencing the physical subject and not vice versa. Yet a conflicting tendency rose throughout the nineteenth century: words that had been essentially metaphorical and flexible in their possible connotations became to some extent victims of the rationalizing tendencies in materialist society. Despite the "heroic" efforts of the decadent poets and symbolists, they began to appear almost one-dimensional, reconstructed, and immobile. For example, the evocative symbolic meaning of the *passage* was lost with the iron construction of the new arcades; and the "threshold," which had acted previously as the demarcation line of a metaphysical crossing into mythic territories, became exclusively used to describe the boundary of a private bourgeois *intérieur*.[38]

Siding with surrealist perception, Benjamin attempts to overcome this limitation by evoking a past multitude of meanings and by returning to the metaphysics of the *passage*. After having established a dialectical image for the more than century-old arcade by incorporating its past rational appearance, its archaic symbolism, and its mythic qualities (present and in retrospect), Benjamin uses arcades as a setting for numerous phenomena in his "prehistory of the nineteenth century," as Adorno fittingly characterized it. Fashion, because of its marginal and ephemeral character, could more easily escape the existing rigidity of attribution. Its varied, ever-changing appearance made it best suited to become the most frequent and most complex of metaphors in the *Passagenarbeit*. Its having been left theoretically unexplored—except by Simmel—further accounts for its significance.

With the emergence of a modern bourgeois society, the importance of history as a philosophical foundation for the present declined, while modernity created a history for itself. Substituting for knowledge handed down through earlier generations was a less examined hope and a positivist expectation in the future. This was partly

**46.**

Jindrich Stýrský, untitled, 1934. Collage on paper, 29 × 46 cm. Published in *Minotaure,* no. 10 (winter 1937).

*The male figure is taken from a fashion illustration by the American Joseph Christian Leyendecker, who introduced the famous Arrow shirt-collar man in the 1910s; the female figure and the background originate from a nineteenth-century painting by the German salon artist Hans Krause.*

due, as Tarde and subsequently Simmel argued, to the ever-growing dominance of "l'époque extériorisée" over "la vie intérieure," and to the modernist belief that technology could create an utopian construct. On a metaphysical level, the change was rooted in the dominance of anticipation over experience.

Apart from an "iconoclastic" attitude toward a past that came to be perceived almost as ballast, this teleological understanding of history had to neglect the revolutionary potential that lay within things to come. "Where progress coagulates into historical norm, the quality of novelty and the emphasis upon unpredictable beginnings are eliminated from the present's relationship with the future," observes Habermas in discussing Benjamin's work.[39] Past experiences are merely additions to the mass of facts with which historicism—that is, a continuous, apparently logical progression of historical facts—fills "the homogeneous and empty time."[40]

While the future is robbed of its ability to exert force, the past becomes without relevance to present time. Also, and even more drastically, the present itself becomes a mere transitional period without any significant value of its own. Early in 1937, in an essay on Eduard Fuchs, a Viennese cultural historian, Benjamin wrote down a number of reflections that would later become part of his fragmented "Theses." His solution to the shortcomings in historicism was to create a new concept of historiography, "whose object is not a ball of mere facticities, but [which] creates it [historiography] out of the counted group of threads which represent the weft of the past fed into the fabric [*Textur*] of the present. (It would be a mistake to equate this weft with a mere causal nexus. Rather, it is a thoroughly dialectical mode. For centuries threads can become lost and are picked up by the actual course of history in a disjointed and inconspicuous manner.)"[41] Here again Benjamin returned to the equation text = textum (a root of which *Textur* is but an inflection). He describes weft yarn from the past inconspicuously woven into present fabric (much as Mallarmé does in section 2.4.2), a construct that again underlines the paradigmatic value that Benjamin attached to fashion in the *Arcades Project*.

To some extent, Benjamin equates the "dialectical" reasoning mentioned in this context with his reading of historical materialism. In the later stages of the *Arcades Project* a number of references to "fetish character" and "accumulation of value" emerged. They focus on Marx's famous evocation of twenty yards of fabric and the one garment that is made from it.[42] In "Walter Benjamin's Historicism," H. D. Kittsteiner describes the "true myth of modernity" as "the myth of complete heteronomy, one in which no gods, heroes, or men appear—only things. It has been told by Karl Marx: it is the story of the birth of money from the mutual reflection of twenty yards of linen and one coat."[43]

At first Marx's example seems arbitrary; one would think that any number of commodities could assume the character of a fetish. Yet in light of Freud's adoption of the term from its anthropological source, it becomes obvious that the aptness of the psychoanalytical coinage of "fetish" arises from its reference, via Marx's earlier use, to a particular aspect of substitution: the sartorial one. The organic product of linen is not only represented by the "equivalent form" of the coat, it is also a raw material that, through the labor process, would become an artificial, inorganic commodity for which it originally constituted a "relative form of value."[44] The sartorial product itself is extremely close to its wearer—a second skin—but as a commodity, not to mention an artificial status symbol, essentially estranged from him or her. It maintains a distinct meaning and value of its own. Therefore it has an additional potential to become a fetish.

As the original point of reference for Marx's dialectics, as well as for his notion of subject and object,[45] Hegel had anticipated the "objective" position of clothing in his *Aesthetics:* fashion has to follow its very own principle, "for the body is one thing, the clothing another, and the latter must come into its own independently and appear in its freedom."[46] Fashion's independence is expressed positively as freedom: a freedom exemplified in creative designs to clothe the human body as well as a freedom to exist without it, as an object that is altered depending on the subject who slips on the clothes. Yet this independence alienates the object, as a commodity, as a fetish, from the body it is originally meant to warm, protect, or cover in modesty. And although not a product of modern times as such, the estrangement of the sartorial commodity from its wearer first became significant in nineteenth-century capitalism with its broadened consumer base.

## ■ **4.5** A Fetish in Fashion

Benjamin begins by including an analytical assessment of the fetish character in the world of commodities found in a 1928 analysis of Marx.[47] In the fashion manuscripts of the *Arcades Project,* he then progresses to a much more revealing evocation that floats between psychoanalysis and a surrealist dreamworld.

■

*In fetishism, the* sexus *puts down barriers separating the organic and the inorganic world. Clothing and jewelry are its allies. It is as much at home with what is dead as it is with living flesh. And the latter directs the accommodation of the* sexus *in the former. The hair is a confined region between both realms of the* sexus. *Another realm reveals itself in the raptures of passion: the landscapes of the body. These have ceased already to be animated, yet are still accessible to the eye, which, of course, as it ventures further, relinquishes its lead through this realm of death more and more to the sensations of touch and smell. Within a dream breasts often begin to swell, dressed like the earth in woods and rocks, and glances have sunk their lives far below the water surfaces that slumber in the valleys. These landscapes are crossed by paths that escort the* sexus *to the world of the inorganic. Fashion itself is only another medium that lures it even deeper into the material world* [Stoffwelt].[48]

■

Unfettered by materialism, the character of the fetish is taken here from its historical, political confines and brought into a dream state, where death and *sexus* meet. This "chance encounter" (partly in a surrealist spirit)[49] is initiated by fashion—we will see how for Benjamin eros and thanatos coexist within it—and the waking from this dream is defined by the last two sentences, where fashion's allure guides *sexus* into the *Stoffwelt:* a world made of fabrics, as well as materially fabricated.

Although the fetish is an integral part of Marx's socioeconomic analysis, it did not relate originally to dialectics. Nor does it relate, as Benjamin recognized in his postulates, to a new concept of history. However, modernity makes it possible for the sartorial fetish to adopt even this most complex of roles. To explain the connection, one

**47.**
Édouard Manet, letter to Mme Jules Guillemet, July/August 1880. Watercolor on paper, 20 × 12.3 cm. Musée du Louvre, Paris.

has to go back to Benjamin's "initiation" into modernity: his translation of the *Tableaux parisiens* by Charles Baudelaire.

In "À une passante" the woman in her black robe passing the flâneur in the street epitomizes modernity, directing the poet's attention to the ephemeral nuance. In gathering and swinging the hem of her dress, specified by Baudelaire's scrutiny as being embroidered as if with festoons, she reveals her leg and thus provokes the erotic and subsequently sublimated thoughts of the beholder. The character of the fetish alludes in the poem both to the commodity, that is, the fashionable detail on the garment, and to the eroticism of the leg, which in itself can be seen only in its sartorial representation: adorned by stocking and shoe—in turn the most common objects of fetishism, as Freud would come to observe.[50]

After 1848 the length of the skirt fell and the *volants* became more numerous. Thus at the time of Baudelaire's poetic observation, the leg could no longer be seen beneath what his contemporary Gautier called the "mass of rich fabrics." The male gaze was forced to console itself with the shoe as a substitution for the original erotic focus on the female upper thigh and pelvis. Freud writes that fetishism originates in the boy's desire to peer at the woman's genitalia from below, that is, from the foot or shoe upward.[51] But it originates equally in the visually impenetrable crinoline fashion of the early 1860s and its subsequent transformation into the long bustled skirts of the 1880s. These forms of womenswear had provided the men, who came into Freud's practice at the turn of the century and after, with their childhood fascination for the shoe as the only visible lead to the female lower body. This remembrance then develops as a neurosis into adult fetishistic tendencies. Thus one can view the symptoms of fetishism, which were prefigured in the psyche, as having been initiated through the sartorial or its visual representation (e.g., in Guys's drawings).

## ■ 4.6 The Confluence of *mode et modernité*

The second paradigmatic value with which Benjamin credited fashion is explained by the sisterhood of *mode* and *modernité*. The sublime ideal within modernity—that is, the true nature of beauty, as Baudelaire defined it through the eyes of the painter of modern life—is found in clothing. It marks the starting point for his modern aesthetics because it possesses a distinct ambiguity, a dual attraction. Drawing on Guys's quest "de dégager de la mode ce qu'elle peut contenir de poétique dans l'historique, de tirer l'éternel du transitoire,"[52] Hans Robert Jauß stresses that fashion

■

*contains a twofold attraction. It embodies the poetical in the historical, the eternal within transitoriness. Beauty steps forth in fashion, not as a well-worn, timeless ideal but as the idea that man forms for himself of beauty, an idea that reveals the mores and aesthetics of his time and that allows man to get closer to what he aspires to be. Fashion demonstrates what Baudelaire calls the "double nature of beauty," which he conceptually equates with modernity: "La modernité, c'est le transitoire, le fugitif, le contingent, la moitié de l'art, dont l'autre moitié est l'éternel et l'immuable."[53]*

■

Modernity defines beauty's double nature as incorporating both aspects of *la vie moderne,* that of historical presence and that of political actuality. And both are linked inseparably in Baudelaire's famous postulate on fashion, and of course in his own sensuality as well.

Benjamin took up the poet's notion some sixty years later and put particular emphasis on the historiopolitical side by ascribing to it an immanent—perhaps revolutionary, perhaps messianic—potential for historical change. For this potential to be realized, he had to find in modernity the time nexus [*Zeitkern*] in which the transitory element of aesthetics coincides with the standstill of the historical present. What Baudelaire established as the ideal of beauty, Benjamin thus transfers to a novel concept of history: "The historical materialist cannot deny himself the concept of a present which is not understood as a transition, but in which time stands still and has come to a stop. For this notion defines *the* present in which he himself is writing history. While historicism presents an 'eternal' image of the past, the historical materialist describes a unique experience in it," he wrote in his reflections of 1940.[54] Between the ideas developed three years before in the essay on Fuchs and the late epistemological fragment above lies a note that defines the time nexus and ties it in with the *Tableaux* poem that

Benjamin had translated and analyzed some fifteen years earlier. In one of the manuscripts of sheaf N (on epistemology and his theory of progress), he notes: "An emphatic refusal of the concept of 'timeless truth' is in order. Yet truth is not simply, as Marxism claims, a temporal form of cognition, but is bound to a time nexus [*Zeitkern*] which is contained in both the known and the knower [*Erkannten und Erkennenden*]. This holds so much truth, as the eternal is rather a ruche on a dress than an idea."[55]

In the encounter on the Parisian boulevard, the flâneur becomes captivated by the image of the woman "balançant le feston et l'ourlet." The transitory movement passing in front of him transfixes the poet. The woman's leg becomes statue-like, not merely in its sublime and "classical" beauty but because time is perceived as standing still, and he finds himself unable to move, "crispé comme un extravagant." The festoon or, for Benjamin, the ruche on the dress becomes eternal; her fashion is immortalized in a momentary time nexus, although it will change so very quickly and its wearer's "beauté fugitive" has already passed from his view. Here one finds the poetic in the historical, since the writer recounts the situation to a reader, and the eternal within the transitory. Constellations like the above were defined by Benjamin, in an aestheticization of Marx's theorem, as "dialectical images." The image of the eternal ruche was singled out and repeated in the fashion manuscript of the *Passagenarbeit*, which directly preceded the surreal description of the fetish.[56]

On the surface it appears as if sexual attraction prompted the poet-flâneur to pause and glance at the woman, and initially of course this is the case. But the desire was a specific one, that of the fetishist: the man whose eroticism is objectified, distanced from any interpersonal relationship. Analyzing Baudelaire's persona in the poem, Benjamin writes: "The 'jamais' is the climax of the encounter, when the poet's passion seems to be frustrated at first but in reality only now bursts out of him like a flame. . . . What makes body twitch spasmodically is not the excitement of a man in whom images has taken possession of every fibre of his being; it partakes more of the shock [*Chock*] with which the imperious desire suddenly overcomes a lonely man."[57] The *Chock*, a Benjaminian term in its idiosyncratic spelling, is the sudden realization or materialization of the metaphysical element in the world. It generates the time nexus

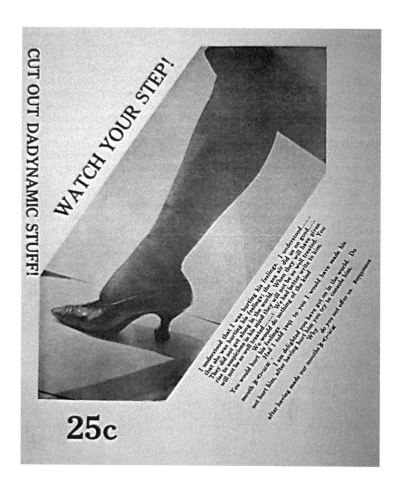

**48.**

Marcel Duchamp and Man Ray, page from *New York Dada,* 1921. Photomontage and typography, 36.8 × 25.6 cm. Richard L. Feigen & Co., New York.

*The image is taken from Alfred Stieglitz's photo* Dorothy True *(1919). "WATCH YOUR STEP!" "CUT OUT DYNAMIC STUFF!" That's how the truly modernist (and ironic)* passante *would appear to the* flâneur *in the twentieth century.*

in which man, whether flâneur, poet, historian, or philosopher, finds the eternal within a transient passage.

■

*Where the thought stops short in a configuration that is saturated with tensions, it gives the latter a* Chock, *by which it crystallizes into a monad. The historical material-ist approaches the historical object only where he encounters it as a monad. Within such a structure he recognizes the sign of a messianic cessation of the event, or, to put it differently, a revolutionary chance in the fight for the oppressed past. He takes cognizance of it in order to blast a specific epoch from the homogeneous course of history; thus he blasts a specific life from the epoch, thus a specific work from the lifework.*[58]

■

As we have seen, Benjamin states in the fashion manuscripts that the "explosive agent" for the historical materialist is to be fashion. Its preference for quotation from the past allows for a clear separation from the continuum of history. The constant ci-tation of clothing styles from the past within the present style liberates Benjamin from the prevalent concept of the *Wirkungsgeschichte*—the history of effects. In this struc-ture, the anticipation of the future by the present directs its understanding of the past. Anticipation wins out over reflected experience (see Tarde in section 3.3.2 above). Friedrich Nietzsche called this concept a "critical view of history," Marx had employed it in historical materialism, and Heidegger ontologized it in *Sein und Zeit*.[59] Benjamin himself looks for "crystallization" and a *Chock* that would enable him to focus on each monad in the past century. Concurrently drawing on historical materialist thought, he aims at isolating the action which he ambiguously saw as both a messianic standstill that grants deliverance and a revolutionary act that could spark a violent conflict. The materialist experience in history can be subsumed under recurrent motifs that illustrate (for example) class conflicts or the relation between base and superstructure. But Ben-jamin frowns on adhering too closely to such orthodox notions. His concern is rather with the aesthetic experience, a singular idea of beauty or of life within an epoch. Fol-lowing again the lead of the Baudelairean flâneur, he prefers the aesthetic reality of an epoch, as embodied in the newest cut, in the latest fashion, to flash momentarily before the eyes of the historian or philosopher.

Acquiring past experience in a way that is solely oriented toward the future renders the present an indistinct place for both the continuation of tradition and unqualified positivism alike; they combine in an objectivity that is essentially *wirkungsgeschichtlich*. Although there are different ways of reading this history of effects—stressing either the continuity within it or its discontinuous character—it is essentially influenced by the anticipation of the future and always regards the past as a "prehistory" of the present.[60] Only when the historian overcomes the tendency "to have the series of occurrences pass through his fingers like the beads of a rosary" is he able to understand the singular constellation that makes up an earlier epoch and, more important, his own. "He thus establishes a conception of the present as 'now-time' which is shot through with splinters of a messianic time."[61] Or, to quote Simmel's earlier metaphor, he recognizes the parts where weft yarn is shot into past's fabric. The hallmark of fashion, to constantly cite from the past in order to propagate the latest "revolution" in style, helps Benjamin reverse the relation between anticipation and experience and dispel the false sense of hope contained in exclusively positivist materialism. And the unashamedly open fetishistic character of the sartorial commodity, in both its materialist and psychoanalytic connotation, encourages a cynical view of society, as it recycles the old in order to generate new commerce. Being supremely realistic about its own limited life span, fashion continually proclaims the rift—through immanent death and rebirth—in the historical continuum, which can only be bridged by a great (tiger's) leap.

Benjamin ascribes to all former epochs a multitude of expectations that had been left unfulfilled: "The past carries with it a secret index, by which it is referred to redemption."[62] The present that eagerly awaits the future is left now with the task of remembering the past and accomplishing what had been expected. For Benjamin there exists no *querelle* between the ancient and the modern but a fusion of the archaic and modernity in the object, positively realized in fashion's potential and negatively expressed in the "hell of commodities" that was part of nineteenth-century Paris. Thus in his dialectical image, above all in the tiger's leap, one conflicting element folds into

**49.**

Erwin Blumenfeld, *The Princess of Pearls* (advertising photo for "Les Bijoux Cartier"), 1939. Photographic print, 28 × 12 cm. Collection Marina Schinz, New York.

*Blumenfeld photographed part of a nineteenth-century fashionable portrait, enlarged its negative print, and combined it with a real string of pearls and hand. Rephotographed—and subsequently published in* Harper's Bazaar *in September 1939—it became a perfect example of fashion's ironic quotation from its own past.*

another. In these images the archaic coalesces with modern aesthetic expression; it contains both the threat of a repetition of past errors and a generic force that counterbalances the destructive potential of modernity. The latter is the "redemption" Benjamin describes, which gives the remnants of commodities from a past century a mythic quality. When fashion makes its own use of these remnants by quoting past attire for new clothing styles, it visualizes and materializes the demand that was raised by Benjamin's dialectical image on a metaphysical level.

In a letter to Benjamin, dating from 1935, Adorno questioned this dialectical image, expressing doubts about both the redemptive and the mythic character of the commodity to which it was to apply: "To understand the commodity as a dialectical image simply means to understand it also as the motif of its own demise and its 'abolition' ['*Aufhebung*'], instead of regarding it as pure regression to the old. On the one hand, the commodity is the alienated object and thus its utility value has withered away; on the other hand it is a surviving object that, having become alien, outlives its immediacy."[63] In discussing the perception of the dated dress either as a quote or as merely of "historic" interest, one has to look at its role in each use as a commodity. The bustled dress from the 1880s, for example, is the commodity whose utility value has died, since no one could wear such a dress expecting anything but to be seen as in disguise or costume. On the other hand, if someone puts on a bustled dress that is a sartorial quote (e.g., a design by Christian Lacroix from the late 1980s), she sports a commodity that, according to Adorno, has "outlived its immediacy" because it has been alienated from its origin and activated for the present. Obviously, a truly fashionable design can never hope to be anything *but* in the present; it will not be capable of overcoming the present, because the design then would cease to exist as fashion and would become an object with another function, perhaps that of the eternal artwork. What the fashion commodity can achieve, however, is to escape its demise by ironically advancing its death and perpetually renewing itself. When the design has been accepted into the sartorial mainstream, the actual innovation dies and the process of inventing and promoting a new style or look begins anew. The "rewriting" of (costume) history thus continues in frequent installments, and by constantly prompting its own "abolition" fashion ideally avoids any regressive tendency. Therefore, the one commodity that is tailor-made as a dialectical image must be clothing, and Benjamin accordingly captures it in the tiger's leap. Adorno concurs with Benjamin in seeing the pressure of future problems demanding a present ready to act with a responsibility toward the past and at the same time aware of the implications its actions carry for the future. In extending this awareness retrospectively to the past, Benjamin created an intricate patterns of a future open to alternatives, a "mobilized" past (visualized by sartorial fashion), and, in their midst, a transient present.

## ■ 4.7 Eternal Recurrence and Redemption

The antithetical tendency of fashion in capitalist modernity, namely eternally recurring motives being sold as novelties, even aesthetic revolutions, is also acknowledged by Benjamin. Yet judging by the space allotted to its discussion in the *Arcades Project,* this sartorial notion was to take second place to fashion's potential as dialectical image.

In linking his study of Baudelaire to the prison writings of the revolutionary Auguste Blanqui, especially to his meditation titled *L'Éternité par les astres* (*Eternity through the Stars*), Benjamin equates the "spleen" with Blanqui's notion that the latest is always old and the old always new[64]—a concept transferred to the sartorial by Simmel. Blanqui wrote: "The number of our doubles is infinite in time and space. . . . These doubles exist in flesh and bone, can be seen in trousers and overcoat, in crinoline and with chignon. These are no phantoms; this is an eternalized reality. . . . The universe repeats itself and impatiently runs in place. Unperturbed, eternity gives the same performances ad infinitum."[65] The invariable repetition imposes a rhythmic pattern that threatens the human spirit in commodified modernity. The "ever-same," which Benjamin observes in Nietzsche,[66] bears down on modernist aesthetics. The novelty in appearance seems to be nothing but the same garments retailored for a new social performance.

Such notions have been employed most forcefully by Jauß to claim that "[I]n the period of modernity since Baudelaire no critic of culture has questioned the aesthetic (and epistemological) preference for the new more decisively than Walter

Benjamin."[67] Quite so, yet his master stroke is the transposition of this critique into the dialectical perception of the novelty's objectification—that is, the tiger's leap in fashion. It is true that fashion repeats itself, but it does so in historical quotation that incorporates the fundamental challenge to linear historicism; through the leap the eternal return is broken, an epoch is thrown from history's continuum. And all this happens under the ironic guise of the conspicuous consumption of the sartorial, which, to the unschooled beholder, offers nothing but a redressing of the old.

In Benjamin's *Tigersprung* quotation, the historical example comes from the opening page of Marx's study on the 1848 Revolution in France, *The Eighteenth Brumaire of Louis Bonaparte.* In it, the cynicism toward proclaimed (political) novelties in old guises is inescapable.

▪

*Men make their own history, but they do not make it just as they please; they do not make it under circumstances chosen by themselves, but under circumstances directly encountered, given and transmitted from the past. . . . And just when they seem engaged in revolutionizing themselves and things, in creating something that has never existed, precisely in such periods of revolutionary crisis they anxiously conjure up the spirits of the past to their service and borrow from them names, battle-cries and costumes in order to present the new scene of world history in this time-honoured disguise and this borrowed language. Thus Luther donned the mask of the apostle Paul, the revolution of 1789 to 1814 draped itself alternately as the Roman Republic and the Roman Empire, and the revolution of 1848 knew nothing better to do than to parody, now 1789, now the revolutionary tradition of 1793 to 1795.*[68]

▪

The idea of citing past revolutions, an idea that is transferred by Benjamin through the tiger's leap to the sartorial (and thus extended from the "masculine" revolt of society to the "feminine" revolutionizing of apparel), appears relevant only in the bourgeois arena. Once the air over the *Tigersprung*'s arena is cleared, the negative infinitude of the "ever-same" is broken and a true historical consciousness makes possible the final leap into freedom. If this means breaking with fashion and forsaking the poetry that lies in designing and wearing clothes and their citations, then it implies a fitting para-

**50.**

Vladimir I. Kozlinsky, *The Dead of the Paris Commune Have Been Resurrected under the Red Banner of the Soviets,* 1921. Painted linocut on card, 72 × 47.7 cm. Russian State Museum, St. Petersburg.

dox: fashion helps make visible a negative aspect that, once challenged and overcome, may serve to eradicate it. Yet such a paradox is nothing new. As Simmel remarked, it is fashion's fate to "die" in each moment of its wider acceptance, while being reborn at the very same instant setting again in motion the cycle of embrace by a sartorial vanguard, dissemination by the media, general following, and stylistic demise.

"Fashion is the eternal recurrence of the new. Are there nevertheless motifs of redemption precisely in fashion?" asks Benjamin, formulating the question vital for his own historiography.[69] For a present that has become transient—and thus, for him and Baudelaire, synonymous with modernity—fashion represents its essence. Not its substance, as fashion's ephemerality makes that impossible, but a concentrated extract; which in embodying the now-time, and providing an open reference to the past can claim to constitute a beckoning future. Benjamin's interpretation of fashion allowed him to combine both the metaphysical side of a messianic past and the materialist side of sociohistorical critique. The latter, although influenced by Engels's and Marx's critical reading of Hegel, consisted not of orthodox dialectics but rather the aestheticizing of the dialectical method, as well as his own application of historical materialism. Because Marxism became influential only at a late stage in the *Arcades Project* (from ca. 1934 onward), the numerous references to a new form of social, cultural, and historical critique always were in progress. But Benjamin's efforts to discard historicism were determined enough that he wholeheartedly embraced its historical-materialist opposite. Examining an intricate historical pattern woven from yarns that symbolize related yet chronologically unconnected occurrences, as in, for example, Parisian *révolutions,* was more important than following the positivist continuum of a superficially observed social fabric throughout the nineteenth century.

Two excerpts on dialectics show the range of interpretation that Benjamin's manuscripts contain. They were written more than a decade apart, and one senses Benjamin's struggle to maintain his original impetus under the constant influx of new stimulations and new ideas on methodology. One is from "Pariser Passagen I," the first notes for the project, which date back to 1927; the other is from the already-discussed "Theses on the Philosophy of History" (1939/1940). Yet a common denominator links

**51.**

Félicien Rops, *The Blow-Up*, 1877. Watercolor on paper, 74 × 53 cm.
Royal Museum of Fine Arts Belgium, Brussels.

*"Concerning* The Blow-Up: *it is a work that will age more than the rest. In twenty years the depicted styles will be forgotten. For the moment, however, they are just 'old-fashioned' and even 'grotesque,' like all past and well-worn fashion. It takes time for it to become 'history.'"—From a letter by Rops, March 1887.*

both, in analytical detail as well as metaphor; not surprisingly it is sartorial fashion. In the earliest notes to his project Benjamin reflected:

■

*It has been claimed that the dialectical method is concerned with mastering the respective concrete-historical situation of its object. This, however, is not sufficient. Because it is equally important to master the concrete-historical situation of the* interest *in the object. The latter notion always is due to the fact that it is prefigured within this very object; moreover, that it renders the object concrete in itself, that it generates a sense of advancement from the object's past existence into a higher concretization of the now-being* [Jetztseins].*Why this now-being* (which is no less than the now-being within now-time [Jetztzeit]) *constitutes in itself a higher concretization—this question cannot be encompassed by the dialectical method within an ideology of progress, but only within a philosophy of history that overcomes this ideology in all its parts. This philosophy would speak of an increasing condensation (integration) of reality, in which all elements of the past (in their own time) possess a higher degree of actuality than in their moment of existence. The way in which it grows accustomed to its own heightened actuality is defined and created by the image itself and through the fact that it is understood properly.—The past, or rather what once has been* [Gewesenes], *has to be dealt with not as before by a historical method but by a political one. The task must be to transform political categories into theoretical ones while venturing to lead them, in the spirit of [revolutionary] practice, to the present only. The dialectical penetration and realization of past configurations is the test on the truth of present action. This means: the explosive in fashion (which always* refers back to the past) *has to be ignited.*[70]

■

The directive to write political history—or, in the case of Max Raphael, who is frequently quoted in the notes, sociological art history—as an aesthetic analysis based on economic facts and the guidelines of historical materialism is transgressed by Benjamin through a direct move into metaphysics. The bibliography for the *Arcades Project* lists Raphael's most important book, *Proudhon Marx Picasso: Trois études sur la sociologie de l'art.*[71] In this book, written and published also in the Parisian exile, Raphael analyzes Picasso's adaptation of "tribal" artifacts that had been brought to France through the politics of colonialism. The sensually drained European artist discovers the artistic expression of a deep and archaic "irrationality" and thus becomes able to position himself against modernity's rationalization. Analyzing two of Picasso's self-portraits, Raphael subsumes the representation of a heightened awareness of the artist's self, from passive, overstrained bohemian in a dark suit to active workman with white rolled-up sleeves,[72] under a general theory. Picasso became able to "realize the relation that exists between physical, psychological, and artistic laws," and this "extending of the horizon of artistic practice refers back to theories of art and leads to a clear distinction between the theory, sociology, and history of art. In particular it reverses the art-historical mode of perception."[73] It is at this point that Benjamin found one of the initial references for his parallel concept of history, as Raphael wrote on the (art-) historical structure: "[O]ne does not proceed anymore from past into present, but from the present into the past. Here are the positive results that the triumphant Marxism has to develop."[74]

This obvious but, in light of existing German bourgeois art history (in the tradition of Burckhardt or Wölfflin), radical view was employed by Benjamin as the starting point for subsequent development and transposition. Like Raphael, he recognized the new impetus within the sociophilosophical definitions of culture and life itself that had been put forward by Simmel (who, as we know, taught at the University in Berlin, where Benjamin and Raphael had studied). Accepting the progress that materialist historians had made in adding and strengthening the social and economic dimension of these definitions, Benjamin nevertheless leaped straight into metaphysical categories in order to arrive at a new historiography that was revolutionary in essence.

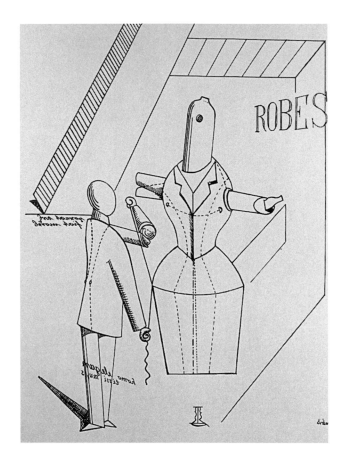

**52.**

Max Ernst, *FIAT MODES—pereat ars* (plate 1), 1919. Lithograph on paper, 43.5 × 32 cm.
Private collection.

*Ernst tailors enigma and irony in the style of* pittura metafisica: *constructing the dress, constructing (wo)man.*

*"A really well-made buttonhole is the only link between Art and Nature."—Oscar Wilde.*

# ■ 4.8  *Tigersprung*

### 4.8.1  The Third Tiger's Leap

*Fashion has the scent of the modern wherever it stirs in the thicket of what has been. It is the tiger's leap into the past. Yet this leap occurs in an arena commanded by the ruling class. The very same leap in the open air of history is the dialectical one, which Marx has understood as the revolution.*

■

This central quotation constitutes the second excerpt on dialectics that illuminates Benjamin's methodology. The arena in which the ruling class cracks the whip had been described and criticized by Marx and Engels. Marxist critics such as Lukács, Raphael, and the young Ernst Bloch transferred these methods to an analysis of art and culture. Benjamin aspired to stretch it even further, hoping to open up the great top above the arena to watch the tiger take the dialectical leap from now-time into the past, in the "open air of history" that had been cleared of iconographic fume.

Yet what is this image of the "leap . . . which Marx has understood as the revolution" and where did it come from? In fact, the concept of the *Sprung* (leap) in materialist thought owes more to Engels than to Marx and was developed, like other elements of materialism, in reference of Hegel—in particular, to his interpretation of objective and natural laws. The earliest use within Marxist theory of the term "leap," which replaced the more tentative *Umschlag* (folding) previously employed, is documented in a letter that Engels sent in July 1858 from a Manchester textile mill to Marx in London: "This much is certain—comparative physiology gives one a healthy contempt for man's idealistic arrogance in regard to other animals. . . . Here too Hegel's stuff about the qualitative leap in the quantitative sequence fits in very nicely."[75]

Hegel's perception of natural history was interpreted subsequently by Engels in his *Dialectics of Nature,* which he wrote between 1873 and 1883 (with additions in 1885/1886) but which remained unfinished. One fragment refuting the prevalent concept of evolutionary, that is, positivist, historical progress states: "These intermediate links prove only that there are no leaps in nature, *precisely because* nature is composed entirely of leaps."[76] Engels had to interrupt this work on the natural occurrence of dialectics—a work that would be his most substantial yet also his most problematic, regarded by many as a vulgarization of the dialectical method—in order to respond to criticism by a German social democrat of the dialectical view of nature, science, and society. Engels's elaborate response (written from the end of 1876 to July 1878) dissected with unconcealed irony the opposing arguments and explained to his critic Hegel's deduction from science to moral philosophy: "This is precisely the Hegelian nodal line of measure relations, in which, at certain definite nodal points the purely quantitative increase or decrease gives rise to a *qualitative leap;* for example, in the case of heated or cooled water, where boiling-point or freezing-point are the nodes at which—under normal pressure—the leap to a new aggregation takes place, and where consequently quantity is transformed into quality."[77] In the *Communist Manifesto* this "qualitative leap" would be the famous phrase "alles Ständische und Stehende verdampft"—"all that is solid melts into air." Progress in nature is never continuous but instead consists of combinations of leaps; and the most significant leap occurs when the form of an object (an element, a configuration, etc.) breaks the continuum and appears in an entirely different state. "In spite of all gradualness, the transition from one form of motion to another always remains a leap, a decisive change."[78]

In the text to which Engels (and later Marx) referred, Hegel had argued against a continuous evolutionary principle. In natural numeric relations (in music or mathematics) quantitative progress, that is, the progression of entities, always must reach a point at which it leaps into qualitative change—where one step suddenly breaks from the expected order to jump back to a relation that had existed much earlier on in the progression. Hegel had written in 1812/1813: "The progression along merely indifferent relations which do change the preceding specific reality (or do not even form one) suddenly interrupts itself, and, while it continues in the same manner quantitatively, a specific relation breaks in through a leap."[79] This leap appears as *actio in distans,* as a relation to something removed; and always it is directed backward, toward the past, as it has to refer to or distinguish itself from a state that existed beforehand. In natural science, these occurrences appear much more dramatically. Without progressing through intermediate stages, one element suddenly changes its appearance into another: water gradually gets colder until it reaches its freezing point, when it instantly alters its aggregate state and "leaps" from a liquid straight into a solid state. The difficulty in understanding this concept, wrote Hegel,

■

*consists in the qualitative transition of something into its other in general and into its opposite; understanding prefers to fancy* identity *and* change *to be of that indifferent and external kind which applies to the* quantitative.

*In* ethics, *in so far as it is considered in the sphere of Being, the same transition from quantitative to qualitative takes place, and different qualities appear to base themselves on differences in magnitude. It is through a more or less that the measure of frivolity or thoughtlessness is exceeded and something quite different comes about, namely crime, and thus right becomes wrong, and virtue vice.*[80]

■

Such a leap, situated in the realm of ethics, became the focal point of Marx's and Engels's interest. The dialectical view of natural phenomena regards it as the essence of Being itself, following Hegel, who had seen the leap as existential: "All *birth* and *death,* instead of being a continued graduality, are rather an interruption of this and are the leap from quantitative into qualitative change."[81]

The idealism found in Hegel's ethics provided only one part of the bases for dialectical materialism. Engels had to transfer his reading of Hegelian dialectics to sociopolitical history. In rewriting (in 1880) his *Anti-Dühring* for socialist monthly published in Paris, he turned natural law into materialist objectivity. The examples for the discontinuous character of the leap were taken no longer from successions of numbers, notes, or chemical compounds but from the series of social configurations throughout human history. In the nineteenth century, the aggregate state of society required change. The dominance of the commodity over humans, which had characterized the successive states within the historical continuum, had to come to an end. A leap *backward* (cf. Hegel's *Science of Logic*) would thus allow the subject to regain his or her original control over the object. Laborers would be alienated from their product no more; the "hell of commodities," as Benjamin termed it, with its abstraction and reification would cease to exist.

The present took dialectical recourse to the past—without nostalgia—and individuals were seen once again as in charge of historical development. This condition, later called by Benjamin the "open air of history," would generate the revolution to liberate the oppressed masses (of consumers). In *La Revue socialiste* Engels described the leap in the historical-materialist tradition as a fusion between theory and practice.

■

*With the seizing of the means of production by society, production of commodities is done away with, and, simultaneously, the mastery of the product over the producer. . . . The extraneous objective forces that have hitherto governed history pass under the control of man himself. Only from time to time will man himself, with full consciousness, make his own history—only from that time will the social causes set in movement by him have, in the main and in a constantly growing measure, the results intended by him. It is humanity's leap from the kingdom of necessity to the kingdom of freedom.*[82]

■

The leap that is here postulated for the first time as a revolutionary event proper was appropriated by Benjamin for his challenge of historicism, which in turn, as we have seen, used fashion as its principal example. But Engels's postulate declares the commodity, and implicitly the dominance of the commodified object over the consuming subject, to be obsolete and harmful to humanity's progress toward the "kingdom of freedom."

In capitalism no commodity is as pronounced as the sartorial one. Its ephemeral character, its quest for changing appearances, demands constant consumption. For the average consumer, following fashion means having to repeatedly restock his or her wardrobe. Obviously, after the leap in the historical-materialist sense we might well be freed from such dependence on the latest clothing. Thus it appears as very ironic that Benjamin would appropriate the liberating tiger's leap of fashion as his tool for mounting a similar revolutionary challenge to history, or at least to the "rewriting" of history—one could surmise that Engels's challenge is geared toward social liberation, while the Benjaminian one rather concerns itself with an attack in the realm of theory. Whether the *Tigersprung* of the late 1930s thus had earned its stripes by progressive development from its origin in the mid–nineteenth century appears debatable. Is it not once again the dreaded victory of style over substance? Or has fashion's ever-changing appearance rather become not only the pacesetter but the very essence of modernity, so that any attack on it implicitly shakes the very foundation of the capitalist system that had generated it?

For Engels, the utopian socialist idea of liberation through deliberate discontinuity in historical progress—that is, through revolution—was scientifically and philosophically founded on the dialectical leap that occurs in the human environment. Yet this intricate theoretical foundation would not suffice for some Marxist critics, who became impatient with the lack of revolutionary practice. Lukács demanded in a 1919 lecture, "The Changing Function of Historical Materialism": "The fundamental tenet of the dialectical method that 'it is not the consciousness of men that determines their existence, but, on the contrary, their social existence determines their consciousness,' has the necessary consequence—when rightly understood—that at the revolutionary turning-point, the category of the radically new, the standing of the economic structure on its head, the change in the direction of the progress, i.e. the category of the leap must be taken seriously *in practice.*"[83] Lukács went to great lengths to determine the *Sprung* in its socioeconomic significance. For him the leap is dialectical not only because it exemplifies the dialectics of nature, but also because the action in itself is dialectical. He maintained that the leap is not a unique event, which would "generate suddenly and without warning the greatest of changes in man's history so far," but is prefigured in what already exists.[84] It thus reclaims a territory that was originally free, but is at present under the dominance of the object. To fully liberate the subject, the turn toward the new has to contain an element of being, which exists, even if one is not initially conscious of it, at least in presentiment. The essence of the leap is "expressed by the fact that on every occasion it denotes a *turning of something qualitatively new;* conscious action directed towards the comprehended totality of society comes to the surface; and therefore—in intention and basis—its home is the realm of freedom."[85] Dialectically, the contents and form of the tiger's leap accommodate themselves in the slow development of society, in order to maintain the leap's character. It is not simply interested in accelerating historical tempi; it wants to reveal the inherent structure prefigured in history. In order to reveal the true reason of historical progress the leap thus has to be, according to Lukács, "*one* step in front of the process, when the revolution shies away from 'the instinct monstrosity of its own purposes' and threatens to waver and fall back into half-measures."[86]

Earlier in his lecturer Lukács had determined the validity of Engels's and Marx's reading of the (originally Hegelian) leap. And here we find the clear connection to Benjamin's *Tigersprung* in history. For Lukács this quote was simply a step toward analyzing revolutionary practice, but for Benjamin it would "clear the air" to illuminate a view of the historical perception of subject as well as cultural object. Thus Benjamin read in Lukács's Budapest lecture, which had been published in German in 1923 (in *History and Class Consciousness*):

▪

*The "leap from the realm of necessity into the realm of freedom," the end to the "prehistory of humanity" were to Marx and Engels more than beautiful but abstract and empty visions providing resounding ornamental phrases with which to round off the critique of the present, but entailing no systematic commitment. They were rather the clear and conscious intellectual anticipation of the path history was to take and their methodological implications reach deeply into the interpretation of current problems.*[87]

▪

The claim that the leap assisted in anticipating the "path history was to take" must have resounded in Benjamin's ears. In this notion he saw the possibility of formulating a critique not merely of the manner in which history apparently progressed and furthered the capitalist system's objectification of the human condition and its alienation of individuals. He was also able to criticize how capitalist history rewrote itself throughout the nineteenth and early twentieth century. Benjamin realized the chance to attack the pattern in the socioeconomic fabric that justifies capitalism by propagating the idea of linear historical progress. And because the main object of this critique was culture, he must have perceived the fitting irony in mounting his challenge by using the primary commodity of modernity, fashion.

Taking Lukács's observation of the ornamentation and beauty in Marx's and Engels's critique into account, Benjamin employed for his metaphor this most expressive element for aestheticizing or beautifying life—through adorning the human form. That choice might have rendered his argument ambiguous, even obscure, yet endowed it with a poetry Benjamin sought in politics and art alike.[88] The dialectical leap is, like fashion, which progresses with ease from one season to the next and never relinquishes its essential characteristics, originally part of the historical continuum. But it soon becomes an apparent cause of discontinuity: each fashion seems to embody the radical new that is going to exist for all time, the ultimate and final break with the progress of the past, the perpetual "revolution" proclaimed almost every season. The leap thus has to take possession of the object inherent in history to realize its (revolutionary) potential. Accordingly, fashion's tiger's leap quotes the past in order to establish absolute novelty.

**4.8.2** The Standstill of the Tiger (on the Catwalk)

There is another metaphoric quality to the leap. The tiger who takes it is able to land almost motionless *on the spot*—as any cat can, whether large or small, even from great heights. Its motionlessness alludes to the dialectical standstill, to the time nexus in which the true revolutionary potential is realized or materialized and thus can be freed. Like the flâneur who is transfixed by the woman's leg and dress, the tiger who meets the ground in an instant finds the place "where the thought stops short in a configuration that is saturated with tensions," as we have seen. And the resulting *Chock* crystallizes this moment in history into a monad that can be evaluated philosophically.

While the term "monad" had represented for Benjamin in his early writings the philosophical entity referring back to Leibniz's concept,[89] he later, in his fragmentary "Theses on the Philosophy of History," imbued it with the notion of time. The monad becomes not simply an idea but its dialectical complement—the concrete that is history: for the flâneur who saunters through *modernité,* "the eternal is rather a ruche on a dress than an idea." Both the instant and the "archaic" object from the past century are filled with the explosive potential of now-time and are regarded as monads, as elements that in their particularity incorporate the whole, like the idea that aims to incorporate totality.

Benjamin's dissatisfaction with the historicism that perceives history's progress as a mere succession of epochs was originally greatly politicized. His view on messianic power runs parallel to the social-revolutionary one. In order to bring to a standstill the progress presided over by the ruling classes—an action nothing short of a revolution—the oppressed masses have to refer back to those that labored before them and who had lost the struggle. They also have to take a tiger's leap into the past!

All this seems far removed from sartorial fashion. Yet fashion is a fundamental impetus for Benjamin's thought. How did he relate this beautifying element of ephemera to the revolutionary struggle? Fashion's significance begins in its archetypal power, the dreamlike quality that every person can relate to: "Fashion stands in the darkness of the experienced instant, but in its collective expression."[90] Whether the term "collective" refers to (Jungian) psychoanalysis (a concept of the archaic vehemently criticized by Adorno as having proto-fascist connotations) or to the definition of a revolutionary crowd, it carries in any case the notion of mass influence and mass power. But does not fashion thus align itself with the undefined and remove itself from the rationale for political engagement? Did not Simmel already observe that the reaction of the lower classes to fashion is decidedly slow and unwilling? In noting in the manuscript sheaf on Baudelaire, "The vogue of fashion breaks on the compact crowd of the oppressed," Benjamin appears to agree with him.[91] Furthermore, one of the pages with fragmentary schemes for the project (rediscovered in 1946 by Bataille in the Bibliothèque Nationale) reads: "Fashion puts its fig leaf always on the spot where the revolutionary nakedness of society is to be found. One small shift and . . ."[92]

So fashion seems to be nothing but an ephemeral covering for social grievances. Indeed, sociologically speaking it appears as precisely that. The power of the commodity elevates the clothing of one particular period to the socially de rigueur. And yet evasive action is taken almost immediately by the designers of a new fashionable style; the accepted sartorial norm ceases to exist and a new form takes its place, which cites an altogether different aspect of the past and thus subverts the object's dominance.

This is fashion's metaphysical coinage, its historical transposition, and for Benjamin it is "canonized dialectics"![93] *Die Mode* may be left in the dark, while politics is out in the open, but it fuels the collective dreams and actions of individuals. The vogue of fashion breaks on the oppressed, but it still showers them with the spray of its influence. Fashion covers a possible societal nakedness, but its constant reshaping and movement carry immanent threats of exposure, as it openly exemplifies—with infinite irony, even cynicism—the facile and fugitive. Benjamin wrote in his first excerpt on dialectics that the concrete-historical situation of the interest is prefigured in its object, and this is nowhere more explicit than in fashion.

"For the philosopher, the most passionate interest in fashion is due to the extraordinary anticipation of it."[94] Although the sensibility of "the painter of modern life" may exceed that of the couturière, and the artist's novel manner of representing a figure may come before a new silhouette is created for *la tigresse,* "fashion is still in much more constant, much more precise contact with the things to come, owing to the incomparable scent of the female collective for what the future holds."[95] And it is not only the similar vocabulary here that establishes the close relation to the tiger's leap. The tiger leaps into the past in an effort to rewrite history, whereas *la tigresse* preserves her scent for sartorial novelties as a means of seduction. One of the "female" collective, Mme de Ponty (a.k.a. Mallarmé), claimed in December 1874: "Laws, orders, plans, bylaws and decrees, as some gentlemen put it, all nowadays promulgate what is fashionable: and no new message of this female sovereign [*la mode*] (which is herself all the world!) will surprise us after a fortnight or two."[96] With an ironic wink the male poet in his female disguise talks about "les messieurs" who claim to define laws that in modernity are now, more importantly, passed also for the dress code, and that would influence the image of Parisian society (and subsequently the rest of Europe and North America) more than would any legal decision. Mallarmé's observation would be echoed faithfully some sixty years later by Benjamin in the *Arcades Project:* "Each season creates in its latest designs some secret signal flags of the things to come. Those who could understand them would learn in advance not only about new trends in art

**53.**
Helen Reiter, *Winter,* ca. 1910. Paper collage, 30 × 22 cm. Staatliche Museen zu Berlin,
Kunstbibliothek.

but also about new law books, wars, and revolutions.—No doubt, this notion contains fashion's greatest attraction, but at the same time the difficulty of rendering it productive."[97] Fashion understands what the future holds while glancing back at the past. Given that Benjamin's historicopolitical concept regards recourse to the past as of paramount importance for a prospective and necessary revolution, fashion with its constant and imperative reference to the past becomes the natural *agent provocateur,*[98] an explosive force for social upheaval.

Like the young Marcel in Proust's *Du côté de chez Swann,* who relived a historical progression in his dream state before waking, before entering present time, the historian has to progress from the literary to the theoretical. "And thus we present," exclaims Benjamin, "the new, the dialectical method of historiography: to go through the past with the intensity of a dream, in order to experience the present as the waking world [*Wachwelt*] to which the dream refers! . . . Each epoch contains such a side turned toward the dream, such a child's side."[99]

The child that buried his face into the pleats and folds of the mother's dress has grown up. He now lifts his head and looks on modernity. But he preserves the dream not only for his comfort and warmth but also to explain to himself, and ultimately to others, his position in history, the condition of his epoch. Thus he finds himself in agreement with the motto by historian Jules Michelet, whom Benjamin quoted at the beginning of the sixth manuscript sheaf: "Each age dreams the following."[100]

## ■ 4.9 Clothed History

To put it materialistically: the structure of modernity came into being with the flowering of monopoly capitalism in the nineteenth century.[101] The historian interested in the cultural repercussions of this economic construct must go back to its origins. Yet rather than looking on it as a mere collection of historical facts, he or she must regard it with the poetical intensity of a dream, as the surrealists would later emphasize, and fuel it with the potential of now-time. Only the dialectical method is appropriate for the immanent dialectics of historical facts, maintained Raphael.[102] That method attempts to find an object from the present and to realize or visualize within it the potential of a past age, which in turn had "dreamed up" or "dreamed of the following age"—that is, the present one. The perception of the dream acts as a guide, as it appears as essentially dialectical itself: at times displaying historical movement, as in Proust's *Recherche,* and at times its standstill as in Baudelaire's "Passante."

When the historian Michelet evaluated his own time, the nineteenth century, he glanced back at the dreams and hopes of former epochs—especially at those from the end of the eighteenth century, namely the ideals of the French Revolution.[103] At that time fashion had dreamed, too, about a future of material and spiritual equality between classes and sexes, made visual also in the revolutionary habit of male and female *sans-culottes* and the unisex long shirts made from calico. In 1795 Chamfort, the "moralist of the revolt," thus had placed the sartorial at the heart of his maxim: "One has to be just before being generous, as one has linen shirts before lace ones."[104]

A century later, contemporary fashion would take a tiger's leap back into this revolutionary past. In her summer collection of 1898, French couturière Jeanne Paquin made an open reference to the "rewriting" of history by creating a dress named after the famous historian. Her design "Michelet" consisted of a sky-blue dress with a colorful, naive embroidery on the upper bodice.[105] It looked like the sophisticated version of a peasant's Sunday wear and was distinguished further by Paquin's trademark: intricate fur trimming on the lapels and hem. For Paquin the design thus constituted a sartorial homage to a historian who had delivered an entire series of lectures at the Collège de France titled "The Education of Woman through Woman" (1850) and who had never tired of emphasizing the role of woman's clothing in society.[106]

Michelet's perception of sartorial significance was described in the diary of the brothers Goncourt, who in March 1864 attended a festivity arranged by the historian in his Parisian home: "We went 'in civvies' to the ball *chez* Michelet where all the women were disguised as oppressed nations: Poland, Hungary, Venice, etc. It was like watching the dance of future revolutions in Europe."[107] The bourgeois historian, with his penchant for political revolt, translated his commitment to equality and liberty into hosting an elegant masked ball for intellectual circles and polite society. He dreamed

**54.**
Studio Jeanne Paquin, "Michelet" model, summer 1898. Ink and watercolor on paper,
24 × 17 cm. Victoria and Albert Museum, London.

of a Europe freed from Prussian and Russian rule, yet his protest might well have been drowned out by the swish of the silken and chiffon *volants* worn by his female guests.

Paquin's collection of 1898 also made a less veiled historical reference to the French Revolution by featuring the "modèle Robespierre," a subdued black dress of heavy silk or poplin with a large belt accentuating restraint and serenity.[108] The black material and its cut symbolized the idea of political rigor, while the belt represented the need for control, as otherwise the striving for moral purity might easily reverse into obsession and *terreur.*

Two seasons later, in the summer of 1899, Paquin took the "rewriting" of history to an even more highly visualized level. The robe "Thermidor," named after the eleventh month of the revolutionary calendar (20 July–20 August), was cut like a Greco-Roman column in cream and off-white silk and taffeta.[109] Pleats ran down the entire dress, and there was—a novelty at that time—no bodice; the waistline was merely indicated by sophisticated stitching. The top of the robe saw a couple of *mouchoir* applications: pieces of thin lace sewn onto the silk to resemble the carved (Corinthian) capital of a column. The adoption of revolutionary ideals, that is, the invocation of the civil virtues within Greek and Roman society, was in this case not symbolized by a contemporary interpretation of a chiton or toga—as in the high-waisted dresses of the Directoire, which would come into vogue again during Paul Poiret's reign as couturier after 1905. Paquin, on the contrary, attempted to reflect on the formative ideals of these ancient societies, bringing the structural element of both architecture and aesthetics in general, the column, back to its "natural" origin and using it to clothe the human figure. She followed what Hegel had demanded of fashion in his *Aesthetics* some seven decades earlier: "The principle for the artistic kind of raiment lies in treating it as if it were architectural. . . . Moreover, the architectural character in wearing and of what is worn must be formed by its own account, according to its own mechanical nature. This very principle is followed in the kind of garment which we see in the ideal sculpture of the elders [i.e., classical Greece]. The mantle especially is like a house in which one is free to move."[110] The "Thermidor" dress demanded that its wearer assume an upright and self-conscious posture. The initial restriction of her movements rendered each gesture into something contemplated, noticeable, even

**55.**
Studio Jeanne Paquin, "Robespierre" model, summer 1898. Ink and watercolor on paper,
22 × 16 cm. Victoria and Albert Museum, London.

significant. In the eyes of those who had witnessed the sartorial "excesses" of the second half of the nineteenth century—notably the crinoline and its multitude of *volants*—Mme Paquin's designs reflected a degree of austerity and restraint. The accent was firmly laid on the fabric (more luxurious than ever) and the cut. The dialectical image inherent in fashion is expressed also in the "Thermidor" design: the element that originally had been perceived as embodying solidity and power, the rising column of stone, in the clothing became its antithesis—flowing silk. However, through the "construction" of the dress the pleats stiffened the material and thus achieved comparable symbolic value (indeed, the Doric column itself is modeled on the Greek female chiton). And because it was seen on a woman, setting it in highly sensuous relation to the human body, the symbolism became even greater and the influence on society appeared more immediate.

Benjamin wrote early on (between 1927 and 1930) in the *Passagenarbeit*: "Fashion. A kind of race for the first place in societal creation. The race is run anew at each moment in time."[111] Fashion functions as much more than a mere social signifier. Clothing is able, like visual art and literature, to depict concepts and ideas. Furthermore it can become their embodiment in the literal sense of the word. Benjamin also noted, "It is obvious that art, in its sociological domain, within the hierarchies founded upon it and in the way it was formed and developed, is much more closely related to what we now regard as fashion than to what we call art."[112]

In order to explain historical process, Benjamin had to analyze social behavior to establish a sociological foundation, a method that Simmel had of course employed earlier in his fashion essay of 1911. This text is the single most frequently quoted source in Benjamin's fashion manuscripts[113]—and in the *Arcades Project* as a whole. Such reliance shows the debt that any astute observer of the sartorial must owe to Simmel. In Benjamin's case, the influence and inspiration seem very direct indeed. His brief curriculum vitae lists the winter semesters of 1912/1913 and 1913/1914 as spent at the University in Berlin; he states, "My main interests were philosophy, German literature, and art history. Consequently, I attended the lectures . . . by Cassirer, Erdmann, Goldschmidt, Hermann, and Simmel in Berlin."[114] Since Simmel left for Strassburg in April 1914, Benjamin could have attended only a very limited number of his lectures, none

**56.**
Studio Jeanne Paquin, "Thermidor" model, summer 1899. Ink and watercolor on paper,
22 × 16 cm. Victoria and Albert Museum, London.

of which is noted in his graduation document.[115] However, the influence of Simmel's writing on Benjamin's work, especially on the manuscript sheaf on fashion, is obvious.

Simmel's vitalism—his *Lebensphilosophie*—has been regarded as favoring phenomenological observations and resisting theoretical constructs. And given his claim of the harmful dominance of the object over the subject in his "tragedy of culture," a rejection of abstraction in his thought seems consistent. Yet his preference for dualism, particularly in explaining fashion, indicates a conceptual integration of conflicting tendencies that would substantially inform Benjamin's later work on dialectics.[116] During the first two decades of the twentieth century, the dual character of fashion was for Simmel, in his guise as neo-Kantian, the means by which conflicting elements in history as well as in society could be reconciled. Benjamin in the third and fourth decades supersedes Simmel's approach with the dialectical image. He attempts to stress analogies—much as Hegel had done "materialistically" with this Kantian term—and provoke a conflict that ultimately has to be "resolved" within the synthesis of a new social (and aesthetic) order. Fashion no longer calmed the *querelle des anciens et des modernes* by incorporating the old and the new. It fueled the past with *Jetztzeit,* with an explosive readiness to be ignited.[117]

The above methodological distinction does not necessarily indicate a conflict between the (purely academic?) social democracy of Sombart, Weber, and Simmel and Marxism; nevertheless a political division remains. In the same way in which Simmel's view on fashion incorporated a complex and sophisticated social critique and philosophy of life, Benjamin's view cannot simply be pinned down as orthodox historical materialism (as is the case with Raphael's historiography). His use of dialectics referred to a greater degree to Marx's early reading of Hegelian terminology for his "Critique of Political Economy" than to historical materialism as the principle of development within social history (let alone in its subsequent usage by Engels, and later by Lenin).

The scheme that Benjamin would have employed for the topic of fashion, and also for the structure of the *Arcades Project* as a whole, reveals itself in the number of manuscripts Benjamin had prepared for his précis, "Paris, Capital of the Nineteenth Century." This particular study was written at the request of one of the directors at the Institute for Social Research in New York, Friedrich Pollock. Completed in May 1935, it ties in with Benjamin's attempt to sketch out his main concept.[118] The same month he wrote to his friend Gershom Scholem that because "I was really alone with my studies on the *Arcades* for the first time in many years . . . the précis, which I had promised without giving it much thought, prompted the work to enter a new phase, in which for the first time it bears more resemblance—even if from afar—to a book."[119] Because of the "incredible difficulties" he had to face, Benjamin at times "reflected with pensive joy on the idea of a dialectical synthesis of misery and opulence that has been an integral part of this research, which has been continually interrupted and revived over the course of a decade, and which has been driven into the remotest of regions. Should the book's dialectic prove to be just as sound, then it would find my approval."[120]

In the précis itself, the subject of fashion is not singled out by a separate chapter heading, although it features in numerous passages throughout the text. In the manuscripts, however, fashion plays a dominant role. This apparent disproportion may be explained by the fact that Walter Benjamin had to cater, for economic reasons, to the interests of the New York Institute and its members, who might not have taken kindly to the stress given to the dialectical analysis of fashion within the prospective work.[121] However, it also reflects the shift of emphasis as his concept developed.

## ■ 4.10 Fashioning the Arcades

Since the various analyses of fashion run parallel to the shifting objective of the *Arcades Project,* it seems appropriate to follow the succession of different schemes in the collection of notes and materials recovered in the Bibliothèque Nationale after Benjamin's death.

The first five pages of the material deal with historical data and outline motives for the project as a whole.[122] Among them one finds a page on Louis Aragon's *Paysan de Paris,* with the heading "the best book on Paris,"[123] as well as a list of reflections on fashion in the second half of the nineteenth century:

*FASHION*

*1866 the head as a cloud high over the mountain's valley of the gown*
*[Benjamin deleted the next line on the shape of lamps]*
*1868 the bosom covered with a fringed carpet*
*—Architectural forms on dresses*
*—Annunciation [Heimsuchung—suggesting also Mary's visitation or affliction] as a*
    *subject for fashion illustration*
*—Fashionable dresses as a theme for confectioners*
*—Motifs of [the next two words could read "fences" and the German for "basket*
    *weave," indicating particular textile patterns] on clothes between 1850 and*
    *1860*
*—The woman as an equilateral triangle (crinoline)*
*—The woman as X—end of Empire—*
    *The jacket as a two-winged door*
    *The gown as a fan*
*Infinitely possible permutations of the fashionable elements*[124]

Across the top of the manuscript Benjamin noted: "Delvau/Falke/Fleurs du Mal"—bib-
liographical references to Alfred Delvau, Jakob von Falke, and, of course, Baudelaire.
The first two were social and cultural historians whose books, published between 1860
and 1867, Benjamin used as source material.[125] It is doubtful that his observations on
fashion were actually based mainly on these writings, as the listed dress styles of 1868
existed only after the publication of the above references. However, the dates on the
manuscript are employed as rough guides rather than a precise chronology. These
notes indicate a method of transferring basic sartorial facts into an aesthetic *précis:* the
construction in clothing patterns becomes an "architectural form" (as had been indicated in the 1860s by Weill, Gautier, etc.); the famous embroidery of black patterns on
a cream dress by Worth (for the princess of Metternich) suggests a lattice fence, while
the overall silhouettes are rendered as geometric abstracts.

**57.**
Unknown photographer, Princess Metternich in a gown by Charles Frederick Worth, ca. 1866.

Benjamin also attempts to trace artistic analogies in fashion: the "head as a cloud" above the fabric that forms mountains and valley, that is, breasts and lap—corresponding with his surrealist contemplation of the fetish as the landscape of dreams—is a poetic evocation of the cumulus hairstyle and the white *poudre de riz* that unified the female face and neckline, which emerged from a luxurious mass of fabric. Gautier's corresponding observation of 1858 comes to mind, in which "cette masse de riches étoffes fait comme un piédestal au buste et à la tête."[126] The "jacket as a two-winged door" that opens over the female body appears much more symbolically charged than the traditional fixation of male writers on bare shoulders and a low-cut decolleté. Finally, the "gown as a fan" appears to be an allusion to the accessorized refinement in the poetry of Mallarmé's "Éventails."

■

*Le sceptre des rivages roses*
*Stagnants sur les soirs d'or, ce l'est,*
*Ce blanc vol fermé que tu poses*
*Contre le feu d'un bracelet.*[127]

■

Benjamin's manuscripts on fashion are rooted within the poetic reflection on *modernité* in the nineteenth century. The sixth page of the notes shows him focusing on two "provisional schemes" for the *Arcades Project.* It serves also as a reminder that Benjamin, like Baudelaire in his *cravate rouge* and *blouse bleue,* had the audacity to combine social and sartorial history, to indicate a relationship between topics as seemingly diverse as urban guerrillas and outfitters:

■

*Provisional scheme*

*Revolutionary praxis*
    *Techniques of street fights and barricades*
    *Revolutionary mise-en-scène*
    *Professional conspirators and proletarians*

*Fashion*

   contemporaine de tout le monde

   *Attempt to lure the* sexus *into the material world* [Stoffwelt][128]

■

Benjamin took "la souveraine de tout le monde," as Mallarmé had ennobled fashion,[129] and rendered it a ruling power not only within a singular period of time, but for
all ages. Fashion becomes, through its ability to take the dialectical leap, a universal
model of contemporariness. Its attempt to guide the *sexus* into the material world (or
world of fabrics) refers both to the psychoanalytical coinage of the fetish and to its earlier definition as commodity in the materialist interpretation of society. Thus manuscript page 7 sets out the following:

■

*Dialectical scheme*

*Hell—golden age*

   *Keywords for this hell: ennui, gambling, pauperism*

   *One canon for these dialectics: fashion*

   *The golden age as a catastrophe*

*Dialectics of the commodity*

   *Take one canon for these dialectics from the "Odradek"*

   *The positive element in the fetish*

*Dialectics of the latest and the most ancient*

   *For these dialectics, too, fashion constitutes a canon*

   *The most ancient as the latest: the* fait-divers

   *The latest as the most ancient: the [Second] Empire*[130]

■

In the later text of excerpts and notes for the *Arcades Project,* the general observations
of the provisional and dialectical schemes are fused with stylistic observations on fashion (of 1866 to 1868), taken from contemporary sources. This method echoes that
of the brothers Goncourts, who in 1862 had described the sartorial fashion(s) of the

previous century as an indicator for its social perversions, which they liked to detail in a cynical manner.[131]

The bourgeois society between the reign of King Louis-Philippe and the end of the Second Empire was characterized by social extremes. On one side was the immense wealth through, in historical-materialist terminology nonproductive, speculation and a resulting obsession with material novelties and perpetually renewed distractions; on the other side was the pauperism that fueled revolts. Benjamin discussed both sides as embodying the futility of fashion's dialectics: the sartorial mode in its eternal recurrence became a prime indicator for the conspicuous consumption that determined the bourgeois lifestyle, as well as advocating a constant revolution—by folding the old into the new, by perpetual referring to its own past.

## ■ 4.11 *Le revers:* The Other Side of Reality

Benjamin specified on page 8 of his manuscripts: "First dialectical step: the arcade turns from a glittering place into one of decay—Second dialectical step: the arcade develops from an unconscious experience into something imbued [with experience]."[132] A relationship with surrealism is introduced through the notion of the dream (and waking) that had found a different expression at the beginning of Proust's *Recherche*. Benjamin conceived the dream as both a historical and a collective phenomenon. He attempted to shed light on the dream of the individual by establishing a canon—but not an explanatory key—of the historical dreams of the collective. Furthermore, the dream and the waking that had been poetic metaphors are here rendered into the constituents of a dialectical construction. "Thesis and antithesis are to be combined in an image of dream change [*Traum-Wandel-Bild*]. Aspects of luster and misery of the arcades are viewed through a dream. Waking is the dialectical folding [*Umschlag*] into synthesis."[133] The folding (*Umschlag* is, literally, the turnup on trousers) marks a reference to orthodox dialectics, as precursor to the "leap" that Engels had adopted from Hegelian terminology as early as 1858, as we have seen (in section 4.8.1 above). In 1867, while working on *The Capital,* Marx had written to Engels about a much more textile than textual example that he regarded as particularly suited to explain exchange value. In this letter he replaced Hegel's leap from quantitative progression to qualitative change again with the *Umschlag,* folding or transformation—perhaps in order to remain within the metaphor in the example.

■

*The economists have hitherto overlooked the very simple fact that the equation* 20 yards of linen = 1 coat *is but the primitive form of* 20 yards of linen = £2, *and thus that the simplest form of a commodity, in which its value is not yet expressed in relation to all other commodities, but only as something* differentiated *from its own natural form, embodies the whole* secret of the money form *and thereby,* in nuce, of all bourgeois forms of the product of labour . . . *incidentally, you will see from the conclusion to my chapter III, where I outline the transformation of the master of trade into a capitalist—as a result of purely* quantitative *changes—that in the text there I quote Hegel's discovery of the* law of the transformation [Umschlag] of a merely quantitative change into a qualitative one *as being attested by history and natural science alike.*[134]

■

Marx's example of the tradesman becoming a capitalist would be rendered by Simmel less abstract and more applicable to a particular quality of life, as he would illustrate the reification in modernity through the transformation of bespoke tailor into anonymous clothing manufacturer (see section 3.2.1 above).

On his part, Benjamin realized that thesis and antithesis need to be integrated into a dialectical image that represents them through dream and change. The moment of waking constitutes a synthesis; and it is perhaps this moment that establishes an absolute method of cognition, when the "inner movement of the absolute," as Hegel characterized the product of dialectical progression, guarantees the preservation of the identities of both subject and object.

The French expression for the "folding" of the text(ile), which was also employed by Benjamin as a synthesis, constitutes another dialectical image: *le revers* is not only "the other," "the reverse," but also the inside of a garment. Throughout the nineteenth century it came to be exclusively used in the German language for the lapels of the jacket, which at that time still prominently displayed their silk lining. In his early study "The Origin of German Tragic Drama," Benjamin quoted a seventeenth-century dramatist, A. A. von Haugwitz, on the allegoric significance of fashion:

■

*Reicht uns den rothen Sammt*
*und dies geblümte Kleid*

*Und schwartzen Atlaß*
*daß man*
*was den Sinn erfreut*

*Und was den Leib betrübt*
*kan auff den Kleidern lesen.*[135]

■

Shortly thereafter he concluded: "Comedy—or more precisely: the pure joke—is the essential inner side of mourning which from time to time, like the lining of clothes that is visible on its hem or lapel [*Revers*], makes its presence felt."[136] This metaphor is carried throughout the *Arcades Project,* and it culminates in the manuscript sheaf on ennui, which, as Benjamin wrote in his notes, epitomized hell in the nineteenth century, a result of the eternal recurrence of fashionable goods and characteristic of both dandy and flâneur: "Ennui is a warm, gray cloth, lined with the most glowing, most colorful silk fabric. We wrap ourselves in this cloth when we dream. We then feel at home in its arabesque lining. Yet the sleeper appears gray and bored under it. And when he awakes and wants to tell us what he has dreamed, this boredom is often all he can speak of. But who is able to turn at once the lining of time inside out? Yet this is exactly what the telling of one's dream means."[137] Thesis and antithesis as decoration and decay in the arcades, or represented as dream and change in modernity, and their respective "folding" (or revers-al) into a synthesis, had to be explored in Benjamin's project—not as a theoretical construct, but for the sophisticated interplay and poetic analogies that the diverse elements might create. Despite the obvious methodological influence of Marx and Engels, it appears that Benjamin, through his focus on fashion, adopted much from Simmel. We should therefore not be surprised when Benjamin states that "the motif of dialectics has to be realized in perspectives [on the city?], in luxury, and in fashion."[138]

For this concept, the tenth manuscript page provides an elaborate, albeit erratic, scheme:

■

*ENNUI*

*First analysis of the decay: Aragon*

| | | |
|---|---|---|
| *Dialectics of the commodity* | Magasins de nouveautés<br>*Failed [subject] matter* | *Theory of collecting<br>Commodity being elevated to the position of allegory]* |
| *Dialectics of sentimentality (Lines from "Traumkitsch"<br>   [Benjamin's gloss on Surrealism, ca. 1925])* | | *Archaeology of (x.).<br>   Dream is the ground in<br>   which things are found.* |
| *Dialectics of the* Flânerie *[the stroll of the flâneur]* | | *The interior as street<br>   (luxury)<br>The street as interior<br>   (misery)* |
| *Dialectics of fashion* | | *Lust and corpse* |
| *The beginning: Representation of today's arcades<br>Their dialectical development: Commodity/perspective<br>The actuality of the arcades in their dream structure* | | *Attempt to define the<br>   character of street<br>   names: no strict analogies<br>Mythological typography:<br>   Balzac* |

| *Thesis* | *Antithesis* |
|---|---|
| *The flowering of the arcades under<br>   Louis-Philippe* | *The decay of the arcades at the<br>   end of the XIX century* |

*Panoramas*                              *Plush*

*Department stores*                      *Failed [subject] matter*

*Love*                                   *Prostitute*

        *Synthesis*

        *Discovery of the arcades*

        *The unconscious knowledge of the past*

          *becomes conscious*

        *Law of awaking*

        *Dialectics of the perspective*

        *Dialectics of fashion*

        *Dialectics of sentimentality*

*Dioramas*

Plush-perspektive

*Rainy weather*[139]

▪

The arcades were firmly established as the stage for dialectical interplay. The materialist observation of the passing fashion from the glass-roofed walkways of the flâneur is seen as an indication of capitalism's constant need to re-dress the commodities. Not only does the appearance of the strolling men and women change with every season, but so does their commodified world in general. The decay of the arcades allows Benjamin to look on them as monads, because their impact is no longer immediate but is removed from the present. As standstills in time they can now be valued, because the "unconscious knowledge of the past becomes conscious" when the individual awakes—a view that contrasts with that of Aragon, who sees the arcade only in a poeticized dream state. The (almost Mallarméan) folding or synthesis of both the textual and visual material is sought, among other places, in the dialectics of fashion, "lust and corpse": fashion's erotic appeal and its imminent death when the next alluring style appears on the scene.

      Benjamin's sartorial metaphors developed, via historical observations, from the Proustian equation of text with *textum* to the paradigmatic value of fashion for *modernité* (echoing and continuing Baudelaire and Mallarmé), further exposing the inherent analogies between the two. A parallel epistemological progression lead him from symbolic and poetic evocation, psychoanalytic interpretation, and surrealist metaphors to the challenge fashion brought against historicism, and finally to the dialectical image and a historical-materialist critique. A more pronounced step toward the latter might have been taken in the completed *Arcades Project;* but it seems likely that such a step would not have been his last.

The précis on Paris of the nineteenth century, situated at an intermediary stage between the early manuscript sheaves and the late fragments on modernity and historicism, contained an observation that marked Benjamin's shift in emphasis toward historical-materialist finality:

■

*Corresponding in the collective consciousness to the forms of the new means of production, which at first were still dominated by the old (Marx), are images in which the new is intermingled with the old. These images are wishful fantasies, and in them the collective seeks both to preserve and to transfigure the inchoateness of the social product and the deficiencies in the social system of production. In addition, these wish-fulfilling images manifest an emphatic striving for dissociation with the outmoded—which means, however, with the most recent past. These tendencies direct visual imagination, which has been activated by the new, back to the primeval past. In the dream in which, before the eyes of each epoch, that which is to follow appears in images, the latter appears wedded to elements from prehistory, that is, of a classless society. Intimations of this, deposited in the unconscious of the collective, mingle with the new to produce the utopia that has left its traces in thousands of configurations of life, from permanent buildings to fleeting fashions.*[140]

■

This historical-materialist view of the folding together of past and present, of the ancient and the modern, made it necessary to analyze the commodity. Fashion, as the transient element that embodies modernity, is best equipped to integrate an archaic past into the most recent past and, in turn, into the present. It fuses the collective unconsciousness (mythic, though not necessarily in a Jungian sense) with the new, as well as with the fetish character of the commodity itself. The poetic element Benjamin sought to introduce into dialectics and its orthodox (i.e., socioeconomic) counterpart are woven together intricately.

In the third passage of the précis, titled "Grandville, or the World Exhibitions," Benjamin elaborates on the latter aspect: "World exhibitions are the sites of pilgrimages to the commodity fetish. . . . [They] glorify the exchange value of commodities. They create a framework in which commodities' intrinsic value is eclipsed. They open up a phantasmagoria that people enter to be amused."[141] Here Benjamin employs Marxist terminology to probe into the "mythic character" of the commodity. The sensibility toward this character derives, as the next chapter explains, from Benjamin's reading of surrealism. The dated object that is removed from its environment proper— as Grandville showed in his fantastic drawings—stands still, becomes isolated, and acquires *a dream potential* that ties it to the Freudian notion of the fetish.

Benjamin's observation on the "theologischen Mucken"[142]—the theological whims (or niceties) of the commodity—underscores that he himself considered its sociopolitical impact to stem not merely from economic formalism but from its elevation to an almost metaphysical level.

■

*The commodity is therefore a mysterious thing [Marx claimed in the first volume of* The Capital], *simply because in it the social character of men's labour appears to them as an objective character stamped upon the product of that labour; thus the social relationship between producers and the sum total of their own labour is presented to them as a social relation, existing not between themselves, but between the products of their labour. Because of this quid pro quo the products of their labour become commodities, social objects whose qualities are at the same time perceptible and imperceptible to the senses.*[143]

■

In contrast, the form of the commodity and the relation between the values of the labor product in which it is represented have no influence on the physical nature of the commodity and the objective relations resulting from it: "It is only the distinct social relation between people that assumes for them this phantasmagoric form of a relation between objects."[144] It is this form that takes on for Marx the character of a fetish, which originates in the peculiar social character of labor that produces the commodity. And this fetish in turn would for Benjamin determine the material character of modernity as such.

The *Arcades Project* must also be read as Benjamin's attempt to single out fashion as the one commodity that is better equipped than any other to transpose myths into objects, one that significantly covers the human body and thus acts as a symbol of a material civilization—as the original rite of passage. "Fashion prescribes the ritual according to which the commodity fetish is worshipped," states Benjamin.[145] It marks an antagonism to the organic, and thus to the subject, since materialism had substituted for the Kantian/Hegelian "man-nature" relation the relationship of "man/subject-commodity/object."

•

*Not the body but the corpse is the perfect object for [fashion's] practice. It protects the right of the corpse in the living. Fashion marries off the living to the inorganic. Hair and nails, midway between the inorganic and the organic, always have been subjected most to its action. Fetishism, succumbing to the sex appeal of the inorganic, is fashion's vital nerve. It is employed by the cult of the commodity. Fashion is sworn to the inorganic world. Yet, on the other hand, it is fashion alone that overcomes death. It incorporates the isolated [das Abgeschiedene] into the present. Fashion is contemporary to each past.*[146]

•

This analysis in the 1935 précis contains most of the elements left in their splintered, multireferential forms throughout the manuscript bundles. Emphatically, Benjamin points to the dialectical opposition of the inorganic and organic that is contained in clothes, a relation transformed poetically in the *Arcades Project* by imbuing the fetish with a connotation of the sexus (see again section 4.5 above). This dialectical relation in fashion is once more interwoven with the other—the incorporation of the most ancient into the latest sartorial style.

But the corollary implied is a problematic one. Benjamin inferred that because fashion is able to conquer death, it also leads the past into the present, thus becoming "la contemporaine de tout le monde" and of all its past epochs. It appears therefore as if two distinct parameters were applied: an ontological one relating to human existence, generated partly through Benjamin's reading of the mythic character of the commodity, and an epistemological one relating to the structure of history, developed from, and partly in opposition to, the orthodoxy of historical-materialist formulas. On a methodological level, this duality also accounts for the problematic relation between Benjamin's own design, the dialectical image, and the conventional look of dialectics in historical materialism. Ultimately, Benjamin would have had to attempt to integrate the two (provided he saw them as separate entities in the first place) into a coherent whole. Thus fashion was to be the ultimate catalyst for an integrated methodology of a completed *Arcades Project*.

## ■ 4.12 Death à la mode

Under the iron construction and glass roof of the arcades, "fashion has opened a dialectical emporium for exchange between woman and commodity. Death is its lanky and loutish shop assistant. He measures the century by the yardstick; in order to economize he also plays the mannequin and conducts the sale, which in French is called *révolution*. Because fashion was never anything but the parody of a colorful corpse, the manner in which woman provokes death, and a communion with decay that is bitterly whispered between loud and memorized cries of joy."[147] But when the tiger takes the dialectical leap, one would assume that the time he jumps back to should have more significance than a mere age of dilapidation and decay. Thus it seems as if Benjamin had sensed the incoherence in equating the fusion of the past into the present with the way in which fashion provokes death. The "Theses on the Philosophy of History," which he would develop from the end of 1939 on, attempted to substitute the hope inherent in a messianic past for the finality of death. Ultimately, perhaps, his dialectics could be proven under only the "open air of history" and not the overarched arcade, bound to decay. Yet in 1935 Benjamin already appeared close to a solution, embedded in the allegory of the exchange emporium because fashion as one element of the relationship is always dialectical in itself. Death plays the shop assistant for fashion and measures out time, or, as Benjamin had written in one of the earliest notes (1927), the interdependence can be reversed: "Death the dialectical central station: fashion the tempo."[148] In either case, be it thesis or antithesis, fashion carries death within itself. If an article becomes fashionable it is already deceased; what one perceives to be the latest cut, the most recent fad, is nothing but a dying echo of the actual innovation. Thus death, as the sales assistant, has to sell his new stock immediately after the last days of the "sale" of the old. There is no finality to this process, and perhaps no hope either. The messianic element in historical materialism, which for Benjamin would bring the classless society, must remain under ceaseless assault from capitalism's logic of prolonging its own life span by designing novel commodities and creating new markets for them.

In Simmel's essays fashion's mortality was explored in its relation to the Bergsonian *durée*. Benjamin would call in his studies preparatory to the Baudelaire essay for the acceptance of death as a purveyor of tradition, in order to counter the "negative infinitude" of *durée*.[149] Fashion's immanent death renders it infinitely transient and constantly moving. That quality explains why, as Simmel observed, "changes in fashion disrupt that inner process of acquisition and assimilation between subject and object which usually does not tolerate a discrepancy between the two."[150] This quotation is featured prominently in Benjamin's excerpts under the heading of fashion. Given the importance ascribed to the individual differentiation of subject and object within the Hegelian conception of dialectics, the dialectical "microcosm" in fashion thus develops into a guarantee for the survival of the methodological system as a whole.

As we have seen, for Simmel one imperative for the gestalt of modernity was the constant struggle of the subject to hold its position against ever-increasing objectification. Thus his emphasis on the dualism within fashion—as well as within art and culture in general—was designed to underline a similar distinction between subject and object. Benjamin employed the "dialectical image" for related reasons, though his concept of *modernité* originates more in poetry than in socioeconomic factors. In chapter 5 of the précis, titled "Baudelaire or The Streets of Paris," he characterized the city as a modern social substratum. For Baudelaire, he wrote, modernity is "a main focus of his poetry. With the spleen he dissipates the ideal ('Spleen et idéal'). Yet modernity always cites primeval history. Here it is realised through ambiguity which is particular to the social circumstances and products of this epoch. Ambiguity is the visual appearance of dialectics, the law of dialectics in standstill. This standstill is utopian and the dialectical image thus an oneiric one."[151] Merely to dream about utopia appears to be a pale substitute; yet when "each epoch dreams up the following"—as he, following Michelet's dictum, was convinced it had to, for poetic as well as for political reasons—the phantasmagoric aspect in looking back at the commodity became as potent as concerted action.

In visualizing modernity, in Baudelaire's poetry as well as in dialectics, Benjamin also wanted to free his points of reference from the confines of their respective historical interpretations. As he found visual expressions for the concepts he meant to discuss, previous one-dimensional reading was superseded and became part of a transitory process—a powerful aid to the interpretation of *modernité* itself.

## ■ 4.13 Consumption, Redemption, or Revolution?

Adorno, the first to receive the 1935 précis, concentrated in his criticism on the dialectical image, as he saw both its potential and the pitfalls in its misinterpretation. Under the premise that no analysis can be separated into "material and epistemological questions,"[152] thereby assuring himself of Benjamin's assent concerning dialectics, Adorno claimed that Michelet's motto represented a crystallization of all the motifs that he regarded as *undialectical* within the theory of the dialectical image. Implicit in this motto, which Benjamin had favored from the beginning, Adorno saw a threefold conception:

■

*[T]he view of the dialectical image as a content of a consciousness, albeit a collective one; its linear, I am tempted to say ontogenetic, reference to the future as utopia; the conception of the "epoch" as the pertinent, self-contained subject of the content of consciousness. I think it highly significant that in this version of the dialectical image, which can be called an immanent one, not only is the original theological force*

*of the concept threatened and a simplification introduced that does not attack the subjective nuance but the truth content itself—but, because of this, precisely the social movement within contradiction is forfeited, for the sake of which you sacrifice theology.*[153]

∎

To position the dialectical image as "dream" within human consciousness implied for Adorno not only disenchantment and a misleading accessibility, but more significantly the loss of "the objective key-potential," which could have legitimized the term materialistically. "The fetish character of the commodity is not a fact of consciousness itself, but it is dialectical in the preeminent sense of producing consciousness."[154] This in turn meant that the fetish character is not pictured by consciousness (or the unconscious) as a dream, but has to be approached with both "desire and anxiety." As the dialectical image takes immanent form, the fetish character loses its dialectical potential. What surrounds the fetish character is reduced to the Saint-Simonian conception of the world of commodities as utopia, but does not account for its reverse—the hell of nineteenth-century capitalism.

The stringency, perhaps even orthodoxy, of dialectics and the dialectical image in Benjamin's discourse became Adorno's main concern. He argued in his letter, as we have seen, that to understand a commodity, specifically a garment or accessory, as a dialectical image means to understand it "as the motif of its own demise and 'abolition,' instead of regarding it as a pure regression to the old."[155] The commodity is an alienated object, with no further use for the subject; but alienated, it surpasses the immediacy of its use value. Thus it becomes "immortal," not through eternal recurrence but by becoming a fetish.

It was obvious to Benjamin that the sole commodity that offers both "regression" to the old, or rather a retracing of history, and "immortality" was sartorial fashion. The recourse to the old, to what has passed, is by no means only regression—in Adorno's negative use of the word—though Benjamin's metaphor of the child and the mother's dress might evoke this psychological aspect. It also exemplifies the attempt to ignite the explosive potential that lies within fashion—which always refers back to the past. Moreover, fashion's immortality is of a particular kind, as it instantly dies when picked up by society and becomes resurrected at the very next moment in order to restart the cycle.

Although Adorno questions Benjamin's view of the fetish commodity, he readily accepts the paradigmatic value that fashion has in this context. In the letter in which he outlined the critique of the dialectical image, he also appraised Benjamin's interpretation of fashion.

∎

*The reference to fashion seems extremely significant to me, but in its structure should be separated from the concept of the organic and related to the living, i.e. not relating to a preconceived notion of "nature." Also, I have thought of the term "Changeant," the shiny and shot fabric, which has expressive significance for the nineteenth century and is obviously bound to industrial processes. Perhaps you could follow this up. Frau Hessel, whose reports in the F[rankfurter] Z[eitung] we always read with great interest, is sure to know all about it.*[156]

∎

Adorno is referring to the point in the précis at which Benjamin singled out fashion's immortality as well as its ability to incorporate the past into the present. A closer reading of fashion's character, as defined by Benjamin, would have already presented Adorno with an interpretation he had sought for the commodity in general. Regarding the distinction between the organic ("a preconceived notion of nature") and the living, one must remember two things: first, ever since Baudelaire (indeed, since Balzac) it has been precisely the artificial aspect of the living that is emphasized by fashion; and second, the (sartorial) object has to relate to nature, because Kant's original subject-object relation, on which Hegel, Simmel, and the rest based their evaluation of fashion's role in modernity, is precisely the juxtaposition of human and nature.

Adorno has reason to insist that the fetish character of the commodity had to be substantiated by quotes from "the person who discovered it."[157] He means of course Marx, who had composed in 1857/1858 his first *Introduction (to the Critique of the Political Economy),* which would prepare the ground for the first edition of *The Capital* in 1867. In this introduction, the definition of the dialectical still relates in essence back to Hegel.[158] Insofar as it pertains to the commodity, it is marked by "production" and "consumption"; its identity is based on a postulate by Spinoza, "[omnis] determinatio est negatio"—that is, each term requires the respective other for its definition.[159] Marx writes, "Production is thus directly consumption, consumption is directly production. Each is immediately its opposite. At the same time, however, a mediating movement takes place between the two."[160] Production mediates the consumption for which it provides the material; otherwise, the latter would have no object. But consumption also mediates production, in creating a subject for which it can produce in the first place. Without production there is no consumption, so much is obvious; but without consumption there cannot be any production either, as there would be no buyers. To a discussion on fashion within Benjamin's *Passagenarbeit,* the next passage in the *Introduction* becomes particularly relevant:

▪

*Consumption produces production in two ways. (1) In that only through consumption does a product become a real product. For example a dress becomes really a dress only by being worn[;] . . . in other words, a product as distant from the mere natural object manifests itself as a product, becomes a product, only in consumption. It is only consumption that, by dissolving the product, gives it the finishing stroke, for [the result of] production is a product not merely an objectified activity, but only as an object for the active subject.*[161]

▪

Adorno had reservations about Benjamin's dictum on fashion in the précis, but from a dialectical viewpoint fashion appears paradigmatic indeed. The "product," which is nothing but the subsequent commodity, is defined through its opposition to the "mere natural object"; therefore it appears as inorganic. But it is not quite inorganic (yet), since Marx maintains that it is only through the act of wearing—the living adorns itself with the inorganic—that the dress actually becomes a dress proper. Consumption, which is also the dissolution of the sartorial, its "death," and appears as a social action that determines the subject, adds the finishing touch (or "finishing stroke," as Marx put it in English in the German original). The organic thus accepts the inorganic; and fashion, as Benjamin maintained in the précis, "mediates" between them: between production and consumption and therefore, on a different level, also between fetish commodity and individual, between (inactive) object and (active) subject.[162]

The initially sensuous and poetic relationship with fashion that Benjamin had sought to describe toward the end was replaced by an emphasis on materialist thought. As the *Arcades Project* progressed, his original conception of describing the myths and phantasmagoria in terms of artistic creation in and of the nineteenth century—from Baudelaire and Mallarmé to Proustian and surrealist remembrance—inevitably directed him toward a notion of modernity with all its sociopolitical implications. The subsequent analysis of those implications began to take over the construction of the "arcades," into which subsequently Marx and the conception of the dialectical image entered, to guide Benjamin toward a social critique and a new concept of history itself.

Each step (or rather flânerie?) inside the arcades was visualized and can be traced through the analysis of sartorial fashion. Whether Benjamin had planned to isolate this image alone as paradigmatic for his "prehistory" of the nineteenth century is open to debate. The incomplete transitoriness of the *Arcades Project* aligns itself with fashion. Much as it is impossible to propose a single reading of Benjamin's unfinished work, so each facet of fashion opens itself up to a number of interpretations, thereby strengthening rather than diminishing its significance.

In the last stages of the work, the essence of Benjamin's methodological approach was captured in his concept of the dialectical image. Its foremost example became the tiger's leap taken by fashion. Whether there was to be a logical progression to the "open air of history" to allow the tiger to take the dialectical leap that would result in revolution, or the open air was meant to be a transient, utopian concept that would lead toward a messianic redemption, the significance of the leap is the same, lying in its poetic and provocative idea. What remains is the form in which all fashion survives and which establishes the *Tigersprung* as the beginning: "Mode ist zündende, Erkenntnis erlöschende Intention," wrote Benjamin before 1927 in his first notes to the "Parisian Arcades" from which the project would grow—"Fashion is an ignited intention, cognition an extinguished one."[163]

5

**The Imagination of** Fashion in Modernity

*Non merci, j'ai l'heure. Est-ce qu'il y a longtemps que vous êtes enfermé dans cette cage?*
*L'adresse de votre tailleur est ce qu'il me faut.*

*André Breton and Philippe Soupault (1920)*[1]

After analyzing fashion's epistemological character, its aesthetic experience, and, in the previous chapter, its "revolutionary" (i.e., political) impetus, I will now conclude with an account of how fashion is employed artistically, as a *metaphor*, as a simulacrum for the human figure and the human character.[2]

In dada and early surrealism, this metaphor became a very potent stylistic element. The late nineteenth century had used clothes symbolically, to represent beauty, open or repressed sexuality, social aspiration, or moral deviation. The human body or mind was shaped by or characterized through dressing. This perception changed with the pronounced reification and commodification that occurred in the early twentieth century. For modern artists, clothing thus was on par with personality in describing a human character. The suit or dress stood for man or woman in the abstract. Often, however, because of increasing alienation in a materialist society, it stood in for him or her.

The empty sartorial shell showed the disembodied, disempowered human; it was representative of a face in the crowd who could not be known and thus had to be judged by his or her appearance. "We are not interested in you as a person," Breton and Soupault seem to declare in the epigraph above, which is taken from their early automatic writing; "what we need is an insight into your clothing—we need the address of your tailor." Because of its tradition in modernity, which the previous chapters have traced, clothing had acquired its own significance, its own definition, its own modus operandi. Therefore clothes, not their owners, could be seen to act out the visual and verbal plays devised by dada and early surrealism. The notion of the (sartorial) shell works as a stylistic device because the fashion depicted or described is not real but *imagined*. It exists first and foremost in the mind of the artist. The more ideally or generically the garments were styled, the more effectively they could be used as metaphors. At the same time, however, the clothing had to be recognizable as particular sartorial items in order to be "understood" by the beholder or spectator; otherwise, the artists could not challenge or subvert their context. Thus these clothes needed to remain material in part, needed to be perceived also as commodities. Yet the dadaists and surrealists imbued them with a "magic" that springs from the perception of everyday objects in a way that is alien to their purpose proper. This process becomes more intricate in clothing, as the garments do not exist as separate entities—as do, for example, objects placed on a table—but normally would be seen on the acting subject (and moving with him or her). Separating or removing them from their usual context thus requires an even greater mental effort; as a result, their alienation is more complete and the sartorial objects become even stranger, even more mysterious.

The separation or removal occurs not only physically but temporally as well. The dadaists and surrealists did not simply invent garments but *quoted* traditional styles of clothing and *mythologized* them—that is, removed them from their time and had them occur as dated fashion on the streets of contemporary Paris. Thus the approach to claim the sartorial as a metaphor is twofold: it relies both on the imagined fashion removed and alienated from its wearer and on the imagined fashion taken from the past and embedded in a modern mythology.

The interpretation of clothes and accessories and their metaphoric use also shows how artists employed the various concepts of sartorial fashion as a paradigm of modernity—from Baudelaire and Mallarmé to Simmel. And it anticipates some of the

**58.**
Hannah Höch, *Da-dandy,* 1919. Collage on paper, 30 × 24 cm. Private collection, Berlin.

Benjaminian methodology in that it intuitively singles out the revolutionary potential within fashion's quotation from the past. For the Da-dandies and for some of the dandyfied surrealists, fashion carried, via the quote, a historical index that they used to evoke the substructures beneath society. The removal of nineteenth-century sartorial items from their context, their alienation from reality, and their transfer into the realm of the mysterious and imaginary create a shift in how these items are perceived. This shift in turn brings independence, which then prepares the sartorial to become a perfectly fitting metaphor.

This preference for the clothes imagined is something we all share. In principle, garments exist to perform a number of simple functions. They may protect, veil, or adorn. They provide shelter from heat or cold; they give dignity and social status to their wearer. We might observe these garments on others or on ourselves. Yet they will never seem like the ones we think about, write about, dream about. When we see clothes draped around the body of a person in the street or that of a mannequin, we will wonder how they might look on us. When we possess them, we want to improve their appearance through various combinations or alterations, provided we have not already grown tired of them.

Accordingly, a piece of clothing may be functional, representative, or decorative; however, it is never representative of *fashion* in its purest sense. Beyond the masquerade of vagaries and passing fads, fashion strives for an ideal, an abstract quality in itself. Although the idea expressed by the word "fashion" differs greatly within different contexts, it always denotes the imaginary and nonexistent or sets the existing in contrast to an ideal. The reality of a garment or accessory is invariably seen in relation to what is imagined to be the most practical, dignified, or aesthetically pleasing. Fashion can thus be described as a composition made, on the one hand, out of clothes that actually exist and form part of a person's appearance and, on the other hand, out of abstract garments—that is, those not really worn but seen on the catwalk, in a magazine, or in a shop window—that fulfill a certain norm or become part of a specific dress code.

Our idea of sartorial fashion might be based on economic circumstances (the fashion industry), on aesthetic considerations (what "looks good"), or on sociological observations (what is worn at a certain time, in a certain place). We arrive at this concept through personal observation or with the help of the media. But fashion's inherent transitoriness will always defy its definition proper. The moment we think we have found an explanation for its erratic behavior, it has passed us by and taken on a different look or form. We might learn what constituted a manner of dressing in the past and inquire into its relation to the present, but to grasp the transcendent and fugitive quality within this particular cultural expression, we are always left speculating about its changing future shape.

This "ahistoricality," which arises because old clothes are constantly revived through quotation and because dated dress acquires dream potential, determines the passage from Benjamin to the metaphoric use of garments in dada and early surrealism. The connection was created through a book by the nineteenth-century illustrator Grandville, titled *Un Autre Monde* (*Another World*), which was partly viewed as the phantasmagoric pendant to Guys's illustrations. In this chapter we see how the book mocks fashion's urge to quote from the past and to dream up future aesthetics, but also how it imagines a new and irrational dress code. Benjamin relates Grandville's manner of quoting to the surrealist fascination with the dated and to its definition of a modern mythology. From *Un Autre Monde* a clearly visible thread runs through to the imagination of poet-flâneurs like Louis Aragon, who distilled from this dated fashion, seen in the Parisian streets and arcades, metaphors to be used in the poetic quest to describe modernity.

The earliest poetry of Aragon's friend Breton provides another approach to the passage from a symbolic view to the metaphoric usage of clothing. Here it is explored through the influence of the (pre)dadaist dandy Jacques Vaché. Breton turned Mallarméan beginnings, clothes designed to dress the soul, into a contemporary perception of *mode et modernité:* fashion as a metaphor for emotional life, while at the same time removed from the living and thus objectified. The nihilist irony of dandies like Vaché would become one of the most effective weapons in dada's arsenal for undermining aesthetic and social structures. This irony expresses itself clearly in the hyperbolic elegance of the dandy's dressing.

As this chapter also deals with garments as described in the writings of the dadaists and early surrealists, I begin with a short excursus on the concept of a written fashion, which precedes concepts of ideal, ironic, and imaginary fashion. This detour might be applicable also to the earlier descriptions of clothes by Baudelaire, Gautier, or Mallarmé. These artists strove, however, for a poetic evocation of actual and existing fashion that could mirror the rhythm of modernity. The twentieth-century writers are interested in not the particular article of clothing or a certain style, but the interplay between the sartorial and language, between the abstraction of clothes or accessories and their subsequent poetic value.

## ■ 5.1 Fashion Written V

In fashion the sublime (and often sublimated) ideal exists as a residue. While the patina of an artwork may well contribute to its standing, the transient character of fashion makes us look forever toward change and requires constant adaption to newly established yet often unspoken laws. Any possible paradigmatic value is literally worn off; and whereas the moral code of a particular society enables us to appreciate an earlier art form, a glance back at fashion reveals it only as outdated and old-fashioned, never "sublime" or "ideal" in a classical or humanist sense.[3] "One just wouldn't wear that today," we say;[4] and it is precisely the physical element in clothes, their interdependence with the human body, that seems to defy any analysis of fashion, any systematic attempt to explain the phenomenon.

Therefore Barthes, in his book on the "fashion system," resorts to the structuralist analysis of the piece of clothing as *described,* as written about: "only written clothing has no practical or aesthetic function: it is entirely constituted with a view to a signification."[5] Barthes intends to present, through the semantics of fashion journalism, a coherent explanation of how a garment constitutes itself; "we might say, then, that the being of a written garment resides completely in its meaning. . . . [W]ritten clothing is unencumbered by any parasitic function and entails no vague temporality."[6] Can we thus assume that when fashion is written about, it loses its transitoriness, seemingly the main obstacle to our complete understanding of it? One must appreciate that Barthes aims at establishing a coherent system. But the nonexistence of a "temporalité floue" means the loss of the hermeneutical potential within fashion, as postulated by Simmel and Benjamin. Their analysis of an abstract fashion, whether one prefers to call it sociological or philosophical, regards the past as a reference for future fashion, in which the outmoded becomes inseparably bound to the not yet fashionable. Real clothing, as seen on the streets of Berlin or Paris, presented for them not an "obstacle," to be explained (away) through an analysis of the "vêtement écrit," but merely an outer appearance of the spirit in fashion, which regards the existing as prehistory to another adaptation of the past.

In Simmel and Benjamin, research into language is important insofar as language provides the source for the fashion material; but it can never exclusively constitute fashion's materiality. However, in Barthes's search for the best corpus to supply a description of fashion, he deliberately avoided literature, since "descriptions from literature proper, although important in a number of great authors (Balzac, Michelet, Proust), are too fragmentary, too variable historically to be of use."[7] The semantic concentration in Barthes's particular way of writing about fashion would thus limit the troubling idiosyncrasies of historic and personal stylistics.

So far I have attempted to join as closely as possible literature and visual art forms in my analysis of fashion—not because the established context of "high art" might lend gravitas to the ephemeral but, quite to the contrary, because fashion's importance reveals itself not only in the fragmentary, as a paradigmatic mode of modernity, but also in the frequency with which it influenced and shaped the œuvre of artists such as Balzac, Michelet, and Proust (to be sure, such a claim is truer of nineteenth-century Parisian society than anywhere else). What concerns us, in Barthes's own words, is the question: "What happens when an object, whether real or imaginary, is converted into language? or rather, when an object encounters language?" In our case fashion (or part of it) provides the object, and its—at times fortuitous—encounter with language functions on the same level as the rapport established between reality and literature: "[I]sn't literature the institution which seems to convert the real into language and place its being in that conversion, just like our written garment?"[8]

It is interesting to see how much more intricate this conversion becomes when the subject of literature is (as, e.g., in Mallarmé's *La Dernière Mode*) fashion itself. The meaning of dress lies in its description, while the importance of literature rests on the skillful rendering of reality into words. However, this reality appeared to exist only outside the folio pages of the magazine, where Mallarmé's fashion was an ideal, imaginary one: a "reality" he dreamed about and evoked by designing a riding habit in prose (see section 2.4.7), making a perfect fashion that could not be worn, even if a couturière had attempted to faithfully follow the poet's instructions. The implicit vagueness of the poetic description corresponded with the necessary transitoriness of the subject.

Herein lies the importance of fashion for literature, indeed for all art forms: because the quest for perfection must be manifest in the imaginary, as no one can hope to achieve it within a context that by definition has to change constantly, it follows that fashion is at its most perfect in art and art is at its most evocative in attempting to celebrate fashion, to "design" or echo a written piece of clothing. "And since Fashion is a phenomenon of initiation," adds Barthes, "speech [*parole*] naturally fulfills a didactic function: the Fashion text represents as it were the authoritative voice of someone who knows all there is behind the jumbled or incomplete appearance of the visible forms; thus, it constitutes a technique of opening the invisible, where one could almost rediscover, in secular form, the sacred halo of divinatory texts."[9] It seems as if someone who talks or writes about fashion "knows everything," even the unconscious process that leads to fashion's appearance. Considered retrospectively, many artists appear to have been aware of the social and aesthetic implications fashion could have for humanity. Their use of a "technique of opening the invisible," of exploring the hidden mechanisms and myths within modern society, closely corresponds with the aim of the surrealists, who hoped that the revelation of the dream state—like what we have observed in Proustian remembrance[10]—could help explain an underlying pattern of creativity, or even creation itself, and thus add the most essential of experiences to human existence. The trigger mechanism that would inspire this exploration of the mythic was to be found in fashion's relation to the past.

## ■ 5.2  Benjamin on Grandville and Surrealism: *The Clothes of Five Years Ago*

The flâneur saunters through the arcades, preferably at night when the gaslights illuminate the shop windows and the ephemeral objects behind the plate glass take on a mystical life of their own. Outside their everyday context, these garments, canes, ties, or umbrellas transcend what is merely factual and become charged with dream potential. They enter the unconscious. The places where they are found, the arcades, are no longer the grand overarched streets of the nineteenth century, filled with luxury commodities and exclusive bars. When Aragon—and later Benjamin—visit them, they possess only a shadow of their former appeal. Yet it is precisely this replacement of the fashionable with reminiscence and remembrance, this shift from reality to myth and imagination, that fascinated poet and philosopher alike.

Benjamin said that his discussion of surrealism constituted an "opaque folding screen placed before the arcades project";[11] it provided not only some of the cultural criteria he was to assemble in his *Arcades Project* but also an exemplary study in critique that veiled more comprehensive intentions. Benjamin's interest can be traced back to 1925,[12] the year after the publication of Breton's first manifesto; it culminated in his 1929 essay "Surrealism: The Last Snapshot of the European Intelligentsia."[13] Commenting on eroticism and the female in surrealist literature (essentially guided by the example of Breton's Nadja), he found that the writer's interest was more directed toward objects than toward the human being: "What are the things she [the female] is close to? Nothing can reveal more about Surrealism than their canon. But where to begin? It has to pride itself in the most amazing discovery." This discovery would correspond very closely indeed with Benjamin's own objective: "It [surrealism] first came across the revolutionary potential that appear in the 'outmoded,' in the first iron constructions [e.g., arcades, locomotives], in the first factory buildings, in early photography, in the objects which are just becoming extinct, the grand pianos, the clothes of five years ago."[14] The sartorial shell, especially after it has undergone a temporal alienation, becomes more important than the human being who might wear it. "Surrealism's potential," as Benjamin wrote in an earlier note for his essay, lay in the manner in which the "enormously tense configurations of the collective that are expressed in fashion can be rendered in service of the revolution."[15]

The collective imagination does not necessarily create fashion, but it is able to determine and accept its impact. The congruences and diversities hidden within the social fabric become apparent in textiles and accessories. Observing them, the historian is able to realize the "revolutionary potential" in a more direct manner, while the artist can employ them as metaphors for another reality. The objectified and increasingly nonobjective world of the commodity that was portrayed by the French poets and artists—in a manner similar to that in the *Passagenarbeit*—appears not merely as the (necessary) evil within modern society, but as a collection of simulacra for the human mind and body. And closest to that body are of course clothes, determined by fashion. Yet they are not observed at the very moment of their desired existence, that is, when worn, but in poetic remembrance, as transient elements that paraphrase the body. The dialectics within the latest fashion, which is always generated through the past, provide an epistemological analogy to the "fortuitous encounter" of different objects on an "unsuitable plane" that was postulated by the surrealists[16]—whereby differences are much more likely to be found in an evocation of the mythic than in actual appearances.

"Thus the new is always the predominant factor, but only where it appears in the medium of the oldest, most familiar, of what lies furthest in the past," wrote Benjamin on the remnants of and repercussions in the Parisian society of the nineteenth century.[17] Here Benjamin alludes to the significant link that lies at the basis of his writing—a link between the past and present imagination, between the nineteenth century and his own time, between dated illustrations and surrealist art. The link is expressed in fashion—in the dialectics of fashion, to be precise:

■

*The drama of how the respectively latest forms itself within this medium of the past constitutes fashion's dialectical drama proper. Only in this way, as a grand manifestation of the dialectical, can we hope to understand the strange books by Grandville, which created a furor around the middle of the century: when he presents a new fan as "éventail d'Iris" and his latest design depicts a rainbow; when the Milky Way is shown as a nocturnal avenue, illuminated by gas candelabra; when the "moon, painted by herself" rests on fashionable plush cushions instead of clouds. Only then does one begin to appreciate that in this most somber, most unimaginative of centuries, the entire dream potential of a society had to flee with doubled speed into the impenetrable, soundless, and misty realm of fashion where the intellect could not follow suit. Fashion is the predecessor—no, the eternal stand-in of surrealism.*[18]

■

The particular style of a dress allows direct access to the past. Through its reference or its quotation it conjures up forgotten dreams of beauty. The once fashionable world with its sartorial fantasies can thus feature in the arts of the present.

Grandville is well chosen as an early example of fashion's transhistorical character. The images that Benjamin describes can be found in *Un Autre Monde*, Grandville's most famous book, published in Paris in 1844.[19] It contains a tour de force through man's imagination, evoking a fantastic world that belongs in equal parts to past, present, and future. The protagonists are three men, who declare themselves "néo-dieux" (thus fitting for Barthes's description of the omniscient writer of divinatory texts) and who explore the "other world" beyond reality. That world, however, appears strangely real and familiar, distinguishing itself by means of the fashion of Grandville's contemporary Paris. In a thinly yet beautifully disguised parable on the Parisian beau monde, one of the (time) travelers spends "a day in Rheculanum," in a classical urban society, where the dress code is portrayed as a fashionable mixture of antique hairstyles, footwear, and postures, coupled with the mid-nineteenth-century clothing of lion and tigresse: fitted waistcoats on bare torsos, velvet dressing gowns worn in the café, and embroidered muslin dresses revealing neck and shoulders covered in *poudre de riz*. On his arrival, the "new god" is greeted by a young man who delivers a concise manifesto of Rheculanum's underlying philosophy:

■

*The clime before you, o beloved mortal of Jupiter, is called antiquity; tradition is cultivated peacefully here, far away from those who want to exploit, comment on, annotate, or expurgate it. Past and present merge here in pleasant alliance. Our task is to show how all the rings of the chain of tradition are linked together, and how the new*

**59.**

Grandville, *A Day at Regulanum: In the Foyer of the Theater* (illustration for *Un Autre Monde*), 1844. Lithograph, 11.7 × 12.7 cm.

*form is bound to the old; we enliven modernity through its contact with antiquity. If
you happen to be familiar with philosophical language, I can tell you that our life is a
progressive and permanent palingenesis.*[20]

■

A complex view indeed, anticipating both Baudelaire and Benjamin! History and fashion are both made up of cycles. They undergo a palingenesis: a spiritual transfer, as well
as the appearance of characteristics from phylogenic ancestors in the course of individual evolution. Yet they remain permanent in their dialectical configuration of
modernity and antiquity—*l'esprit moderne* in intimate contact with *l'esprit antique.*
Moreover, the initiation of the protagonist into this society worked sartorially: "Behold," the young guide advised his visitor, "the attire you are wearing does not sufficiently link the past and the present for it to conform to tradition."[21]

     The importance of the dated quote for this curious society is shown, as the
"néo-dieu" soon discovers, by adopting a tragic muse. In particular, the rape of Lucre-
tia, "the innocent and guilty spouse," has been dramatically revived.[22] When the protagonist ventures to enter the couture house of Mlle Aspasia on the forum,[23] in order
to pay his compliments to the head of the house, all disciples of the "temple"—that is,
all seamstresses and *premières,* equipped with scissors, spindles, and pairs of com-
passes—threatened to stab themselves to death publicly should he dare to desecrate
their sanctuary still further. Apart from needling at the salons of the couturières re-
served so exclusively for the female, her taste and fashion, Grandville thus creates a sophisticated but ironic frame of references around the classical mode.

     The early 1840s, when *Un Autre Monde* was created, saw the beginning of the
"crinolinization" of fabrics. Flannel, silk, cashmere, and so on were carefully interwoven with horsehair, to make them stiff and protruding. An increasing number of *volants*
were added to skirts and thus a development was introduced that would find its (most)
ridiculous culmination in the tightest corsets and broadest crinolines of the second half
of the 1860s.[24] Grandville counterbalances the beginning of this restrictive progress
by alluding to the classical fashion of the Directoire, which existed from 1795 well into
the first decade of the nineteenth century (though the actual political "directoire exé-
cutif" of five equal members itself lasted only from 1795 to 1799). After the French

**60.**

Grandville, *A Day at Regulanum: Unsociable Lucretias Threaten Suicide if I Come a Step Closer* (illustration for *Un Autre Monde*), 1844. Colored lithograph, 7.8 × 15.3 cm.

Revolution the waistline of the dress had moved to a new height just under the bust; flowing fabrics such as muslin, batiste, poplin, and even percale were tailored to almost transparent chemises. Light tunics and the *Caraco tablier* had been cut off at the knee and were worn over a toga slit at the front.[25] Garments consciously re-created the antique ideal of a society full of republican virtues. Yet in Jacques-Louis David's painting of Napoleon's coronation (1804), one already begins to detect a change in the dresses of Josephine and her ladies-in-waiting, which had been designed by Leroy and Mme Raimbaud. The fabrics had become less transparent and the sleeves were now puffy and decorated with lace. Soon afterward a "medieval" lace collar was added to the rather low neckline, while the skirt became shorter. Fashion subsequently moved via a rococo revival toward the Romantic mode. Around 1820 the waistline reached its "natural" position again, and *la ceinture Maria Stuart* had the bodice end in a point. The year 1832 saw the establishment of the first corset factory in Bar-le-Duc, and by 1845 the skirt was as voluminous as ever, brushing the floor.

Thus by the time of Grandville's book, the change within female fashion throughout the first decades of the nineteenth century had traversed history: from classical antiquity through medieval times to the fifteenth and sixteenth centuries. The fantastic reintroduction of dresses echoing (and mocking) the Directoire in *Un Autre Monde* brought the transient cycle back to the time of its author's childhood. Grandville had history repeat itself, and the rather pessimistic ending of the book (titled "The End of One and the Other World"), when the three new gods find themselves reunited, shows a disenchantment with the artful, the fantastic, and, ultimately, the fashionable:

.

*"After having based glory on material success, one naturally had to base art on fashion."*

*"Also, fashion still reigns undivided. Muscardins, incroyables, dandies, fashionable folk, lions, have succeeded each other without weakening its power in the least. The same absurdities still exist in different guise.*

*"The tailors,*

*"The shoemakers,*

*"The tie salesmen,*

*"The corset makers,*

*"The seamstresses,*

*"The purveyors of waistcoats,*

   *"are executors of fashion's sublime works. Feminine dictator, absolute monarch, it leads a procession of henchmen and executioners. Today everybody is more or less its victim."*

   *"Clothes no longer make the man, since there are no simple men, but it rather makes the solicitor, the barrister, the advocate, the member of parliament, the peer, the minister."*

   *"Tell me who your tailor is, and I will tell you who you are."*[26]

■

One wonders whether this would prompt Breton and Soupault's later wish to learn of the bespoke tailor's address.

   The critique of the ephemeral and transient, which force humans into constant adaptation and render true (i.e., by definition eternal or humanist) values hard to appreciate, indicates Grandville's weariness toward civilization. The images in *Un Autre Monde* became a satire on the Parisian vanity fair of luxury goods, modish distractions, and escapist vagaries. Yet the succession of fashions that provided the artist with material for his "collage" of history were far more successful in evoking underlying ideas and concepts that an introspective list of historical facts ever could be. Without the rapid change of sartorial fashion in the space of a mere five decades, Grandville could not have hoped to make his artful irony work. As paradigm of modernity, fashion was for him much more inspiration than impediment. Like Baudelaire (as well as Gautier and others), Grandville was ready to embrace the ephemeral in *modernité* in order to create an aesthetic framework that could in turn serve as basis for a modernist critique of bourgeois society and its escapist distractions. Half a century later, his erstwhile artistic positivism turned into the attacks on art by the dadaists, who mockingly threw dated clothing styles together in their masqueraded performances. The early surrealists, in contrast, glanced back to appreciate the imaginary potential in Grandville's fantasies on fashion. Like Grandville, separately quoting individual garments in *Un Autre*

**61.**

Grandville, *Fashion* (illustration for *Un Autre Monde*), 1844. Colored lithograph, 18.4 × 14.1 cm.

*The volatile character she is, fashion as "la souveraine de tout le monde" spins the wheel of fortune to decide which style to quote, which garment to revive next. A coterie of male dandies looks on admiringly. According to Grandville's illustration, the year 1992 would have seen the revival of the Jacobin cap of the French Revolution. The artist's prophecy was only slightly incorrect: it was to be 1989 (the bicentenary of the Revolution) when the summer collection by Jean-Paul Gaultier prominently featured this very cap.*

*Monde,* they dissociated the sartorial item from its purpose and turned it into a metaphor.

If the "néo-dieux," as a satirical version of the omniscient narrator, actually stood for Grandville's dissatisfaction with the superficial and represented his longing for the eternal and sublime, it follows that the artist himself attempted to put deeper meaning into his depictions of clothes. Accordingly, just before establishing the relationship between Grandville and surrealism in the quote discussed above, Benjamin credits Grandville with *abstracting* fashion so that it transcended the natural law of cause and effect: "Grandville's masking of nature—of the cosmos as well as of fauna and flora—in the spirit of the midcentury fashion, makes history, in the figure of fashion, evolve from the eternal cycle of nature."[27]

## ■ 5.3 *Mythe et mode*

If fashion emerges from the eternal cycle determined by natural law, and thus positions itself outside the historical narrative, it may possess valuable potential for hermeneutics. Yet we cannot expect to ascertain historical facts merely from looking at clothes. This is not to say that no factual investigation is possible; but fashion will always remain too transient and ephemeral to simply explain historic causality—though its changes are very often anticipated.[28] Obviously, a sartorial style at, for example, a certain point in the nineteenth century might be regarded as a reflection of contemporary society. But because of its transcendent autonomy it can never be seen as simply mirroring that society; instead, it projects forward.

Therefore it is not the complexity of fashion in the abstract that will reveal cultural processes to us. We need to concentrate further on its objectification; "We need a concrete, materialist focus on the things closest to us," as Benjamin demands.[29] Once again, the curious ambiguity of the revolutionary and the messianic surfaces: for Benjamin, only the object that is liberated from historical continuity and thus approaches the realm of the mythic and surreal is suited to reveal the revolutionary potential that is independent from its cultural framework. Yet this object, if sartorial, also must reflect the social circumstances of its creation by repeatedly referring to its own past.

The perception Benjamin and the surrealists had of the last century was not always distanced enough for them to gather the complementary pieces needed for an overall interpretation. Thus they, too, had to bow to the impressions that the object close to them was ready to reveal, hoping that by learning from its myth they could free some of its subversive and poetic power. They liked to concentrate on the (sartorial) fragment in order to stimulate their imagination. Their choice of how to view its possible meaning—through the lens of literature or of metaphysics—was open, and indeed the difference may be only a matter of semantics. Benjamin writes: "'Mythology,' as Aragon put it, moves things once again away from us. Only the explanation of the congenial and conditional is important. The nineteenth century is, as the surrealists said, the sound that intervenes in our dreams, which we interpret in awakening."[30] Here, Benjamin appears not to appreciate Aragon and seems to discard mythology too readily. Otherwise, what are those sounds within our dreams—the "turned-down collars" of the past century, as Proust had called them? They are the myths that have to be deciphered, yet quite different from the legends of an ancient time that were transcribed to serve a moral purpose. They are a part of a *modern mythology,* eternalizing the ephemeral, and lending it hermeneutic and poetic justice. As we will see, the myth frees an object like the mannequin from the normative and evolutionary confines of historicism and endows it with subversive power, a power that complements the transient beauty of the clothes that adorn it.

The *Arcades Project* had to deal with the awakening from the nineteenth century,[31] and Benjamin felt that surrealism's interpretation of dreams remained somewhat sleepy and imprecise. This view, which at first appears too simplistic, becomes valuable in light of the divergence between surrealism and dada. It hints, veiled and retrospective as it is, at the poetic shortcomings that would impede surrealism's feel for modernity: a feeling that must remain at the core of any analysis of contemporary society aiming to venture beyond aesthetic judgment. Benjamin later found it necessary to distance his *Passagenarbeit* from the *mythologie moderne* of Aragon's *Le Paysan de Paris,* a source that once had been so formative and inspirational. Thus in regard to "Passage de l'Opéra," a chapter used as the starting point for his *flânerie* through the arcades of the nineteenth century, Benjamin makes an epistemological observation: "While an impressionistic element lingers on in Aragon—the 'mythology'—and this impressionism should be held responsible for many nebulous philosophemes [juridical concept and categories] of his book—what matters here is the dissolution of 'mythology' into the space of history. Of course, that can only happen through the awakening of a knowledge not yet conscious of what has gone before."[32] This late addition to the *Arcades Project* was stimulated by the discovery of what historical materialism could mean for the project's underlying structure. Elsewhere, Benjamin similarly sided with the "communist" Aragon of the mid-1930s, agreeing with him insofar as both contradicted their own (intellectual) past and distanced themselves from earlier writings—in Aragon's case, *Le Paysan de Paris*.[33] In 1927, when the impact of Louis Aragon's early writing had been formative—*Le Paysan* seemed "the best book on Paris"—Benjamin had affirmed to a friend: "It struck me that you put together Aragon and historical materialism, *voilà exactement mon point-de-vue à moi*."[34]

It is very striking indeed how Aragon and Benjamin stand together in evoking the old arcades and the outmoded yet inspirational display of fashion inside them. Both started off with a celebration of the ephemeral, one discovering its mythic power and the other its potential for the transient. Both subsequently progressed to a description of how the sartorial object projects the beholder into the past; Aragon praised its poetic potential, while Benjamin underlined its challenge to historicism. And both turned finally to the "other" within the object, the evil side of the commodity, to commit themselves—in political practice or theory—to a political line based on historical materialism. Thus no condemnation of the once-favored commodity, fashion, could have been harsher than Aragon's declaration in 1929:

■

*Fashion is the word that the lovers of weaknesses and those who revere reassuring divinities have invented as a sort of mask to disfigure the future. One must accept the challenge; one has to accept that fashion, in the most discredited meaning of the word, women's fashion, this frightening and frivolous history of changing hats, may become the vulgar symbol of what disqualifies any activity one day. This is merely to the benefit of life, the only concept that qualifies against all others and that is not to be challenged.*

*The idea of what is modern and modernity. Do use these words without worrying about what people will make of this passage in our text.*[35]

■

A profound pessimism, perhaps even a thinly veiled disgust, coined Aragon's text. Michelet's nineteenth-century call, "Avenir! Avenir! . . . chaque époque rêve la suivante"—published for the first time only a few months before Aragon's "Introduction à 1930" and used by Benjamin as the epigraph for "Paris, Capital of the Nineteenth Century"—was thus contravened by a new motto with which Aragon prefaced his text: "L'Avenir n'est qu'un mort, qui, s'étendant, *revient*" (The future is nothing but a dead one, who, spreading full length, *comes back*).[36]

Ironically perhaps, that latter message—so true of fashion's characteristics in modernity—would be used by Benjamin (influenced by Simmel's earlier studies) to argue *against* the damnation of fashion as mere ephemeral flippancy. The future, as represented by the constant change toward the new, is doomed to die quickly. Fashion, as we have seen, carries this death within itself and succumbs as soon as it becomes conspicuous in the public sphere, only to return in a novel form at the very next moment. However, fashion never presents merely "a sort of mask to disfigure the future," as Aragon writes, but wears its intention on its braided sleeve for everyone to see. That this intention may be to make political and social activity vulgar and external must be accepted only when, as Benjamin set out to prove, fashion's hermeneutic potential outstrips its dependence on materialistic society.

From the historical-materialist viewpoint, fashion may be nothing but the futile celebration of the commodity and a symbol of unjust class antagonism. As Aragon stressed in the third part of his book *Les Beaux Quartiers* (1936), the modern mythology of the *passage* becomes lost in the feeble, fashionable, and restricted world of the "Passage Club."[37] The author's objective was to describe *Le Monde réel*—Aragon's title for his (socialist-)realist trilogy of the 1930s, of which *Les Beaux Quartiers* became part 2[38]—instead of the *sur-réel,* the mysterious, mythic elements behind the manifestations of modern life.

This, however, is Aragon in his "midlife." In the earlier part of his career he followed Baudelaire, Mallarmé, and others in defining *modernité* not simply as constituting the confrontation between the new and the old, or the conflict of the ephemeral and transitory with the classical and sublime; *modernité* for them was created by the contact of a subjectivist sensuality with the real world and its objects. This understanding, set in the strange world of the arcades, comes to the fore in Aragon's first two novels, *Anicet ou le panorama, roman* and *Le Paysan de Paris;* the former was written at the time when dada still represented "haute couture,"[39] the latter when surrealism had not yet become *en vogue.*

Anicet, Aragon's alter ego and a mystified flâneur, passes through the modern world of the commodity, muttering to himself the poetry of sensual perceptions: "The setting in which my sensibility delights, I herewith baptize *Passage des Cosmoramas.*"[40] The onrush of impressions within this "cosmoramic arcade" was so prodigious that the protagonist seemed unable to maintain his sense of direction: "How to escape this enchanted forest? I do not know the magic words that could break the spell. I am looking around anxiously without understanding a thing. Suddenly, an inspiration flashes before my very eyes. High above me I read the words: ALL CLOTHES MADE TO MEASURE. The curse is lifted, thank God; I am saved."[41] Did the sign act as a signifier for the familiarity of clothes that protect and warm their wearer, or was it rather an ironic fingerpost pointing toward Anicet's principal interest among all the commodities, namely male apparel?

Even if the sign indicates a possible way out of the profusion of images and products, the adventure in the arcade has only just begun: "I still find myself in the arcade in which my sensibility delights. Only it is night in the world, and the shops have won the battle of electricity against daylight. Because I am returning from a long journey, I am contemplating this landscape with the eyes of a stranger, without really understanding its meaning or having any clear idea of the exact point in space and the exact time in the century I live in." Nighttime is the prerequisite for the dream state, even if it only the artificial nightfall generated by the roofed arcade. The protagonist of Aragon's novel thus dreamed and found himself looking at alienated objects; and because they were unfamiliar, he saw them in a different, magical light. When he wakes

**62.**

Germaine Krull, *Passage du Ponceau* (detail), before 1933. Gelatin silver print,
21.8 × 11.6 cm. Theodor W. Adorno Archiv, Frankfurt a.M.

much later, he—like Marcel in *La Recherche*—have traveled centuries, and remembers them essentially in their sartorial objectification. For the time being, however, Anicet continues to "dream": "On my right and on my left, the mannequins of two tailors; undoubtedly, the bodies under these visible clothes have no notion of them anymore. Their heads, legs, hands definitely have strayed into another period. I transport myself therein and by a curious reversal of values, I can only perceive around me hands, legs, heads, coats, gloves, and old-fashioned trousers."[42] The dreamer-flâneur is thrown into the past by the fragmentary artifacts of modernity that have passed their fashionable sell-by date. This projection into the past is not generated by the modish garments of that particular season (autumn 1920), but by the "clothes of five years ago"— which, because of their datedness, rise above fashion's "superficial" claim to be contemporary and can be appreciated by the most commonplace of consumers. These very clothes become thus symbols for a transitory passage in history: they are evocative of the past while still part of the present sartorial mode. The area of fashion represented by these slightly outmoded clothes is a far cry from the rue de la Paix (Paris's principal mile of haute couture between the 1870s and 1930s). While the vanguard of fashion moves forward, the old-fashioned remnants it leaves behind continue to exist without immediately becoming historic objects. Their status is that of a cross-reference. They testify to the latest change in fashion while no longer being part of it. In the strictest sense, they do no longer exist as fashion yet are still being worn on the side street (or what has nowadays become known, ironically perhaps, as the "high street") instead of the catwalk.

The showroom dummies that flank the passage of Anicet's *flânerie* into the past have their mythical predecessors in Breton and Soupault's *Les Champs magnétiques,* published earlier in the same year. The last passage in prose of this original *écriture automatique* evokes, under the heading of "Gants Blancs" ("White Gloves"), a setting that is remarkably similar to the panorama in *Anicet:* it is night in the city and the sophisticated flâneur, in formal attire complete with white gloves, passes along the boulevard, through "magical squares" and the "illuminated panorama of breasts"[43]— an earlier version of the manuscript even mentioned a journey through the "lights of the arcades."[44] When two of these "subterranean travelers" meet by chance, they decide to roam together through this "other world." And as in Grandville's book, the end of their perilous journey sees them surviving only in outer appearance, as mannequins dressed in suits made to measure.

▪

*Their soul's entrance once open to every wind is now so obstructed that they no longer offer to hold a misfortune. They are judged according to the clothes that no longer belong to them. Most often they are two very elegant mannequins devoid of both heads and hands. Those wishing to assume good manners bargain for their dress in the display window. When they pass the next day, the fashion is no longer the same. The stiff collar which is to some extent the mouth of these shells makes way for a stout pair of gilt pincers which when one is not looking seize hold of the shop window's prettiest reflections. At night it merrily swings from side to side its label on which all could read: "The season's latest novelty." Whatever is inhabiting our two friends gradually emerges from its quasi immobility. It gropes its way forward obtruding a fine pair of stalked eyes. The body in complete phosphorous formation remains halfway between the day and the tailor's shop. It is connected by delicate telegraphic antennae to the sleep of children. The mannequins down there are made of cork. Life-belts. Those charming codes of polite behaviour are far away.*[45]

▪

The "two friends," with whom the authors perhaps identify, live on borrowed time, lent to them like the clothes they do not own. Fragmented like the mannequins in Aragon's novel, they have to remain immobile, exposed to the greed of those who are unable to grasp the ideas hidden in transitoriness and who always return to find that "the fashion is no longer the same." However, the showroom dummies possess lives of their own. Breton and Soupault credited them with a sense of the supernatural, of the surreal, even of the subconscious, a state of mind comparable to the "sleep of children" (cf. the slumber of the young Marcel). Anicet himself conferred on the dummies a related potential to evoke turned-down collars, that is, to generate past epochs through their display of contemporary yet dated clothes.

This dialectical concept of the latest and the old(-fashioned), of integrating past and present into a single object, becomes obvious in a man's bespoke suit. This partic-

**63.**
Eugène Atget, *Avenue des Gobelins,* 1925. Albumen-silver print, 24 × 18 cm. The Museum of
Modern Art, New York. Print by Chicago Albumen Works, 1984. Abbot-Levy Collection.
Partial gift of Shirley C. Burden. Copy print © 2000 The Museum of Modern Art, New York.

ular article of clothing is subjected to constant change and is thus always contemporary. But by the same token it becomes abstracted, via the sartorial tradition, into a stable system of signification—that is, the dress code of the bourgeois male—and thus is rendered essentially historical.

To understand the distinction between dada and early surrealism, the following (structuralist) excursus—centered on the male suit—is important. When it comes to using clothes as a metaphor, dada embraces somber dandyism with all its finesse, nuances, and ironic irreverence, while surrealism sides with the imaginary and the artistic aspirations pertaining to the *habit*.

## ■ 5.4  Fashion Written VI: A Structured (Pur)Suit

In an essay of 1957 that explored most of the ideas that would later form the core of *Système de la mode,* Barthes attempts to undertake a structuralist inquiry into the dialectical status fashion can assume.[46] He begins with the linguistic classification, distinguishing *langage* (language as an abstract means of communication), *langue* (the language spoken within a sociological framework, a cultural grouping, or a society), and *parole* (the individual manner of speaking every individual uses for him or herself). These distinctions are analogous to the differences between *vêtement* (clothing in general), *costume* (as national or cultural sign of recognition), and *habillement* (individual sartorial expression).[47] *Langue* is here an institution, "a body abstracted by constraints,"[48] like the formal attire that constraints the corporeal; *parole* is the part within the institution that is momentarily chosen by the individual and actualized as a means of communication, both verbal and sartorial—whether by the poet/couturier clothing a body (of work) in the most sophisticated of ways or by the man in the street, speaking and dressing as he sees fit.

A decade later, with the publication of *Système de la mode,* Barthes abandoned the tripartite distinction above and had *vêtement* and *costume* trade places. Thus *costume* was reduced to the most general of meanings, while *vêtement* became equivalent to the Saussurean *langue.*[49] One reason for this change can be traced back to an earlier essay, "Les Maladies du costume de théâtre," which Barthes republished in conjunction with "L'Activité structuraliste" as an important early example of his methodological approach.[50] In this essay the term *costume* was exclusively employed to denote clothes worn on stage or in films. Therefore it seems as if the shift in meaning from *costume* to *vêtement* became necessary because the latter word had no overtones of masquerade or garb. Yet by substituting *vêtement* for *costume,* Barthes lost something important in his application of clothing to writing (in its historic and cultural context): the literal connotation of the male suit—*le costume* in French. Because *langue* is defined as a "structural institution," the homonym of the suit, the sartorial institution in men's fashion since the nineteenth century, provides its best equivalent in clothing. For the purpose of my discussion it thus seems more fitting to retain Barthes's earlier classification. He wrote in 1957:

▪

*It is important to observe that a matter of personal dressing* [un fait d'habillement] *first of all constitutes a deteriorated state of* costume. *Yet it can be transformed again into a secondary* costume, *when the deterioration functions as a collective sign, as a value: for instance,* costume *might imply originally making use of all buttons of the shirt; subsequently* habillement *might neglect to button the two uppermost ones; such a cadence might thus become a matter of* costume *itself, the moment it becomes a normative constituent of a certain group (dandyism).*[51]

▪

Personal stylistics in bourgeois men's fashion are restricted to small variations on a limited number of garments. This limitation had become paradigmatic since the "great masculine renunciation"—that is, the time after the French Revolution when the European male "abandoned his claim to be considered beautiful. He henceforth aimed at being only useful."[52] That meant discarding brightly embroidered brocade coats, breeches, and silk stockings in favor of the (uni)formal suit made from plain and somber fabrics. The elaborate aristocratic dress code gave way to simplicity and an almost "democratic" egalitarianism in man's apparel.

As fashion is driven by the constant interplay between individual expression and mass appeal, the former became manifest within modernity in the fragmented detail. To appear "aristocratic" (in the Baudelairean coinage of spiritual aristocracy) no longer depended on putting on the distinct attire of the upper echelons, but on paying close attention to the subtle nuances of clothes, which shapes were—in theory—common property.[53] The arbiters of fashion laid emphasis no longer on the possession of clothing but on the ability to make a sophisticated choice, to accessorize (choosing one's tie became a most significant example in Balzac) and to *wear* the garment correctly. Echoing this quest for nuance and individual distinction, and anticipating the Barthesian communication between *habillement* and *costume,* the painter and stage designer Jean Hugo remembered in his memoirs the infinite sartorial discourse of the 1910s and '20s:

■

*The buttons on the jacket were the words of a language: buttoning only the top one signified an archaic and indifferent attitude toward the garment; closing merely the bottom one was a display of affectation and lack of taste; buttoning all three equaled German rigidity, the top two betrayed repressed coquetry; should one therefore close the two bottom ones or only the one in the middle? We debated this endlessly. And because one saw at that time also many jackets with four buttons and some with just two, which obviously changed the premises of the debate, the subject matter appeared inexhaustible.*[54]

■

Through its minimal variation the male suit establishes a set of values; it becomes a sartorial institution whose structure is rooted in the past, in this case in the second half of the nineteenth century, when the overall appearance of the suit to be worn later by Hugo, Aragon, Breton, and ultimately by Barthes had first become de rigueur. Its variations, such as buttoning thus correspond with *la parole:* the way in which individual language is fashioned at a particular instance, yet clearly within the boundaries of previously established *costume/langue.* Thus it is the incessant play between personal expression and social rigor that constitutes fashion and propels it along.

Barthes continues:

■

*Fashion is always a matter of* costume, *but its origin can be representative of two distinct movements. At times fashion is a matter of* costume *that is artificially elaborated by specialists (haute couture, for example); sometimes it is constituted by the propagation of a simple matter of* habillement, *reproduced on the collective scale for a number of diverse reasons. For our present age the first process (the dispersion of a matter of* costume *in matters of* habillement*) occurs most frequently in female fashion, while the second (the expansion of a matter of* habillement *to a matter of* costume*), at least in terms of sartorial details, can be found principally in men's fashion (what one could call the "Brummellization" of fashion).*[55]

■

Beau Brummell, the English dandy of the late eighteenth and early nineteenth century, is taken here as the model for the elevation of a sartorial idiosyncrasy—his "rebellious" introduction of a suit comprising redingote, *gilet,* and long trousers, all in plain unobtrusive colors—to the level of a dress code, of a "structural institution." This came about not so much because of the influence the dandy himself exerted on his contemporaries as because of his compliance with a new aesthetic experience that was—in a Kantian sense—"disinterested." The fashionable attire was no longer a completely subjective statement, an extravagant display of wealth and status, but was subjugated to a general rule, to a moral code that declared the virtues of eschewing everything ostentatious and displaying individuality through well-chosen details rather than grand gestures. In a sense Brummell reified Kant's categorical imperative in coining a standard attire that could act as general law for the enlightened male, while retaining the significance of an individual sartorial maxim that would always appear to be integral to that law. Brummell's *parole* (his "fait d'habillement") also becomes *langue-costume* because in reflecting a restrained simplicity to confront the increasing rapidity of change in contemporary life, it anticipates attitudinal patterns toward an emerging modern culture.

"Dandyism is a complete theory of life," wrote Barbey d'Aurevilly in his famous essay on Brummell and dandyism, "and its material side is not its only side. It is a way of existing, made up entirely of shades, as is always the case in very old and very

**64.**

Jacques Vaché, *Self-portrait,* ca. 1917. Pen and ink on paper. Published in
*La Révolution Surréaliste,* no. 2 (January 1925).

*"Dandyism is the assertion of the absolute modernity of Beauty."—Oscar Wilde.*

civilised societies, where comedy becomes so rare, and the properties hardly have the better of boredom."[56] The dandy's elegant impertinence is not merely a matter of attire—it is a *habit* (in the literal sense of the word). Barbey d'Aurevilly greatly admired this headstrong quest to retain individuality in a commodified existence:

■

*Incredible though it may seem, the Dandies once had a fancy for torn clothes [as Baudelaire observed, a true dandy can have the sartorial appearance of a "chiffonnier"]. . . . They had . . . their clothes torn, before wearing them, through the whole extent of the cloth; so that they became a sort of lace—a cloud. They wanted to walk like Gods in their clouds! The operation was difficult and tedious of execution; a piece of pointed glass was employed for the purpose. There you have a true detail of Dandyism, where clothes go for nothing, in fact they hardly exist.*[57]

■

The perception of individuality as an artistic necessity can be expressed in different ways. One can introduce from outside a new concept or shape, decidedly different from existing forms, like the novelties haute couture claims to discover in each season, while remaining rooted in its tradition and quoting the past at every present moment. Or one can undermine the structure from within, seemingly adhering to the moral or aesthetic law but employing irony ("la comédie rare" of Barbey d'Aurevilly) and surprise to make an impact on unsuspecting beholders and subvert their expectations: "Dandyism . . . while still respecting the conventionalities, plays with them. While admitting their power, it suffers from and revenges itself upon them, and pleads them as an excuse against themselves; dominates and is dominated by them in turn: a double a mutable character!"[58]

## ■ 5.5 Dada's Dandyism and Surrealist Imagination

Dandified and heightened individualism is also employed in the stylistic revolt of certain art movements. The purported disinterestedness held to be a prerequisite for the aesthetic experience of the dandy can show itself in a nihilist disinterest in (artistic) creation.[59] In Paris of the 1920s different attitudes toward distance and disinterestedness were displayed among one and the same group of artists.

The surrealist movement celebrated new "discoveries" that were introduced partly from other areas into the arts: for example, the interpretation of dreams, the importance of the sub- and unconscious, *explosante-fixe,* and the novel concept of "convulsive beauty." In contrast, their dadaist predecessors never claimed to have discovered anything. Their distinction from existing art and culture existed not in decree but in the nuance, in the intellectual challenge offered by an almost imperceptible fragment. Dada appeared to follow bourgeois law, down to the request for black tie in Zurich's Cabaret Voltaire; but this outward adherence to the rules made its subsequent nihilist irony all the more cutting.

The opposition of "interest" and nihilism would later form the basis of the divergence in the movements' respective attitudes toward fashion. Surrealism—Breton's poetry, as we will see, provides a particularly apt example—looked almost exclusively at the woman. The *langue-costume,* coupled with woman's erotic appeal, was essentially imagined, and its highly subjective interpretation of clothing became *parole* and *habillement;* thus the surrealists enacted Barthes's postulate on female fashion. The male Da-dandies (e.g., Vaché, Cravan, Rigaut), on the other hand, concentrated on the ironic treatment of, or distance from, inherent structures. This stance was exemplified in fashion by the nineteenth-century monocle, which was worn with contemporary suits; and in literature by semantic assaults, wordplay, and nihilist irony, which tore at the seams of the sublime. The aesthetic experience of dada therefore served as an example of an idiosyncratic *habillement-parole* ready to become *costume* and *langue.* Yet at the same time its practitioners recognized that art and fashion are both ephemeral and subject to the same increased rate of change in modernity.

In chapter 1 I touched on the distinction between *le mode,* as the equivalent of a rationale or method, and *la mode,* as the expression of the ephemeral and fugitive (see sections 1.2.3 and 1.2.4). It is also obvious that the surrealists regarded themselves and their movement as making an earnest contribution to art and its theory. For example, they took seriously and rationalized their shared obsession with (fetishism about?) woman and her *habillement,*[60] as well as their attempt to alter *parole* in order to generate an wider aesthetic change. In this respect again they stood in contrast to the dadaists, who regarded nonsense as the preferred way to attack artistic pretensions. But through their shared penchant for the tailored male *costume,* the dadaists challenged the fundamentals of *langue*—seen both as language and institution—much more seriously and vigorously. This challenge begins during the Great War; it originated in the letters and personal appearance of a Da-dandy *avant la lettre,* Jacques Vaché.

## ■ 5.6 Fashion Written VII: Tailoring Irony

In *Anicet,* Aragon used his roman à clef to include a veiled self-portrait of the artist as flâneur that epitomized the transition from nuance to assertion, from Da-dandy to revolutionary poet. In the text the protagonist Harry James—the nom de guerre/plume Vaché used in his last letters from the front line—is guided by a cultivated disinterestedness. He is portrayed as the epitome of the nihilist dandy: "What consolidates our admiration for Harry James is the fact that one never knows whether he will kill himself tomorrow without reason, or commit an amazing crime; one detects in him an ill-disciplined strength. He is the truly modern man who can't be subjugated to being only a spectator."[61]

The particular interest in clothes of this "truly modern man" became evident in his correspondence, which also provided source material for Aragon's portrait; it can be seen as well in the memories of those who had come in contact with Vaché—as much as his habitual distance allowed such intimacy. "At the front, he seems mostly obsessed with the luxury of his clothes and with very refined garments, which in the heart of this cataclysm that is destroying minds and bodies seems strangely 'displaced'—and this word is to be taken literally."[62] His was also the "displacement" of a particular expression of male elegance that had been elevated to a moral stance and aesthetic standard, simply through Vaché's uncompromising attitude toward life. A letter to Aragon, addressed "dear friend and mystifier," read: "I'm pleased to live beatifically, like 13 × 18 cameras = It's much like any other way of waiting for the end. I am gathering strength and save myself for future acts. You'll see what a jolly jumble our

**65.**

Jacques Vaché, *Those Gentlemen,* September 1918. Ink and crayon on paper, 31 × 12 cm.
Private collection.

future will be, and how it will enable us to kill people!! . . . I also do some experimenting so as not to get out of practice, right?—but I must just keep my intimate jubilations to myself because of the spies of Cardinal Richelieu."[63] Appearance and customs had to be maintained even in the face of destruction—or perhaps especially then, as only extreme situations such as war, revolution, or scandal could really test the dandy's "virtues." Thus Richelieu's spies also might have been sent to supervise Vaché's behavior and style under duress, since the rue de Richelieu had been the Parisian equivalent of London's Savile Row during the first half of the nineteenth century; and the cardinal after whom it was named had long been synonymous with a life of intellectual and habitual dandyism.[64] During the first months of being dispatched to the front, Vaché bitterly complained about having been drafted into the army, as any young recruit would. However, in his case it was not so much the cruelty of war and the likelihood of being shot that upset him, but rather the absence of civil apparel: "Above all, I desire to be a civilized animal, in a black suit (a black suit!) with white cuffs (!!) and patent leather SHOES (shoes in patent leather!!!)—and to reside in the extremely cosmopolitan foyer of a very foreign palace hotel, where there are many green plants and rastaquoères."[65] He hoped for "displacement" or alienation and for the preservation of his sanity by completely ignoring his surroundings. Although he made numerous sketches and collages of his comrades in the trenches, he maintained a pronounced inward distance. In the letter above such distance and disinterest is presented through his personal style of dress. The black suit clothed him in a manner that went back to the early part of the nineteenth century and thus removed him from the harsh reality of his present situation. Vaché expressed his wish to appear incognito in a strange place as a *rasta(quouère),* a man of unknown (and often doubtful) material resources, who is immaculate in dress and orthodox in his behavior. Echoing this ideal other dadaists, especially Francis Picabia, would elevate the *rasta* to become the sophisticated standard-bearer for the subversion of bourgeois society and the beau monde.[66]

In Aragon's novel, Anicet attends a gathering of the high society dressed in a black suit with a "waistcoat of gray silk, which was all that was known of [him]." He has a nocturnal encounter with the princess Marina Mérov, who appears before him in a "gown colored like the night, painted with symbolic constellations." Given this

**66.**

Studio Meyer and Pierson, *The Beautiful Comtesse de Castiglione,* between 1853 and 1857.
Albumen print, ca. 21 × 13 cm.

*The comtesse de Castiglione—whom Maurice Leblanc rendered immortal in one of his* Arsène Lupin *novels
—left an album of 288 photos of her son, of members of the court of Louis Napoléon III, and, above all,
of herself in hundreds of splendid gowns and dresses, worn over a period of four years. Thus fashion indeed
ensured her immortality.*

sartorial preamble, the conversation naturally has to focus on poetry and symbolist ethics. Evoking the spirit of *La Dernière Mode* and its author, the princess judges: "To be complete and understood, you should have written: I put on my evening clothes as I would put on nice feelings. . . . I certainly prefer the end of the piece, because you have successfully repeated the rhyme *rie,* which gives the whole poem a distinctly Mallarméan tone."[67] Like fashion, literature loses its momentum once it has spread from the vanguard to a wider audience—even if that is merely a literary soirée. The fashion in dressing a body and dressing a poem is disseminated, and thus the capacity to surprise or scandalize is greatly diminished in the eyes of the poet. Enter the dandy Ange Miracle, who further robs Anicet of any remaining illusions by affirming his judgment about the present society as a world where "only snobs, who dress each morning as people of taste, are tolerable from time to time" and where emotions become reified and impersonal: "you might well think that once in their wardrobes the mannequins undress each other and make love."[68] Both Ange Miracle and Anicet are, of course, part of this societal malaise. Their critique is partly self-denial; and this denial in turn becomes an intricate part of both the dandy's and the dadaist's moral outfit. The Dadandy is distanced not only from others but also from his own persona, as all the things he ridicules in his fellow men must be observed as mercilessly within himself.

As modernity wore on, the dandy's position became increasingly precarious. He was no longer alone in his supreme individualism, as Brummell had been; nor could he always claim his part in a aristocratic coterie, as the Comte de Montesquiou and Prince Radziwill could before the turn of the century. While the bourgeoisie grew steadily in numbers, the dandy found it more and more difficult to maintain his distance and the required disinterestedness. Any sartorial nuance was so quickly spotted, commented on, and aped that dandyism became almost an intellectual game of outwitting the crowd rather than the distinctive manner of existence that it had been during most of the nineteenth century. Some of the dadaists recognized this shift, and their critical eyes could not help but see their own individualism as a mere hybrid form of bourgeois attitudes and customs. However, at his best, the Da-dandy was able to turn this condition to his (artistic) advantage. He was part of the bourgeoisie, loathed his affiliation with it, and yet wore its outward signs: suit, collar, and tie. The intellectual nuance—

as much as the sartorial—became a weapon in the aesthetic arsenal. The monocle thus became a favored accessory because it separated the critical eye from too direct confrontation with the opposition: fake accusations and forged criticism were launched by the dadaists against their own performances of the night before (a technique skillfully employed by Tristan Tzara and Walter Serner; see section 5.9.1 below). Yet beyond the ironic play with artistic conventions, self-contradiction was employed also to withdraw from any alliance with other literary models.

In his "memoir" *Lautréamont et nous,* Aragon used a clothing metaphor to evoke this notion: "To turn inside out Pascal's sleeve, Vauvenargues's jacket, La Rochefoucauld's pockets, is an operation that has to question the meaning beyond the gesture: . . . this contradiction of contradictions."[69] To be sure, dada could not escape the need to relate to artistic tradition. Like fashion, it quoted its past to proclaim a novel, exciting, and unexpected form (collage, montage, ready-made, performance, etc., which used existing commodities and parodied artistic techniques) each new season; and while the bourgeois audience readied itself to appreciate the new, dada had taken already another step, disavowed last week's manifestation as "old-fashioned," and preserved its aesthetic impetus through aloofness and detachment from the art scene while secretly preparing to launch the next trend. But there is a negative side to these tactics. Its oppositional stance seemed to make dada unable to follow through on any programmatic artistic exploration. In the end it had to lose its sense of irony and perish in its own nihilism, exhausted by constant self-denial. (Surrealism was of course only too ready to pick up the pieces and the protagonists.) Yet the Da-dandies retained their distance, even to themselves, by exposing the structures within their own artistic productions. They stripped bare the idea, so that it stood naked for everyone to see.[70] Thus the scandal, despite constituting a main attraction in dada's artistic vocabulary, could be put into perspective very quickly: "It is totally erroneous," remarks Anicet to Ange Miracle, "to believe that men invented formal attire on the day that they conceived the idea of nudity. Because this idea implies that of clothing and therefore the idea of diseases and cold. . . . Our mental nudity appalls the spectator and if we write, we write about ourselves. Poetry is a scandal like any other."[71] Fashion is far from constituting the "dressed" in contrast to the "naked"; it is the synthesis of the two. Fashion, like dada's self-preserving sense of irony, reveals more than it conceals. Indeed, the dadaists only had to "write about themselves"; their *parole* and *habillement* were designed to become structural institutions, because only then could they assert their denial of experience and cut up the *langue* or *costume* again.[72]

The male artist found it comparatively easy to be structurally ironic. If a woman around 1920 intended to subvert society's sartorial customs, she must have found it difficult to identify one single piece of clothing that could be altered or added to in order to achieve ironic (self-)denial.[73] But all a man had to do was to put on his suit (*le costume*) and subvert its somber respectability with, for example, the anachronistic monocle, a false beard, a revolver, or an eccentric hairstyle. Such additions turned the suit at once from well-cut attire into a caricature of the bourgeois uniform.[74]

That one item of clothing so dominated (and continues to dominate) male fashion accounts for its significance in modernity. Baudelaire's and Gautier's *habit noir,* the black wool suit of Montesquiou and Mallarmé,[75] the dark attire of the nightly flâneur all share the same frame of reference and are part of the same tradition. "It is quite obvious," claims Barthes, "that there is ceaseless movement between *habillement* and *costume,* a dialectical exchange that, in terms of *langue* and *parole,* can be defined as veritable *praxis.*"[76] This dialectical exchange between *habillement* and *costume* is crucial; the instant when a novel nuance (of the suit, for example) enters the public consciousness and the moment when this sartorial style is so common that it loses its importance as fashion, becomes "just" clothing and thus has to be challenged anew, are pivotal points within modernity. The shortened life span of fashion increases the likelihood that a certain suit will become "extinct"—five years after its sale, as Benjamin says—and thus will be capable of evoking the past. Tzara confessed in his "Manifeste Dada" of 1918: "I like an ancient work [of art] for its novelty. It is nothing but the contrast that connects us to the past";[77] and the following year fellow dadaist Pierre Reverdy quipped: "A touch of criticism / He turns his coat."[78] Such observations lead to the critique that "Dada teaches us that art is as ephemeral as fashion."[79] And fashion, as the poetical hermeneutics of Benjamin declare, is as fundamental as art in awakening remembrance.

**67.**

Unknown photographer, *Salon Dada* at the Galerie Montaigne, Paris, June 1921.
Gelatin silver print. Private collection, Paris.

*The inscription on the balustrade reads: "Here you see ties and not violins, here you see bonbons and no
spouses"* (mariés *in the original)—a gibe at Cocteau's fashionably modernist drama* Les Mariés de la Tour
Eiffel, *replaced here by real fashion in form of assorted, candy-colored neckties.*

This point finally brings us back to Anicet, whom we left at the tailor's window looking at the dummies, whose clothes were preserved as part of the modern mythology of the arcade. Anicet asks himself:

■

*But what style is adopted by these fragmentary beings? In the top hats and pumps, I recognize the Second Empire. I find myself between two rows of financiers and snobs: one of them in a suit of Nankin silk in cornflower blue, who came back to drive in a tilbury along the allée de l'Impératrice; the other with long sideburns à l'autrichienne, the cravat billowing under his chin, the briefcase in grain leather under his arm, and whistling a quadrille that his feet have danced already. Next I see a peer; while the fourth wears tight-fitting trousers molded on his thighs like a timid nymph, a waistcoat in velvet, with rings on each finger; this handsome blackbird I recognize as a dressmaker, because of the journalists that surround him; this cavalier, who is a bit too tanned, belongs to the entourage of the Brazilian emperor; here a pretty boy, there a cocodès.*[80]

■

The tiger's leap into the past is not concerned simply with historic garb. It places the mannequins—the real ones, not those who, according to Aragon, flock to the salons—in a life that the poet has dreamed up for them. In his literary exploration of the sartorial Aragon occupies the transition between dada's irony and the surrealist imagination. As Da-dandy he uses clothing to subvert the bourgeois structure; as surrealist writer he celebrates the potential of clothing to metaphorically evoke a modern mythology.

## ■ 5.7 Aragon and Breton: *Le cabinet des cravates*

Between 1920 and 1926, Aragon was an insatiable nightwalker. The three great documents of his *flâneries*—*Anicet* of 1920, "Une Vague de rêves," of 1924, and *Le Paysan de Paris,* published in 1926—describe the protagonist's meandering strolls through the capital and his search for the mythic element in contemporary objects.[81] Since nothing seems to excite him more than the latest sartorial commodities, the flâneur's path in all three texts leads him inevitably to the tailors' shop windows. Though exhibitions in museums or galleries might have provided intellectual stimulation, it was left to the ever-changing displays of the tailors and dressmakers to stir his poetic inspiration. Aragon reminds his lover in 1923: "In the shops everything attracts your attention. I looked at men's clothes."[82] In order to explain the genesis of fashion, employed as a generic term for the various objects meant to adorn the human figure in Aragon's *mythologie moderne,* we can look at how the perception of the narrator-flâneur changes over the course of the three documents.

■

*There is a window display . . . of a tailor, where striped trousers and fitted jackets attach themselves to a slanting white background. They stun mortal souls sensitive to the wonder that a garment can suffice in itself. The window display of the second tailor consists of bales of wool in three or four shades of gray, in bluish pearl-gray; chiné fabrics in beige, red, and green, in large or small checks, on the bias or straight, decorated with assorted dots.*[83]

■

In the first text of 1920 the author appears as an impressionable window-shopper, looking with childlike wonder at the choices displayed in the tailor's shop. He perceives the commodities both disinterestedly, with the "objective" eye of a photographer, and transfixed, with the admiration of the consumer who wishes to slip into one of these suits or have one made to measure from the fabrics on display. Four years later in "Une Vague de rêves," the setting observed remains the same, but it gives a different impression.

■

*There is a surrealist light: the moment when the cities go up in flames, it falls on the salmon-colored decoration of stockings; . . . it lingers till late on the avenue de l'Opéra at Barclay's, when the ties transform themselves into phantoms; it is the ray of pocket lights shining on murders and lovemaking.*[84]

■

Perhaps it was the more sophisticated setting—not the old-fashioned arcade, but the stylish place Vendôme and avenue de l'Opéra next to the rue de la Paix—or perhaps it was just the onset of night; in any case, the sartorial objects now possess an air of the supernatural, the surreal. They reach below the visual surface and evoke the erotic and mysterious. The clothes and accessories turn toward objectified myths that lie embedded in the subconscious fabric of modern life.

Two years later, in 1926, Aragon describes the adventures of a Parisian peasant who travels the length and breadth of the city, devoting space once more to the detailed observation of shop windows, which displayed hats, canes, suits, dresses, and so on. At the end of his day's journey, however, he is content neither with merely describing his experiences nor with poetically transforming them. He now renders them part of a dream, "Le Songe de paysan," which begins:

■

*There is an unthinkable disorder which exists in this world: the extraordinary thing about this is that men should have habitually sought beneath the surface appearance of disorder for some mysterious order, one that comes naturally to them, that merely expresses an innate desire within them, and they have no sooner introduced this order into things than they start going into raptures about it, making this order the basis of an idea, or alternatively explaining this order by an idea.*[85]

■

Here, the purportedly disinterested loses out to the metaphysical. Aragon now argues against the Kantian rationale that aspires to establish an order for each objectification of human life. In aesthetic experience, but not exclusively there, disorder should remain disorder to generate imagination. Dreams become explicit attempts to digest this experience, not schematic explanations that limit it.

■

*It is clear that this is not simply a matter of feeling: if I have chosen order and disorder as the terms of this dialectic it is only with a view of demonstrating accessorily, while simultaneously providing an example of this dialectic, the vulgar approach which has permitted men to conceive the universe in terms of a divine inspiration*

*that is repugnant to any genuine philosophical scheme. My dream is concerned,
above all, with the way the mind works.*[86]

.

In Aragon's view, the task of metaphysics was not to argue for God's existence but to
search for "the notion, or knowledge of the concrete."[87] And because the concrete
had to retain an aspect of the human, the sartorial object clothing the body recurs as
a metaphor throughout Aragon's writing up to 1930.

If, as Barthes argued, *l'habillement*—individualized sartorial style—remains an
empirical fact and should be approached phenomenologically, whereas *le costume* is
an institution and should be analyzed as the proper object of both sociology and history,[88] then one can argue that the generic term *le vêtement,* under which any existing
garment or accessory falls, accordingly becomes a *metaphysical* fact, since it depends
neither on personal nor on social preferences, but remains conceptualized. And because the conceptual value of sartorial fashion emerges in its genetic link with modernity, surrealist poets—for example, Aragon and Roger Caillois—were able to create a
metaphysical *mythe moderne* at the very point where literary tradition joined the original concept: "This taste for modernity is far reaching, since Baudelaire as well as Balzac
extend it to the most futile details of fashion and dressing. Both studied fashion for
themselves on the basis of moral and philosophical questions, as it represents an immediate reality in its most critical, most aggressive, perhaps most irritating aspect, but
equally in one that is experienced most generally."[89] To become part of a literary tradition in which a metaphysical view of fashion continued to thrive was especially significant for the surrealists. Although they emphasized how their ideas led them to a
radically different approach to writing, especially in poetry, they accepted that they
were part of a continuous tradition in French literature (the title of the first journal
edited by Breton and others, *Littérature,* which was suggested by Paul Valéry, is not just
ironic; it also pays homage, albeit satirical at times, to its feuilletonistic predecessors).
Tracing their roots to poets such as Nerval, von Arnim, Baudelaire, Mallarmé, and Verlaine; "discovering" hitherto marginalized poets such as Corbière, Lautréamont, Rimbaud, and Roussel; and accepting patronage from writers such as Valéry and Gide,

members of the surrealist movement were iconoclastic mainly in their manifestos; their poetic existence drew heavily on their forefathers' reputation and influence.[90]

Such (mocking of) tradition became evident in their attire as well: while Aragon was busy discovering the spirit of his modern mythology, he also tried to express the notion of past periods in contemporary clothing, through carefully researched additions to his suits. His erstwhile "disciple," the Alsatian surrealist Maxime Alexandre, remembered:

■

*For the time being, I would like to come back to Aragon and talk about his walking sticks, his neckties, and about what these accessories displayed or concealed. . . . I have described already how he bought his silk scarfs in antique shops, and, on reflection, it must have been the lure of these shops that made him buy the foulards . . . , since he also acquired his walking sticks there. The shops where one could find the most beautiful foulards and the most elegant walking sticks (preferably with ivory knobs or handles) were situated on the boulevard de Raspail. Here, one could also find neckties; and they were very important indeed those ties! Foulards, walking sticks, and neckties were integral parts of the Parisian flâneur's apparel.*[91]

■

Brought back not from antiquity but at least from the antique shop, the tie as the ultimate *parole* within the rigidity of the *costume masculin* (in its Saussurean and sartorial sense) operated not only as a metaphysical connection that transcends history but also as a link within literary tradition.[92] In 1891 Edmund and Jules de Goncourt had paid a visit to the dandy and *poète-dilletante* Comte de Montesquiou-Fezensac. On arrival it had not been Whistler's etchings or the Japanese artifacts that caught their eyes, but "[o]ne original room: the dressing-room. . . . And in the middle of this dressing-room, a little glass show-case revealing the delicate colours of a hundred or so ties."[93]

A very similar observation appears in Alexandre's memoirs. He told a story he had heard from Breton, who visited Aragon in an exclusive hotel in Biarritz, where the latter spent the summer with the English heiress Nancy Cunard. "Aragon said to me: 'Come to the hotel with me, I want to show you our nice accommodation.' I let him drag me along, and it was indeed the best hotel in Biarritz. He opens his wardrobe

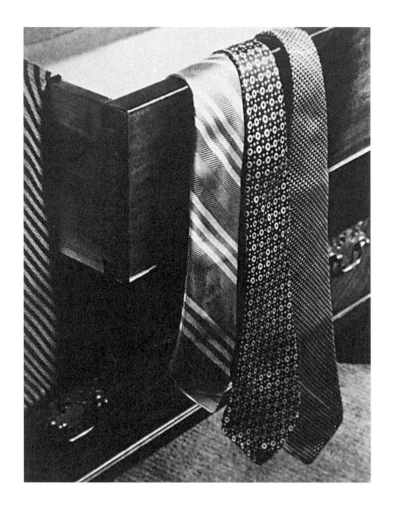

**68.**
Paul Outerbridge, *Ties Hanging from Drawer,* ca. 1926. Platinum print, 11 × 9 cm.
The Estate of Paul Outerbridge Jr., Santa Monica.

and says: 'Have a look!' It was filled with ties. I say: 'Fabulous, the amount of ties you have.'"[94] The similarity is too close to be coincidental. Breton would have known the journals by the Goncourt brothers, an inexhaustible source of anecdotes and criticism of the artistic life of the nineteenth century. If he presented the story to Alexandre in this manner, he must have had the earlier memoir in mind, knowing that his young listener—unschooled in the French literary tradition—was unlikely to make the connection.

However, while the Goncourts looked upon the *cabinet de cravates* as one element within the refined attitude of Montesquiou, Breton did not necessarily regard the parallel presentation of shades of neckties in the mirrored wardrobe as a historical continuation of dandyesque attitudes. For him such a display hinted at a psychological anomaly, an obsession. He therefore extends the proportions of the tie collection in his story, and what originally was an assembly of tasteful reminders of past and present fashion becomes an aberration: "'That's nothing,' says Aragon, 'just hold on a moment!' He heads for the chest of drawers and pulls out the top one: full of ties. 'Oh, that's great!' He pulls out the second drawer: equally filled with neckties. 'But that's not all,' and Aragon opens an enormous suitcase, packed with ties. That really blew me away."[95] Fashion had by the second half of the 1920s lost nearly all of its hermeneutic potential for Breton. He would assess a garment or accessory, when it could not be found on the body of a female (or, better, discarded beneath it), only in the psychoanalytical context. For example, in his "Rêve de la cravate, du 26 août 1931," recorded and analyzed in *Les Vases communicants,* the tie with a "Nosferatu" motif, which Breton acquired, held no appeal as an adornment; nor did it represent anything beyond the arbitrary object of association. Hence his complaint: "I hate that incomprehensible ornament of masculine dress. I reproach myself now and then for giving in to such a pitiful custom as that of knotting every morning in front of a mirror (I try to explain this to the psychoanalysts) this bit of material, which is supposed to enhance with a careful little nothing the already idiotic look of a jacket with lapels."[96] Not the attitude of a dandy, one has to say. Yet in an earlier phase in Breton's artistic development dandyism had held for him a strong appeal indeed, and literary tradition had instructed him in the paradigmatic value of fashion for modernity.

## ■ 5.8 Vaché and Breton

### 5.8.1 Initiation and Imitation

*Enfin, hors la critique littéraire, un dandy de 1913 est devenu un homme* extrêmement *élégant, dont la tenue ne va pas sans étude ni sans méditations, et qui peut s'intéresser aux plus hauts sujets comme aux plus infimes . . . mais sans paraître toutefois attacher la moindre importance à ce qui l'occupe tant.*

*Marcel Boulenger (1913)*[97]

In 1913 the seventeen-year-old Breton began a diverse series of poems that would be published some six years later by his former classmate René Hilsum. The name of his publishing house, which was to be inaugurated by this collection of poetry, became the topic of fervent discussion. Breton favored "À l'incroyable"—the name of a chain of shoe stores in and around the French capital that aimed to make itself part of a sophisticated tradition by adopting the nickname used for the dandies of the eighteenth and nineteenth century. Their mutual friend Louis Aragon intervened with the suggestion that prevailed, "Au Sans pareil," which in turn was borrowed from the shop signs of contemporary *magasins de nouveautés.*[98] The title eventually chosen for Breton's book denoted a commercial establishment in almost the same vein: *Mont de piété*—a pawnshop where clothes, watches, pieces of jewelry, and so forth could be exchanged for money under the auspices of a municipal government.

The fifteen poems of the volume—as well as a number of related pieces that were not included in the book—demonstrate an artistic coming of age, "a collection of works of a *période révolue,*" as the author's protégé Henri Pastoureau later put it.[99] The use of *révolue* indicated that this period was "past," but the term is also synonymous with "complete" or "accomplished." During it, Breton turned from late symbolist tradition to modernity and dadaesque collage, passing through phases of diverse literary preferences that would come to make up the stylistic ingredients for the avantgarde he set out to create.

A number of rough divisions can be made within *Mont de piété.*[100] The earliest poems—"Rieuse" (1913), "L'An suave" (April 1914), "D'or vert" (May 1914), and "Hymne" (August 1914)—reflect an attitude that Breton later described in a letter to his friend Théodore Fraenkel: "Mallarmé reigned: no idolatry on my part, but a sort of worship for a manifest deity. I believed in the exclusive heroics of living for the bijou."[101] The same bijou—in the sense of precious object—was celebrated by Marguerite de Ponty, a.k.a. Mallarmé, in the first issue of *La Dernière Mode.* "Let us seek out the bijoux in themselves. . . . Speaking of lace, we desire it at any cost, this work emerging from the hands of fairies proper, who will never know any mediocrity. Underskirts, bonnets, tunics, fans, parasols: in Chantilly; underskirts, tunics, fans, delicate sunshades: in *application de Bruxelles* [needlepoint]; one cannot deny oneself making a choice!"[102] The young Breton believed in the quest for the refined element, the beautiful nuance, the ornament that beyond its ephemeral character aims at evoking a dandyism of the word by maintaining a semantic disinterestedness and a distance from everyday *langue,* thereby turning poetic language into the most precious of structures.[103]

His early poetry is distinguished by his choice of metaphors; these form the fabric of his collection *Mont de piété.* Fashion, true to "l'esprit mallarméen," features in all the poems in one form or another. Fashion appears as a garment circumscribing the "ornamental woman," as an accessory or an action (like needlework) that describes a character or situation, as an evocation of the world of haute couture, or, ultimately, as its cutting up within *l'esprit nouveau.* Clothes, as well as the woman who wears or produces them, remained at the core of Breton's poetic sensibility during this period. Years later, he would remember a dream, described in the first issue of *La Révolution Surréaliste,* which in spirit and vocabulary reflects on his early poetic impressions.

■

*The first part of this dream is devoted to the realization and presentation of an outfit* [costume]. *The face of the woman for whom it is designed has to assume here the role of a simple ornamental motif, like those that can be seen repeatedly in the railings of a balcony or in the pattern of cashmere. . . . The human truth within such features is no less pronounced and its repetition in various elements of the attire, notably in the hat, . . . does not allow for individual consideration. . . . The form of the attire is such that it does permit the human shape to subsist.*[104]

■

The relation between the erotic and the sartorial, between the female and her garments, was, like the poems she emerges from, dominated by utmost artificiality. "I have heard Valéry in the past criticizing some jeweled excesses in my very first poems," remembered Breton of his former "mentor," who had asked: "Who is that marvelous woman of whom one discusses nothing but her pearl strings and rivers of diamonds [bijoux, once again], which were not worthy of the place they were covering?"[105]

In "Rieuse" ("She Who Is Cheerful"), the earliest poem of the collection, the subject appears in "unclothed whiteness,"[106] a purity that had not yet been conquered by realities. In "D'or vert" ("On Green Gold"), the poet creates a fairylike creature, nonexistent but for the garment which covers her—"Je t'évoque, inquiet d'un pouvoir de manteau"—who appears to vanish within the embroidery she designed herself:

■

*Ton col s'effile, orné de rinceaux par la treille.*
*Il semble, à voir tes mains, qu'elles brodent couleur*
*De feuillage une soie où te fondre, pareille.*

■

The character would remain at a distance, and the poet's last impression of her would be of nothing but the dress:

■

*Je sens combien tu m'es lointaine et que tes yeux,*
*L'azur, tes bijoux d'ombre et les étoiles d'aube*
*Vont s'éteindre, captifs du ramage ennuyeux*
*Que tôt figurera ton caprice de robe.*[107]

■

In "L'An suave," dedicated to the painter Marie Laurencin,[108] Breton introduced the poetic subject sartorially again: "Un châle méchamment qui lèse ta frileuse / Épaule nous condamme aux redites."[109] In this poem, fair hands do not embroider but dissipate, but the woman described remains once again tangible only through her accessory, in a facile way, like the fabric around her shoulders. The textile—as well as the shoulder—is hardly tactile, compared to the objective description in the verse of Apollinaire (who had dedicated a poem to Laurencin as well).[110] In his piece titled "1909," Apollinaire does not evoke the symbolism of the fabric but "disinterestedly" presents the simplicity of its cut and construction, thus reflecting a distinctly modern spirit that prefers principle over decoration.

∎

*La dame avait une robe*
*En ottoman violine*
*Et sa tunique brodée d'or*
*Était composée de deux panneaux*
*S'attachent sur l'épaule*[111]

∎

Simplicity also appears in another of Breton's early poems—composed in 1913 but not included in *Mont de piété*—where the focus on the sartorial went beyond evocation to become more realistic. The poet recorded in a playful, lightly ironic way the conversation of seamstresses (the "Lingères" of the title) who are embroidering lace for a dowry:

∎

*Bous, dentelle. "Auriez-*
*Vous pris la manchette?"*
*Boudant tes lauriers,*
*Soupire, Fanchette.*[112]

∎

Since *manchette* denotes not only the piece of cloth that closes the sleeve but also an occasional poem,[113] the term exemplifies again the poet's wish "to live for the bijou." Yet with the new century, the Mallarméan nymphs, fauns, and fairies now became much more mundane and, in Breton's case, also autobiographical rather than poetic, since his mother worked as a couturière and very likely employed a number of girls to finish lace pieces for her.[114]

**69.**
Anders Zorn, *Lace Makers,* 1894. Oil on canvas, 42 × 48 cm. Zornsamlingarna, Mora.

In 1915, the year after he wrote "L'An suave," Breton was drafted into the French army and eventually sent to work at the municipal hospital in Nantes. He compared this period of his life with going through "the school of weary and numbing work" that Rimbaud had described.[115] And it was indeed Rimbaud, together with his interest in Alfred Jarry and Francis Jammes and the continuing correspondence with Valéry and Apollinaire, who began to transform his poetry. That transformation is visible in pieces such as "Décembre" (1915) and "Âge," a poem in prose dated "19 février 1916" and soon afterward dispatched to Apollinaire. Of interest is Valéry's comment on that poem: "Now I see the inspiration you gain. A noble illness takes its course."[116] This inspiration, coupled with the curious descriptiveness that Breton observed in Apollinaire's poetry, manifests itself in the prose-poem through clothing: "Chemises caillées sur la chaise. Un chapeau de soie inaugure de reflets ma poursuite. Homme. . . . Une glace te venge et vaincu me traite en habit ôté. L'instant revient patiner la chair."[117] Breton's gradual change of attitude, toward the sartorial metaphor as well as poetic perception in general, culminated in late spring 1916. The previous year had been one of intellectual torpor, brought on for the most part through the drudgery of army life. By summer Breton, who still fought for new forms of expression, must have been exhausted by the effort to rouse his still-dormant creativity. Yet change was at hand. It would come in the figure of an anglophile dandy. Breton remembered:

■

*It was at Nantes . . . where I became acquainted with Jacques Vaché. He was still receiving treatment for a calf wound at the hospital in the rue du Boccage. One year older than myself, he was a red-haired young man of great elegance. . . . Confined to bed, he busied himself with drawing and painting a series of postcards for which he devised strange captions. Poses, such as you find in men's fashion magazines, were almost the only style he used in these drawings. He loved those glabrous faces, those hierarchical attitudes which you notice in bars. Every morning he spent a good hour arranging one or two photographs, some goblets, and a few violets on a piece of lace covering a small table within reach. During that time I composed Mallarméan poetry.*[118]

■

Mallarmé, in fact, had ceased to be his main model—*poèmes rimbaldiennes* would have been closer to the truth. Yet whatever his literary models, Breton confessed: "I was going through one of the most difficult times of my life; I began to realize that I was not doing what I wanted to do."[119]

But the young student of medicine was not the only one who came under the influence of Vaché. On his hospital bed the convalescent dandy was attended to by a nurse, Jeanne Derrien. She, too, was born in Nantes, where she had known Pierre Bissière, a close friend of Vaché and, like him, part of the coterie of dandyesque, semi-anarchist pupils at the Lycée de Nantes, who had created an uproar with their journal *Le Canard Sauvage* in August 1913. In retrospect, though the poetry published in the journal seems adolescent and stylistically derivative of symbolism, the more reflective texts, reviews, and criticism anticipate some of the undiluted energy of later Dada publications.[120] Vaché and Derrien became friends and he addressed to her, between July 1916 and January 1918, a total of forty-three letters from the front, profusely illustrated with studies of men in both their civil and military apparel. The pictured suits were designs by Vaché reflecting a dandified ideal, whereas the uniforms showed the gritty reality of the "fashion in the trenches"; some sartorial descriptions, observed especially among the British officers, oscillated between the designed and the real.[121]

Derrien and her brother Édouard both played a part in a small enterprise set up by Vaché. He leafed happily through piles of fashion journals and magazines, drawing from their inspiration a number of scenes on postcards depicting fashionably attired characters. These were often then clothed with bits of fabric, as Aragon remembered: "I would like to point out that in 1916 in Nantes, Jacques Vaché designed collages with pieces of fabric on postcards, in editions of twelve that he sold for two francs apiece, and that depicted scenes from the military life of that time, with extremely elegant characters, the women very 'Vie Parisienne.' I ask those who still possess some of them to please come forward."[122] Alternatively, Derrien's brother cut wooden silhouettes after the sketches, which Vaché then filled with line drawing or paint.[123] Needless to say, these figures were the "glabrous men with hierarchical attitudes" whom Breton claimed to have noticed in bars—most of them idealized self-portraits of Vaché (see fig. 71). He described emphatically his friend's vision: "Male elegance steps out of

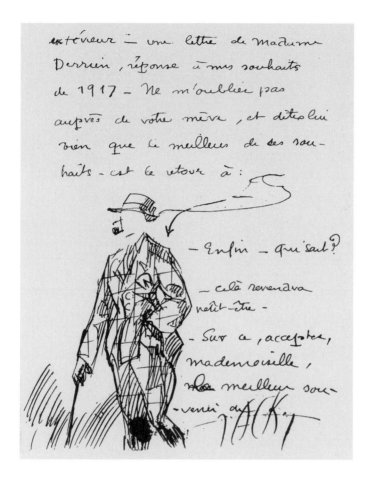

**70.**

Jacques Vaché, illustration in a letter to Jeanne Derrien, January 1917.
Ink on paper, 26 × 21 cm. Private collection, Nantes.

*"I dream of nicely felt Eccentricities or of some pretty and comical insidiousness that causes a lot of deaths, all the while dressed in a softly tailored, light suit; sporting. Can you show me beautiful shoes, open and garnet-colored?"—Jacques Vaché, 1917.*

**71.**
Jacques Vaché (with Édouard Derrien), wooden cutouts. Contemporary photo by P. Trawinski.

the ordinary. The cover of the *Miroir des Modes* is the color of water bathing the sky-scraper in which it is printed. Human bellies set on pilings make excellent parachutes, by the way. The smoke escaping from these top hats frames in black the honorary diploma that we wanted to show our friends and acquaintances."[124] The combination of Vaché's individual dandyism and his fascination with the "look" of fashion magazines made a great impression on Breton. He, too, started leafing through the illustrations, admiring fabrics and designs. Given his dissatisfaction with the lack of development in his earlier "symbolist" poems that had dealt with garments and female apparel, it appears logical that Breton would now adopt a different attitude toward the subject.

The result of this change is "Façon" (as in "fashion," "workmanship," "manner," "mode," etc.), a poem written in June 1916; the author, defying for once the chronological arrangement that ruled *Mont de piété,* showed the great importance he attached to it by placing it at the beginning of his collection. Also, it was the only poem emphasized by the use of italics.

■

*FAÇON*

*Chéruit.*

*L'attachement vous sème en taffetas*
*broché projets,*
*sauf où le chatoiement d'ors se complut.*
*Que juillet, témoin*
*fou, ne compte le péché*
*d'au moins ce vieux roman de fillettes qu'on lut!*

*De fillettes qu'on*
*brigua*
*se mouille (Ans, store au point d'oubli), faillant*
*téter le doux gave,*
*—Autre volupté, quel acte élu t'instaure?—*
*un avenir, éclatante Cour Batave.*

*Étiquetant*

*baume vain l'amour, est-on nanti*

*de froideur*

*un fond, plus que d'heures mais, de mois? Elles*

*font de batiste: À jamais!—L'odeur anéantit*

*tout de même jaloux ce printemps,*

*Mesdemoiselles.* [125]

■

Here, Breton continues the imagery of the seamstresses stitching and embroidering the cloth. Yet these are not the patient hands working away "in the fake daylight of the lamps," as in the earlier "Lingères."[126] These modern girls, no phantoms or fairies but part of a self-confident workforce to be addressed as "Mesdemoiselles," are now employed by the Parisian couture-house of Chéruit to which the poet dedicates his piece. A commentary that Breton wrote in 1930 stresses the impact that the fashion journals at Vaché's bedside had made on him: "'Façon' attached itself to the margins of countless *journaux de mode* that delighted the author during that time."[127]

Once again artistic inspiration originated in the interplay of *mode et modernité.* Proust also confirms such interplay in his *Recherche,* where he remembers the painter Elstir (i.e., Claude Monet) advising him on the importance of haute couture as the yardstick for the contemporariness and actuality of portraits. According to Elstir, only very few designers possessed both the artistry and style to make their gowns representative of the character of modern times and thus worthy of depiction, while at the same time retaining a link to the past, to aesthetic tradition. "You see, there are very few good dress-making houses at present, one or two only, Callot—although they go in rather too freely for lace—Doucet, Chéruit, Paquin sometimes."[128]

With "Façon," Breton entered for the first time the exclusive world of the rue de la Paix (Doucet, Paquin after 1900) and the place Vendôme (Chéruit, located next to the Ritz and Paquin before 1900). Later, in "Une Vague de rêves," Aragon, and with him other dadaists and surrealists (such as Robert Desnos and Pierre Unik),[129] would follow; and Breton himself would return to this fashionable realm with the last poem of his *Mont de piété* in 1919. As an aspiring young designer, the couturier Paul Poiret remembered his ambiguous impression at his first meeting with Mme Chéruit: "I have never seen anything more troubling than this pretty woman in the middle of so much elegance."[130] So too in "Façon" we find no longer feminine charm but a sophisticated, distanced—"have we guaranteed / by our coldness / a foundation"—elegance that determines the value of both the poetic subject and the writing itself.

■

*L'attachement vous sème en taffetas*
*broché projets,*
*sauf où le chatoiement d'ors se complut.*

■

Everything lies in the make and making of dress and poem; the more complex they were, the more fitting for modernity. The composition of Breton's verses reflects this belief. The first stanza consists of lines of twelve syllables (alexandrines), the second lines of eleven syllables, and the third lines of thirteen syllables, although the rhythm and syntactical breaks make it hard to follow the internal structure of the verses.[131] Its *façon*—12–11–13—thus appears similar to the measurements for a couture dress: shoulder width (or bust), tightened waistline, and wider hip size. Although the piece seems to be in free verse, the deliberate refusal to alternate feminine and masculine rhymes and the breaking up of rhymes—the words at times following each other, at times arhythmically separated—is meant to challenge readers and make them search even harder for possible coherence within the syntactical and poetic fabric. Valéry was quick to recognize Breton's idea:

■

*Here comes Façon which, in the rue de la Paix, between the phials by Coty, accepts savagery in multicolored metaphors, which he, the follower, does not wear out, but prefers to follow some young girl or reverie with precious expression.*

*Is Rimbaud loitering? The brain on the pavement at the corner of the rue des fines Capucines?*[132]

■

To dream of the "precious," combined with the sartorial fetish to which, inspired by Vaché's fascination, he gave new value, becomes Breton's aim. In his amorous pursuit of the female there comes a moment when he is challenged to bring the two "objectives"—sex and dressing—together by entering À la Cour Batave, a well-known lingerie shop near the porte Saint-Denis. Aragon recalls in his memoirs:

- 

*[Breton] found himself not far from what used to be the Cour des Miracles, off rue Réamur, and he saw before him, rising into the sky, the high windows of the store À la Cour Batave, which now won't strike you anything as impressive as when I was told about them: one of the very first poems that my new friend showed me when he met in 1917 had been "Façon," written in 1916, which André kept very close (and which, before being printed, carried as epigraph the name of a couture house Chéruit, written by a woman, the woman who made "Façon" in 1916, as he wrote to me a bit later) and whose lines I never forget " . . . a future, the dazzling Cour Batave!"[133]*

- 

Alas, the courted seamstresses of the couture house appear indifferent. They continue to label "balm vain love" and work on the batiste fabric. "Forever!" is their defiant reply when asked whether they will resist seduction for hours, even months. But no bitterness or despair grips the poet, since he has found a voice more contemporary than before. "Theme, language, aim, design, metric, everything is new, in future fashion and *façon*," as his mentor Valéry affirms.[134] Breton has escaped the deadlock in his quest for a new mode of expression. That this break has ephemeral high fashion as both its subject and its catalyst is hardly ironic; indeed, it is logical. Not only Baudelaire but also Mallarmé and Rimbaud would have volunteered to give their (modernist) approval, as Pastoureau noted: "In a poem like 'Façon,' Rimbaud enters with Breton the couture house of Chéruit—although Mallarmé still follows them at a distance."[135] And this distance was smaller than one might think; on the arm of Mallarmé walked, of course, Marguerite de Ponty.[136]

Yet the female fashion in Breton's writing hints merely at a newly found *parole*. The Chéruit piece alters the stylistics but not the substance of *langue-costume*. Leaving Mallarmé, especially in his later phase, at a distance so that one can walk beside Rimbaud hardly implies radical change. By following Vaché, however, whose "male elegance," as Breton had put it, "steps out of the ordinary," he found a focus on male apparel that would prove to be far better suited to change artistic perception. He became thus able to anticipate Barthes's structuralist approach, as any alteration or subversion of this subject would inevitably change *le costume* and thus (poetic) language per se.

In *Anicet,* Aragon baptized his portrait of Breton by choosing a name composed from a line of "Façon": "batiste: À jamais!" became Baptiste Ajamais.

■

*It was then [as Aragon remembers his friend's conversion after July 1916] that he encountered Harry James, the modern man of whom the heroes of popular novels, American serials, and adventure films were but fragmentary reflections. Who could say what happened between these two men? A mystery! But when, a few months later, Baptiste Ajamais came back to Paris—in a way similar to that of someone who, having looked long enough into a mirror, would recognize himself if he met himself in the street—one could notice a profound change in him, the sign of great resolutions and a certain air about him which gave food for thought to many people.*[137]

■

Obviously, the average man looks in the mirror not to catch a glance at someone who has found a novel artistic expression, but rather to spend time adjusting his tie or brushing his lapels, thereby assuming the distinct and distinguished presence fit for urban modernity. Like Vaché, the true modernist looks to tradition not for inspiration but rather for the remains of a self-conscious reflection of his or her own apparel and appearance. "Are you sure that Apollinaire is still alive," asks Vaché early in 1917, "or that Rimbaud even existed? For me, I don't think so."[138] And a few weeks later he writes: "The same with modernity—it's constant and yet killed off every night—We ignore MALLARMÉ, without hatred, but he's dead anyway—But we don't recognize Apollinaire anymore."[139]

What Simmel realized in a sociological context, Vaché restated metaphorically: *la modernité,* like *la mode,* dies every night. In order to keep ahead, or to keep one's distance, depending on whether one wishes to appear as avant-gardist or dandy, one has to embrace the fragmentary and the novel: "of slicing romanticism with telephone wire . . ."[140] Consciously or not, Breton took his advice and began to view Rimbaud from the same distance he previously had accorded late Mallarméan symbolism. He took issue with Rimbaud by employing another sartorial metaphor from the supply in his pawnshop *Mont de piété.*

■

*FORÊT-NOIRE**

                                                                    *Out*

*Tendre capsule        etc melon*

*Madame de Saint-Gobain trouve le temps long seule*
*ne côtelette se fane*
                    *Relief du sort*
*Où        sans volets        ce pignon blanc*
   *Cascades*
                *Les schlitteurs sont favorisés*

                                            *Ça souffle*
que salubre est le vent               *le vent des crémeries*

                *L'auteur de l'Auberge de l'Ange Gardien*
*L'an dernier est tout de même mort*
*À propos*

                    *De Tubingue à ma rencontre*
                    *Se portent les jeunes Kepler Hegel*
                    *Et le bon camarade*

**RIMBAUD PARLE.*[141]

■

In this poem set in the Black Forest, the protagonist Rimbaud speaks through the author Breton. Pastoureau attempted to interpret this poem, after consulting Breton himself; he suggests that "here, permission to speak is given to Rimbaud at a moment that has to be regarded as indeed critical for the course of his life, since it is undoubtedly the very instant when the rupture occurs between the poetic persona that he had been and the entirely different persona that he would become."[142] Is it the pervasive sense of reality, in Rimbaud's refusal to "create" any more poetry thereafter, that turns the poetic persona into the "other"? The key to Breton's poem lies in Paterne Berrichon's nineteenth-century biography of Rimbaud: Paul Verlaine has learned that his erstwhile lover, after their disastrous sojourns in London and Brussels (where Verlaine spent two years in prison for shooting Rimbaud), has relinquished art and found employment in Germany as a private tutor for children. Verlaine, fresh from his prison sentence, lovesick and filled with religious fervor, rushes to meet the younger poet. Dressed like a tramp he creates a scene in front of Rimbaud, who has settled nicely into his new bourgeois life. In order to avoid any further melodrama, the embarrassed and furious Rimbaud takes Verlaine for a walk. Once deep in the woods, he lets fly his anger and beats Verlaine bloody.[143] Pastoureau sets this episode in relation to Breton's poem:

■

*Rimbaud is meant to start speaking at the very moment when he gets back on his feet, having left his companion knocked out on the ground. The "solution" in his previous language is accompanied by a "lyrical" movement that is likely to reconcile "a manner of expression in the last degree clownish and exaggerated," which he has already renounced, and to introduce a certain "umour," similar to the one Jacques Vaché was to find, when he himself aspired to success in all things vulgar and mean.*[144]

■

For Rimbaud, Breton, and Vaché (though the latter chose to abandon any claim to literary immortality), a rupture between the lyrical in poetic tradition and *modernité* is necessary to find individual expression. Sartorial reality, not symbolic masquerade, becomes their mutual aim. The embarrassment and disgust Rimbaud felt when confronted with the bohemian rags of Verlaine provoked the confrontation.[145] Rimbaud wanted "Out" and emphasized this point physically. After knocking down Verlaine he picks up his "Tendre capsule etc melon" and walks away toward a new mode of expression. The ironic overtones within the comfortably bourgeois accessory of the "melon" are underlined by the "etc.," as if there had been numerous poetic descriptions of the bowler hat, like "tender capsule," before. This irony was related to the "umour," coined by Vaché as an *Ubu*-esque satire that ridiculed life, death, culture.[146] It is embodied by someone who laughs at himself: "But—of course, this isn't definitive and umour derives too much from a sensation of not being very difficult to express—I think that it's a sensation—I was going to say SENSE—also—of the theatrical (and joyless, too) futility of everything."[147] This is nihilism that opposes past and present in equal measure, but reaffirms aesthetic principles—principles to be viewed from a great distance. Irony is directed not only against literary tradition but against oneself. It attaches itself to the ephemeral and fragmentary in fashion. Change becomes the ever-present savior from the perils of linear narratives as well as successive or progressive movements: "Oh! enough—enough! and even too much!—a black suit, trousers with sharp creases, highly polished shoes. Paris—striped cloth—pyjamas and uncut books—where are you going tonight? . . . nostalgic things that died from before the war—And then—what next??" How, Vaché asked Breton at the very beginning of their correspondence, could they go on? And one possible answer was both *Ubu*-esque and full of "umour": "We'll have to laugh, won't we?"[148]

In order to be able to satirize what exists, one must be well versed in its rules—able to live them in the manner of Barbey d'Aurevilly's archetypal dandy, who respects customs only to subvert them the very next instant. The bohemian past of the adolescent Rimbaud, who had been known to discard the minimal contents of his wardrobe through the hotel window, claiming that nudity liberated his body, prepared him for the later change in attitude when he would switch to ostentatiously bourgeois attire.[149] By the same token, it is his intimate knowledge of avant-garde and traditional art that allows Vaché to form his critique and to stay distanced through his adherence to ephemeral fashion. Their knowledge of both *costume* and *coutume* provided them with the *langue* that comes to be cut up into an individual, modern *parole.*[150]

For (the unassumingly dressed) Breton, the task was going to be more difficult. Drawing on the poetic tradition of past decades proved a dead end, and only the metaphorical usage of clothing and accessories prevented his lyric from becoming a routine expression. By late spring 1919 Breton felt it time to renew his quest for modern expression. Once again his shop, called *Mont de piété*, parted with a sartorial item; this time it was

■

## Le Corset Mystère

**Mes belles lectrices,**

à force d'en voir de **toutes les couleurs Cartes splendides,** *à effets de lumière,* Venise


Autrefois les meubles de ma chambre étaient fixés solidement aux murs et je me faisais attacher pour écrire :

**J'ai le pied marin**


nous adhérons à une sorte de **Touring Club** sentimental

## UN CHÂTEAU À LA PLACE DE LA TÊTE

*c'est aussi le* **Bazar de la Charité Jeux** très amusants pour tous âges ;
**Jeux poétiques,** etc.

Je tiens Paris comme — pour vous dévoiler l'avenir — votre main ouverte

**la taille bien prise.**

■

On this final poem of his first collection, which marks an intermediary break in his early poetic development, Breton comments: "One of the most authentic of collages. (Cutout advertisements alternate with ready-made commonplaces and minute fabrications.) One can still read the rather beautiful sign of 'Le Corset Mystère' on the first floor balcony of a house in the rue de la Paix."[152] The sign advertised a corset that had been patented by Mme Guillot at the beginning of the twentieth century. This special undergarment was labeled "mysterious" because it could not be detected under the gown, as it replaced stays with stiffened fabric, yet nevertheless shaped women's figures to fit into the tight bodices of their day and evening wear. Breton's surreal evocation of this item of clothing was first published in June 1919 in *Littérature,* issue 4, which also carried on its flyleaf an advertisement for *Mont de piété* ("to be published on the 20th of June").[153] The poem thus was made to represent the entire book, indicating the importance that the author attached to it (rivaled only by "Façon," which begins the collection).

Max Ernst, at that time working far away in Cologne, uses the very same image of the "mysterious corset"—that is, a garment that has gained metaphorical independence from the body or is alienated from it—for a cover study of his own first collection of work.[154] It seems only logical that both works, though independently produced, shared the same frame of reference and poetic postulate. Ernst's series of lithographs is titled *"FIAT MODES—pereat ars."* This ironic adaptation of the humanist motto "fiat iustitia et pereat mundus" remains the epigraph to the relationship of fashion and modernity: "Art may perish, LET THERE BE FASHION." The French word *modes* stands out from the Latin in the motto as a distinctly modern and "quite beautiful sign," like the neologism *modernité* that Baudelaire had introduced in his prose midway into the nineteenth century.

While "Façon" is skillfully tailored after a poetic pattern, "Le Corset Mystère" appears as an assemblage of diverse cutouts combined on one sheet of paper.[155] The lines of the poem combined words the author saw on one of his strolls through the rue de la Paix with an ironic address to his audience, "Mes belles lectrices"—a salutation used in both Mallarmé's *La Dernière Mode* and in Breton's and Vaché's source of inspiration, the magazine *Le Miroir de Modes.* It also made use of ready-made expressions: for example, the fashionable credo "we are members of a kind of emotional Touring Club," which reappeared a few months later in Tzara's *Bulletin Dada;*[156] automatism, like "a castle instead of a head"; the flâneur's promise "to hold Paris . . . like your open hand"; and finally a line referring back to the garment of the title, which will

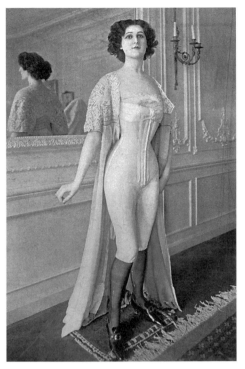

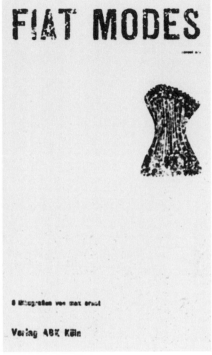

**72.**
Madame Guillot, underwear for theater and town (*corset mystère*), 1900s. Photo by Chéri-Rousseau and Glauth. Published in *Les Modes,* no. 96 (winter 1908). Staatliche Museen zu Berlin, Kunstbibliothek.

**73.**
Max Ernst, study for the cover label of *FIAT MODES—pereat ars,* 1920. Block pull and typography on card, 23.3 × 14.7 cm.

generate "her elegant figure." Breton considered his cut-up composition "the most authentic collage" since, as he later told Aragon, "I didn't write one line, believe you me."[157]

However, his attempt to preserve a semantic construct and its limited range of references (to fashion and to Paris, particularly its beau monde or bohemia) made "Le Corset Mystère" neither a poem in the free dadaist spirit, which proposed the combination of words pulled out of a hat or assembled from newspaper scraps,[158] nor an anticipation of automatic writing. In terms of literary models it remains a hybrid form, influenced by Apollinaire and displaying the associative leaps of Rimbaud or Lautréamont. But it also owes a considerable amount to Vaché's writing. His letters to Breton were collages of observations, dialogues, and words on shop signs or in shop windows, often carefully drawn so that they evoked different typefaces and interspersed with sketches.

■

—*Blanche Acétylène*

    *Vous tous!—Mes beaux whiskys—Mon horrible mixture . . .*
    *ruisselant jaune—local de pharmacie—Ma chartreuse*
    *verte—Citrin—Rose ému de Carthame—*
    *Fume!*
        *Fume!*
            *Fume!*
    *Angusture-noix vomique et l'incertitude des sirops—*
    *Je suis un mosaïste.*
    *"Say, Waiter—You are a damn' fraud, you are—"*[159]

■

Breton's sent the first transcript of "Le Corset Mystère" to Aragon in May 1919; it echoed Vaché's style and, once set up in type, it looked like a collage of press cuttings. Breton's correspondence with Vaché from that time displays an even rougher, less stylized approach. The last letter to his friend in Nantes, actually written after Vaché's death (news of which took over a week to reach his friends in Paris), is a more direct version of Vaché's carefully written and drawn letter-collages. Bonnet describes its physical appearance:

▪

*The letter from 13 January is composed of a multitude of cutouts glued onto two pages, as was Breton's habit at that time: a variety of fragments from newspaper or magazine articles; pages torn from a calendar; pieces of a wrappers for a chocolate bar; parts of diverse labels; the portrait of a masked character "The Man with Two Faces," probably lifted from a film program or journal, with the words: "That's You Jacques!"; a caricature of Clemenceau in woman's clothing, complete with large hat and umbrella. Breton's text ran between these collages.*[160]

▪

Vaché made up his letter-collages from firsthand experience. He quoted himself, what other people said to him, signs he had seen, or scenes he chose to depict. Breton, in contrast, assembles secondhand information, texts he has read and cut out, while the information he wants to convey is coherently composed in between the fragments. For Vaché the cutting-up technique was integral to expressing the experience of modern life; for Breton it was confined to the realm of art.[161] In "La Confession dédaigneuse," he reflects on this: "I think [Jacques Vaché] reproached me for my leanings toward modernism."[162]

The same difference between the two can be seen in their use of fashion as the pivotal point of reference. For Vaché it was his *costume,* the male fashion that he wore himself, that constituted an individual and subtle challenge to *langue,* to sartorial and social norms alike. But Breton's early work is concerned from the outset with female clothing, beginning with the most ephemeral accessory and progressing to actual dress and then to lingerie and corsets; a tentative approach by the young poet through the layers of fabric toward the nude female form, which would be celebrated so excessively in surrealism. Because the topic was women's clothing, his experience of it had to remain distanced and secondhand, mediated through notions of sexuality, love, disgust, fear, and so on. Up to 1919, throughout his first formative phase, Breton is content to observe style, both in female fashion and in poetry, that is, *parole.*

This style first is borrowed from symbolism, where the clothing had been imbued with spirituality; then is fused with the exclamations of Rimbaud and Lautréamont, who saw clothes as the mysterious shell or armature of the body; and finally, under the influence of Vaché, executes a turn toward the written and visual collage. The last phase is dominated by the sartorial commodity, which Breton quotes from fashion magazines or shop signs. He thus moves toward *modernité* as the aesthetic mirror of social reification, and in Breton's first book clothing becomes progressively independent from its wearer. As a theme or metaphor the corporeal subject steps back while the object advances.

### 5.8.2 *L'éternel carré de dentelle*

Vaché could influence his friend and admirer only so far; to actually live by clothes was asking too much of Breton, even if they provided an ample source of inspiration. In 1917 Vaché wrote to Derrien about the particular comfort he needed while stuck in the trenches: "It is a bit small in here, but I still keep close to my camp bed[,] . . . the eternal square of lace, and my favorite drawings—*well.*"[163] This piece of lace that he used to dress his collages and puppets acts as a reminder of Barbey d'Aurevilly's "espèce dentelle," described in the context of dandyism and Brummell, as well as of Mme de Ponty's last article for *La Dernière Mode*.[164] We have seen how he acquired this habit the previous year while he was confined to bed and how Breton juxtaposed his memory of Vaché "arranging one or two photographs, some goblets, and a few violets on a piece of lace covering a small table" with his own composition of "Mallarméan poetry" during that same time. Is one to take this as an expression of analogous sentiments, the "eternal square of lace" as the material equivalent to Mallarmé's refined sensibility?[165] Years later, in the second half of the 1930s, Breton qualifies his earlier recollection with psychoanalytical hindsight: "Except as a type of finery, Vaché no longer retains a superego of pure simulation, a genuine *dentelle* [both "lace" and "nicety"] of its own. An extraordinary lucidity confers an unforeseen—yet willfully macabre and most alarming—turn to his relationship with 'self.'"[166]

Vaché's dandyism styles self-negation to be the only proper means of existing. No commitment or postulate could make him assume any given position. Since his creativity, like that of his friends Breton, Aragon, and Fraenkel, was primarily channeled into poetry, he had to translate his attitude into the negation of literature as a sublime expression. Yet this expression was somewhat ambiguous because it referred to tradition and similarly adhered to the avant-gardist change of structure while maintaining a fixed set of literary values. In modernity, it is fashion that alternates in a similar manner between the sublime notion of art and its futile antithesis. According to Barthes it creates "a dialectic of the serious and the futile, i.e., if the frivolity of Fashion were *immediately* taken absolutely serious, we would then have one of the most elevated forms of literary experience: i.e. the very movement of the Mallarméan dialectic apropos Fashion itself (*La Dernière Mode*)."[167]

The "literary experience" is transferred into the physical world by Vaché in an attempt to "live" fashion under precarious and difficult circumstances, in the trenches and the hospital. "L'éternel carré de dentelle" is a miniature cosmos that contains his philosophy. It is serious and futile at the same time, both challenge and self-negation. As part of Vaché's sensibility, it marks the move from the sublime to the ironic. It becomes an accessory to his clothes or, when he is undressed and tucked into the hospital bed, even their representation. The sartorial is the passage from the sensuous to sense.[168]

Vaché thus sides (inadvertently, to be sure) with Hegel, who confirmed in his *Aesthetics* that "clothing is simply what really emphasises the posture and is in this respect to be regarded as an advantage because it deprives us of an immediate view of what, as purely sensuous, is without significance, and shows us only what is related to the situation expressed by posture and movement."[169] The dandy, especially the literary-minded one, duplicates, consciously or not, Hegel's premises: "This is how, in clothing, the sensual and tangible is dissolved in the intelligible. The clothes of the dandy thus fit into a signifying structure."[170] The "invisible finally opens up" as Barthes has demanded (as we saw at the beginning of this chapter), and control of the significance of the sartorial, whether in the equation of *costume* and *langue,* or purely in the use of fashion as a paradigm for modernity, passed from Vaché to Breton. For the latter it would remain catalyst and subject of the poetic, as the transition to real life seemed impossible and far too distracting from the "sublime" artistic tasks that the leader of the surrealists would set himself. This particular paradigm of fashion—which began in 1913, matured structurally in 1916, and ended in 1919—would, after Vaché's death and the publication of the "Pawnshop," never again feature prominently in Breton's work.

## ■ 5.9 Modern Mythology

The increased dominance of the object over the subject within the "tragedy of culture" observed by Simmel aided to varying degrees the Parisian modernists around Breton in the 1910s and early 1920s. Imbuing humans with a mystery behind their outer appearance, these artists had to find a way to make the mysterious become manifest. Unanimously, they chose clothes and accessories as symbolic of hidden fantasies and phantasmagories: close to the wearer's skin, yet nevertheless independent in its aesthetic and mythic expression.

By definition, myths belong to the collective, as Jung explained in regard to the unconscious—a view many writers such as Breton and Caillois were to eventually embrace.[171] However, there also exists an individualized myth, as Aragon established in his Parisian *flâneries* up to the mid-1920s, not an individual interpretation of a common perception but a creation in one's very own vocabulary. Thus it is not the collective unconscious but the poetic perception of the object, shaped via literary tradition, that creates modern mythology. Like fashion's set code of dressing, which applies to the general public, so certain myths become an integral part of society. Yet, even as individuality determines the choice of clothes of modern men and women through their awareness of tradition, the mythic that extends beyond the individual dominates avant-garde artists who attempt to remain indifferent to set historical and aesthetic customs. The *mythologie moderne* had a deliberately limited scope of expression. Where clothes were concerned, only half a dozen garments and accessories recurred as metaphors within dadaist and surrealist writing and visual arts: the hat, monocle, tie, dress, glove, and shoe. The mythology attached to these commodified sartorial objects is challenged by each artist in turn who wishes to oppose conventional usage in both society and the avant-garde.

Two metaphors in particular exemplify the exploration of individual myths that worked against the continuation of both the aesthetic and historic order. One, the monocle, was a metaphor proper; the other could be regarded as a metaphoric composite of two opposite elements: the locomotive and the top hat.

### 5.9.1 Monocularity

In the first issue of the new series of *Littérature* (March 1922), Breton recalls a strange dream. He found himself at the beach, where he witnessed men shooting at two birds; once tracked down, they turned out to resemble cows or horses. The animal that was unwounded appeared to watch over the other one, which died with "a curious expression in its eyes." One of these eyes remained dull, while the other was luminously colored.

■

*It was then that Monsieur Roger Lefébure who, I do not know why, found himself among us, seized the phosphorescent eye and used it as a monocle.*

*Seeing this, one of the onlookers thought it well to report the following anecdote:*

*Recently, as is his custom, Monsieur Paul Poiret was dancing in front of his clients, when suddenly his monocle fell to the ground and broke.*

*Monsieur Paul Éluard, who happened to be present, was kind enough to offer him his own, but it suffered the same fate.*[172]

■

This peculiar dream might well have had its precedent in reality. Poiret, still the most famous couturier at that time, had (through his sister Nicole Groult) become friends with the artistic coterie around Picabia in Barcelona; he kept himself informed of the activities that led to the formation of the group Dada in June 1916 (including Arthur

Cravan) and the publication of the first issue of *391* (January 1917), Picabia's journal, which carried the spirit of Dada throughout Europe and across the Atlantic.[173] Issue 8 of this magazine, produced in Zurich in February 1919, featured a "society column" by "Pharamousse" (Picabia himself); it advertises, next to the activities of the members of the avant-garde in Paris, New York, Barcelona, and Zurich, "Paul Poiret gowns and coats, rue du Faubourg St–Honoré."[174]

Thus when Breton recalls this anecdote, a number of artists had already begun to admire the material creations (and perhaps the financial generosity) of the couturier. "The Dadas are definitely ready for Paul Poiret," declares Picabia and immediately follows this statement with the observation that "morality is ill-disposed in a pair of trousers."[175] One has to wonder whether his declaration referred only to what is concealed by the trouser rather than to the couturier's unprecedented attention to its fabric and cut.

Poiret's studio might well have received Éluard or some other dadaists, though neither they nor their partners were able to afford the designer's exorbitant prices.[176] A few months after Breton's dream was published, Picabia's lover Gabrielle Buffet introduced Man Ray to Poiret; this encounter instigated his career as a fashion photographer, which was to run parallel to his work as the chronicler of dada and surrealism.[177] That these two strands within his photography are closely related is apparent in his photos for Tzara's essay "D'un certain automatisme du goût," published in *Minotaure* in December 1933, where both the author and the photographer explored the resemblance between the different shapes of women's hat and female genitalia.[178] Tzara transfers the paradigmatic importance of fashion as the "transitory and fugitive expression of beauty," asserted by Baudelaire in the 1850s, into the subconscious of its wearer. The modern mythology cherished by the dadaists and early surrealists took on distinctly sexual overtones, or rather undertones. However, Tzara did not participate in the "psychoanalytical" interpretations of modern society and its objects that were favored by the surrealists. His essay is decidedly ironic (dadaesque in essence); it describes the hat models as overtly symbolic yet clearly antiphallic, thus subtly subverting the Freudian view.[179]

**74.**
Man Ray, photograph for Tristan Tzara's essay "On a Certain Automatism of Taste,"
12 × 18 cm. Published in *Minotaure,* nos. 3–4 (winter 1933). Collection Skira, Geneva.

Tzara qualifies his own distinctive and omnipresent accessory, the monocle, with a similar degree of narcissism and irony: an open admiration for the object coupled with hidden ridicule for its pretentious appearance. Wearing the monocle was more of a necessity for him than for any other of the Parisian dadaists; his sight had been poor since childhood.[180] Yet seen from the more important stylistic angle, the monocle reflects the power of fashion to break up linear historic progression through its quotation from past models. In Tzara the two reasons for *monocularity* are combined: it continues an aesthetic and literary tradition—the artist as sophisticated dandy; and ironically subverts that tradition—through that ahistorical/transhistorical accessory, the glance of contempt and ridicule strikes the unsuspecting beholder or reader. For the young French dadaists at the end of the Great War, these views appeared at the same time foreign and familiar and so their attraction was doubled instantly. Historically, the monocle first glistened in the eyes of the Da-dandies from central Europe—Zurich, Bucharest, or Berlin—where the grand bohemians Walter Serner and Tzara, as well as Raoul Hausmann and Richard Huelsenbeck, sported the eyeglass to complete their dandified dressing.

In Paris, in contrast, the tradition of poet-dandy, which was mirrored in the monocles of men such as Barbey d'Aurevilly (see his essay on Brummell, where the term "dandy" was first defined in French), Robert de Montesquiou (the ruling literary amateur and full-time snob in Paris from 1885 to 1914), and Whistler, marked the remembrance of the beau monde as extolled in Proust's *temps perdu*. For Proust's protagonists, the correct insertion of the eyeglass wins entrée into an enclosed sophisticated world. "Odette approved that Swann, his elegance elusive to the forces of dandyism, added, out of necessity, a provocative monocle to his apparel."[181]

Subversive satire combined with nihilism and the display of profound ennui formed an integral part of efforts of the German, Swiss, and Romanian dadaists to confront bourgeois bigotry. Politically committed, they were always ready to discard the monocle if the conflict demanded it. At the beginning of 1917, Walter Serner epitomized the dadaist nihilistic distance in Zurich with his *haute-bourgeois* attire—black morning coat, striped trousers, pearl-gray cravat—and his advice "that each young man should as early as possible acquire a cachet that serves as support for his outer

**75.**

Paul Helleu, *Portrait Made while Whistler Posed for Boldini,* 1897. Drypoint on laid paper, 35 × 26.1 cm. Library of Congress (Pennel Collection), Washington, D.C.

*"I am very happy to answer the reproach of 'perfect uselessness.' How so? Is there not still something completely useless left in a time that utilizes everything, even the superfluous? And not just something useless, but something that has realized perfection within its uselessness? I do not mean to jest, but herein lies something that allows us to dream. . . ."—Jehan Durieux on the monocle, 1921.*

ego."[182] However, if the situation became serious, when the struggle for expression had to take precedence over pose, Serner was prepared to replace the accessory with substance: "At the age of twenty, one has to spit out the monocle, at thirty remove the cigarette behind the ear," as he wrote in his manifesto of 1919.[183] The protest, though sophisticated, must be regarded as merely adolescent if action does not follow attitude. But what if one is not prepared to remove the eyeglass while engaging in a struggle—whether physical or intellectual? The advantage of keeping a monocle in the eye during a fight is the impression it conveys of utmost contempt and disrespect. While Tzara and Éluard were battling out their different views on stage of the Théâtre Michel, Tzara's reserve as well as the position of his monocle was rattled by Éluard's fists, but both would remain in place during the course of further conflicts.[184] Whistler had taken an even tougher stance when confronted by a hostile opinion. The *Echo de Paris* described in 1890 a thrashing administered by the painter to an unfortunate critic, after which "The artist exited refreshed, in good form and smiling from the encounter. Even his monocle had not left its rightful place in the right eye." Mallarmé would dispatch this review to Whistler in London, calling the account "well placed and beautifully described."[185]

Picabia's cover for *Littérature* of February/March 1923 offered an ironic solution to the hazard that the fragility of the eyeglass posed within the course of action. His drawing depicts a muscular athlete wearing nothing but black trunks and a monocle, which is fixed by a cord to his right nipple.[186] Here, the eyeglass becomes part of the physique, and the modernist quest for athleticism is combined with the sophistication of the Da-dandy. It was matched in real life by the Berlin dadaist Raoul Hausmann, who liked to be photographed with naked torso and monocle, which complemented each other as he acted out the modern obsession for stylized, "geometric" perfection of the body.[187] Tzara observes this attitude in an article written for *Vanity Fair* in 1922 on the Dada congress in Weimar, where "Raoul Hausmann, the poet-dancer and Czechoslovakian dadaist attended with his monocle."[188]

The Da-dandy is capable of putting himself on display, in clownish costume or even undressed; yet the eyeglass would always act as a transparent barrier, setting a symbolic distance between him and the rest of society. His role and integrity remain

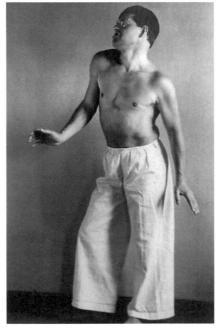

**76.**
Francis Picabia, cover illustration for
*Littérature,* February 1923. Ink on paper, ca.
30 × 20 cm.

**77.**
August Sander, *Raoul Hausmann Dancing,*
1929. Vintage print, 22.5 × 15 cm. © 2000
Die Photographische Sammlung/SK Stiftung
Kultur-August Sander Archiv, Cologne;
DACS, London.

intact, as the criticism and ridicule hurled at him from the audience is reflected in the eyeglass and thrown back into the face of adversity. In both inactive ennui as well as performed nonsense, the monocle of the dadaist ensured his distance and protected his artistic raison d'être.

In the same spirit as these activities in Berlin, Barcelona, Zurich, and Geneva, Vaché, who went as far as to negate his own creativity, renewed the monocle as a symbol of nihilistic ennui and irony in France. His position, originating from nineteenth-century dandyism in London and Paris, was coupled with his idea of *umour,* as we have seen. Vaché's letters dispatched from the Franco-German front to Breton, Theodore Fraenkel, and Aragon restate the metaphor of stylized boredom again and again: for example, "I take my crystal monocle and a theory for troubling paintings for a walk around villages in ruin."[189] Even incessant bombardment did not stop aesthetic reflections, whether they were deep or remained on the glistening surface of the glass. "I am very bored behind my glass monocle, I dress in khaki and knock the Germans about," he wrote a few months later to Fraenkel,[190] characterizing his situation as more mundane than mysterious—the crystal monocle becomes ordinary glass. In August 1917 he sent the following erratic lines, reaffirming that the tradition of modernity had to be simultaneously acknowledged and dispensed with.

▪

*We neither care for ART nor for artists (down with Apollinaire) AND how RIGHT TOGRATH IS TO ASSASSINATE THE POET! However, since this is so, it's necessary to gulp down a drop of acid or old lyricism, doing it in a lively jerk—because the locomotives go fast.*

*The same with modernity—it's constant and yet killed off every night—We ignore MALLARMÉ, without hatred, but he's dead anyway—We don't recognize Apollinaire anymore—BECAUSE—we suspect them of creating art far too consciously, of slicing romanticism with telephone wire and not knowing the dynamos. THE STARS are still disconnected!—it's boring—and then sometimes they speak so seriously!— A man who believes is a curiosity. BUT SINCE SOME PEOPLE ARE NATURAL HAMS . . .[191]*

▪

In the space of two paragraphs Vaché dismisses Mallarmé, the *esprit nouveau* of Apollinaire and Max Jacob, of André Gide and the editor-cum-writer Pierre Reverdy. He then concludes his attack with a self-portrait: "Two deadly blazing eyes and the crystal circle of a monocle—having a tentacled typewriter—I would like that better."[192] Yet even a typewriter holding one captive could much more easily be dispensed with than the eyeglass; the irony in defiantly wearing this accessory had to outweigh any literary production: "Naturally, written irony is unbearable—but naturally You are well aware that *umour* is not like irony—that's the way it is,—what do you want, that's just the way things are—in fact, all this is amusing—how amusing indeed! (and if we killed ourselves also, instead of merely going away?)"[193]

The black humor of Vaché belongs equally to the nihilist and the Romantic modes. His experiences seem to have taught him that there was no escape from ennui, least of all through writing a poem or novel. The trenches made it clear that reality had nothing to offer but barbarism and barbed wire. Thus he turned more and more toward a Romantic idea of the dandy, supported by his penchant for *le genre anglais*, popular cinema, and magazines. The roman à clef by Jean Sarment, a close friend of Vaché from his schooldays, imagined a last reunion of the Groupe de Nantes, when the nineteen-year-olds presented each other with parting gifts:

■

> *Each of us gets his envelope. Each writes with grave irony the following in-*
> *scription:*
> "*Cendre de nos rêves.*"

> *—Oh! remarks Bouvier [i.e., Vaché]. He lets the monocle drop from his eye as*
> *if overcome by nostalgia, and, just to be different, he inscribes in his small*
> *crooked writing the following words in green ink [in English]:*
> "*Ashes of our dreams.*"[194]

■

Even if a character like Jacques Bouvier-Vaché were to be overcome with a real sentiment such as regret or nostalgia, a quickly raised eyebrow, a deliberately dropped eyeglass as the ironical quotation of a dated accessory, saves him from losing distance as well as composure. He concentrates on the minute object in order to forgo any pondering of the "important" questions in life. Breton remembers this habit in his portrait of Vaché for the *Anthology of Black Humor:* "The red hair, the 'deadly blazing' eyes, and the glacial butterfly monocle supply his continually desired dissonance and isolation. His personal negation"—a character trait that was curiously common among the Da-dandies Vaché, Cravan, Rigaut, and perhaps Tzara—"is as complete as possible, under the disguise of pure form pushed to the limit: all 'the exterior signs of self-respect' were there, yet a self-respect of some automatic adhesive kind to what the spirit finds as the most insensate."[195] The principal among these ambiguous signs of appreciating tradition and customs, as well as pose, is the *papillon glacial,* the "glacial butterfly" that filters and screens off the *papillon noirs* that might be observed by the mind's eye.[196]

In the honored tradition of eyeglass wearers stood also the dandy-writer Jacques Rigaut, whom his "employer," the society-painter Jacques-Émile Blanche (himself greatly afflicted by dandyism), describes: "Our Jacques was an eternally bored sensualist"—his "graceful dandyism was out of place; nevertheless he made himself into more than just a listener."[197] Rigaut combined his preference for certain accessories with a distinct unwillingness to pay for them: "He coveted the buttons of uniforms or liveries. Armed with a special pair of scissors he cut them off in the Metro, at the gate of barracks, or while chatting to huntsmen, without the good people whom he duped being at the least suspicious. . . . He preferred . . . monocles and women's lipstick. The more trivial a task was, the more he appreciated it."[198]

Like Vaché's concept of nihilist irony, Rigaut's pleasure principle is based on the small singular element, combined with the temporal and spatial distance that remains crucial to the dandy's survival. It is not sufficient for the *umour* that subject and object, individual and society, merely exist within a "comical contrast."[199] The subject, furthermore, has to incorporate a reflection, a doubling of the contrast within his own contradiction. For the Da-dandy, negation is categorical *and* imperative. The *umour* reflects the individual within himself and within the society that is out to negate him. Thus the small reflecting piece of glass becomes the perfect vehicle for distance, reflection, and an ironic—that is, an ahistorical or transhistorical—negation of the individual, for it positions him—through the quote—outside linear historical progression. Moreover, by stealing (to which Rigaut confessed) the stylistic element that is imbued with traditional meaning, he adapts it to an ironic and subversive cause, and it becomes a potent weapon in Dada's arsenal.

The dadaist adventurer Arthur Cravan, who said of himself that "I get up London-style and go to sleep in an Asian way—London-style means monocle,"[200] seemed, as Oscar Wilde's nephew, destined to assume the role of dandy supreme. André Salmon remembers him from early Dada times (ca. 1914): "Before me, I see once more Arthur Cravan as a speaker. On the slopes of Montmartre, in the *Cercle de la Biche*. Taut, pale, clean-shaven, bloody, monocled."[201] During that time Aragon, still in the throes of dandyism that would influence *Anicet,* was introduced to Cravan's uncle: "André Gide had a charm that made me admire Oscar Wilde. But when I found myself alone in facing this Englishman, who dressed rather too well and glanced at me through his monocle, I felt like breaking some shop windows and crying: Get away you ponce!"[202] Although the monocle still might have been on occasion too awe-inspiring for the young French artists, its connection with (literary) dandyism, together with the fact that the accessory adorned the face of Vaché and others, opened their eyes to the *rastaquouère* and dadaesque character that Tzara would import soon from Switzerland. In Geneva, at the beginning of 1920, Serner had staged a "Grand Bal Dada," which coincided with an exhibition of dadaist painting, sculpture, and photography at the Galerie Moos, renamed for the occasion "Galerie Dada." "[T]he gallery assistants were bombarded with insults by the clean-shaven and monocle-wearing performers"—whose cultivated appearance caught them completely unawares—"and . . . Serner, in the middle of his opening address, descended into the main room and started dancing a tango with one of the film stars who were present."[203]

However, this was to be the last spectacle, since the animated Tzara, and with him Dada's impetus, had already left for Paris. In January 1920, Breton, Éluard, Aragon, and Soupault went to greet him at Gabrielle Buffet's apartment. "They all came together, to brace themselves for possible disappointment, after such a long and arduous period of waiting. And when he [Tzara] finally arrived, the first contacts were marked by a certain awkwardness. In their imagination, the moral superiority of this individual should be matched by physical grandeur. Yet the great man was small and sported a monocle."[204] Despite Tzara's reputation, Breton and Aragon, who were well aware of the implication of the eyeglass, felt that they were encountering another distanced, aloof dandy of erratic behavior, displaying either the remnant of a nineteenth-century pose or an anarchic spirit like that of Cravan or Vaché—in any case, not the person they hoped would further their avant-gardist cause. Yet they soon recognized in Tzara a source of immense practical energy, which he was only too ready to share with the French dadaists. His Francophile literary education in Budapest and his ability to fight for artistic progress within a deeply unappreciative society—a situation very familiar to the dadaists in Zurich, especially to those who were politically active—made him perfectly suited to impart a new artistic dimension to Paris.

Tzara includes a hidden self-portrait in the first act of an unpublished piece of theater, which he labeled a pantomime, written in Paris between his two great dramas *Le Cœur à gaz* (1921) and *Mouchoir de nuages* (1924). It features an ironic mise-en-scène in the tradition of Alfred Jarry (if not *Ubu*-esque, at least *umourique*), where the director, mounted on a little horse—a "dada," to be sure—instructs the audience at the beginning:

■

> *I am the director of this performance.* (Noise from the orchestra.)
> *I lead the action.*
> *Here I represent the author, his piece, and his ideas.* (Noise from the
> orchestra.)
> *But who is the author?*
> *A young man who has suffered enough to be permitted to wear a monocle
> and even be frivolous.* (Noise . . .)[205]

■

In the 1910s and 1920s, the combination of eyeglass and frivolity was by no means customary; the association had to be earned through endurance. In the past, a monocle stood for aristocratic pose and the insolence of "le prince dilettante," as a source from the mid–nineteenth century describes: "To insert the monocle . . . [his] tic consisted in closing the eye, accompanied by a certain movement of the lips and a certain movement of the suit. . . . The figure of an elegant man always has to have . . . something convulsive and rigid [*convulsif et crispé*]."[206] This, of course, is precisely what

Baudelaire (and later Benjamin) postulates as the experience of *modernité* (see "À une passante" in section 1.7 above). The Baudelairean flâneur who stops in the middle of the street "crispé comme un extravagant" is "forced" to hold the same artificial, unnatural pose assumed by the wearer of the monocle to prevent his accessory from falling out. Bodily movement, gesture, and facial expression become rigidly fragmented and mechanical, a representation in miniature of the increasing alienation between subject and object. Therefore, it seems only natural that the "invention" of the monocle in the first decade of the nineteenth century coincided with the rise of commodities and the objectification of modern society.[207] Its deliberate impracticality and the notorious difficulties it posed within the course of everyday life made it the perfect symbol for a position outside the pace of ordinary society. The eyeglass challenges and subverts the pragmatic and renders the wearer a statue-like commodity himself, while helping him maintain an ironic and malicious distance from the group in which he seemingly participates.[208] By merely adjusting its place or having it drop from the eye with a twist of the eyebrow in pretended surprise or actual disapproval, the wearer economizes enormously on his expressions. Thus he ironically reflects an age that is obsessed with labor-saving devices, while at the same time the delicateness of the small piece of glass or crystal forbids that its wearer actually participate in any form of labor whatsoever.[209]

The ahistoric and asocial connotation of the monocle, skillfully blended by Tzara with a nihilistic attitude of heightened individualism during the late 1910s and early 1920s, made the French artists grouped around Breton and Aragon again appreciative of its original meaning. Thus between 1919 and 1924 (the time span between the division after the Congrès de Paris and the formulation of the first surrealist manifesto) the eyeglass becomes again a cherished accessory for the young dadaists in the French capital. In March 1920, *DADAphone* (issue 7 of the magazine *Dada*) introduces to the public the portraits of its leading contributors. It features photos of Philippe Soupault and Georges Ribemont-Dessaignes, whose faces were adorned by a monocle in the right eye, while Breton opted for dark-rimmed glasses and Paul Dermée for a tennis racket.[210] A picture taken some months later depicts Jacques-André Boiffard, Max Morise, and Benjamin Péret as a dandyesque ensemble: two out of three sport the

**78.**
Max Ernst, *The Meeting of Friends,* 1922. Oil on canvas, 130 × 195 cm.
Museum Ludwig, Cologne.

**79.**
Unknown photographer, portrait of Jacques Rigaut, Tristan Tzara, and
André Breton, ca. 1921. Gelatin silver print, 9 × 18 cm.

eyeglass. (Right eye again: apart from Vaché, only one drawing of Tzara ever depicts the monocle worn in the left eye of a dadaist, and in that case the transposition was surely due to Picabia's technique of copying from photographs.) In Max Ernst's famous peinture à clef *Le Rendez-vous des amis* (1922), Péret's round eyeglass marked the center of the canvas, a reflection of the circular constellations on the nocturnal sky behind the group of friends. When the dadaists again posed for the opening of Ernst's first exhibition in Paris, at the gallery Au sans pareil (2 May 1921), Péret joined Breton and Soupault in monocularity,[211] while Jacques Rigaut chose to impress only with his immaculate suit. Tzara, of course, did not need an occasion to justify the eyeglass, and Ernst's son Jimmy later recalls wondering "whether he wore that monocle also in his sleep."[212] His monocular elegance, as well as Rigaut's sartorial one, enticed Breton to pose with them in a 1921 photo as a dandyesque triad in black suits and shining eyeglasses, heads and body lined up in a parallel expression of aestheticism.

Once again, it would be Picabia's mock journalism that proves the most astute account of this artistic fashion:

∎

*The Dadaists . . . held a discreet court[;] . . . the doctoral Louis Aragon wore his genius in his buttonhole and posed like Jean Lorrain would have liked to, facing André Breton, who was animated, courteous, very seductive[,] . . . who hoisted a monocle framed in tortoiseshell until, according to J.-E. Blanche, he started resembling Plato for his marbled preface to Max Ernst's obscenities. . . . Jacques Rigaut, a handsome mannequin from the rue de la Paix, kept close to a shaven-headed Benjamin Péret.*[213]

∎

Even rival artists felt compelled to adorn themselves with the ubiquitous symbol: "In the midst of the ballroom . . . stood Georges Casella, who, after an expression by St. Mallarmé, 'cried monocles.'"[214] And that same spring, in the magazine *Cannibale*, readers were told how "M. Georges-Armand Masson told Dada to kick up more fuss. He encourages us to demolish the old routine bar, otherwise he would cash in on us with a cheque. Picabia declares that he does not expect anything less. Tzara also has a mad and virgin plaything. Ribemont-Dessaignes also has a monocle."[215] A new bar with the glabrous clientele ("les rastaquouères") evoked by Breton from Vaché's drawings has to be established; and for a short time at least, it seemed as if this bar was truly *en vogue*—only to be replaced by the flâneur's café in Aragon's later novels.

The plain glass monocle that was worn by Tzara, Hausmann, and others in everyday life, the "monocle d'écaille" favored for the grander occasion, and the crystal eyeglass Vaché had dreamed about became even more precious in Breton's imagination. An unedited piece for *Poisson soluble* presents a sophisticated world where Proust meets Lautréamont: "A game of golf was the foible of the screw at the back of the vessel, as the swindlers who dressed in gray morning coats and wore diamond monocles made themselves heard."[216] Aragon in the same year transfers the setting mundanely to the capital: "If the Parisian houses were mountains, they would be the ones reflected in Max Morise's monocle."[217] This observation finds its visual analogy in Man Ray's famous documentation of the "séance du rêve éveillé," where Morise's monocle distinguishes the profile of a man who, as the only one in an overcoat and with hat in hand, appears to be a stranger passing through.[218] He regards with polite disinterest the carefully arranged tableau vivant, marked by the look of intense concentration on the faces of Breton, Éluard, and Jacques Baron. He made sure that he would be ready to leave when ennui took over.

Although the Parisian members of Dada—especially Breton, because of the impact that Vaché had made on him—praised the principles of dandyism, negation, and *umour,* the very symbol of those principles, the monocle, never took on significance greater than that accorded its earlier use as a mask or disguise. For most of the modern artists it continued to belong to nineteenth-century (aesthetic) snobbery, and thus it distinguished its wearer only by dressing him up. Even if they were ready to appreciate the sartorial commodity as such, they had difficulty realizing its inherent potential for protest and challenge—a challenge generated through a pose that disrupts, through its self-conscious and ironic quotation, the linearity of historical progress. The monocle could never become the self-evident accessory that it had been, under different premises, for writers such as Barbey d'Aurevilly, Eugène Sue, Montesquiou, or the Comte de Villiers de l'Isle-Adam. Its appeal during the late 1910s and early 1920s would remain tied primarily to its retrospective and not its disruptive character. One of the few artists—and the only one within the Parisian avant-garde as the nineteenth-

**80.**
El Lissitzky, untitled (*Jean Arp with " Navel-monocle"*), 1922–1924. Stiftung Hans Arp und Sophie Taeuber-Arp e.V., Rolandseck.

*"The wearers of glasses are in fashion. The majority of eggs wear sunglasses nowadays. A cloud transforms itself into a necktie and the above-mentioned mechanical doll knots this tie around its neck."*
*—Jean Arp, 1924.*

century dandies died out and the new ones (including Cravan, Vaché, and Rigaut) killed themselves, in a manner of speaking—who continued to wear the monocle beyond the change of fashion from dada to surrealism is Tzara; correspondingly, he was also one of the very few to fully appreciate the difference between *à la mode* and *la mode,* that is, between vagary and style.

In 1924, the year that saw the publication of Breton's manifesto, which set the movement's new direction, also produced a divisive winner of the established Prix du Nouveau Monde. Reverdy, the editor of *Nord-Sud* (a magazine devoted to the Apollinairean *esprit nouveau;* see Vaché's contemptuous remark on Reverdy earlier in this chapter), was chosen over Tzara, whose novel *Faites vos jeux* had been serialized the previous year in the rival *Les Feuilles Libres.* René Crevel—the lone mediating voice during the various quarrels between artistic circles—resigned because of the jury's decision and because he realized the impossibility of maintaining the spirit of dada within surrealism. For him, dada required a fascination for fashion that was no longer shared by the new, self-professed stalwarts of the avant-garde: "We could see Tristan Tzara again, the monocle in his eye and a multicoloured scarf around his neck. Impassive, he witnessed all the little intrigues: *Faites vos jeux,* he seemed to tell his friends of late who never forgave him for writing a proper novel. But he knew what he had to preserve."[219]

### 5.9.2 On Locomotives and Top Hats

As Breton and his artistic allies moved from dada's nihilism to surrealism's more constructive, perhaps scientific attitude toward creation, former friends became first rivals then enemies. Tzara's refusal to be "serious" cost him Breton's sympathies; and when Breton set out to work in 1922 on the committee for the Congrès de Paris, organized to investigate the spirit of modernity, he and Tzara clashed in an argument that curiously took the shape of a debate about the respective modernist merits of the locomotive and the top hat.

Breton chose the most tentative and descriptive of titles for his project, "Congrès pour la détermination des directives et la défense de l'Esprit Moderne" (Congress to Determine Directives and the Defense of the Modern Spirit), and the opening presentation conveys the same general and placatory tone, intended to include as many avant-garde efforts as possible: "The undersigned of this article have not intention whatsoever, beyond all their individual characteristics, even characteristics of groups or schools, the example of which we have seen in art with impressionism, symbolism, unamism, fauvism, simultanism, cubism, orphism, futurism, expressionism, purism, dada, etc., to work toward the creation of a new intellectual family and to preserve links that many will judge illusory."[220] Yet in his Barcelona conference, Breton allows much less room for individual expression and aligns the movements so that they may become part of progressive evolution—a thought alien to dada. This effort culminates in his definition of *l'esprit moderne:* "All in all, I regard cubism, futurism, and dada not as three distinct movements, but rather as all three taking part in a more general movement whose perspective or dimension we do not yet know. . . . [T]o consider cubism, futurism, and dada in succession means to follow the development of an idea that at present has reached a certain zenith and is waiting for a new impulse to continue describing the curve to which it has been assigned."[221] This notion that there is a historical narrative and a logical, stylistic progression in the arts, even if viewed through the seemingly contradictory postulates of successive movements, is opposed by Tzara, as he gently plays down dada's impact: "Modernism does not interest me at all. And I think it is very wrong to say that dadaism, cubism, futurism have a common basis. The two latter tendencies were based, above all, on the principle of reaching technical or intellectual completion, while dadaism was never based on any theory and was but a protestation."[222] For him, the essence of *modernité* lay neither in the evolution of visual perception, as in cubism, nor in the celebration of technical progress, as in futurism. By the same token, *modernité* could not lie in the arts' "discovery" of the unconscious or in automatism, as the surrealists would have it. The object and the objective are to be seen not as part of a historical progression, but as standing in contrast to or at least detached from it—as the ephemeral and transitory in culture.

For Breton, however, the program had to be concerned with continuous evolution. *L'esprit moderne* and his Barcelona lecture were in fact very close to Apollinaire's *l'esprit nouveau* and his conference of 1917. One of the principal advocates of *l'esprit nouveau* and the founder of purism, Amédée Ozenfant, indeed sat on the committee for the Parisian congress five years later. Together its members formulated the questions that needed to be addressed in 1922:

■

*All those who in taking action do not place themselves under the tutelage of the past are invited to make themselves known. We are going to count our numbers on both sides.*

      *To determine the ideas, here are two of the numerous questions that the congress will have to examine:*

      *Does the modern spirit still exist?*

      *Among the objects that are said to belong to modernity, is a top hat more or less modern than a locomotive?*[223]

■

The program appears highly ambiguous. If Breton intends to rally all those "not under the tutelage of the past," why does he attempt to establish a link with tradition by asking about the continuation of a modern spirit? Moreover, why choose the top hat and locomotive as particular metaphors of such a spirit, since both have their origins in a past epoch, the nineteenth century?

      Whereas the futurists celebrated twentieth-century inventions such as the motorcar and the airplane, Breton and his committee single out the locomotive, a mode of transportation invented in 1804 (the word itself entered the French language in 1823).[224] And what about the top hat? How can the ultimate bourgeois accessory, which determined the look of the Parisian streets throughout the latter part of the previous century, be indicative of a modern spirit? Breton's question as to which of the two objects is "more or less modern" appears curiously academic, as both had already become part of cultural tradition.[225]

      Like the monocle, these two metaphors that are regarded as examples of the spirit of *modernité* are not recent historical or sociological facts. They emerge, under novel auspices, from literary tradition. Whereas Tzara attempts to "create" anew via negation and ironic quote, Breton draws on the past to support the principles he claims to be contemporary: though he comes closer perhaps to devising a "modern mythol-

**81.**

Karel Teige, *The Return Ticket* (cover for the book of that title by Vítězslav Nezval), 1933.

Collage and typography on card, 21.3 × 13.5 cm. ÚDU AVČR, Prague.

ogy," he leaves himself open to the charge of remaining "impressionistic," a reproach that Benjamin would raise against Aragon (see section 5.3 above). The argument about what constitutes *modernité* or the modern spirit dominated the public correspondence between Breton and Tzara during February 1922. Tzara's open refusal to participate in the congress immediately drew an aggressive communiqué: "Straightaway, the undersigned, who are all members of the organizing committee, would like to warn against the activities of a certain individual, known as promoter of a 'movement' that came from Zurich, who is no longer reasonable *and nowadays does not respond to reality any more.*"[226] The xenophobic tone of this text, which attacks one particular dissident, makes it hard to credit the congress's initial claim of seeking an open, international forum for debate. Tzara's defiance must have touched a raw nerve. A day later "the promoter from Zurich" reacts with customary irony in a letter that deflates the intentions of the committee: "Regarding the honor that is bestowed upon me by the committee of the congress in occupying itself so intensively with my person, I can but raise my top hat in salute and put it on a locomotive that travels with high speed toward unknown territories of critique." More important, he considers Breton and his allies "far from qualified to organize the diverse tendencies of modern art."[227]

Because dada was regarded by the dadaists as an end in itself and as "not modern,"[228] Tzara believes it unnecessary to throw his (top) hat into the ring. The ironical treatment of Breton's metaphors defused their pretension and at the same time referred locomotive and top hat back, intentionally or not, to the nineteenth century and thus to one of their inspirations from literary history.

At the time of Baudelaire and Gautier, the enthusiasm for *modernité* and its inventions seemed boundless. Old beliefs were thrown out while society advanced at full speed into a future that seemed to promise much. In some explanatory notes for his collection of poems titled *Les Chants modernes* (1855), Baudelaire's friend Maxime du Camp lends the locomotive (and also fashion) iconic status for the modern age. When the devil is ironically set against the locomotive, the machine clearly carries the day: "He [the devil] raced through the night, vomiting flames, howling, crying, and carrying with him legions of little devils and sorcerers; but a locomotive dragging along its convoy spits even more flames, roars even louder, carries more people away than he

**82.**
Émile Bernard, *Pont d'Asnières,* 1887. Oil on canvas, 46 × 54 cm. The Museum of Modern Art, New York. Grace Rainey Rogers Fund. Photograph © 2000 The Musuem of Modern Art, New York.

does."[229] Alas, the actual poem celebrating the locomotive has none of the energy and vigor ascribed to the machine. It may be enthusiastic, but to the reader it seems long and one-dimensional.[230] Two decades later Ix., Mallarmé's alter ego who signs the society column of *La Dernière Mode*, approaches the subject in a more complex and reflective manner. Contemplating the transitoriness of existence within modernity, as exemplified by the speed of railway travel to a fashionable sea resort, (s)he writes:

■

*One learns everything on the spot, even beauty; how to hold one's head; one has to learn it from someone; that is to say, from everyone, like the manner in which to wear a dress. Shall we escape this world? we are part of it; so back to nature? one travels through it at full steam, in its external reality, with its landscapes, its places, to get somewhere else: a modern image of its insufficiency for us! For if the pleasures we know within our four walls were to relinquish their season's lead for open-air games, long rambles through the woods, or regattas on the river, where we are keen to rest our eyes in an oblivion created by the vast and naked horizon, would we not find therefore a novel perception able to appreciate the paradox of intricate and complex outfits that the ocean has embroidered at the bottom with its froth?*[231]

■

There is no rest for the fashion-conscious eye of modern men and women; even the sky and sea are turned into decorated garments, and the beholder can always prevent agoraphobic meditation on nature's vastness by recourse to a novel object of clothing. In 1919 Tzara ridicules a setting that seems a parody of both Mallarmé's high-minded "journalism" and the impressionist (or fauvist) paintings of Deauville or similarly fashionable spots. "There is a joke for each fellow, and the totality of jokes is called literature. Superimposed, seedy cylinders with shawls visit the seaside."[232] Although certainly not a critique of Mallarmé (or Proust's Balbec) in particular, Tzara's *L'Antitête,* which incorporates the piece here quoted, proposes the counterpoint to literary commonplaces: "Oh! the joys of love! What excessive pleasure! The clients are terrified. Even under the skin of the locomotive."[233] Given the associative connections retained in dada's verbal nonsense, one might speculate that Tzara is portraying a fashionable

**83.**

Max Ernst, *The High Chant of the Holiday Maker in Winter* (illustration for *La Femme 100 têtes*), 1929. Collage on paper, 8 × 24 cm. Private collection, Cologne.

group that is driven to anguish and despair rather than to the sea resort, as he provides a cynical, modern antidote to symbolist refinement in both subject and language.

In the fifth issue of *La Dernière Mode,* Ix. anticipates some of Tzara's cynicism by viewing the locomotive as a true parable of *modernité,* a black modernist cortege in the tradition of Baudelaire's take on the black tailcoat as the aptly ironic attire for the crude bourgeoisie of the nineteenth century: "Who knows whether the moving procession of this afternoon and of tomorrow does not take place for the last time, in its traditional way, which will be disturbed one day by the introduction into its midst of the locomotive, with its haste, its noise, and its mourners mingling in the carriages?"[234] And Mallarmé also uses the black top hat to evoke a poetic modern world. His "Billet à Whistler" (written in 1890) begins:

■

*Pas les rafales à propos*
*De rien comme occuper la rue*
*Sujette au noir vol de chapeaux;*
*Mais une danseuse apparue*[235]

■

The surrealist Max Morise transfers such an encounter—more cinematic than symbolist—to the present. In an essay on the relation of surrealism and painting in which he demands modern objects and contemporary settings, he asks: "Who is that woman in white who passes in her motorcar through the crowd of men in top hats?"[236]

From the 1830s, when the name of a French hatter Gibus became synonymous with the top hat,[237] the headgear began to represent bourgeois society, its morality and aspirations. Worn on the barricades by those fighting for constitutional principles, it was prominently displayed in Eugène Delacroix's *La Liberté guidant le peuple* (1830).[238] It then was adapted as the literal support for the crown of the bourgeois king Louis-Philippe, as the dualistic symbol of the July monarchy. From the mid-1860s on, the *tromblon* (a top hat with widened brim) began to assume its status as a must for the fin de siècle *élégant* (see James Tissot's painting *Le Cèrcle de la rue Royale,* 1868). By the first decade of the twentieth century, the *tube*—whether *clair* (daytime, summer resort) or *noir* (evening, grand occasion)—already appeared dated and reminiscent of a more sophisticated age. It was an accessory left to the melancholic dandy who liked to dream in front of this "cylindrical and black mirror in which trams and coaches are obscurely reflected, like trees and clouds in the dark waters of the sea."[239]

For the generation of Mallarmé, the poet who had once initiated its symbolism and poetry, the black cylindrical headgear remained a sartorial prerequisite, so normative still that perceptions of it invariably had to leave the commonplace and take flight to the metaphysical. One of Mallarmé's very last pieces of writing was the reply to a questionnaire by the journal *Le Figaro* in January of 1897, a year that was celebrated as the centenary of the top hat's invention.

■

*Sir, You find me alarmed at the prospect of touching on such subject matter. You have remarked—obviously it has not escaped your attention—that on his head, contemporary man wears something somber and supernatural. You might have the courage, perhaps, to explore this mystery in a newspaper column: I, on my part, am led, quite singularly, to a meditation, and I expect at least some volumes of a compact edition, numerous, abstruse, to be produced in which science will solve this mystery and then progress beyond it. One could, I should think, omit all disturbing metaphysics here, of the machine or of finery or of what this dark meteor represents, and confine oneself to the actual fabrication of hats, as the questionnaire helpfully indicates; for example, as you suggest, to explore the question whether this modern complement, called the top hat, will haunt the dawn of the twentieth century.*[240]

■

It was to be indeed of great significance for the twentieth century, especially in its function as a metaphor for the Parisian artists after the Great War; yet it would work precisely by evoking the "disturbing metaphysics of the machine" that Mallarmé chose to omit. Mondor in his biography gave an example of how the poet's imagination is spurred by the appearance of a top hat, in this case, in a manner that indeed inclines toward the mechanical. Mallarmé once more dreams of steam, as in his evocation of modern travel: "Together with Méry [Laurent] and H[enri de] Régnier, Mallarmé went one evening in July to the Bois de Boulogne, close by the boating lake. . . . Breaking the sheet of water and reflecting the crimson sunset, was a man alone in his boat, who

**84.**

Unknown illustrator, page from *La Mode Pratique*, no. 6 (6 February 1897), with an anonymous essay titled "The Centenary of the Top Hat." Lithograph, ca. 30 × 50 cm. Staatliche Museen zu Berlin, Kunstbibliothek.

rowed with gravitas and elegance, dressed all in black and bedecked, incredibly, by a top hat: 'Look,' said Mallarmé, 'an imaginary navigator: the handsome hat replaces the smokestack of his dreams.'"[241] The wearer of the top hat finally reaches the water as "promised" in Ix.'s society column—although it is not the ocean but merely a pond in the park. His black cylinder still gives off steam, only this time it is a boat's chimney, not the funnel of a locomotive. Visiting Vaché in hospital, Breton is struck by the same image. "The smoke escaping from these top hats frames in black the honorary diploma that we wanted to show our friends and acquaintances," he quips while looking at the layout of the fashion magazines beside his friend's bed.[242]

The visual similarities between top hat and smokestack—a connection heightened by the two separate meanings of the word *cylindre*, which denotes both headgear and part of a machine—are obvious.[243] The *tube noir* was fashion's expression of the industrial age, an equivalent to the pumping piston inside the steam-emitting engine. Fashion journals, from *La Dernière Mode* to the *Miroir des Modes*, celebrated the appeal of the commodity and thus implicitly the success of capitalism as well. The more chimneys erected to denominate the prosperity of the factory owners, the more numerous grew the shiny tubes of the hats covering the bourgeois of the Second Empire.

Thus Breton's question, intended to trace an expression of the modern spirit, seems justified after all. Yet what element in this metaphoric compound had to be regarded as more important for modernity, the hat or the machine? It came down to a veiled decision about what had been more influential for *l'esprit moderne* or modern mythology: the stylized forms of the object, as in French cubism and purism, or the dynamics of the engine. "Here are some wise men of our time," writes Breton in early 1920; "Lautréamont, Apollinaire have nursed a universal admiration for the umbrella, the sewing machine, the top hat. . . . I consider a veritable modern mythology about to be formed."[244] Apollinaire observes the top hat in his *Calligrammes* in the same simple, almost purist and descriptive mode that he had used earlier to describe the dress that covered the woman's shoulder.

■

*Un chapeau haut de forme est sur*
*Une table chargée de fruits*

**85.**
Draner [Jules Renard], *At Messr. Independent Painters by Draner* (detail),
1879. Ink on paper. Bibliothèque Nationale, Paris.

*Les gants sont morts près d'une pomme*
*Une dame se tord le cou*
*Auprès d'un monsieur qui s'avale* [245]

▪

The top hat in its stereometric form is easy to reduce to circle, rectangle, or cylinder, while the uniform block of color and its clear lines facilitate its abstraction. Picasso's *Still Life with Hat,* for example, dating from the winter of 1908/1909, could have served easily as a visual source for Apollinaire's poem.[246] The Cézannesque composition depicts some fruits next to the stiff black cylinder at the center, all spread out on a floral green tablecloth. Ironically, the dadaist Richard Huelsenbeck hoped, at the time of Apollinaire's poem and his art criticism that championed cubism, that the cubist painters would exclusively use modern imagery: "The old perspective is dissolved through Picasso and the cubists, the models flee, and the most beautiful easels and top hats vanish from this world."[247]

Although the top hat was regarded by some as a remnant of dated aesthetics, it was seen by others as the purist symbol of the new reification. Thus any assessment that attempted to regard one of Breton's two metaphors as more modern than the other seemed to underestimated their inherent dualism. The historian Sanouillet observes: "Progressively . . . the theme of the congress began to develop and, at equal measure, it began to show itself less and less worthy of interest in the eyes of the dadaists: once the mysterious haze that surrounded Breton's real intentions was lifted, nothing seemed to be left except the prospect of a new, muffled dialogue between the ancient and the modern, of an empty and 'drawn out *querelle* between tradition and invention' that had been resolved long ago in poetry and love by Guillaume Apollinaire."[248] Fashion functions so well as the paradigm of modernity because its objects are ambiguous in themselves; they incorporate modernity and antiquity. Fashion is modern not despite the old but precisely because it carries the past within itself, or is remodeled by it. The dualism of modern society and its subjects is mirrored *en miniature* in the dual characteristics of its objects: new and old, ephemeral and sublime, transitory and eternal. Accordingly, the top hat is both the nineteenth-century bourgeois headgear and an abstract entity of high aesthetic value; it is at once modern and mysterious, due to its uninterrupted existence as a potent accessory for more than a hundred years. As Benjamin observes, the surrealists retained a pronounced interest in the rediscovery of the nineteenth century and its dark symbols. One of the surrealist muses was Fantômas, the *gentleman-cambrioleur,* who became during his nocturnal excursions part of the modern mythology. "Already," Caillois claims, "he has imposed on our imagination the vision of a large, dormant city over which a gigantic Fantômas, masked, clean shaven, in black suit and top hat . . . extends a very powerful grasp."[249]

For Dada and its nihilist irony, the cylinder of both top hat and locomotive belonged to a different category. The Cabaret Voltaire in Zurich had witnessed numerous times its instigator Hugo Ball wrapped in cylinders—most expressively in 1917, when he recited one of his phonetic poems from inside a white tube that doubled the length of his head, further topped by a black *Zylinderhut* while he was gently waving the flag of the German *Kaiserreich.* Such political satire was revived by Tzara in a less purposive but equally controversial form for the Parisian "Festival Dada" at the Salle Garveau in May 1920: "On the podium, occupied on any other evening by a conductor waving his stick ceremoniously in front of some sixty musicians, now stood six dadaists, dressed in black, their heads concealed by enormous cylinders of white bristol board (as if their stiff collars suddenly had decided to grow), who shuffled around mournfully. There was no respect left toward anything!"[250]

The previous year Tzara had incorporated this image, adopted from Ball, into a poem titled "Unveiled Optimism" that he would publish only three years later, after the sad break with the surrealists of the congress.

■

*L'OPTIMISME DÉVOILÉ*

*pour:*

*. . . . .*

*l'ennui d'argent*
*une nuit d'ordre supérieur*
*un cylindre d'azote couvert d'un chapeau haut-de-forme*

*. . . . . . . . . . . . . . . . . . . . . . . . . . . . . . . . . . . . . . . .*

*la moins chère et la plus résistante*
*en vente*
*partout*
*toujours*[251]

■

At the same time, back in Geneva, another Dada performance (re)introduced the locomotive. A journalist hidden behind the pseudonym of "Zy.," who in fact was the dadaist Serner, reported for *La Tribune de Genève* on the proceedings: "A one-step was danced by two coupling locomotives (who, as Franc-Nohain said, were following their locomotifs). Commentator Brosjadam expressed it ingeniously by onomatopoeia."[252]

The term "locomotif" should be understood also etymologically, as referring to the "locomotive system" of an organism (e.g., the human body). It denotes subjects or objects moving independently from a spot. This spot or standpoint also marks the status quo in aesthetic experience. Thus Tzara proclaims in his manifesto of 1918: "The new painter creates a world where the objects are also the means, no doubt resulting in a clearly defined and sober piece of work. The new artist protests: he does not paint any symbolic or impressionist reproductions but creates directly in stone, wood, iron, tin, rocks, locomotive organisms can be turned completely by the limpid wind of a momentary sensation."[253] He protests against the approach of most cubist painters, who regard an object merely from different angles, and of the Futurists, who were concerned essentially with a succession of objects in their movement. For Tzara, the spirit of modernity lies in the complete autonomy of the object that is regarded through constantly changing modes of perception. This self-sufficient mobility requires no artwork for its depiction, evaluation, or documentation. The object, as it appears to the beholder, becomes the artwork via the subject's inspiration and imagination (perhaps most potently realized visually in Marcel Duchamp's ready-mades). Therefore the question that would be put later to Tzara, concerning the superior modernity of top hat or locomotive, can be of no concern to him. He considers both as equally transitory within a true *esprit moderne*. The all-too-literal reading of Breton's metaphoric composite—for example, as in Robert Delaunay's cover study for *Littérature,* in which the member of the committee depicts a top-hatted man before the smokestack of a locomotive, its steam enveloping the title of the magazine[254]—further disillusioned Tzara and proved the validity of his critique and satire once again. In mockingly removing his top hat to place it over the engine's funnel, he does more than attempt to prevent the buildup of a smoke screen that is artificially created by what he sees as superfluous arguments. Tzara wants both metaphors to be sent into the wilderness, "toward unknown territories of critique," because only such a dismissal could prevent new hierarchies from forming.

His gesture was appreciated—by some at least. Picabia in his habitual ironic irreverence writes: "The perfidious Tristan Tzara has quit Paris for the damned dance halls on the outskirts,[255] he has decided to put his top hat over a locomotive: obviously much easier than putting it over the Victory of Samothrace." Whether Tzara in fact would go as far as to place a wreathe on the moving machine, thus partly siding with the futurist dismissal of the sublime, is questionable; any copycat maneuver must appear pathetic and disgrace the individual who considered doing it. "When Ribemont[-]Dessaigne[s] one day felt in the mood, he put on a top hat in order to resemble a locomotive. The result was pitiful."[256]

Such vitriol fueled the progressing, yet hardly progressive, feud about the reasoning behind the Congrès de Paris. Instead of attempting to remain constantly at the vanguard of artistic development, Breton might have listened more closely to Vaché's advice about "assassinating the poet." Following Apollinaire's decree to radically dispense with the sublime at regular intervals, the Da-dandy proposed to punctuate the rapid tempo of modernity with a more self-directed assault on one's sensibility. "[I]t's necessary to gulp down a drop of acid or old lyricism, doing it in a lively jerk—because the locomotives go fast."[257] The speed of modern life requires deliberate interruption, but it seems doubtful that this break can be achieved by blocking a smokestack with a top hat, or that the gesture amounted to anything more than bestowing on the locomotive a modernist laurel crown. The object simply becomes a commodity unless its impact is questioned—not exclusively by sociopolitical critique but also by artists who explore its ambiguity and multifaceted character.

The "other" in modernity's mad tempo is vividly expressed in Stanislaw Witkiewicz's drama *Szalona lokomotywa* (*The Mad Locomotive*) of 1923. Sexual tension,

**86.**
Robert Delaunay, cover study for *Littérature*, 1922. Ink on paper, 20 × 17 cm.

psychopathic energy, and enormous speed are combined in a flurry of action inside the driver's cab of an express train. The catastrophic consequences of the last act present a nihilist alternative to the otherwise positive view of the engine. The machine was ready to transport helpless individuals to destruction, and the Polish author literally refrained from offering any escape from reality within the pace of modern life. The driver and stoker, their wives, and lovers, and the passengers were destined not to reach a sea resort. They would perish in the horrific accident resulting from human inability, or unwillingness, to stop the locomotive.[258]

In 1928 another author transported reality into the composite metaphor of topper and engine. The poet Osip Mandelstam often used clothes as simulacra for the human being. His world was as absurd and fantastic as the one evoked by surrealist poetry. In "The Egyptian Stamp," a story set between the February and October Revolutions of 1917, Mandelstam describes a journey where "the top-hatted locomotive with its chicken pistons was outraged at the weight of the *chapeaux-claques* and muslins."[259] Here, the sartorial remnants of the nineteenth century appear only as ideological ballast that hinders social progress. As a victim of this progress, Mandelstam's protagonist Parnok has his beloved coat repossessed by his tailor. With the loss of the garment—whose function is similar to that of the symbolic coat in Gogol's famous story—its wearer loses his social status. The incomprehensible action by the tailor and the utter confusion of his victim-turned-outcast are part of the parable for the tumultuous time of 1917. Here, the poetry of locomotive and top hat appears already anachronistic.

In contrast, Aragon's nocturnal pairing of top hat and locomotive in *Anicet*—written in 1920, two years before Breton's questionnaire for the congress—seems rather placid, though the story is equally effective in its accidental character and dreamlike setting. Aragon skillfully renders the objects, especially through their surreal combination, part of a modern mythology that redefines how both objects are perceived. "These seven men in top hats did not surprise even the rare passersby. . . . They had taken the rue aux Ours. The steam clock said three in the morning. A steam whistle made Anicet turn: like a bad omen, a real goods train with a real locomotive slowly crossed the rue Étienne-Marcel."[260] This nocturnal meeting of sophisticated

**87.**

Unknown photographer, *Negative Locomotive,* ca. 1929. Printed negative, ca. 23 × 14 cm. Private collection, Paris.

*"This century of locomotives . . . cannot include . . . a population adorned and decorated in dazzling colors. One must render oneself harmonious with the machines and products of contemporary industry."*
—*Gustave Geffroy, ca. 1888.*

fashion and vapor-producing industry allows the reader to contemplate a possible symbolism (perhaps similar to the encounter of umbrella and sewing machine) behind the objects. Although the *hauts de forme* must have seemed out of place (and thus dandified) on the streets of 1920 Paris, the effect was once again created not by the contrast of old static forms versus the movement of the modern, but by the combination of unrelated, independent entities. *La mode et la modernité,* in this case *habit noir* and sooty black machine, are guidelines for a society preoccupied with the consumption and assimilation of merchandise and commodities. The artists' task is not simply to emphasize the ephemeral, transitory, and ambiguous within these objects. They must put them into perspective and open up paths toward a possible way to counterbalance this "hell of the commodity," as Benjamin termed it; perhaps the artists must even find a solution.

In order to defuse the heated debate between the artists who once had been grouped under Dada's banner, Breton adopted on the eve of the congress a strategy of ironic deflection, not dissimilar from Tzara's. "In the meantime, Philippe Soupault and myself have tried without much success to create a diversion: a number of top hats," Breton writes in the fourth issue of the new series of *Littérature,* "but it becomes clear very quickly indeed that we are living a compromise."[261] It becomes obvious that this compromise was one of customs (literary and social), when one looks at the candor of Breton and Soupault's first collaboration on the top hat in the pages of *Les Champs magnétiques:* "What separates us from life is something very different from that little flame running over the asbestos like a sandy plant. Nor do we think about the flown-away song of the gold leaves of an electroscope that one used to find in certain top hats, even though we used to wear one of that kind when in society."[262] With hindsight, fellow surrealist Jacques Baron judged this attempt to maintain ironic distance to be ill-advised. He thought the series of covers facile and misleading in view of what was to follow with the publication of *La Révolution Surréaliste:* "After the top hats of Man Ray, who had been too polite to be honest, Picabia designed a scandalous cover. The titles went crazy: 'Lits et ratures' or 'Erutérail.' Also, the contents themselves were far from complacent. No charming columns any more. . . . A particular manner of keeping up with things and of establishing the ephemeral was reflected in Breton's text 'The

**88.**
Man Ray, cover for the new series of *Littérature,* March 1922. Ink on paper, 25 × 20 cm.

Year of the Red Hats.' In that year [1922], the fashion among women was indeed to wear hats of this passionate color."[263] During the period of the Congrès de Paris, however, the text titled "year of the red hats" was much less precise than the sartorial evocation by Aragon—as one would expect from a professional flâneur. He describes the aftermath of the congress as a purging of unwanted elements from the newly established movement. "At that time there was a tribunal de Salut Dada, and by no stretch of the imagination could one have foreseen that the Reign of Terror would, one day, give way to the Directoire, with its games, its dandies [Incroyables] and open dresses."[264] The postdadaist terreur saw the top hat perish as metaphor and poetic subject, like so many other sartorial elements (cf. the monocle). The sophistication of fashion accessories came to be viewed as a futile snobbery that endangered artistic and sociopolitical integrity.[265]

If accessories continued to be used at all, the focus turned away from their significance as marking the objectification of modern life to the hitherto neglected psychological undercurrent. In the "Second Manifeste du surréalisme" of 1930, Breton quotes from a discussion at the Société Médico-Psychologique of December 1929, when psychologist Pierre Janet singles out the top hat: "In support of Dr. de Clérambault's opinion, I am reminded of some of the surrealists' methods. For example, they take five words absolutely at random out of a hat and make various series of associations with these five words. In the 'Introduction to Surrealism' they tell a whole story with these two words: turkey and top hat."[266] Janet here refers to some lines from Breton's Poisson Soluble, which in October 1924 was published in a volume with the "Manifesto of Surrealism" (misnamed "Introduction to Surrealism" by the doctor).[267] It is surprising, however, that he makes no comment on the psychology of the accessory proper, especially since Clérambault's expertise in investigating neurotic attitudes toward clothing and accessories was unrivaled.[268] The psychological connotations of this most phallic of headgears certainly account for its frequent occurrences in dada and early surrealism; yet no direct link or interpretation comparable to Breton's analysis of his tie was ever attempted by the artists.[269] Hats continue to appear in surrealist art. However, the accessory is confined to the ephemeral realm of female fashion, as in the "year of red hats" above, or in Tzara's seminal "D'un certain automatisme de goût."

The locomotive, the mechanical expression of moving from a spot, made one last appearance. This time the emphasis was put on its regression, as it seemed to become a modern antiquity. In *L'Amour fou* (1937), Breton attempts to define the notion of convulsive beauty (as postulated in his aesthetic credo—"Beauty will be CONVULSIVE or will not be at all"): "I regret not having been able to furnish, along with this text, the photograph of a speeding locomotive abandoned for many years to the delirium of a virgin forest."[270] In her commentary Bonnet suggests that this image originated in a poem by Blaise Cendrars, written some twenty years earlier.

■

*Envoyez-moi la photographie de la forêt de chênes-lièges*
*qui pousse sur 400 locomotives abandonnées*
*par l'entreprise française.*[271]

■

The composer Georges Auric, a fellow organizer of the congress, remarked ambiguously on Cendrars's poetry at the preparation for Cocteau's show *Les Mariés de la Tour Eiffel:* "Concerning Cendrars; to compare a poem by him with the poor *Mariés . . . ,* is like establishing a parallel between a locomotive and an Italian straw hat out of the pieces by Labiche."[272] One wonders whether Auric sees Cendrars's lines as steamrolling through the reader's mind or he simply means to praise their ultimate *modernité.* Again the parallel of locomotive and hat was established, only this time the cheaply decorated female headgear that was used in operettas, not the top hat, was invoked. The criticism now shifted to questioning substance instead of attitude. Cendrars's imagery was again echoed by Breton in his poem "Facteur cheval," where he conjures up the self-contradictory image of an immobile locomotive, overgrown by nature and devoured by its own past:

■

*Sans un regard pour la locomotive en proie aux*
*immense racines barométriques*
*Qui se plaint dans la forêt vierge de toutes ses*
*chaudières meurtries*[273]

■

**89.**
Anonymous photograph published in *Minotaure,* no. 10 (winter 1937).

The untouched, uncivilized virgin forest stands for an innocent dream-state; it acts as the Romantic ideal of a brake on modern progress. The speed of the machine is stopped by mysterious overgrowth, possibly for all time. The unconscious takes control of objectification, and the myth begins to cover the dynamics of contemporary life.

We have seen that Breton's attitude once had been much more "Mallarméan" in its poetic depiction of the locomotive and its train. In 1921 he sided with the modern in declaring, on occasion of Ernst's exhibition, that contemporary art was better equipped than ever to reflect life: "Thanks to the cinema, today we have the means to let a locomotive arrive in a painting."[274] In the "year of the red hats," the fashionable cinematic influence makes its presence felt again. Breton narrates an imaginary scenario: "I was traveling over a viaduct, paling at the idea of those louts that they employ on locomotives to whistle through their fingers. . . . I arrived at the gare d'Est-Ceinture at the time when the factory gates opened . . . and all the passengers seemed mad about a field of lilies."[275] This text was integrated into *Poisson soluble*, whose first chapter stressed once more the parallels between the mechanical and the sartorial as expressions of *modernité:* "She walked along and came into a compartment that was similar to those of the carriages of trans-European express trains. . . . I coughed a number of times and the train in question slipped through tunnels, sending suspension bridges to sleep. . . . I did not find us again until much later, she in an extremely vibrant dress, that made her look like the gear of a very new machine, me blending in as much as possible in the impeccable black suit that I have not taken off since."[276] As they travel at full steam, the dress of the female passenger becomes as much a part of modern machinery as the top hat funnel, while the author's black suit marks him out as the typical exponent of both male sartorial sobriety and the modern spirit. In 1937, however, when the anonymous photo that Breton had missed as an illustration for his essay was used for a text by Péret, the title reversed the symbolism of the engine. The locomotive no longer traveled through tunnels and over bridges, but is now forced to indefinite standstill: "Nature devours progress and overtakes it," Péret titled his text. The "telephone wire," described by Vaché as slicing Romanticism, is rolled out again, "but quickly, the forest has grown tired of plucking that string"; and the smokestack of the train, previously so evocative in its form, was only left to "smoke orchids."[277]

The progress of modernity driven along by the "locomotives orphelines dadaïstes"[278] came to a halt in surrealism; Marcel Noll's early characterization of Breton as "a village of humor and awareness of disaster, something like a top hat,"[279] no longer held true. Péret concludes in his essay that "the woman of the forest, who has licked for long at her prey, will swallow it like an oyster."[280]

If Péret intended to connect this image to the overgrowth that swallowed mobility and movement, it helps explain the attitude toward monocle, top hat, and locomotive. Because of its edge and clarity and the accompanying tendency toward negation, which was at first admired, dada was subsequently viewed by avid surrealists as too modish and clever for its own good. Thus its metaphors were consumed whole by the new art movement, as if shut inside an oyster. Yet the surrealists were unable to digest the pearl that their artistic predecessors had left inside the shell, and fashion's responsibility for modernity was handed back from artist to designer. Commodity and artwork would grow nearer in years to come, but the poetic rendition of the sartorial would never occur again as potently as it had done in the century between 1840 and 1940.

# Conclusion

The idea that there can be a proper conclusion to fashion's relationship with modernity appears absurd. Both *la mode* and *la modernité* live on incessant change, self-fertilizing quotation, and constant adaptation to new parameters that ensure their continuance. The tiger's leap will continue to occur and fashion (as well as modernity) likewise will continue—in neither a linear nor logical manner—because of novel citations of its own past.

One must refrain at all costs from historicizing fashion. It is best observed en passant. In writing that, I leave this book itself open to accusations of being insubstantial. Yet to observe something in passing by no means implies that its beauty is not fully appreciated, its meaning not grasped, or its substance not understood or thoroughly engaged. On the contrary, only the particular perception of the flâneur—whether dandified and artistic, like Baudelaire and Aragon; historical, like Michelet; sociological, like Simmel; or philosophical, like Benjamin—is able to capture the fleeting impression that is characteristic of *modernité* and *mode* alike.

Fashion is transitory by nature. Thus we must bow to the ephemeral impression revealed to us in the minute sartorial element, the small detail of an artwork, the subordinate clause in a piece of literature. In the overall picture, we find only constant change; it is in each quickly observed detail that the true character of modernity lies.

Evaluating fashion within a historical construct can be attempted only in conjunction with modernity—specifically, within European metropolitan societies from the mid–nineteenth century to the beginning of the Second World War. Since the ever-changing aesthetics of *modernité* has now done away with the absolute notion of beauty, informed by aesthetic tradition, we can appreciate fashion as her congenial sister without petrifying its own "relative beauty." Like fashion, modernity dies every night, as Simmel and Vaché had remarked in 1906 and 1916, respectively. Like the aesthetic expressions of *modernité*, fashion is always reborn in the form that is most fitting for the relevant cultural and social circumstances. This erratic rebirth is made possible by fashion's quotation from its own sartorial sourcebook and by modernity's "remembrance of things past." The things and objects drawn on thus either become part of a modern mythology, alienated and imagined in new surroundings, or appear as ironic citations.

When Aragon, in his "Introduction à 1930," discussed *modernité* as the historical and the actual quality both to remember and to create through remembrance, that is, quotation, he concluded by considering a fundamental question:

■

Modernité *is a temporal function that expresses the sentimental reality of certain objects, whose novelty is not their main characteristic, but whose efficiency is due to the recent discovery of their expressive value. Or, if you will, in which one discovers a new use that surpasses the one that is known, so that the former becomes forgotten. . . .*

*Look on the modernist objects and what links them to life—the street, ads, machines, mannequins, shop windows, etc., which have been transformed during the years we are concerned about. Can one not find, right at the heart of all these elements, a common element that confers* modernité *upon them? And if so, is it not*

*feasible that this very element has stood out and that it marks, during the same pe-*
*riod, a history of ideas that isn't any different from that of the street, for example?*[1]

■

The claims of a "paradigm shift," a "postmodern condition," or even a misunderstood "end of history" can be read as attempts to ring in the end of modernity. Rightly understood—and the commodities of fashion essentially make such an understanding possible—modernity will continue as long as capitalism and bourgeois societies exist. Fundamental economic, ecological, or political changes might cause the revolution that renders the parameters of modernity obsolete. Until such time, we are left to critically engage with continuous modernity and with the growing investigation and analysis of fashion's fundamental role within it.

Therefore, in view of Baudelaire's original postulate with which I began this book—namely, to *dégager,* to extract "from fashion whatever element it may contain of poetry within history, to distill the eternal from the transitory"[2]—Aragon's question regarding which element is common to all the varied expressions of modernity can have only one answer: fashion.

**90.**

M.v.S., title page of *Wiener Mode,* no. 8 (detail) (January 1897). Pencil and watercolor on paper, 32 × 13 cm. Staatliche Museen zu Berlin, Kunstbibliothek.

*Perhaps the tiger is tired after its leap, and even fashion has to rest once in a while.*

# Notes

## Introduction

1. The French is used here to distinguish the particular aesthetic quality of the modern—as coined by Gautier, Baudelaire, et al.—from the more sociological and political implications that shape the English word "modernity." Ergo: *modernité* = aesthetic or stylistic modernity (but not "modernism").

2. In section 1.2.3, I discuss why the feminine gender of this word is so significant.

3. For representative French writers, see the works of Perrault, Baudelaire, Compagnon, and Lefebvre listed in the selected bibliography. Other authors range from Marx to Habermas, Giddens, Wellmer, and beyond—again, see the bibliography.

4. Notable examples include studies by Perrot, Hollander, Wilson, Fortassier, Steele, Chenoune, Wigley, and Poschardt (see the bibliography).

5. That there is no woman among this group, despite the topic's orientation toward the "feminine," says more about the artistic and academic mores and tradition of the period discussed than, I hope, any hidden prejudices on my part.

6. Walter Benjamin, "Über den Begriff der Geschichte," in Benjamin, *Gesammelte Schriften,* 7 vols. (Frankfurt a.M.: Suhrkamp, 1974–1989), 1.2:701; trans. Harry Zohn as "Theses on the Philosophy of History," in Benjamin, *Illuminations* (London: Pimlico, 1999), 252–253 (translation modified).

7. Obviously, fashion can leap to any period, yet it appears that the "classical"—i.e., the Greco-Roman—ideal is the preferred point of repose because it combines aesthetic and civic virtues.

In an interview during the Olympic Summer Games of 1996, the victorious ex-GDR track cyclist Jens Fiedler explained that the expression *Tigersprung* is used in cycling for the final, desperate body push of the bike over the finish line. This perhaps suggests that Benjamin's dialectical image has been adopted to the vocabulary of Marxist-Leninist (sport) politics.

8. Eric Hobsbawn, *The Age of Extremes: The Short Twentieth Century, 1914–1991* (London: Joseph, 1995), 178; see also his collection *On History* (London: Weidenfeld & Nicolson, 1997) and his article "To See the Future, Look at the Past," *Guardian* (London and Manchester), 7 June 1997, 21.

9. The more recent school of "deconstructivist" fashion, lead by the "Antwerp Six" in the late 1980s, has its origins more in the anarchic spirit of punk than in the structuralist foundations of Derrida's ideas. Significantly, the label itself comes from an American journalist who previously had seen an exhibition of new architecture that had been labeled "deconstructivist." Such double transpositions are more likely to occur because of visual parallels than because of underlying principles.

We must also remember that one of the most lucid explorations of structuralism was conceived through the look at fashion in Roland Barthes's *Système de la mode* (Paris: Seuil, 1967) and its preparatory studies (see section 5.4).

10. The allocation of the ideas of quotation and self-reference to what has been called postmodernity just goes to prove that the impact of *modernité* is far from being past. Jean-François Lyotard, as one of the apostles of the postmodern condition, has turned on its head the traditional art-historical cycle of the avant-garde, the fashionable, and the established (later the "classical")

through which an artwork changes its significance, in order to describe the paradox of a post-modern consciousness.

See section 3.6 on Simmel's and Habermas's postulates of an "unfinished modernity."

## 1. Baudelaire, Gautier, and the Origins of Fashion in Modernity

1. "All modernity is supplied by the reader. Le chapeau—etc." Stéphane Mallarmé, *Le "Livre" de Mallarmé,* by Jacques Scherer (Paris: Gallimard, 1977), 148 (A). It is likely that the word *chapeau* denotes a short article (of writing) rather than actual headgear, yet Mallarmé's juxtaposition of terms is far from accidental—*mode* and *modernité* are bound together from the start.

2. Gabrielle Chanel always insisted that fashion does not equal art. Yet the question that remains is whether fashion is capable in principle of submitting itself to artistic or theoretical analysis.

3. The only two recent studies addressing Baudelaire's relation with fashion and modernity (that I know of) are an essay by Robert Kopp, "Baudelaire: Mode et modernité," *Cahiers de l'Association Internationale des Études Françaises,* no. 38 (May 1986), 173–186, and a book by Gerald Froideveaux, *Baudelaire: Représentation et modernité* (Paris: Corti, 1989). Although both go some way in explaining the importance of fashion for Baudelaire's aesthetic experience and indeed establish the connection to modernity in their titles (Froideveaux's chapter 3 is titled "La Mode, scène de la modernité"), neither actually discusses sartorial fashion. Yet without a (detailed) appreciation of fashion's sensuality, an understanding of these aspects in Baudelaire's work must remain one-dimensional.

4. Gustave Geffroy, *Constantin Guys: L'Historien du Second Empire* (1904; reprint, Paris: Crès, 1920), 48–49.

Robert T. Denommé, in *The Naturalism of Gustave Geffroy* (Geneva: Droz, 1963), 195, reckons that this book "was inspired by Baudelaire's article on the illustrator." The word "inspired" has to be interpreted very broadly: some 300 drawings by Guys were acquired by Tony Beltrand from Baudelaire's laundress, to whom the impoverished poet had given them to pay off some of the debts he had run up having his white shirts and ties professionally starched; some of the most beautiful of these sketches were then bought by Geffroy, who subsequently built his book around the examples. See *Gustave Geffroy et l'art moderne* (Paris: Bibliothèque Nationale, 1957), 37–38.

5. Charles Baudelaire, "Le Peintre de la vie moderne I: Le Beau, la mode et le bonheur," in Baudelaire, *Œuvres complètes,* 2 vols. (Paris: Gallimard, 1975–1976), 2:684; trans. J. Mayne in Baudelaire, *The Painter of Modern Life and Other Essays* (London: Phaidon, 1995), 1–2.

6. André Blum, *Histoire de costume* (Paris: Hachette, 1952), 52.

7. The magazine was produced and edited by La Mésangère from 1799 or 1800 up to his death in 1831. For a much more extensive discussion of the engravings, see T. H. Parke, "Baudelaire et La Mésangère," *Revue d'Histoire Littéraire de la France* 86, no. 2 (March–April 1986), 248–257.

8. Charles Baudelaire, *Correspondance,* ed. Claude Pichois and Jean Ziegler, 2 vols. (Paris: Gallimard, 1973), 1:550.

9. Here Baudelaire reveals a bias toward masculine fashion—as befits someone who was a self-confessed dandy in his youth. After having described "the idea which man [the male aesthete?] creates for himself," he continues: "The women who wore these costumes were themselves more or less like one or the other type, according to the degree of poetry or vulgarity with which they were stamped." Baudelaire, "Le Peintre de la vie moderne I," 684; trans. in Baudelaire, *The Painter of Modern Life and Other Essays,* 2.

The habit in artists and theoreticians of equating men's clothing with substance and women's wear with futile adornment is further discussed later in this chapter.

10. Charles Baudelaire, "Le Peintre de la vie moderne IV: La Modernité," in Baudelaire, *Œuvres complètes,* 2:694; trans. in Baudelaire, *The Painter of Modern Life and Other Essays,* 12.

11. First published in the feuilleton of *Le Figaro,* 6 November, 29 November, 3 December 1863, 3.

12.

•

2. **MODE** *(mo-d'),* s.f.*//**1**° Manner, fantasy. . . . **2**° Temporary usage that depends on taste or caprice. . . . **4**° Modes in the plural denote fit or adjustments, fineries in fashion; but in this sense, it does not mean to speak of anything but that which pertains to women's clothing. . . .*

**†MODERNITÉ** *(mo-dèr-ni-té),* s.f. *Neologism. Quality of what is modern. On one side, the most extreme modernity; on the other, the austere love of antiquity. TH. GAUTIER,* Moniteur univer[selle] *8 July 1867.*

•

É[mile] Littré, *Dictionnaire de la langue française: Tome second: Première partie* (Paris: Hachette, 1869), svv. "mode," "modernité."

Although he first planned his dictionary at the same time that Baudelaire would begin his autobiographical *Mon cœur mis à nu* (1859), Littré never displayed any congenial appreciation of fashion (or modern life)—whether in theory or in his own attire. Thus he is described as "the patient philologist, the austere disciple of Auguste Comte who was never seduced by the mysteries of dandyism, and who could not attach himself to them at all"; Simone François, *Le Dandysme et Marcel Proust: De Brummell au Baron de Charlus* (Brussels: Palais des Académies, 1956), 15.

13. Littré, *Dictionnaire de la langue française*, s.v. "moderne." The history of this dispute goes back to Charles Perrault's *Parallèle des anciens et modernes en ce qui regarde les arts et les sciences: Dialogues* (Paris: Coignard, 1688–1696); see Hans Robert Jauß's introduction to a new edition (Munich: Eidos, 1964) as well as his *Literaturgeschichte als Provokation* (Frankfurt a.M.: Suhrkamp, 1970), 11–106. On the *querelle,* see section 3.3.1.

14. On Gautier and *Le Moniteur Universel,* see Robert Snell, *Théophile Gautier* (Oxford: Clarendon, 1982), 148–149, 154, 192, 202.

15. Théophile Gautier, "Eugène Plon. Thorvaldsen, sa vie et son œuvre," *Le Moniteur Universel: Journal Officiel de l'Empire Français,* no. 189 (8 July 1867), 1.

16. Théophile Gautier, "Salon de 1852," *La Presse,* 25 May 1852. See Stéphane Guégan, "Modernités," in *Théophile Gautier: La Critique en liberté,* ed. Stéphane Guégan, Les Dossiers du musée d'Orsay, no. 61 (Paris: Réunion des musées nationaux, 1997), 47.

Robert Kopp, in "Baudelaire: Mode et modernité," 174–175, also aims to prove Littré incorrect in dating the first occurrence of *modernité* in Gautier's œuvre. For him, the first significant usage comes in an essay of 1855 that Gautier wrote for *Le Moniteur Universel* on that year's Universal Exhibition; reprinted in Gautier, *Les Beaux-Arts en Europe,* 2 vols. (Paris: Lévy, 1855–1856), where he, in a critique of Winterhalter, establishes an "ideal for elegance beyond antiquity and the eternal figures of beauty" (2:144–145). In an article on Balzac, Gautier then emphasizes a sharp opposition with antiquity, writing that "nobody is less classical" than the author of the *Comédie humaine.* This text was published simultaneously in *L'Artiste* and *Le Moniteur Universel* in April and May 1858; it is reprinted in Gautier, *Portraits contemporains* (Paris: Charpentier, 1874), 45–131.

17. See the fashion for grand *Expositions universelles* in Paris from 1855 onward.

18. Charles Baudelaire, "Salon de 1848 X: Du chic et du poncif," in Baudelaire, *Œuvres complètes,* 2:468; trans. J. Mayne in Baudelaire, *Art in Paris, 1845–1862: Salons and Other Exhibitions Reviewed by Charles Baudelaire* (Oxford: Phaidon, 1965), 92 (translation modified).

19. Charles Baudelaire, "Journaux intimes XIII: fusées no. 20," in Baudelaire, *Œuvres complètes,* 1:662.

20. Walter Benjamin, "Zentralpark," in Benjamin, *Gesammelte Schriften,* 7 vols. (Frankfurt a.M.: Suhrkamp, 1974–1989), 1.2:664; trans. L. Spencer (with M. Harrington) as "Central Park," *New German Critique,* no. 34 (winter 1985), 37.

21. Ibid., 665; trans., 38.

22. Théophile Gautier, *De la mode* (Paris: Poulet-Malassis & de Broise, 1858), 10–11. This minute volume was published in a single "collectors'" edition of thirty copies.

23. Ibid., 25–26.

24. The perception of a substantial distance between fashion and reality can be found regularly in the writing on the sartorial, from Stéphane Mallarmé to André Breton.

25. Gautier, *De la mode,* 27–28.

26. For Balzac's use, see Antoine Compagnon, *Les Cinq Paradoxes de la modernité* (Paris: Seuil, 1990), 17; trans. F. Philip as *The Five Paradoxes of Modernity* (New York: Columbia University Press, 1994), 5.

27. François-René, Vicomte de Chateaubriand, "Journal de Paris à Prague," in Chateaubriand, *Mémoires d'outre-tombe,* vol. 5 (Paris: Dufor, Mulat & Boulanger, 1860), 527.

28. Horace Walpole, letter "to Cole, Friday 22 February 1782," in *Horace Walpole's Correspondence with the Rev. William Cole,* ed. W. S. Lewis and Dayle Wallace, vol. 2 (London: Oxford University Press, 1937), 305.
    *The Oxford Encyclopaedic Dictionary* (Oxford: Clarendon, 1989), s.v. "modernity," makes two etymological references, "modern-us" and "modernité (Littré)," before giving alternative definitions of "modernity": "1. The quality of condition of being modern: modernness of character"—

here the first occurrences are dated to 1627 (Hakewill) and 1782 (Walpole)—and "2. Something that is modern," 1753 (Walpole) and 1884 (*Harper's Magazine*). Of these, that by Walpole in 1782 bears implications comparable to those within Littré's definition of 1859. Obviously, the English use is earlier than the French, yet the cultural environment and social conditions of nineteenth-century France imbue *la modernité* within qualities distinct from the English and align it with *la mode*.

29. *Le mode* is of course also a term in philosophy, especially in logic; e.g., "mode d'emploi"—as Littré rightly states in his *Dictionnaire de la langue française*, s.v. "mode."

30. It is hardly accidental that in this patriarchal society the challenge should belong to the female sex. Yet the caprice is far from flimsy and unsubstantial; artists like Mallarmé were able to celebrate fashion and the feminine without patronizing it (too much).

31. "What is pure art according to the modern idea? It is the creation of an evocative magic, containing at once the object and the subject, the world external to the artist and the artist himself." Charles Baudelaire, "L'Art philosophique," in Baudelaire, *Œuvres complètes*, 2:598; trans. in Baudelaire, *The Painter of Modern Life and Other Essays*, 205. This passage in Baudelaire's posthumously published text (it was written ca. 1859) can be related to Friedrich Schelling's conception of cognition and the self.

Georg Simmel, whose perception of fashion and reification is discussed in chapter 3, would be the first to systematically analyze the "female world" and its social and theoretical connotation. Such inquiry hitherto had belonged exclusively to the realm of the *journal des modes* and their contributors, who included Balzac, Barbey d'Aurevilly, and Mallarmé.

32. Henri Lefebvre writes that "Baudelaire's poetry inaugurates a pathway for poetry and modern art which Rimbaud, Lautréamont, Mallarmé and Valéry (to name but a few) will later pursue. In these poets, and in poetry since Baudelaire, there is a demented hope which is disalienating in terms of the everyday life they reject, and the bourgeois society they despise, but alienating and alienated in all other respects. It is a powerful hope, fruitful yet ineffectual: the hope of turning the abstract into everyday reality, since everyday reality itself is nothing more than an abstraction." Lefebvre, *Introduction à la modernité* (Paris: Minuit, 1962), 175; trans. J. Moore as Lefebvre, *Introduction to Modernity: Twelve Preludes, September 1959–May 1961* (London: Verso, 1995), 175.

33. Charles Baudelaire, "Le Peintre de la vie moderne IX: Éloge du maquillage," in Baudelaire, *Œuvres complètes*, 2:716; trans. in Baudelaire, *The Painter of Modern Life and Other Essays*, 33.

34. Baudelaire, "Le Peintre de la vie moderne IV," 694–695; trans. in Baudelaire, *The Painter of Modern Life and Other Essays,* 12.

35. See Telenia Hill, "Conception de la modernité," *Cahiers de l'Imaginaire,* nos. 14–15 (1997), 54; Kopp, "Baudelaire: Mode et modernité," 180; and Malgorzata Kobierska, "Epistémé moderne," *Cahiers de l'Imaginaire,* nos. 14–15 (1997), 62.

36. More on this shift in viewpoint—and Benjamin's interpretation of Baudelaire—is found in chapter 4.

37. See W. Freund, *Modernus and andere Zeitbegriffe des Mittelalters* (Cologne: Böhlau, 1957), 2, 5, 16; the shift in the meaning of *modernus* to "only" has been established in the fifth century, the shift to "new" in the twelfth.

38. The full quotation reads: "Fashion and modernity are temporal, instantaneous phenomena, and yet they have mysterious connections with the eternal. They are mobile images of an immobile eternity." Lefebvre, *Introduction à la modernité,* 172; trans. as *Introduction to Modernity,* 171 (translation slightly modified).

39. Baudelaire, "Le Peintre de la vie moderne IX," 716; trans. in Baudelaire, *The Painter of Modern Life and Other Essays,* 32.

40. Baudelaire, "Le Peintre de la vie moderne I," 684; trans. in Baudelaire, *The Painter of Modern Life and Other Essays,* 1.

41. Baudelaire, "Le Peintre de la vie moderne IV," 695; trans. in Baudelaire, *The Painter of Modern Life and Other Essays,* 13 (translation slightly modified).

42. Marcel Proust, *À l'ombre des jeunes filles en fleurs,* part 2 of *À la recherche du temps perdu* (Paris: Gallimard, 1988), 302; trans. C. K. Scott Moncrieff and T. Kilmartin as *Within a Budding Grove,* part 2 of *Remembrance of Things Past* (London: Chatto & Windus, 1981), 1013.

43. Alexandre Weill, *Qu'est-ce que le propriètaire d'une maison de Paris, Suite de Paris inhabitable* (Paris: Dentu, 1860), 2.

44. Gautier, *De la mode,* 28–29.

45. Ibid., 13–14, 11.

On a textual level, the "folds" (of the text) could be read as affirmation of the male (philo-sophical and literary) thought in contrast to feminine style (in poetry and prose); see sections 2.4.1 and 2.4.2.

46. Baudelaire, "Salon de 1846, XVIII: De l'héroïsme de la vie moderne," in Baudelaire, Œuvres complètes, 2:494; trans. in Baudelaire, Art in Paris, 1845–1862, 118 (translation slightly modified).

47. Honoré de Balzac, "Traité de la vie élégante," La Mode (October 1830); in Balzac, Œuvres complètes, vol. 39 (Paris: Conard, 1938), 162.

The often-cited observation by J. C. Flügel on "the great masculine renunciation" (see The Psychology of Clothes [London: Hogarth, 1930], 132), that it was man's decision to abandon any claim toward being beautiful and henceforth confine himself to being useful, is not accurate. Masculine apparel did not cease being beautiful; it was the concept of beauty, especially mod-ernist beauty, that changed because of the shift of social parameters after the Revolution. Flügel's view was curiously one-dimensional in ascribing beauty to woman and rationality or expedience to man. If anything elaborate would routinely be equated with beauty and anything somber or re-straint with mere utility, works in whole epochs in art should cease to be considered "beautiful."

48. Max von Boehn wrote about the "downright devastating inroad of black into male fashion." See Die Mode: Menschen und Moden im 19. Jahrhundert, 4 vols. (Munich: Bruckmann, 1905–1919), 1:91–92.

49. Honoré de Balzac, "Physiologie de la toilette," La Silhouette, 3 June 1830; in Balzac, Œuvres complètes, 39:47.

50. Baudelaire, "Salon de 1846, XVIII," 493; trans. in Baudelaire, Art in Paris, 1845–1862, 117 (translation slightly modified).

51. Baudelaire, "Salon de 1846, XVIII," 494; trans. in Baudelaire, Art in Paris, 1845–1862, 117 (translation slightly modified).

For Antony, see Alexandre Dumas, Antony: Drame en cinq actes, en prose (Paris: Auffray, 1831). The piece was set explicitly in the present. Ironically, the only "ancient" reference was pro-vided by the costume ("manteau grec") that the author felt appropriate to slip on for his photo on the frontispiece.

In his memoirs, Dumas writes: "The day will come when a modern author arrives who is bolder than all the others, and he will take contemporary manners, existing passion, and hidden vices, and bring all three to the stage dressed in white tie, black suit, strapped trousers, and patent leather shoes. And oh! everybody will recognize themselves as in a mirror and grimace instead of laughing, attacked at the very time of their approval." Dumas, *Mes mémoires,* vol. 21 (Paris: Cadot, 1854), 131. He thus anticipates Baudelaire's more famous call at the end of his "Salon de 1845" for the true artist, him "who can snatch the epic quality from contemporary life and can make us see and understand . . . how great and poetic we are in our cravats and our patent leather boots." Baudelaire, *Œuvres complètes,* 2:407; trans. in Baudelaire, *Art in Paris, 1845–1862,* 32 (translation slightly modified).

52. Mallarmé would make the same observation in 1862, in one of his earliest poems; "Contre un poëte parisien"; see section 2.4.3.

53. Baudelaire, "Salon de 1846, XVIII," 494; trans. in Baudelaire, *Art in Paris, 1845–1862,* 118 (translation slightly modified).

54. Théophile Gautier, "Salon de 1837," *La Presse,* 8 April 1837, [3].

55. Charles Baudelaire, letter to his brother Alphonse, dated "[Lyon], le 17 mai [1833]," in Baudelaire, *Correspondance,* 1:18; trans. R. Lloyd in *Selected Letters of Charles Baudelaire: The Conquest of Solitude* (London: Weidenfeld & Nicolson, 1986), 6 (translation slightly modified).

56. Eugène Marsan, *Les Cannes de M. Paul Bourget. Et le bon choix de Philinte. Petit manuel de l'homme élégant. Suivi de portraits en references, Barrès, Moréas, Bourget, Alphonse XIII d'Espagne, Taine, Barbey d'Aurevilly, Baudelaire, Balzac, Stendhal* (Paris: Le Divan, 1923), 236; the first version of this text (some 30 pages in length) had been published in 1909 under the title *Les Cannes de M. Paul Bourget.*

For an idiosyncratic literary treatment of Baudelaire's taste in fashion (especially cashmere trousers), his dandyism, and his resulting financial difficulties, see Michel Butor, *Histoire extraordinaire: Essai sur un rêve de Baudelaire* (Paris: Gallimard, 1961), 45–54.

57. See Georges Poulet (with Robert Kopp), *Wer war Baudelaire?* (Geneva: Skira, 1969), 30.

58. Le Vavasseur is quoted in Jules Bertaut, "Baudelaire dandy," *Monsieur,* no. 33 (September 1922), 4. On his "poetic fabric," see Poulet, *Wer war Baudelaire?* 33.

59. Unpublished letter by Champfleury [Jules Husson] to Eugène Crepet, dated 7 August 1887; in Baudelaire, *Œuvres complètes,* 2:1553.

60. See Boehn, *Die Mode,* 1:97.

61. Boehn, *Die Mode,* 2:13.

62. On Baudelaire's invariable black suit and his "interior dandyism," see André Ferran, *L'Esthétique de Baudelaire* (Paris: Nizet, 1968), 50–72, esp. 60–61, 70.

63. The painting is in the depot of the Musée de Versailles; the photograph was formerly in the collection of Claude Pichois, Paris.

64. See Charles Baudelaire, "Salon de 1845, I: Quelques mots d'introduction," in Baudelaire, *Œuvres complètes,* 2:352; and "Salon of 1846," in ibid., 415.

65. See Marcel Ruff, "La Pensée politique et sociale de Baudelaire," in *Littérature et société: Recueil d'études en l'honneur de Bernhard Guyon* (Paris: Desclée de Brouwer, 1973), 67.

66. Charles Baudelaire, "Des moyens proposés pour l'amélioration du sort des travailleurs," *La Tribune Nationale,* 6 June 1848; in Baudelaire, *Œuvres complètes,* 2:1055. On *La Tribune Nationale,* see Jules Moquet and W. T. Bandy, *Baudelaire en 1848: "La Tribune Nationale"* (Paris: Émile-Paul Frères, 1946).

67. Charles Baudelaire, letter to Sainte-Beuve, dated "Brussels, Tuesday, 2 January 1866," in Baudelaire, *Correspondance,* 2:563; trans. in *Selected Letters of Charles Baudelaire,* 240 (translation slightly modified).

68. Baudelaire, "Avis," *La Tribune Nationale,* April 1848, in Baudelaire, *Œuvres complètes,* 2:1042.

69. "My wild excitement in 1848 / What was the nature of this excitement? / The taste for revenge. Natural pleasure in destruction / Literary excitement; memories of my reading." Charles Baudelaire, "Mon cœur mis à nu, V," in Baudelaire, *Œuvres complètes,* 1:679; trans. Christopher Isherwood in Baudelaire, *Intimate Journals* (1930; reprint, London: Methuen, 1949), [27].

70. Baudelaire, "Avis," 1042.

71. "Enivrez-vous" is the title of Baudelaire's prose poem published in *Le Figaro,* 7 February 1864, which later became no. 33 of the *Spleen de Paris* (in Baudelaire, *Œuvres complètes,* 1:337).

72. Karl Marx, "Kritik des Hegelschen Staatsrechts," in Karl Marx and Friedrich Engels, *Werke,* vol. 1 (Berlin: Dietz, 1988), 233; this unfinished manuscript was written between March and August 1843 (trans. as "Contribution to the Critique of Hegel's Philosophy of Law," in Karl Marx and Friedrich Engels, *Collected Works,* vol. 3 [London: Lawrence & Wishart, 1975], 32).

73. Chapter 3 examines how Gabriel Tarde and Georg Simmel transposed the notion of exteriority of spirit into a less politically charged analysis.

74. Karl Marx, *Der 18. Brumaire des Louis Bonaparte,* in Marx and Engels, *Werke,* vol. 8 (Berlin: Dietz, 1988), 115–116; the text was written immediately after the events, December 1851 to March 1852; trans. as *The Eighteenth Brumaire of Louis Napoleon,* in Marx and Engels, *Collected Works,* vol. 11 (London: Lawrence & Wishart, 1979), 104.

75. "Politically realized," that is, if we accept the proclamation of the Third Republic (4 September 1870) as a partial redemption of the promises from 1848—although Blanqui, Flourens, and other revolutionaries were once more forced underground.

76. Walter Benjamin, "Über den Begriff der Geschichte," in Benjamin, *Gesammelte Schriften,* 1.2:701; trans. Harry Zohn as "Theses on the Philosophy of History," in Benjamin, *Illuminations* (London: Pimlico, 1999), 252–253 (translation modified).

77. *Katzensprung* (a cat's leap) is the German expression for something very close, something that is just a stone's throw away. In the figure of the *Tigersprung,* in which a big feline takes one great leap to land motionless on a distant spot, the historical-materialist attitude has found both a precise and poetic metaphor.

78. Charles Baudelaire, "Critique littéraire: Théophile Gautier [I]," in Baudelaire, *Œuvres complètes,* 1:115.
    Earlier in this essay, Baudelaire recalled the first encounter with his poet-friend: "I thought that his looks were not as impressive as they are today, but already majestic and gracefully at ease

in his flowing garments" (107). Subsequently a parallel is drawn to Gautier's poetry: "His poetry, majestic and precious at the same time, works beautifully, like courtesans wearing their most magnificent clothes" (126). The description is a perhaps unintended yet indeed prophetic irony, given Gautier's later role as the arriviste "reporter" to the court of Louis Napoleon.

On the relationship between Baudelaire and Gautier, see also the commentary in Charles Baudelaire, *Théophile Gautier—Deux études,* ed. Philippe Terrier (Neuchâtel: À la Baconnière, 1985).

79. Jules Michelet, *L'Amour* (Paris: Hachette, 1858), xlii; trans. J. W. Palmer as *Love* (New York: Rudd & Carleton, 1860), 37.

80. Charles Baudelaire, letter to his mother, dated "[Paris], 11 December 1858," in Baudelaire, *Correspondance,* 1:532; trans. in *Selected Letters of Charles Baudelaire,* 120.

81. In a way, both bourgeois served the revolution: Baudelaire wrote his pamphlets and is said to have fought on the barricades, while Michelet defiantly returned to the Collège de France during and after February 1848, only to have his lectureship suspended once more by the emperor in 1851. That suspension prompted the liberal historian to refuse to swear the oath to Louis Napoleon (a requirement for all those employed by the French state) in the following year.

82. Charles Baudelaire, "Le Peintre de la vie moderne XII: Les Femmes et les filles," in Baudelaire, *Œuvres complètes,* 2:719; trans. in Baudelaire, *The Painter of Modern Life and Other Essays,* 36.

83. Gautier, *De la mode,* 5–6.

84. Charles Baudelaire, "Le Peintre de la vie moderne X: La Femme," in Baudelaire, *Œuvres complètes,* 2:714; trans. in Baudelaire, *The Painter of Modern Life and Other Essays,* 31.

85. Charles Baudelaire, "Le Spleen de Paris, XXV: La Belle Dorthée," in Baudelaire, *Œuvres complètes,* 1:316; trans. F. Scarfe in *Baudelaire,* vol. 2, *The Poems in Prose* (London: Anvil, 1989), 107. The poem was written ca. 1861.

86. Baudelaire, "Le Peintre de la vie moderne XII," 720; trans. in Baudelaire, *The Painter of Modern Life and Other Essays,* 36.

87. Ibid.; trans., 37.

88. Walter Benjamin, "Über einige Motive bei Baudelaire," in Benjamin, *Gesammelte Schriften,* 1.2:623; trans. Harry Zohn as "Some Motifs in Baudelaire," in Benjamin, *Illuminations,* 166. First published in *Zeitschrift für Sozialforschung,* no. 8 (1939 [i.e., 1940]), 50–89.

89. Charles Baudelaire, "À une passante," first published in *L'Artiste,* 15 October 1860, and included in the first edition of *Les Fleurs du mal* as piece no. 93; in Baudelaire, *Œuvres complètes,* 1:92–93. A translation in prose is provided by F. Scarfe in *Baudelaire,* vol. 1, *The Complete Verse* (London: Anvil, 1986), 186:

▪

*To a Woman Passing By | The darkening street was howling around me when a woman passed on her way, so tall and slender, all in black mourning, majestical in her grief, with her stately hand lifting and swaying the scallop and hem, | light-footed and noble and with a statuesque leg. And I, tense as a man out of his wits, drank from her eye—a pallid sky in which the tempest brews—that gentleness which bewitches men, that pleasure which destroys. | A flash of light— then darkness. O vanishing beauty, whose glance brought me suddenly to life again, shall I never see you once more except in eternity? | Elsewhere, far from here, too late or perhaps never? For whither you fled I know not, nor do you know whither I am bound—O you whom I could have loved, O you who knew it!*

▪

90. Charles Baudelaire, letter of 13 December 1859, in Baudelaire, *Correspondance,* 2:627.

91. The Roman catalogue edited by Gilda Piersanti, *Constantin Guys: Il pittore della vita moderna* (Rome: Savelli, 1980), features a huge selection from the drawings that once belonged to Baudelaire (some of them later passed on to Geffroy) and that are now kept in the depot of the Musée Carnavalet in Paris; a quarter of the listed works show women of various classes, shapes, and postures, all lifting the dress to reveal shoe, foot, and part of the leg (see the depot nos. ieD 856, 860, 862, 865, 866, 869, 870, 908, 918, 929–932, 936, 939, 969, 978, 979, 1067, 1069, 1100, 1121, 1164, 1176, 1178, 1281). Obviously a *poncif* by the artist to increase the commercial appeal and recognizability of his work, it also shows an obsessive interest that borders on the fetishistic.

92. The drawing that Geffroy reproduced in *Constantin Guys,* 47, is titled *Au bal;* thus the movement could be that of a dance step. However, most titles are descriptive notes given by various editors and none of them are contemporary. Additionally, the lack of jewelry and the lace bonnet in this particular drawing appear to set the scene outside, in the daytime, and not necessarily

within a ballroom at night. An early London publication on Constantin Guys—which also contains the first complete English translation of Baudelaire's *Le Peintre de la vie moderne*—titled *The Painter of Victorian Life* (London: The Studio, 1930) reproduced this drawing on its frontispiece with the title *Femme se retroussant* (Woman hiking up her dress).

93. Geffroy, *Constantin Guys,* 49, 81.

94. André Fontainas, *De Stéphane Mallarmé à Paul Valéry: Notes d'un témoin 1894–1922* (Paris: Bernard, 1928), [28]; the entry is dated "22 December [1897]."
    In Jean-Michel Nectoux, *Mallarmé: Un Clair Regard dans les ténèbres: Peinture, musique, poésie* (Paris: Biro, 1998), 211 (no. 25), the drawing is thought to be titled *Femme en crinoline bleu;* but since its whereabouts are unknown, speculations about the precise look of Guys's work have to remain academic.

95. See Charles Baudelaire, "Le Peintre de la vie moderne V: L'Art mnémonique," in Baudelaire, *Œuvres complètes,* 2:698; and Rudolf Koella, *Constantin Guys,* exhib. cat. (Winterthur: Kunstmuseum, 1989), 32.

96. Charles Baudelaire, "Sur mes contemporains: Théodore de Banville," *Revue Fantaisiste,* 1 August 1861; in Baudelaire, *Œuvres complètes,* 2:167.

97. Théodore de Banville died in 1891, yet the drawing had been passed on long before that. Banville's label as an "intermediary" also derives from his leading position within the group of poets known as Parnassiens. Their anthologies (1866, 1871, and 1876) combined the poetic tendencies of l'*art pour l'art* in, e.g., Gautier, with the formal rigor of Baudelaire, Banville, and also Mallarmé. In discussing Mallarmé's fashion journal in the following chapter, I will again refer to some of the Parnassiens, including Coppée and Mendès.

98. Marguerite de Ponty, "La Mode," *La Dernière Mode,* no. 4 (18 October 1874), 2; in Stéphane Mallarmé, *Œuvres complètes* (Paris: Gallimard, 1945), 763.

### 2 Mallarmé and the Elegance of Fashion in Modernity

1.

▪

**André Courrèges:** *"And the marriages of cotton and synthetic fabrics render the fibers capable of protecting you from climatic changes outside. Cotton preserves the intrinsic quality of warmth inside it. Marriages like these make you feel very comfortable indeed!"*
**Jean-Pierre Barou:** *"Those things were never discussed by Mallarmé although he occupied himself also with fashion."* (Laughs.)
**Courrèges:** *"But Mallarmé lived in his age. I myself live with a washing machine!"*

▪

Interview from spring 1983 in the appendix of Eugénie Lemoine-Luccioni, *La Robe: Essai psychanalytique sur le vêtement* (Paris: Seuil, 1983), 157–158.

2. Charles Baudelaire, "Le Peintre de la vie moderne I: Le Beau, la mode et le bonheur," in Baudelaire, *Œuvres complètes,* 2 vols. (Paris: Gallimard, 1975–1976), 2:684; trans. J. Mayne in Baudelaire, *The Painter of Modern Life and Other Essays* (London: Phaidon, 1995), 1–2.

3. On Mallarmé and *modernité,* see Jean-Pierre Richard, *L'Univers imaginaire de Mallarmé* (Paris: Seuil, 1961), 297–304 ("mythological enclosure," 301); and Judy Kravis, *The Prose of Mallarmé: The Evolution of a Literary Language* (Cambridge: Cambridge University Press, 1976), 84–100.

4. Mallarmé's daughter would later judge: "Poetry was really part of his nature. . . . Verses embroidered on the uniformity of fabric stretched over a wall." Letter to Catulle Mendès, dated "Nantes, 5 November 1916," in "Mallarmé par sa fille," *La Nouvelle Revue Française,* no. 158 (1 November 1926), 518.

5. Albert Thibaudet, *La Poésie de Stéphane Mallarmé: Étude littéraire* (Paris: Gallimard, 1926), 316, 327.

6. According to the study by Pascale Saisset, "Stéphane Mallarmé et la mode," *La Grande Revue,* April 1933, 203–222, the poet simply accepted the "bad taste in clothes" prevalent in his time and did not endeavor to change the sartorial excesses that, for instance, imprison and hinder women's movement.

7. See Paul de Man, "Literary History and Literary Modernity," in de Man, *Blindness and Insight: Essays in the Rhetoric of Contemporary Criticism* (New York: Oxford University Press, 1971), 156–161, which deals in particular with Baudelaire's *Le Peintre de la vie moderne.*

8. See Gilles Deleuze, *Le Pli: Leibniz et le baroque* (Paris: Minuit, 1988), 43–44.

9. See J. C. Flügel, *The Psychology of Clothes* (London: Hogarth, 1930), 137.

10. Charles Baudelaire, "Le Peintre de la vie moderne IV: La Modernité," in Baudelaire, *Œuvres complètes,* 2:695.

11. Stéphane Mallarmé, letter to the poet Henri Cazalis, dated "Tournon, Monday evening [May 1866]," in Stéphane Mallarmé, *Correspondance,* ed. Henri Mondor and Lloyd James Austin, 11 vols. (Paris: Gallimard, 1965–1985), 1:216.

12. Paul Verlaine, "Charles Baudelaire," *L'Art,* 30 November 1865; in Verlaine, *Œuvres en prose complètes* (Paris: Gallimard, 1972), 605.

13. Stéphane Mallarmé, "Sur le beau et l'utile," in Mallarmé, *Œuvres complètes* (Paris: Gallimard, 1945), 880. In 1848 Gautier had published an article on Ingres's studio that was titled "Du beau antique et du beau moderne"—showing again that perceptions of beauty require an element of the dialectical.

14. Méry Laurent (Anne-Rose Louviot, 1849–1900) was a patron of the arts and lover of, among others, Edouard Manet and, from 1883 onward, Mallarmé. See figure 15, quoting from Henri Mondor, *Vie de Mallarmé* (Paris: Gallimard, 1941), 415–416.

15. "White Japanese mischievous / I cut myself as soon as I rise / For a dress a piece of the blue turquoise / sky of which I dream. | Extravagant dress of a Persian divinity / And inside even more fairylike / To change them into hers Méry / Decorated by our fanciful dreams. | Always true to my friendships / Clothed in a silvery blue reflected light / Would you for any reason doubt me! / That only my dress will change. | I do not know why I keep wearing / My moonlight-colored dress / Since I, a goddess, might / very well wear none." Stéphane Mallarmé, "Photographies," in Mallarmé, *Œuvres complètes,* 115–116.

16. See Gotthold Ephraim Lessing, "Laokoon oder über die Grenzen der Malerei und Poesie" (1765/1766), in Lessing, *Werke,* vol. 3 (Leipzig: Fock, 1895), 284–285, 353.

17. The color of Laurent's gown is significant. Not only were the covers of *La Dernière Mode* blue but so was the dress that opened the first issue of the magazine (3); see also "la robe bleu-rêve" created by Charles Frederick Worth that was discussed in issue 5 (3, again).

    In the Romantic tradition, the artist longed for the cosmic impression of a complete work of art, symbolized by the "*blaue* Blume Sehnsucht" (Novalis)—the blue flower of yearning.

18. As will become clear later in the chapter, the refusal to observe and record even the most minute of these changes would prove fatal for Mallarmé's magazine.

19. For a fuller account of modernity's changes in social and artistic configuration, see, e.g., Werner Busch, *Das sentimentalistische Bild: Die Krise der Kunst im 18. Jahrhundert und die Geburt der Moderne* (Munich: Beck, 1993).

20. Stéphane Mallarmé, "Autobiographie," letter to Verlaine dated "Paris Monday 16 November 1885," in Mallarmé, *Correspondance,* 2:303 (also in Mallarmé, *Œuvres complètes,* 664).

    See also Jean-Pierre Faye, "Lexique," in *La Mode, l'invention,* Change, no. 4 (Paris: Seuil, 1969), 91–92.

21. Roland Barthes, *Système de la mode* (Paris: Seuil, 1967), 246 n. 2; trans. M. Ward and R. Howard as *The Fashion System* (London: Cape, 1985), 242 n. 11. On the relation between the structuralist and symbolist, see Lemoine-Luccioni, *La Robe;* and Mary Lewis Shaw, "The Discourse of Fashion: Mallarmé, Barthes, and Literary Criticism," *Substance,* no. 68 (1992), 46–60.

22. Barthes, *Système de la mode,* 246; trans. as *The Fashion System,* 242.

23. Stéphane Mallarmé, letter, dated "Besançon, Tuesday 14 September [1867]," in Mallarmé, *Correspondance,* 2:259.

24. Marguerite de Ponty, "La mode," *La Dernière Mode,* no. 8 (20 December 1874), 2; in Mallarmé, *Œuvres complètes,* 831.

25. See George Woodcock, *Anarchism* (London: Penguin, 1977), 276, 286.

26. Stéphane Mallarmé, letter, in Mallarmé, *Correspondance*, 2:26 n. 3; the editor establishes the date of the letter as 7 April 1872.

27. Claudius Popelin (1825–1892) would appear to have been an ideal choice as illustrator. Not only a talented painter who specialized in small-scale works in enamel, he also skillfully decorated fans (some of which are kept in the Musée d'Arts Décoratifs in Paris) and composed dandified poetry himself. He was also the (rather unfaithful) lover of the Princess Mathilde, who, according to the Goncourts, was one of the first patrons of the couturier and collector Jacques Doucet.

28. Stéphane Mallarmé, "Symphonie littéraire," *L'Artiste* 35, vol. 1, no. 3 (1 February 1865), 57–58; in Mallarmé, *Œuvres complètes*, 261–265.

29. Comtesse d'Orr, "L'Art et la mode," *L'Artiste* 35, vol. 2, no. 1 (1 July 1865), 20; and no. 11 (1 December 1865), 260.
　　On the occasion of his previous contribution in 1862, Mallarmé first had met his friend Nina de Villard, whose interest in literature and fashion would become instrumental in the sartorial descriptions in La Dernière Mode a dozen years later. Significantly, Mme de Villard was also the Comtesse de Callias.

30. Arsène Houssaye, *Les Confessions: Souvenirs d'un demi-siècle 1830–1880*, vol. 3 (Paris: Dentu, 1885), 361. "Diana" was Mlle de F——, the adolescent heiress to a banking empire.

31. Ibid.

32. See the letters dated 21 and 26 September 1874 by Charles and Constance Wendelen to Mallarmé concerning financial arrangements; in Mallarmé, *Correspondance*, 5:223–225.

33. Marasquin, "Nos six premières livraisons," *La Dernière Mode*, no. 6 (15 November 1874), 10; in Mallarmé, *Œuvres complètes*, 810.

34. The illustrators were Henri Polydore Colin and Louis David; in the first issue of the new series, two illustrations in the text were credited to the pairing of illustrator-engraver "F. Pecqueur and Trichon" (the latter a well-known Parisian maker of woodcuts). Wendelen and Mallarmé envisaged a luxury edition of each issue that would contain hand-colored lithography. Very few of these survive, and thus it is not clear whether they accompanied all eight issues; see the catalogue edited by Yves Peyré, *Mallarmé 1842–1898: Un Destin d'écriture* (Paris: Gallimard/Réunion des

musées nationaux, 1998), 173, no. 147, where three of these lithographs are credited to L. René (with coloring by M. Huguet).

35. Théodore de Banville and Edmond Morin, "Promenade galante," in *Sonnets et eaux-fortes* (Paris: Lemerre, 1868), 13. Originally, Mallarmé was supposed to contribute to the volume as well (his "sonnet en yx"); see Mondor, *Vie de Mallarmé,* 274. Mallarmé had become first acquainted with Lemerre when the latter published the *Parnasse Contemporain.*

Edmond Morin (1824–1882) was a pupil of Charles Gleyre; he worked in London between 1850 and 1857 and helped to found the English art magazine *Pen and Pencil;* he then became a regular contributor to the Parisian journals *Le Monde Illustré* and *Vie Parisienne,* for which he documented fashion and costume designs. On the relationship between Morin and Mallarmé, see a letter by the painter inquiring about a summer residence for "his editor," in Mallarmé, *Correspondance,* 4:587-588. It seems quite telling that instead of "Popelin"—the masculine form of a weaving technique—Mallarmé would turn to employ "Morin"—a particular yellow dye for textiles.

36. See le Marquis de Villemer, *Nouveaux portraits Parisiens,* illus. Morin (Paris: Librairie International, 1869), illustration facing 7, *La Femme qui laisse de bons souvenir,* which is very similar to the later frontispiece of *La Dernière Mode;* or Gustave Droz, *Monsieur, Madame et Bébé,* illus. Edmond Morin (Paris: Havard, 1878), illustration on 309, titled *En famille,* which is almost a copy—in subject as well as style—of Morin's work for Mallarmé.

37. Stéphane Mallarmé, letter, dated "Paris, 6 August 1874," in Mallarmé, *Correspondance,* 2:47–48.

One of the very few advertisements among "Les Maisons de confience" to appear in almost every issue was that of "Madame LEMERRE / (ANCIENNE MAISON LAROCHE) / Fournisseur de Son Altesse Royale l'Infante / d'Espagne. / Modes pour Enfants et jeunes Desmoiselles / 44, passage Choiseul." Obviously, the editor's wife greeted the first issue of Mallarmé's magazine with much professional interest.

38. Stéphane Mallarmé, letter, dated "6 November 1874," in Mallarmé, *Correspondance,* 2:50–51.

39. Zola was quick to chastise Mallarmé's "limitations" caused by his expressed preference for form: "Monsieur Mallarmé was and remains the most typical poet of this group. In his work all the folly of formalism exploded. . . . In short, one finds here the theory behind the Parnassiens,

but pushed to a point where the mind begins to buckle." Émile Zola, "Les Poètes contemporains," in Zola, Œuvres complètes, vol. 12 (Paris: Cercle du livre précieux, 1969), 379–380.

40. Marasquin, "Nos six premières livraisons," 9; in Mallarmé, Œuvres complètes, 808.

41. Ibid.

42. See Charles Baudelaire, "Le Peintre de la vie moderne III: L'Artiste, homme du monde, homme des foules et enfant," in Baudelaire, Œuvres complètes, 2:687–694.
    It is also interesting to relate the character of Ix. to Mallarmé's sonnet of 1868 "en yx" (ibid., 1488–1491), where the masculine endings in the first eight lines become feminine in the sestet—a prosodic equivalent to a male poet turning into a female fashion journalist?
    On the letter x, see Robert Greer Cohn, Toward the Poems of Mallarmé (Berkeley: University of California Press, 1965), 276–277.

43. "Correspondance avec les Abonnées," La Dernière Mode, no. 5 (1 November 1874), [9]; in Mallarmé, Œuvres complètes, 792.
    The page ends "please address your orders directly to Madame Charles; in regard to payment, you are requested to send a postal order made out to Monsieur Marasquin, Publishing Director, along with your order." Thus we find the additional roles of M. and Mme Charles Wendelen as an exclusive mail-order business of their time.

44. Luigi Gualdo, postscript to a letter, dated "Venise, 27 August [1874]," in Mallarmé, Correspondance, 5:221–222 n. 3.

45. Luigi Gualdo, letter, dated "Milan, 30 November [1874]," in Mallarmé, Correspondance, 5:222 n. 3.

46. Shaw offers a structuralist interpretation: "Under the cover of fashion, they [Mallarmé and Barthes] seem to link literature and its criticism to an inarticulable feminine signified" ("The Discourse of Fashion," 46).

47. La Dernière Mode, no. 6 (15 November 1874), [1].

48. Marguerite de Ponty, "La Mode," La Dernière Mode, no. 6 (15 November 1874), 2; in Mallarmé, Œuvres complètes, 797.

49. Unpublished letter from the end of October or beginning of November 1874; in Mallarmé, *Correspondance,* 4:587.

    The Comtesse de Callias's social position emphasized the significance of her sense of style: "Between 1863 and 1882, Nina hosted the most lively and intellectually challenging salon in Paris." Ernest Raynaud, *La Bohème sous le Second Empire: Charles Gros et Nina* (Paris: L'Artisan du livre, 1930), 72; see also 86–89, on Nina de Villard's sartorial style.

50. See Ix., "Chronique de Paris," *La Dernière Mode,* no. 6 (15 November 1874), [4]; in Mallarmé, *Œuvres complètes,* 801–802. Zola's *Les Héritiers* is discussed following the description of the costume.

51. Marguerite de Ponty, "La Mode," *La Dernière Mode,* no. 4 (18 October 1874), 2; in Mallarmé, *Œuvres complètes,* 761–762.

52. Ibid.

53. Michel Butor, "Mode et moderne," in *La Mode, l'invention,* 23. Reprinted in Butor, *Répertoire,* vol. 4 (Paris: Minuit, 1974), 409.

54. The illustrator Edmond Morin once alluded to the political persuasion that Mallarmé shared with him. On occasion of dealing with a landlord, he warned the poet: "You will congratulate yourself in the end if you stay away from any political discussion (where he [the landlord Monsieur Colliaux] is terrible, and you won't find any common ground)." In Mallarmé, *Correspondance,* 5:377.

55. Sacher-Masoch confessed to his diaries: "There is a female type that continues to be my obsession since my earliest youth. . . . The woman with the tiger's body, idolized by man, although she torments and degrades him." Another facet within the metaphor of the Benjaminian tiger's leap is *la tigresse:* the promiscuous and dominating female who devours one lover after the other; see, e.g., Sacher-Masoch, "Ein weiblicher Don Juan" and "Leibeigenschaft," in *Aus dem Tagebuche eines Weltmannes* (Leipzig: Kormann, 1870), 76–80, 167–175.

56. Maximilienne de Syrène, "De l'élégance (1)," *Moniteur de la Mode,* 20 April 1843; in J. Barbey d'Aurevilly, *Premiers articles (1834–1852),* ed. André Hirschi and Jacques Petit (Paris: Les Belles lettres, 1973), 86.

57. J. Barbey d'Aurevilly, "Fragment," in *Œuvres romanesques complètes,* vol. 2 (Paris: Gallimard, 1966), 1161. The piece was written between 1833 and 1835.

58. Maximilienne de Syrène, "De l'élégance (1)," 86.

59. [Maximilienne de Syrène], "Revue critique de la mode," *Le Constitutionnel,* 13 October 1845); in Barbey d'Aurevilly, *Premiers articles,* 93.

60. Théophile Sylvestre, "Jules Barbey d'Aurevilly," *Le Figaro* 8, no. 672 (25 July 1861), [1].
The attire of the aging Barbey d'Aurevilly repeatedly occasioned malicious gossip and bemused observation in Edmond and Jules de Goncourt's *Journal: Memoires de la vie littéraire,* 4 vols. (Paris: Fasquelle & Flammarion, 1956); see, e.g., 2:1065 (9 May 1875), or 3:454 (12 May 1885). The campness of Barbey's frock coat and the late coloring of his hair are also the subject of much sniping by Bourget (an archenemy) and by the Parnassien Coppée.

61. Barbey d'Aurevilly referred repeatedly to the pitiless "vanité tigre des Dandys." See *Du Dandysme et de George Brummell,* in Barbey d'Aurevilly, *Œuvres romanesques complètes,* 2:720.

62. See Baudelaire, *Œuvres complètes,* 2:1293.

63. [Maximilienne de Syrène], "Modes," *Le Constitutionnel,* 3 April 1846; in Barbey d'Aurevilly, *Premiers articles,* 311.

64. Jacques Boulenger, *Sous Louis-Philippe: Les Dandys* (Paris: Ollendorf, 1907), 358.

65. The increased competition among fashion magazines at the upper end of the market—during the 1870s in Paris there existed at least twenty sophisticated fashion journals, including five exclusive weeklies that could be compared to *La Dernière Mode*—and the costliness of Mallarmé and Wendelen's publication (it was the second most expensive) also contributed to its demise.
See two works by Annemarie Kleinert, "La Dernière Mode: Une Tentative de Mallarmé dans la presse féminine," *Lendemains* 5, nos. 17–18 (June 1980), 167–178, and *Die frühen Modejournale in Frankreich: Studien zur Literatur der Mode von den Anfängen bis 1848* (Berlin: Schmidt, 1980).

66. Charles Wendelen, letter, dated Paris, 12 January 1875, in Mallarmé, *Correspondance,* 5:226.

67. Stéphane Mallarmé, letter, dated Monday, 25 January 1875, in Mallarmé, *Correspondance,* 2:52.

The very next day Coppée replied: "This goes without saying. The moment you are no longer editor-in-chief of *La Dernière Mode,* I will cease to be part of this journal. I have received a letter today by one *Baronne de Lomaria*—if I have read it correctly—who asks me to continue my collaboration. I will not reply, very simple" (Mallarmé, *Correspondance,* 4:588).

The critic and writer Remy de Gourmont would judge in 1890: "*La Dernière Mode,* alas! has fallen into the hands of a woman who turns it into a banal journal of historicized silliness, of which there are too many around." Gourmont, "La 'Dernière Mode' de Stéphane Mallarmé: Trouvailles et curiosités," *Revue Indépendante,* (February 1890); in Gourmont, *Promenades littéraires, deux-ième série,* 9th ed. (Paris: Mercure de France, 1913), 45.

68. Philippe Burty, undated letter in Mallarmé, *Correspondance,* 4:587.

69. Mme de P[onty], "Conseils sur l'éducation," *La Dernière Mode,* no. 7 (6 December 1874), 10; in Mallarmé, *Œuvres complètes,* 828.

70. Paul Valéry, "Je disais quelque fois à Stéphane Mallarmé," first published as a foreword to *Poésies de Stéphane Mallarmé* (Paris: Société des cent une, 1931); in Valéry, *Œuvres,* vol. 1 (Paris: Gallimard, 1957), 650–651; trans. M. Cowley as "I Would Sometimes Say to Mallarmé . . . ," in *The Collected Works of Paul Valéry,* vol. 8 (London: Routledge and Kegan Paul, 1972), 280–281 (translation slightly modified).

Valéry's interpretation goes beyond merely considering phonetic qualities; however, his use of terms such as *langage* and *parole* is not yet to be understood in a structuralist sense.

71. See Charles Baudelaire, "Le Peintre de la vie moderne V: L'Art mnémonique," in Baudelaire, *Œuvres complètes,* 2:697–700.

72. Walter Benjamin, "Zum Bilde Prousts," in Benjamin, *Gesammelte Schriften,* 7 vols. (Frankfurt a.M.: Suhrkamp, 1974–1989), 2.1:311; trans. Harry Zohn as "The Image of Proust," in Benjamin, *Illuminations* (London: Pimlico, 1999), 198 (translation not used).

73. Benjamin, "Zum Bilde Prousts," 311.

74. Marguerite de Ponty, "La Mode," *La Dernière Mode,* no. 1 (6 September 1874), 3; in Mallarmé, *Œuvres complètes,* 715.

75. Remy de Gourmont, "Stéphane Mallarmé et l'idée de décadence" (1898), in Gourmont, *La Culture des idées* (Paris: Mercure de France, 1900), 113, 132; trans. G. S. Burne as "Stéphane Mallarmé and the Idea of Decadence," in Gourmont, *Selected Writings* (Ann Arbor: University of Michigan Press, 1966), 67, 76 (translation slightly modified).

76. Gourmont, "La 'Dernière Mode' de Stéphane Mallarmé," 34–35, 45.

77. André Fontainas, *De Stéphane Mallarmé à Paul Valéry: Notes d'un témoin 1894–1922* (Paris: Bernard, 1928), 36–37.

78. Apropos of Constantin Guys, Baudelaire had written: "The more beauty that the artist can put into it, the more valuable will be his work; but in trivial life, in the daily metamorphosis of external things, there is a rapidity of movement that calls for equal speed of execution from the artist." Charles Baudelaire, "Le Peintre de la vie moderne II: Le Croquis de mœurs," in Baudelaire, *Œuvres complètes,* 2:686; trans. in Baudelaire, *The Painter of Modern Life and Other Essays,* 4.

79. Kravis puts forward an interesting notion about Mallarmé's prose on a whole as "preparing a spectacle but not yet constituting it," thereby touching on the problematic of procedural aspects in modernity; see *The Prose of Mallarmé,* 88.

80. See Mallarmé, *Correspondance,* 1:260 n. 2.

81. "In the linguistic realm, *figures* [of speech], which ordinarily play the role of accessories—which are introduced merely to illustrate or emphasise a meaning, and which therefore seem to be extrinsic, as if they were ornaments that could be stripped from a discourse without affecting its substance—become essential elements in Mallarmé's reflection: the *metaphor* in particular, instead of being displayed as a jewel or used as a momentary expedient, seems to have the value here of a symmetrical relation based on the essence of things." Valéry, "Je disais quelquefois à Stéphane Mallarmé," 658; trans. as "I Would Sometimes Say to Mallarmé . . . ," 291 (translation slightly modified).

82. Marguerite de Ponty, "La Mode—Bijoux ('Paris, le 1er août 1874')," *La Dernière Mode,* no. 1 (6 September 1874), 2; in Mallarmé, *Œuvres complètes,* 711–712. The previous month, the editor of the *Gazette des Beaux-Arts,* Charles Blanc, had completed his series of articles on the "grammaire des arts décoratifs." In February 1874 female apparel had been his topic, in March

he had written on lace, during May and July on jewelry, and the descriptions had come full circle with some aesthetic reflections on gowns and dresses by the end of July. If Mallarmé had leafed through these articles—and given the standing of the *Gazette,* that seems very likely—Blanc's writing might have suggested some of the topics in *La Dernière Mode,* at least in its first issue of August 1874.

83. Three months later, Mallarmé—or rather Ix.—elaborates on "the perspicacious genius of the architect"; Ix. "Chronique de Paris," *La Dernière Mode,* no. 7 (6 September 1874), 4; in Mallarmé, *Œuvres complètes,* 818.

In his "Autobiographie," Mallarmé describes to Verlaine his written ideal: "A book that is an architectural and premeditated book" (301).

84. Ix., "Chronique de Paris," *La Dernière Mode,* no. 1 (6 September 1874), 4; in Mallarmé, *Œuvres complètes,* 716.

85. Ibid.

86. Ibid., 717.

87. Ibid.

88. Miss Satin, "Gazette de la Fashion," *La Dernière Mode,* no. 5 (1 November 1874), [3]; in Mallarmé, *Œuvres complètes,* 783.

89. Marguerite de Ponty, "La Mode," *La Dernière Mode,* no. 4 (18 October 1874), 2; in Mallarmé, *Œuvres complètes,* 763.

90. "[M]y gown / Bleached in an ivory chest" set against "a sky / Bestrewn by birds amidst the embroidery / Of tarnished silver." Stéphane Mallarmé, "Ouverture ancienne d'Hérodiade," in Mallarmé, *Œuvres complètes,* 42 (the poem was composed ca. 1866); trans. H. Weinfield in Mallarmé, *Collected Poems* (Berkeley: University of California Press, 1994), 26.

91. "Often the poet's vision strikes me / An angel with a fawn-colored cuirass—he brandishes for exquisite pleasure / A dazzling sword, or, white dreamy vision, he wears the cope, / The byzantine miter and the sculpted baton. | Dante, crowned with bitter laurels, drapes himself in a shroud, / A shroud made of night and serenity: / Anacreon, naked, laughs and kisses the grapes / not know-

ing that vines have leaves in summer. | Covered with starry sequins, dazzled by azure skies, the great bohemians, / In their pale blue costumes, playing their gay tambourines, / Pass, their heads whimsically crowned with rosemary. | How I dislike, oh my Muse, you queen of poetry, / Whose hair is surrounded by a golden halo, / The sight of a poet dancing in his black suit." Annotated reprint in Auriant, "Sur des vers retrouvés de Stéphane Mallarmé," *La Nouvelle Revue Française*, 21, no. 236 (1 May 1933), 837; in Mallarmé, *Œuvres complètes*, 20–21.

92. The idea that Mallarmé's readership was imaginary has, to my knowledge, only once been hinted at, but its implications have never been discussed. In 1941 Mondor wrote that in *La Dernière Mode* "tout est de la main, de l'encre de Mallarmé . . . la lectrice alsacienne . . . les correspondantes anonymes" (*Vie de Mallarmé*, 361).

93. "Correspondance avec les Abonnées," *La Dernière Mode*, no. 2 (20 September 1874), [9]; in Mallarmé, *Œuvres complètes*, 742.

Geneviève Mallarmé recalled her father's aesthetics: "He was so sure in his taste. In regard to everything. . . . When I was still a child he told me: 'You can obtain a nice effect with the simplest of things, with mere nothing, provided that it is chosen with taste and works as an ensemble'"; in "Mallarmé par sa fille," 519.

94. "Correspondance avec les Abonnées," *La Dernière Mode*, no. 4 (18 October 1874), [9]; in Mallarmé, *Œuvres complètes*, 776.

95. Constance Wendelen, letter, in Mallarmé, *Correspondance*, 5:224–225.

96. "Correspondance avec les Abonnées," *La Dernière Mode*, no. 5 (1 November 1874), [9]; in Mallarmé, *Œuvres complètes*, 793. The Franco-Prussian War had ended in 1871 with the Treaty of Frankfurt.

97. Marguerite de Ponty, "La Mode," *La Dernière Mode*, no. 8 (20 December 1874), 3; in Mallarmé, *Œuvres complètes*, 833.

98. The masthead stated in September 1874: "Prix / lf25 le numéro avec / gravure coloriée / 0f80 le numéro sans / gravure coloriée / - Abonnements / - PARIS / Un an . . . 21f / Six mois . . . 13f / DÉPARTEMENTS / Un an . . . 26f / Six mois . . . 14f / ÉTRANGER / S'adresser pour la liste des / prix, établie d'après les / taxes postales, aux bu- / reaux du journal." In Mallarmé, *Correspondance*, 5:224.

99. Charles Wendelen, letter, dated "Paris 21 September 1874," in ibid.

100. Constance Wendelen, letter, dated "Paris 26 September 1874," in ibid., 224–225.

101. "Correspondance avec les Abonnées," *La Dernière Mode,* no. 7 (6 December 1874), [9]; in Mallarmé, *Œuvres complètes,* 826–827.

102. Marguerite de Ponty, "La Mode (On nous harangue et nous répondons . . .)," *La Dernière Mode,* no. 8 (20 December 1874), 2; in Mallarmé, *Œuvres complètes,* 830.

103. Ibid., 831.

104. Stéphane Mallarmé, "Remémoration d'amis belges" (1890), in Mallarmé, *Œuvres complètes,* 60.
    See Deleuze, *Le Pli,* 43; as well as the setting by Pierre Boulez, *Pli selon pli* (composed between 1957 and 1962), whose score transposes the folds of the text-ile—i.e., the multitude of meanings and structural levels—into a disparate confluence of percussion, woodwinds, and voice (esp. in part 3, "Improvisation II sur Mallarmé: Une Dentelle s'abolit").

105. Marguerite de Ponty, "La Mode," *La Dernière Mode,* no. 6 (15 November 1874), 2; in Mallarmé, *Œuvres complètes,* 797.

106. Ix., "Chronique de Paris," *La Dernière Mode,* no. 1 (6 September 1874), 5; in Mallarmé, *Œuvres complètes,* 718.

107. Ibid., 718, 719.

108. See "Autre éventail (de Mademoiselle Mallarmé)," in Mallarmé, *Œuvres complètes,* 58; this "feuillet d'album" was composed in 1884.

109. See Jean-Pierre Faye, "Mallarmé: L'Écriture, la mode," in *La Mode, l'invention,* 56.

110. Marguerite de Ponty, "Explication de la lithographie à l'aquarelle du jour . . . ," *La Dernière Mode,* no. 2 (20 September 1874), 3; in Mallarmé, *Œuvres complètes,* 730.

111. This analogy is inherent, for example, "dans les plis jaunes de la pensée / Traînant, antique, ainsi qu'une toile encensée" (In the yellow folds of thought, still unexhumed, / Lingering, and like an antique cloth perfumed), as he had written in his "Ouverture ancienne d'Héroiade," 42; trans. in Mallarmé, *Collected Poems,* 26.

112. See "[A] gently quivering fold of her skirt simulating the impatience of feathers toward an idea"; Stéphane Mallarmé, "Ballets: Crayonné au théâtre" (1886), in Mallarmé, *Œuvres complètes,* 306.

113. Marguerite de Ponty, "La Mode: Toilette d'une princesse ou d'une parisienne," *La Dernière Mode,* no. 8 (20 December 1874), 3; in Mallarmé, *Œuvres complètes,* 832–833.

114. Marguerite de Ponty, "La Mode," *La Dernière Mode,* no. 3 (4 October 1874), 2; in Mallarmé, *Œuvres complètes,* 745–746.
  In the final issue Mallarmé would emphasize that his program was "but to show an outfit for a great lady chosen among others, and thus summarize the resulting metamorphosis in the Costume, the signs of which can be seen already day by day." Marguerite de Ponty, "La Mode: Information chez les grandes faiseuses . . . ," *La Dernière Mode,* no. 8 (20 December 1874), 3; in Mallarmé, *Œuvres complètes,* 833.

115. Paul Verlaine, "Les Hommes d'aujourd'hui: Stéphane Mallarmé," in Verlaine, *Œuvres en prose complètes,* 793–794. The essay was written between 1885 and 1886 and has only survived as a quote in Henri Mondor, *L'Amitié de Verlaine et Mallarmé* (Paris: Gallimard, 1939).

116. Mallarmé, "Autobiographie," 303.

117. André Fontainas would later recall a meeting with Mallarmé in 1895; "when I told him, he showed real signs of joy, repeating so happily that it mystified us: 'Ah! I used to write for fashion journals!'"; *De Mallarmé à Valéry,* [38].

118. Henry Charpentier, "La Dernière Mode de Stéphane Mallarmé," *Minotaure,* nos. 3–4 (May 1933), 25–29.

119. See Henry Charpentier, "De Stéphane Mallarmé," *La Nouvelle Revue Française* 14, no. 158 (1 November 1926), 537–545; also "La Poésie de Mallarmé," *La Nouvelle Revue Française,* 1923;

"Les Mardis de la rue de Rome," *Les Marges,* 10 January 1936; or "À Valvins chez Mallarmé," *Visages du Monde,* 15 January 1939.

120. "Gravures noires du texte—4. Peigne et coiffure virgile," *La Dernière Mode,* no. 4 (18 October 1874), 1, the illustration is printed on 4; in Mallarmé, *Œuvres complètes,* 761.

121. See, e.g., Max Ernst, "Le Fugitif," in Max Ernst and Paul Eluard, *Les Malheurs des immortels* (Paris: Librairie Six, 1922), 42, whose title potently evokes the symbolism of the main motif, a luxurious *gilet.* See also Ernst, *Une Semaine de bonté ou Les Sept Éléments capitaux* (Paris: Bucher, 1934), especially the last chapter, titled "L'Ile de Paques," in which the profiles of nineteenth-century women and their hairdos are depicted in a manner closely resembling the chosen detail from Mallarmé's magazine.

122. "Gravures noires du texte—Jeune fille de quatorze ans," *La Dernière Mode,* no. 8 (20 December 1874), [5], inside cover illustration; in Mallarmé, *Œuvres complètes,* 830.

123. Charpentier, "La Dernière Mode de Stéphane Mallarmé," 25.

124. Ibid. Mallarmé's daughter emphasized his "courteous reserve in manner"; in "Mallarmé par sa fille," 517.

125. Charpentier, "La Dernière Mode de Stéphane Mallarmé," 25.

126. Ibid.

127. Ibid.

128. Ibid. "The silk of time's balsam" ("Quelle soie aux baumes de temps") is a reference to the opening line of Mallarmé's untitled sonnet, written in January 1885, "on tissues and fabrics"; in Mallarmé, *Œuvres complètes,* 75, 1500–1501.

129. Charpentier, "La Dernière Mode de Stéphane Mallarmé," 25.

130. Remy de Gourmont wrote: "Nevertheless, in the case of Mallarmé and a literary group, the idea of decadence has been assimilated to its exact opposite—the idea of innovation." Gour-

mont, "Stéphane Mallarmé et l'idée de décadence," 121; trans. as "Stéphane Mallarmé and the Idea of Decadence," 71.

131. From Balzac to Zola and beyond, a tradition of social and psychological realism would at the same time attempt to reconcile life with modernist aesthetics.

132. Paul Valéry, "Stéphane Mallarmé," lecture at the Université des Annales on 17 January 1933, first published in *Conferencia,* April 1933; in Valéry, *Œuvres,* 1:677; trans. J. R. Lawler as "Stéphane Mallarmé," in *The Collected Works of Paul Valéry,* 8: 267 (translation slightly modified).

133. Mallarmé, "Symphonie littéraire," 261.

134. Paul Valéry, "Existence du symbolisme," in *À l'enseigne de l'alcyon* (Maastricht: Stols, 1939); in Valéry, *Œuvres,* 1:700; trans. M. Cowley as "The Existence of Symbolism," in *The Collected Works of Paul Valéry,* 8:231 (translation not used).

135. "Poets have the resource of long articles in magazines and journals: some, like Théophile Gautier, earned their living by it [see his remark on the neologism *modernité* and journalism]; whereas Baudelaire succeeded badly at it, and Mallarmé worse still." Gourmont, "Stéphane Mallarmé et l'idée de décadence," 129; trans. as "Stéphane Mallarmé and the Idea of Decadence," 75 (translation slightly modified).

136. Valéry, "Je disais quelquefois à Mallarmé," 653; trans. as "I Would Sometimes Say to Mallarmé . . . ," 284.

137. Geneviève Mallarmé, letter, dated "12 May 1896"; in Mallarmé, *Correspondance,* 8:142.

138. "Mallarmé par sa fille," 520.

139. Geneviève Mallarmé, letter, dated "[Paris,] Wednesday [29 April 1898]"; in Mallarmé, *Correspondance,* 10:157–158.

## 3 Simmel and the Rationale of Fashion in Modernity

1. "Fashion's potential for abstraction, which is founded in its very being, lends through its 'estrangement from reality' a certain aesthetic style to modernity itself, even in nonaesthetic areas; this potential is also developed within a historic expression." Georg Simmel, "Die Mode: Zur philosophischen Psychologie," in Simmel, *Philosophische Kultur: Gesammelte Essais* (Leipzig: Klinkhardt, 1911), 34.

2. The switch to German indicates the focus of chapters 3 and 4 on Simmel's and Benjamin's writings. Like the Romance languages, and unlike English, German reflects the etymological sisterhood between sartorial fashion and modernity.

3. Jürgen Habermas, "Georg Simmel als Zeitgenosse," afterword to Georg Simmel, *Philosophische Kultur: Über das Abenteuer, die Geschlechter und die Krise der Moderne: Gesammelte Essais* (Berlin: Wagenbach, 1983), 246 (my emphasis); trans. M. Deflem as "Georg Simmel on Philosophy and Culture: Postscript to a Collection of Essays," *Critical Inquiry* 22, no. 3 (spring 1996), 407–408 (translation modified).

4. See Otthein Rammstedt, foreword to *Simmel und die frühen Soziologen,* ed. Rammstedt (Frankfurt a.M.: Suhrkamp, 1988), 7–9 and passim. The critical edition of Simmel's complete works is being prepared under the auspices of members of the sociology faculty at the University of Bielefeld (Germany), a work that began in 1989.

5. See the studies by David Frisby: "Georg Simmels Theorie der Moderne," in *Georg Simmel und die Moderne,* ed. H.-J. Dahme and O. Rammstedt (Frankfurt a.M.: Suhrkamp, 1984), 9–79; *Fragments of Modernity: Theories of Modernity in the Work of Simmel, Kracauer, and Benjamin* (Cambridge: Polity, 1985); and the ambiguously titled *Sociological Impressionism,* 2d ed. (London: Routledge, 1992). Extensive and thought-provoking as these studies are, Simmel is presented in Frisby's analyses very much as a sociologist of his time and, alas, as not much more. Other essays on Simmel and his relationship to modernity that have been published by Anglo-American or German authors—e.g., Deena and Michael A. Weinstein, "Georg Simmel: Sociological Flâneur Bricoleur," *Theory, Culture, and Society* 8 (1991), 151–168; Brigitta Nedelmann, "Georg Simmel as an Analyst of Autonomous Dynamics: The Merry-Go-Round of Fashion," in *Georg Simmel and Contemporary Sociology,* ed. Michael Kern, Bernhard S. Phillips, and Robert S. Cohen (Dordrecht: Kluwer, 1990), 243–257; or Julika Funk, "Zwischen Last und Lust: Mode und Geschlechterdif-

ferenz bei Georg Simmel" (Labor and Lust: Fashion and Gender Difference in Georg Simmel), *Metis* 6, no. 12 (1997), 26–43)—eschew historical differences and are concerned mainly with other topics. I find the best understanding of Simmel's intellectual origin and impact in his contemporaries working outside the confines of sociology, most notably Siegfried Kracauer, Georg Lukács, and Walter Benjamin.

6. See Georg Simmel, *Kant* (Munich: Duncker & Humblot, 1904), a collection of sixteen lectures given at the University of Berlin.

7. Georg Simmel, "Zur Psychologie der Mode," *Die Zeit* (Vienna), 12 October 1895, 20–24. Significantly, it was Charles Darwin's son who first applied evolutionary theory to social studies and who first found a logical focus in the evolution of female apparel; see George H. Darwin, "Development in Dress," *Macmillan's Magazine* 26 (September 1872), 410–416.

8. Georg Simmel, *Philosophie der Mode* (Berlin: Pan, 1905).

9. See Michael Landmann, "Georg Simmel: Konturen seines Denkens," in *Ästhetik und Soziologie um die Jahrhundertwende: Georg Simmel,* ed. Hannes Böhringer and Karlfried Gründer (Frankfurt a.M.: Klostermann, 1976), 3–11.

10. Simmel, "Die Mode," 29–64.

11. Ibid., 39–40.

12. Georg Simmel, *Die Philosophie des Geldes,* 2d ed. (Leipzig: Duncker & Humblot, 1907); in Simmel, *Gesamtausgabe,* ed. O. Rammstedt (Frankfurt a.M.: Suhrkamp, 1989ff.), 6:633–634; trans. T. Bottomore and D. Frisby as *The Philosophy of Money,* 2d ed. (London: Routledge, 1990), 457 (translation slightly modified).

13. Georg Simmel, "Der Begriff und die Tragödie der Kultur," *Logos* 2 (1911–1912), 1–39; see also his lecture, *Der Konflikt in der modernen Kultur* (Munich: Duncker & Humblot, 1918).

14. Simmel, *Die Philosophie des Geldes,* 641; trans. as *The Philosophy of Money,* 462 (translation slightly modified).

15. Max Weber, "Kritische Studien auf dem Gebiet der kulturwissenschaftlichen Logik," in *Gesammelte Aufsätze zur Wissenschaftslehre,* 2d ed. (Tübingen: Mohr, 1951), 215–290; trans. E. A. Shils and H. A. Finch as "Critical Studies in the Logic of the Cultural Sciences," in Weber, *The Methodology of the Social Sciences* (Glencoe, Ill.: Free Press, 1949), 113–188.

16. Weber, "Kritische Studien," 238; trans. as "Critical Studies," 136 (Rickert's original remark is paraphrased by Weber on 234; trans., 132).

17. *Die Zeit,* founded in 1894, was mainly devoted to mainstream liberal discussions on political life in Europe. However, its feuilleton remained on a remarkably high level through 1904, soliciting contributions from D'Annunzio, Dostoyevsky, Mackay, Mallarmé, Rilke, Schnitzler, Tolstoy, and Wilde and publishing essays by Conrad, Hofmannsthal, Kraus, Loos (his first published piece), Maeterlink, Sombart, Zola, and many others. Simmel's article on fashion fits well into this modernist environment for an educated readership.

18. Georg Simmel, "Fashion," *International Quarterly* 10 (1904), 130–155. The essay was translated either by W. D. Briggs, who had previously brought Simmel's "Tendencies in German Life and Thought" into English (published in the predecessor of the *International Quarterly,* the *International Monthly*), or by Albion Small, the editor of the *American Journal of Sociology,* which would reprint the original essay in 1957. Small became Simmel's promoter and contributed to the influential position Simmel occupied in the Chicago School.

19. See the following essays in Rammstedt, ed., *Simmel und die frühen Soziologen:* Alexander Deichsel, "Das Soziale in der Wechselwirkung. Ferdinand Tönnies und Georg Simmel als lebendige Klassiker" (64–85); David P. Frisby, "Soziologie und Moderne: Ferdinand Tönnies, Georg Simmel und Max Weber" (196–229); and Heinz-Jürgen Dahme, "Der Verlust des Fortschrittsglaubens und die Verwissenschaftlichung der Soziologie. Ein Vergleich von Georg Simmel, Ferdinand Tönnies und Max Weber" (222–274).

20. "Irritatingly complicitous" was Adorno's complaint, according to Habermas; see "Simmel als Zeitdiagnostiker," 245; trans. as "Georg Simmel on Philosophy and Culture," 406.

21. See the editorial note in Simmel, *Die Philosophie des Geldes,* 726.

22. Karl Joël, "Georg Simmel," *Die Neue Rundschau* 30 (1919), 242, 245.

23. Ibid., 245.

24. Ix., "Chronique de Paris," *La Dernière Mode,* no. 1 (6 September 1874); in Stéphane Mallarmé, *Œuvres complètes* (Paris: Gallimard, 1945), 717—discussed above, section 2.4.3.

25. Simmel, "Zur Psychologie der Mode," 22.

26. Simmel, "Fashion," 130.

27. Georg Simmel, *Philosophie der Mode;* in Simmel, *Gesamtausgabe,* 10:9.

28. Simmel, "Fashion," 130; see also *Philosophie der Mode,* 9.

29. Charles Baudelaire, "Le Peintre de la vie moderne I: Le Beau, la mode et le bonheur," in Baudelaire, *Œuvres complètes,* 2 vols. (Paris: Gallimard, 1975–1976), 2:685-686; trans. J. Mayne in Baudelaire, *The Painter of Modern Life and Other Essays* (London: Phaidon, 1995), 3.

30. Simmel, "Die Mode," 29.

31. "Aus dem nachgelassenen Tagebuch von Georg Simmel" (From the Posthumous Diary of Georg Simmel); quoted at the beginning of Fritz Landsberger, "Georg Simmel," in *Europa-Almanach,* ed. Carl Einstein and Paul Westheim (Potsdam: Kiepenheuer, 1925), 75.

32. Charles Baudelaire, "Salon de 1845," in Baudelaire, *Œuvres complètes,* 2:407; trans. J. Mayne in Baudelaire, *Art in Paris, 1845–1862: Salons and Other Exhibitions Reviewed by Charles Baudelaire* (Oxford: Phaidon, 1965), 32 (translation slightly modified).

33. Ferdinand Tönnies, "Considération sur l'histoire moderne," *Annales de l'Institut International de Sociologie* 1 (1895), 247.

34. Simmel, *Philosophie der Mode,* 10.

35. Ibid.

36. Jean Desmarets de Saint-Sorlin, *La Comparaison de la langue et de la poësie Françoise, avec la Grecque et la Latine, et des Poëtes Grecs, Latins et François* (Paris: Thomas Jolly, 1670).

37. Ibid., 9–10.

38. Charles Perrault, *Parallèle des anciens et des modernes. En ce qui regarde les arts et les sciences. Dialogues,* 2d ed., 2 vols. (Paris: Coignard & Coignard Fils, 1692–1693), 1:76–77.

39. Throughout modern times, from Perrault through nineteenth-century Manchester or Lyons (see the weavers' revolts) to contemporary sweatshops in Southeast Asia, textile production, especially of refined and luxurious fabric or garments, has always taken place under the most appalling conditions for the industrial workforce. Since everybody has to be clothed and increasingly expects to have a wide choice in clothing, the industry has to engage in the greatest degree of exploitation in order to generate profits.

On another level, the seventeenth-century fashion of delicate silk stockings rendered the leg a unified plane; individual muscular play or particular details of the skin became concealed and abstracted. Fashion thus hid human imperfection and approached a classical physical ideal, ironically not remote at all from the white marbled leg of an antique statue; see Baudelaire's *passante* and her idealized "jambe de statue," which would both generate and epitomize the aesthetic experience in modernity.

For a materialist view, see Karl Marx, *Das Kapital,* in Karl Marx and Friedrich Engels, *Werke,* vol. 23 (Berlin: Dietz, 1993), 680–685; trans. as *The Capital,* vol. 1, in Karl Marx and Friedrich Engels, *Collected Works,* vol. 35 (London: Lawrence & Wishart, 1996), 612–615, on the conditions of stocking makers in nineteenth-century England.

40. Perrault, *Parallèle,* 1:140, 142.

41. Ibid., 2:47–48; see also the figure of l'Abbé, the advocate for the modern, on the "beautez universelles & absoluës" and "particulières & relatives" (48–49).

42. Simmel, "Fashion," 132.

43. Georg Simmel's review of Tarde's book was published in *Zeitschrift für Psychologie und Physiologie der Sinnesorgane* 2 (1891), 141–142.

44. See Klaus Christian Köhnke, "Von der Völkerpsychologie zur Soziologie: Unbekannte Texte des jungen Georg Simmel," in Dahme and Rammstedt, *Georg Simmel und die Moderne,* 411–412.

45. Gabriel Tarde, *Les Lois de l'imitation* (Paris: Alcan, 1890), 268. On the proximity of Simmel's and Tarde's perceptions and style, and an account of the subsequent conflict between subjectivist spontaneity and Cartesianism, emphasized by Tarde's and Durkheim's sociology respectively, see Terry N. Clark's introduction to Gabriel Tarde, *On Communication and Social Influence* (Chicago: University of Chicago Press, 1969), where Tarde is also described as being "stigmatized as an inchoate and imprecise philosophical and literary writer" (1)—a stigma that Adorno, in his correspondence with Benjamin, attached equally to Simmel; see, for example, Benjamin, *Briefe,* 2:785 (trans. M. R. and E. M. Jacobson as *The Correspondence of Walter Benjamin, 1910–1940* [Chicago: University of Chicago Press, 1994], 581), or Theodor W. Adorno, "Einleitung zu Benjamins 'Schriften,'" in *Noten zur Literatur,* vol. 4 (Frankfurt a.M.: Suhrkamp, 1974), 111; trans. S. W. Nicholson as "Introduction to Benjamin's 'Schriften,'" in Adorno, *Notes to Literature,* 2 vols. (New York: Columbia University Press, 1992), 2:224.

46. Simmel, "Die Mode," 31.

47. See Georg Simmel, "Über eine Beziehung der Selektionslehre zur Erkenntnistheorie" (On a Relationship between the Laws of Selection and Epistemology), *Archiv für systematische Philosophie* 1 (1895); in *Philosophie der Kunst* (Potsdam: Kiepenheuer, 1922), 120–121.

48. See Georg Simmel, *Lebensanschauung: Vier metaphysische Kapitel* (View of Life: Four Chapters on Metaphysics) (Munich: Duncker & Humblot, 1918), 120.

49. Simmel, *Philosophie der Mode,* 10–11. This metaphysical distinction had still been a physiological, perhaps psychological one, in the 1895 text ("Zur Psychologie der Mode," 23).

50. See Immanuel Kant, introduction (part 9) to *Kritik der Urteilskraft,* in *Werkausgabe,* vol. 10 (Frankfurt a.M.: Suhrkamp, 1978), 46–47; trans. J. C. Meredith as *The Critique of Judgement* (Oxford: Clarendon, 1952), 36–39.

51. Simmel, *Die Philosophie des Geldes,* 255.

52. Simmel, "Fashion," 133.

53. This view of "invention" in haute couture is almost obsolete today, of course, since the various designers increasingly "communicate" with each other, reflecting mutual references, shared economic pressures, the influence of trend forecasting, and multiplied media exposure.

54. Tarde, *Les Lois de l'imitation,* 270. On Tarde and his perception of imitation and invention, see Michael M. Davis, *Psychological Interpretations of Society* (New York: Columbia University, 1909), 84–190, esp. chaps. 9 and 10 (143–190), which present the first analysis of Tarde's *Les Lois de l'imitation* in English.

55. Tarde, *Les Lois de l'imitation,* 269. "The ages and societies among which reigns exclusively the prestige of the ancient are those where, as in antique Rome, *antiquity,* besides its meaning proper, signified *a thing that is loved.* 'Nihil mihi antiquius est—nothing is more dear to me,' said Cicero" (ibid.).

56. Charles Baudelaire, "Le Peintre de la vie moderne IV: La Modernité," in Baudelaire, *Œuvres complètes,* 2:695; trans. in Baudelaire, *The Painter of Modern Life and Other Essays,* 12.

57. Tarde, *Les Lois de l'imitation,* 270.

58. Simmel, *Philosophie der Mode,* 11.

59. See Werner Sombart, "Wirtschaft und Mode: Ein Beitrag zur Theorie der modernen Bedarfsgestaltung" (Economics and Fashion: A Contribution to the Theory of Modern Consumerism), in *Grenzfragen des Nerven- und Seelenlebens,* no. 12 (1902), 1–23.

See also Walter Troeltsch, *Volkswirtschaftliche Betrachtungen über die Mode* (National Economic Observation on Fashion) (Marburg: Elwert, 1912); published transcript of his inaugural lecture at Marburg University, which further developed Sombart's and Simmel's observations.

60. Georg Lukács, quoted in Elisabeth Lenk, "Wie Georg Simmel die Mode überlistet hat" (How Georg Simmel Outwitted Fashion), in *Die Listen der Mode,* ed. Silvia Bovenschen (Frankfurt a.M.: Suhrkamp, 1986), 421–422.

61. Ibid., 422.

62. Pierre Bourdieu, "Haute Couture et Haute Culture," in *Noroit,* no. 192 (November 1974), 1–2, 7–17, and nos. 193–194 (December 1974–January 1975), 2–11; in *Question de sociologie* (Paris: Minuit, 1980), 200; trans. R. Nice as "Haute Couture and Haute Culture," chap. 16 of Bourdieu, *Sociology in Question* (London: Sage, 1993), 134–135.

63. Caroline Rennolds Milbank, *Couture* (London: Thames & Hudson, 1985), 342.

64. For a discussion of Loos and Le Corbusier in their relation to fashion, see Mark Wigley, *White Walls and Designer Dresses* (Cambridge, Mass.: MIT Press, 1995); regarding van de Velde and clothing, see Radu Stern, *À contre-courant: Vêtements d'artistes 1900–1940* (Berne: Benteli, 1992), 9–19, 90–111.

65. Analysis of sexual mores will be left to psychological rather than sociological investigation.

66. Siegfried Kracauer, "Georg Simmel: Ein Beitrag zur Deutung des geistigen Lebens unserer Zeit" (Georg Simmel: A Contribution to the Spiritual Life in Our Time) (1919–1920), 15, 16; unpublished typescript, the Archives of German Literature in Marbach a.N.

67. See ibid., 29.

68. Siegfried Kracauer, "Georg Simmel," *Logos* 9 (1921), 328 (a much abbreviated and modified version of the earlier typescript).

69. See Hans Simmel, "Auszüge aus den Lebenserinnerungen," in Böhringer and Gründer, *Ästhetik und Soziologie um die Jahrhundertwende,* 247–255.

70. Adolf Loos, "Die Fussbekleidung," *Neue Freie Presse* (Vienna), 7 August 1898; in Loos, *Ins Leere gesprochen* (Vienna: Prachner, 1987), 119; trans. J. O. Newman and J. H. Smith as "Footwear," in Loos, *Spoken into the Void: Collected Essays, 1897–1900* (Cambridge, Mass.: MIT Press, 1982), 57.

71. Adolf Loos, "Die Herrenmode," *Neue Freie Presse* (Vienna), 22 May 1898; in Loos, *Ins Leere gesprochen,* 56; trans. as "Men's Fashion," in Loos, *Spoken into the Void,* 11. See also Oscar Wilde's well-worn aphorism, "If one is noticed in the street, it means one is not well dressed."

72. Guillaume Apollinaire, "L'Émigrant de Landour Road," in *Alcools* (Paris: Gallimard, 1927), 100; this collection of poems dating from 1898 to 1910 was first published in 1913 (Paris: Mercure de France). "His hat in his hand he stepped right foot first / Into a smart and by-appointment-to-the-King tailor's / Which tradesman had just beheaded several / Dummies dressed in unexceptionable clothes"; trans. O. Bernard in Apollinaire, *Selected Poems* (London: Anvil, 1986), 73.

73. Loos, "Die Herrenmode," 57; trans. as "Men's Fashion," 12.

74. Kracauer, "Georg Simmel," 328.

75. Quoted in Michael Landmann, "Bausteine zur Biographie," *Buch des Dankes an Georg Simmel,* ed. Kurt Gassen and Michael Landmann (Berlin: Duncker & Humblot, 1958), 33. There were of course other—conservative and anti-Semitic—reasons for refusing Simmel a professorship.

76. See the account of Proust's *pardessus,* made to the cut and style of the one he "designed" for his fictional character Baron de Charlus, in Marcel Plantevignes, *Avec Marcel Proust* (Paris: Nizet, 1966), 41.

77. See Pierre Bourdieu, *La Distinction: Critique sociale de jugement* (Paris: Minuit, 1979).

78. Jürgen Habermas, "Die Moderne—ein unvollendetes Projekt," in *Kleine politische Schriften (I–IV)* (Frankfurt a.M.: Suhrkamp, 1981), 447; trans. S. Ben-Habib as "Modernity: An Incomplete Project," in *The Anti-Aesthetic: Essays in Postmodern Culture,* ed. Hal Foster (Seattle: Bay Press, 1983), 5.

79. Habermas, "Die Moderne—ein unvollendetes Projekt," 447.

80. Jürgen Habermas, *Der philosophische Diskurs der Moderne: Zwölf Vorlesungen* (Frankfurt a.M.: Suhrkamp, 1985), 145; trans. F. Lawrence as *The Philosophical Discourse of Modernity* (Cambridge: Polity, 1987), 119–120 (translation modified).

81. Shierry Weber Nicholson, quoted in Martin Jay, "Habermas and Modernism," in *Habermas and Modernity,* ed. R. J. Bernstein (Cambridge: Polity, 1985), 125.

82. Jürgen Habermas, *Legitimationsprobleme im Spätkapitalismus* (Frankfurt a.M.: Suhrkamp, 1973), 110; trans. T. McCarthy as *Legitimation Crisis* (Cambridge: Polity, 1988), 78 (translation modified).

83. Simmel, "Begriff und Tragödie der Kultur," 119.

84. Georg Simmel, *Kant,* 6th ed. (Leipzig: Duncker & Humblot, 1924), 99.

85. Ibid., 100, 101.

86. Baudelaire, "Le Peintre de la vie moderne IV," 695; trans. in Baudelaire, *The Painter of Modern Life and Other Essays,* 12.

87. In his analysis of the temporal element Simmel understandably refers to Bergson's particular notion of memory. In his study on the aesthetics behind Rembrandt's art, Simmel compared life to "a past that becomes present"; Georg Simmel, *Rembrandt* (Leipzig: Wolff, 1916), 43.

88. See also the definition of the "modern" at the beginning of Perrault's *Parallèle.*

89. Habermas, *Der philosophische Diskurs der Moderne,* 19; trans. as *The Philosophical Discourse of Modernity,* 9 (translation not used).

90. Ibid., 20; trans., 10.

91. Ibid.; trans., 10—modified, because *Nachahmungsmotiv* is translated as "imitation," which, sociologically speaking, it is not.

92. Walter Benjamin, "Über den Begriff der Geschichte," in Benjamin, *Gesammelte Schriften,* 7 vols. (Frankfurt a.M.: Suhrkamp, 1974–1989), 1.2:701; trans. Harry Zohn as "Theses on the Philosophy of History," in Benjamin, *Illuminations* (London: Pimlico, 1999), 252–253 (translation modified).

93. Simmel, "Die Mode," 34.

94. Karl Marx and Friedrich Engels, *Manifesto of the Communist Party,* in Marx and Engels, *Collected Works,* vol. 6 (London: Lawrence & Wishart, 1976), 487. The English translation renders the rather prosaic "alles Ständische und Stehende verdampft" as a much more poetic phrase, although it does omit the original political implication contained in the term *ständisch,* i.e., pertaining to "trade" or "class."

95. Simmel, "Die Mode," 35.

96. Theodor Wiesengrund Adorno, paralipomena to *Ästhetische Theorie* (Frankfurt a.M.: Suhrkamp, 1973), 468; trans. C. Lenhardt as *Aesthetic Theory* (London: Routledge & Kegan Paul, 1984), 436 (translation slightly modified).

97. Georg Wilhelm Friedrich Hegel, *Vorlesungen über die Ästhetik,* vol. 1, in *Werke,* vol. 13 (Frankfurt a.M.: Suhrkamp, 1986), 51; trans. T. M. Knox as *Aesthetics: Lectures on Fine Art,* 2 vols. (Oxford: Clarendon, 1975), 1:31. The lectures were delivered four times—1820/1821, 1823, 1826, and 1828/1829—and the text was later compiled from Hegel's own papers and subsequent notes; the translation is based on the second edition by H. G. Hotho (1842), generally regarded as the most complete and authoritative.

98. Adorno, *Ästhetische Theorie,* 469; trans. as *Aesthetic Theory,* 437 (translation slightly modified).

99. This reading of Habermas's and Adorno's interpretation is obviously a very selective one, which claims completeness in regard to only one topic: fashion.

100. Simmel, "Fashion," 135.

101. Ibid.

102. Herbert Spencer, "Fashion" (chapter 11 of *The Principles of Sociology,* 2.4), in *A System of Synthetic Philosophy,* vol. 3 (London: Williams & Norgate, 1882), 208; see Simmel, "Die Mode," 36.

In the 1930s Harold Nicolson wrote "Men's Clothes," an essay that begins: "It is related of Mr. Herbert Spencer that he possessed a suit which had been specially made for him. He only wore this suit when he was feeling irritable, but he sometimes wore it for weeks at a time. It was made all in one piece and of a soft soothing Jaeger sort of texture. He entered the suit from the middle, huddling his angry legs into the lower part, as if he was putting on bed-socks; working his impatient head into the upper part, as if entering a bathing-dress. Then down the front was an arrangement for lacing the thing together. . . . Clearly such a system would be soothing to the nerves. But it was not aesthetic. . . . The angry suit ceased to soothe; it irritated gratuitously; it became the shirt of Nessus excruciating to the wearer. . . . And next morning he would dress in a neat suit of grey tweed, and be again his bright and petulant self." Nicolson, in *Small Talk* (Leipzig: Tauchnitz, 1938), 36–37.

103. See John Bellers, *Essays about the Poor, Manufactures, Trade, Plantations, & Immorality . . .* (London: Sowle, 1699), 9: "The Uncertainty of Fashions doth increase Necessitous Poor. It hath two great Mischiefs in it. 1st the Journey-men are Miserable in Winter for want of Work, the Mercers and Master Weavers not daring to lay out their Stocks to keep the Journey-men imploy'd, be-

fore the Spring comes and they know what the Fashion will then be. 2[ndly.] In the Spring the Journeymen are not sufficient, but the Master Weavers must draw in many Prentices, that they may supply the Trade of the Kingdom in a quarter or half a year, which Robs the Plow of Hands, drains the Country of Labourers, and in great part Stocks the City with Beggars, and starves some in Winter that are ashamed to Beg." Quoted in Marx, *Das Kapital,* 503–504; trans. as *Capital,* 1:450–451.

104. Tarde, *Les Lois de l'imitation,* 270.

105. Werner Sombart, *Liebe, Luxus und Kapitalismus: Über die Entstehung der modernen Welt aus dem Geist der Verschwendung* (Love, Luxury, and Capitalism: On the Origin of a Modern World through the Spirit of Wastefulness), 2d ed. (Berlin: Wagenbach, 1992), 192–194; the book originally appeared in 1922 under the title *Luxus und Kapitalismus.*

106. Simmel, "Fashion," 136.

107. See Georg Simmel, "Exkurs über den Fremden" (Excursus on the Stranger), in *Soziologie: Untersuchungen über Formen der Vergesellschaftung* (Sociology: Studies on Forms of Socialization) (Leipzig: Duncker & Humblot, 1908), 685–691.

108. Ibid., 687–688.

109. Simmel, *Die Philosophie des Geldes,* 285–286; translated as *Philosophy of Money,* 432.

110. Simmel, "Exkurs über den Fremden," 687–688.

111. Simmel, *Philosophie der Mode,* 15.

112. Ibid.

113. Simmel, "Die Mode," 38.

114. Charles Baudelaire, "Salon de 1846, VVIII: De l'héroïsme de la vie moderne," in Baudelaire, *Œuvres complètes,* 2:494; trans. in Baudelaire, *Art in Paris, 1845–1862,* 118.

115. Charles Baudelaire, "Journaux intimes X: fusées no. 46," in Baudelaire, *Œuvres complètes*, 1:657; trans. Christopher Isherwood in Baudelaire, *Intimate Journals* (1930; reprint, London: Methuen, 1949), [11]. Elsewhere in the "Fusées," Baudelaire scattered notes for further literary projects on fashion; e.g., "Un chapitre sur / La Toilette / Moralité de la Toilette. / Les Bonheurs de la Toilette" (694); or for an essay on "Modes de ces époques" (in "Titres et canevas," 590). These notes date from the early 1860s and were developed in conjunction with his work on *Le Peintre de la vie moderne*.

As close observers of all literary developments, the brothers Jules and Edmond de Goncourt thus published in 1862 a book titled *La Femme au XVIIIᵉ siècle* (Paris: Librairie Nouvelle) that included many an observation on contemporary fashion.

116. Simmel, "Die Mode," 39.

117. Ronald Firbank, "A Study in Temperament," in *The New Rythum, and Other Pieces* (London: Duckworth, 1962), 27; the story was written ca. 1905.

118. Simmel, "Zur Psychologie der Mode," 23.

119. Georg Simmel, "Henri Bergson," *Die Güldenkammer* 4, no. 9 (June 1914), 516.

120. Simmel, "Fashion," 139.

121. Simmel, *Philosophie der Mode*, 17.

122. A few months earlier, Proust had published the first volume of *La Recherche*, which begins with the fusion of past into present within a dream; see section 4.4, above.

123. See Simmel, "Henri Bergson," 523–524.

124. Gilles Deleuze, *Le Bergsonisme* (Paris: Presses Universitaires de France, 1966), 49; trans. H. Tomlinson as *Bergsonism* (Cambridge, Mass.: MIT Press, 1988), 55.

125. See Deleuze, *Le Bergsonisme*, 57, 61–62; see Theodor W. Adorno, *Kierkegaard*, in *Gesammelte Schriften*, vol. 2 (Frankfurt a.M.: Suhrkamp, 1979), 50–51. Adorno refers to Søren Kierkegaard, *The Concept of Anxiety*, ed. and trans. R. Thomte (with A. B. Anderson), vol. 8 of *Kierkegaard's Writing* (Princeton: Princeton University Press, 1980), 29–35.

126. Walter Benjamin, "Über einige Motive bei Baudelaire," in Benjamin, *Gesammelte Schriften,* 1.2:643; trans. Harry Zohn as "On Some Motifs in Baudelaire," in Benjamin, *Illuminations,* 181 (translation modified).

127. Ibid., 643; trans., 181 (translation slightly modified).

128. Simmel, "Die Mode," 40–41.

129. Kracauer, "Georg Simmel: Ein Beitrag," 24.

130. Adolf Loos, "Herrenhüte," *Neue Freie Presse* (Vienna), 24 July 1898; in Loos, *Ins Leere gesprochen,* 122; trans. as "Men's Hats" in Loos, *Spoken into the Void,* 53.

131. Simmel, "Fashion," 140.

132. Simmel, *Philosophie der Mode,* 20.

133. Immanuel Kant, "Vom Modegeschmack," in *Anthropologie in pragmatischer Hinsicht,* in *Werke,* vol. 7 (Berlin: Reimer, 1917), 245; trans. V. L. Dowdell as "On Taste in Fashion," in Kant, *Anthropology from a Pragmatic Point of View* (Carbondale: Southern Illinois University Press, 1978), 148.

134. Harry Graf Kessler was born in Paris in 1868, educated in England, and spent most of his life traveling around the world, with Berlin as the fixed point of his political and cultural interests. He thus appears as the embodiment of Pan-European modernity. The philosopher Hannah Arendt would recall him later as "terribly elegant, although his face was pinched with weariness. He balanced his frailty on a cane, waiting with increasing impatience for someone who had not arrived. . . . As an aspirant myself, I was always curious about those who had been born to clean linen, casual friendship, fine china, and the best cuisine. Not that I aspired to possess and employ them, but rather, like Count Harry, to possess them and then disdain their transparency and irrelevance. I recalled these feelings as I observed his gray suit and gray silk tie, his white handkerchief breaking the edge of his breast pocket, and the yellow tea rose in his buttonhole"; quoted in Arthur A. Cohen, *An Admirable Woman* (Boston: Godine, 1983), 46.

From symbolism to dada, from Mallarmé and Hofmannsthal to Heartfield, Count Kessler assimilated the avant-garde, always ready to encourage and support it, but always anxious to keep his distance—the epitome of the refined dandy.

135. See Georg Simmel, "Der Bildrahmen: Ein ästhetischer Versuch" (The Frame: An Aesthetic Essay), *Der Tag,* no. 541 (1902); in *Gesamtausgabe,* vol. 7 (Frankfurt: Suhrkamp, 1995), 86–93. Liebermann's and Simmel's criticism is directed against the Jugendstil/art nouveau custom of integrating a decorated frame into the artwork in order to approach the ideal of the complete artwork, if only on a rather banal level (as done by, e.g., Franz von Stuck and, at times, Max Klinger). See also Simmel's "Exkurs über den Adel" (Excursus on Nobility) (1908), where the nobleman, in particular someone of Count Kessler's sophistication, is regarded in a parallel to the artwork as an "island within the world" (in Simmel, *Soziologie,* 741).

136. Bernhard Zeller, ed., "Aus unbekannten Tagebüchern Harry Graf Kesslers," *Jahrbuch der Deutschen Schillergesellschaft,* no. 31 (1987), 18–19. The club discussed was the *Deutsche Künstlerbund* (the German Confederation of Artists), founded in December 1903 in Weimar with Count Kessler as its vice president. Max Liebermann, Henry van de Velde, and Simmel's friend the painter Reinhold Lepsius were all among its founding members. It seems likely, despite the lack of documented evidence, that Simmel was an original member as well. London's Athenaeum Club, which was their model, included among its members scientists as well as intellectuals in letters and the arts; it still exists.

137. Hans Simmel, "Auszüge aus den Lebenserinnerungen," 261.

138. Ibid., 261–262.

139. Simmel, *Philosophie der Mode,* 25–26.

140. Benjamin, "Über einige Motive bei Baudelaire," 622; trans. as "On Some Motifs in Baudelaire," 164 (translation slightly modified).

141. Siegfried Kracauer, "Das Ornament in der Masse," *Frankfurter Zeitung,* 9–10 June 1928; in Kracauer, *Der verbotene Blick* (Leipzig: Reclam, 1992), 172–185; trans. T. Y. Levin as *The Mass Ornament: Weimar Essays* (Cambridge, Mass.: Harvard University Press, 1995). Kracauer had studied philosophy and sociology under Simmel at the University of Berlin between 1907 and 1909.

Unlike former students Ernst Bloch, Georg Lukács, or perhaps Benjamin, Kracauer continued to correspond with his old professor.

142. Obviously, such a cultural observation would become politically significant. The exiled Siegfried Kracauer would discuss the prefiguration of fascism and totalitarian culture in general in his collection of essays on the cinema titled *From Caligari to Hitler: A Psychological History of the German Film* (London: Dobson, 1947).

143. Simmel, "Fashion," 147–148.

144. Ibid., 148.

145. Ibid., 149.

146. Ibid., 150.

147. Ibid., 151.

148. Simmel, "Die Mode," 58; see his "Die Großstädte und das Geistesleben" (Cities and Cultural Life), *Jahrbuch der Gehe-Stiftung zu Dresden,* no. 9 (1903), 27–71 for a more general investigation of the topic.

149. Simmel, *Philosophie der Mode,* 32–33.

150. Émile Langlade, *La Marchande de modes de Marie-Antoinette Rose Bertin* (Paris: Albin Michel, 1911), 63; trans. A. S. Rappoport as *Rose Bertin: The Creator of Fashion at the Court of Marie-Antoinette* (London: Long, 1913), 56–57 (translation amended).

151. Simmel, "Zur Psychologie der Mode," 24.

152. See Simmel, *Philosophie der Mode,* 33.

153. Ibid.; see Simmel's connection with Marx in section 3.7.

154. Simmel, "Fashion," 152.

155. Simmel, "Zur Psychologie der Mode," 24; remarkably, Simmel used the term "dialectical" only in his study on fashion written in the nineteenth century (the reference is omitted from all subsequent ones; cf. "Fashion," 152, or *Philosophie der Mode,* 33–34).

156. The fixed center and point of repose in classical art appears to limit the "points of attack," as Simmel found. One wonders whether there was indeed a side to him that, despite all the significance he ascribed to fashion, harbored the fear that the *Ersatzreligion* art (characterized as essentially bourgeois by, e.g., Benjamin and Adorno) might be threatened by the influence of the ephemeral.

157. See Gilles Deleuze, *Le Pli: Leibniz et le baroque* (Paris: Minuit, 1988), 20, 164–165, and passim.

    Kracauer would defend Simmel's analogies by maintaining that they are to be perceived not as "fruits of baroque arbitrariness" but as goals in themselves ("Georg Simmel," 338).

158. Simmel, *Philosophie der Mode,* 36.

159. See Charlotte-Elisabeth, duchesse d'Orléans, *A Woman's Life in the Court of the Sun King: Letters of Liselotte von der Pfalz, 1652–1722,* ed. Elborg Forster (Baltimore: Johns Hopkins University Press, 1984), 87.

160. Simmel, "Fashion," 154.

161. Roland Barthes, *Système de la mode* (Paris: Seuil, 1967), 246 n. 2. trans. M. Ward and R. Howard as *The Fashion System* (London: Cape, 1985), 242 n. 11.

162. Ibid., 245-246; trans., 242.

163. This half sentence was added in *Philosophie der Mode,* which then omitted the following clause.

164. Simmel, "Fashion," 155: see "Zur Psychologie der Mode," 24; *Philosophie der Mode,* 36–37; and "Die Mode," 63–64.

165. Pierre Bourdieu, "Haute Couture et Haute Culture," 202; trans. as "Haute Couture and Haute Culture," 136.

## 4  Benjamin and the Revolution of Fashion in Modernity

1. "Fashion is the eternal recurrence of the new. Are there nevertheless motifs of redemption precisely in fashion?" Walter Benjamin, "Zentralpark," in Benjamin, *Gesammelte Schriften,* 7 vols. (Frankfurt a.M.: Suhrkamp, 1974–1989), 1.2:677; trans. L. Spencer (with M. Harrington) as "Central Park," *New German Critique,* no. 34 (winter 1985), 46.

2. The title of Benjamin's second précis, written in March 1939 by request of the Institute for Social Research in New York so that he might secure founding for his ongoing project.

3. The bibliography that aims to list all publications on Benjamin up to 1986 has fashion as a topic of only two essays—and both mention the subject merely in passing. Few critics—to my knowledge—have ventured to explain Benjamin's relationship with fashion. Anne, Margaret, and Patrice Higonnet, in "Façades: Walter Benjamin's Paris," *Critical Inquiry* 10, no. 3 (spring 1984), 391–419, touch very briefly on fashion (405–406); Susan Buck-Morss, in *Dialectics of Seeing: Walter Benjamin and the Arcades Project* (Cambridge, Mass.: MIT Press, 1989), presents fashion as one aspect among many in the *Arcades Project* (see 99–101); while the elaborately titled contribution by Doris Kolesch, "Mode, Moderne und Kulturtheorie—eine schwierige Beziehung. Überlegungen zu Baudelaire, Simmel, Benjamin und Adorno" (Fashion, Modernity, and Cultural Theory—Difficult Relations: Reflections on Baudelaire, Simmel, Benjamin, and Adorno), in *Mode, Weiblichkeit und Modernität* (Fashion, Femininity, and Modernity], ed. Gertrud Lehnert (Dortmund: Ebersbach, 1998), 20–46, formulates a relationship between fashion and modernity, but simply lists the various contributors to that relationship without exploring further the intricate connections among them. Other authors, like Hans Robert Jauß in his essay "Tradition, Innovation, and Aesthetic Experience," *Journal of Aesthetics and Art Criticism* 46, no. 3 (spring 1988), 375–388, arrive, through a reading of *la querelle* and Baudelaire, at the paradigmatic value of fashion for Benjamin (cf. 383), but then leave the subject unexplored.

4. Walter Benjamin, letter dated Berlin-Grunewald, 17 March 1928, in Walter Benjamin, *Briefe,* ed. Gershom Scholem and Theodor W. Adorno, 2 vols. (Frankfurt a.M.: Suhrkamp, 1978), 1:464; trans. M. R. and E. M. Jacobson as *The Correspondence of Walter Benjamin, 1910–1940* (Chicago: University of Chicago Press, 1994), 329. Benjamin's letters were edited by his friends Scholem and Adorno for publication in 1975; the complete edition is currently being published in Germany (the years 1910 to 1937 have already been covered in five separate volumes).

5. Theodor W. Adorno, *Ästhetische Theorie* (Frankfurt a.M.: Suhrkamp, 1973), 265–266; trans. C. Lenhardt as *Aesthetic Theory* (London: Routledge & Kegan Paul, 1984), 255 (translation slightly modified).

The example of Picasso's *Lichtmalerei* is perhaps too singular and not very fortunate. Adorno wrote this passage around 1967/1968, at a time when Henri Clouzot's film, which included the famous footage of the artist drawing with a candle, marked a peak in the postwar reverence for Picasso in Germany. Adorno was himself of course never free from fashionable influences in the cultural sphere. A more "avant-garde" German critic would probably have referred to the use of light in paintings by "Zero" artists such as Otto Piene and Günter Mack (from ca. 1963), rather than to Picasso's work.

6. Walter Benjamin, letter dated Berlin-Grunewald, 17 March 1928, in Benjamin, *Briefe,* 1:464; trans. in *The Correspondence of Walter Benjamin,* 329.

7. Hans Mayer, *Der Zeitgenosse Walter Benjamin* (Frankfurt a.M.: Jüdischer Verlag, 1992), 66; see also Denis Hollier, in his biographical note for Mayer, in *Le Collège de Sociologie,* ed. Hollier (Paris: Gallimard, 1979), 447–448; trans. B. Wing as the foreword to *The College of Sociology (1937–39),* ed. Hollier (Minneapolis: University of Minnesota Press, 1988), 21.

8. Professor Mayer, letter to the author, 12 October 1993.

9. Benjamin had known, for example, of the imprisonment of his brother Georg since 1938.

10. Walter Benjamin, *Das Passagen-Werk,* ed. Rolf Tiedemann, in Benjamin, *Gesammelte Schriften,* 5.1:494, and 5.2:1015.

11. Baudelaire had reminisced (as an adult) about the scent of a skirt in his poem "Le Léthé," the mythical river that prompts humans to forget their earthly past: "Dans tes jupons remplis de ton parfum / Ensevelir ma tête endolorie, / Et respirer, comme une fleur flétrie, / Le doux relent de mon amour défunt" (Swathe my head in thy skirts swirling / Perfumes that one never borrows, / Perfumes of some flower unfurling / Leaves like loves that hate their morrows). Charles Baudelaire, "Le Léthé" (second stanza; part of the collection "Les Épaves"), in Baudelaire, *Œuvres complètes,* 2 vols. (Paris: Gallimard, 1975–1976), 1:155; trans. J. M. Bernstein in *Baudelaire, Rimbaud, Verlaine: Selected Verse and Prose Poems* (New York: Citadel, 1947), 33.

12. Walter Benjamin, "Zum Bilde Prousts," in Benjamin, *Gesammelte Schriften,* 2.1:312; trans. Harry Zohn as "The Image of Proust," in Benjamin, *Illuminations* (London: Pimlico, 1999), 198–199 (translation modified).

13. Benjamin, *Das Passagen-Werk,* 495.

14. See Baudelaire's exclamation: "Mais le génie n'est que l'enfance retrouvée à volonté" (But genius is nothing more nor less than *childhood recovered* at will). Charles Baudelaire, "Le Peintre de la vie moderne III: L'Artiste, homme du monde, hommes des foules et enfant," in Baudelaire, *Œuvres complètes,* 2:690; trans. J. Mayne in Baudelaire, *The Painter of Modern Life and Other Essays* (London: Phaidon, 1995), 8.

15. The martial metaphors may appear peculiar here, but we will come to see how fashion and the notion of revolution interact closely in both Benjamin's concept of remembrance and his "Theses on the Concept of History."

16. See Charles Baudelaire, *Tableaux Parisiens* (Heidelberg: Weißbach, 1923). The volume was published as a bilingual edition; preceding the German translation is a text by Benjamin titled "Die Aufgabe des Übersetzers" (trans. Harry Zohn as "The Task of the Translator," in Benjamin, *Illuminations,* 70–82). His original manuscript for the *Tableaux* translation was written between 1920 and 1921.

17. Benjamin and Hessel were approached by the publisher after the previous attempt to bring *À côté de chez Swann* into German had ended in a "great editorial and critical fiasco." See Benjamin, *Briefe,* 1:431; trans. in *The Correspondence of Walter Benjamin, 1910–1940,* 304.

18. See Benjamin, *Briefe,* 1:412, 432; trans. in *The Correspondence of Walter Benjamin, 1910–1940,* 289, 305.

19. Benjamin, *Briefe,* 1:492; trans. in *The Correspondence of Walter Benjamin, 1910–1940,* 349 (the translators use the unevocative "hatching" for the German *spinnen*). See also notes to the essay "Zum Bilde Prousts," in Benjamin, *Gesammelte Schriften,* 2.3:1044–1047.

20. Benjamin, notes for "Zum Bilde Prousts," 1057.

21. Walter Benjamin, "Neoklassizismus in Frankreich," in Benjamin, *Gesammelte Schriften,* 2.2:627.

22. Walter Benjamin, letter dated 28 December 1925, in Benjamin, *Briefe,* 1:406–407; trans. in *The Correspondence of Walter Benjamin, 1910–1940,* 286 (translation not used). For Proust's disagreement with Thibaudet, see Marcel Proust, "À propos du 'style' de Flaubert," *Nouvelle Revue Française* 7, vol. 14, no. 76 (1 January 1920), 72–90; see also his *Contre Sainte-Beuve* (Paris: Gallimard, 1971), 586–600.

23. Benjamin, *Briefe,* 1:407; trans. in *The Correspondence of Walter Benjamin, 1910–1940,* 286 (translation slightly amended).

24. Théophile Gautier, *De la mode* (Paris: Poulet-Malassis & de Broise, 1858), 5–6.

25. See, e.g., Samuel Weber, *Return to Freud: Jacques Lacan's Dislocation of Psychoanalysis* (Cambridge: Cambridge University Press, 1991).

26. See once again Walter Benjamin, "Über den Begriff der Geschichte," in Benjamin, *Gesammelte Schriften,* 1.2:701.

27. See Walter Benjamin, notes on "Paris, die Haupstadt des XIX. Jahrhunderts," in Benjamin, *Das Passagen-Werk,* 1206–1254.

28. Rolf Tiedemann, "Einleitung des Herausgebers" (editor's introduction), in Benjamin, *Das Passagen-Werk,* 12–13.

29. Irving Wohlfahrt, "Re-fusing Theology," *New German Critique,* no. 39 (fall 1986), 5.

30. See Tiedemann, "Einleitung des Herausgebers," 38, and Wohlfahrt, "Re-fusing Theology," 5.

31. *Dictionnaire de la langue française* (Paris: Larousse, 1992), s.v. "passer."

32. Benjamin, *Das Passagen-Werk,* 617.

33. Ibid., 580.

34. Ibid.

35. Marcel Proust, *Du côté de chez Swann,* part 1 of *À la recherche du temps perdu* (Paris: Gallimard, 1987), 5–6; trans. C. K. Scott Moncrieff and T. Kilmartin as "Overture" to *Swann's Way,* part 1 of *Remembrance of Things Past* (London: Chatto & Windus, 1981), 5–6. See also Benjamin on "the child's side of the dream" in *Das Passagen-Werk,* 1006.

   For the relationship between Proust's and Benjamin's epistemologies, see, e.g., Henning Goldbæk, "Prousts *Recherche* und Benjamins *Passagen-Werk:* Eine Darstellung ihrer Erkenntnistheorie," *ORBIS Litterarum,* no. 48 (1993), 83–95.

36. In 1965 Adorno referred back to Benjamin and, through him, to Proust and surrealism when he wrote: "What Surrealism adds to illustration of the world of objects is the element of childhood that we have lost; when we were children, those illustrated papers, already obsolete by then, must have leaped out at us the way Surrealist images do now." Theodor W. Adorno, "Rückblickend auf den Surrealismus," in *Noten zur Literatur,* vol. 1 (Frankfurt a.M.: Suhrkamp, 1958), 157; trans. Shierry Weber Nicholsen as "Looking Back on Surrealism" in Adorno, *Notes to Literature,* vol. 1 (New York: Columbia University Press, 1991), 88.

37. Roland Barthes, *Système de la mode* (Paris: Seuil, 1967), 144; trans. M. Ward and R. Howard as Barthes, *The Fashion System* (London: Cape, 1985), 136–137.

38. See also Benjamin's reflection on etymology in *Das Passagen-Werk,* 617–618.

39. Jürgen Habermas, *Der philosophische Diskurs der Moderne: Zwölf Vorlesungen* (Frankfurt a.M.: Suhrkamp, 1985), 22; trans. F. Lawrence as *The Philosophical Discourse of Modernity* (Cambridge: Polity, 1987), 12 (translation slightly modified). (The English rendition had to be changed because the translator read *des unvorhersehbaren Anfangs* as "predictable beginnings" instead of "*un*predictable beginnings," which obviously changes the phrase's relation to novelty.)

40. Benjamin, "Über den Begriff der Geschichte," 702; trans. Harry Zohn as "Theses in the Philosophy of History," in Benjamin, *Illuminations,* 254.

41. Walter Benjamin, "Eduard Fuchs, der Sammler und der Historiker," *Zeitschrift für Sozialforschung,* no. 6 (1937); in Benjamin, *Gesammelte Schriften,* 2.2:479; trans. K. Tarnowski as Benjamin, "Eduard Fuchs: Collector and Historian," *New German Critique,* no. 5 (spring 1975), 37 (translation slightly modified).

Benjamin might have adopted the metaphor from Simmel, who in 1907 had warned in his preface to the third edition of *Die Probleme der Geschichtsphilosophie* (Problems in the Philosophy of History) that one of the "violations of modern man" is a particular understanding of history: "It renders the soul as a simple connection of social threads that have been spun throughout history, and dilutes its productivity to merely administrating the legacies of our species." Georg Simmel, "Die Probleme der Geschichtsphilosophie," in Simmel, *Das Individuelle Gesetz* (Frankfurt a.M.: Suhrkamp, 1987), 31.

42. See, e.g., Benjamin, *Das Passagen-Werk,* 808–810; on the character of the fetish, see also 806.

The example of the linen and the coat can be found in Karl Marx, *The Capital,* trans. S. Moore and E. Aveling, vol. 1, in Karl Marx and Friedrich Engels, *Collected Works,* vol. 35 (London: Lawrence & Wishart, 1996), 59–69 and passim. Marx makes a distinction between the weaving of the linen as "concrete work" and the tailoring of the coat as "abstract work" (68–69), he also hints at the fashionable connotation and the sociocultural implication of the "braided" coat (61–62).

Helmut Salzinger, *Swinging Benjamin,* rev. ed. (Hamburg: Kellner, 1990), 111, writes: "Benjamin read in Lukács's work that all social life in capitalism is but an exchange of commodities. Which means that in capitalism each and every manifestation of life takes on the shape of a commodity. This thought, which in Lukács remains abstract, has been applied by Benjamin to the artwork and thus rendered concrete. In portraying Baudelaire as a producer among producers, he showed that there is no difference in the nature of products. As commodities, the *Fleurs du Mal* and Marx's coat are the same thing."

43. H. D. Kittsteiner, "Walter Benjamins Historismus," in *Passagen: Walter Benjamin's Urgeschichte des XIX. Jahrhunderts,* ed. Nobert Bolz and Bernd Witte (Munich: Fink, 1984), 196; trans. J. Monroe and I. Wohlfarth as Kittsteiner, "Walter Benjamin's Historicism," *New German Critique,* no. 39 (fall 1986), 214 (translation not used).

The English language version of this article wrongly translates *Rock* (= "coat" in nineteenth-century German usage) as "skirt" (the contemporary meaning of the word). Thus to avoid altering the meaning of the metaphor discussed, I have preferred to use my own translation.

44. Obviously, as linen itself is woven from plant fibers, it is itself manufactured and to some extent an artificial product. But as a basic material it remains unfinished, while the tailored coat is not—it can only be altered or cut up.

45. Marx clearly criticizes the "mythic" side of Hegelian dialectics, however; see the 1873 after-word to the second edition of Marx, *Das Kapital,* in Karl Marx and Friedrich Engels, *Werke,* vol. 23 (Berlin: Dietz, 1993), 27; trans. as *The Capital,* 1:19–20. Benjamin in his reading of Marx would repossess the mythic or "messianic" qualities without mentioning Hegel.

46. Georg Wilhelm Friedrich Hegel, *Vorlesungen über die Ästhetik,* in *Werke,* vol. 14 (Frankfurt a.M.: Suhrkamp, 1986), 408; trans. T. M. Knox as *Aesthetics: Lectures on Fine Art,* 2 vols. (Oxford: Clarendon, 1975), 2:747.

47. The quotation in Benjamin, *Das Passagen-Werk,* 245, comes from Otto Rühle, *Karl Marx: Leben und Werk* (Hellerau: Avalun, 1928), 384–385; for a discussion of the commodity fetish as phantasmagoria in Benjamin, see Henrik Stampe Lund, "The Concept of Phantasmagoria in the *Passagen-Werk,*" *ORBIS Litterarum,* no. 48 (1993), 96–108, esp. 98.

48. Benjamin, *Das Passagen-Werk,* 118. The term *Stoffwelt* can also be translated literally as "world of fabric"—surely an intentional ambiguity, given Benjamin's metaphorical style.

49. The "surrealist" fetish—that is, the adoption of a signifier from "tribal" cultures into West-ern modernism—essentially takes second place to Benjamin's exploration of the Freudian and Marxist notions of the fetish character.

50. See Sigmund Freud's "Fetishism" (1925), trans. James Strachey in *The Standard Edition of the Complete Psychological Works of Sigmund Freud,* vol. 21 (London: Hogarth, 1961), 152–154.

51. Ibid., 155.

52. Charles Baudelaire, "Le Peintre de la vie moderne IV: La Modernité," in Baudelaire, *Œuvres complètes,* 2:694.

53. Hans Robert Jauß, *Literaturgeschichte als Provokation* (Frankfurt a.M.: Suhrkamp, 1970), 54–55. Baudelaire's quote can be found in "Le Peintre de la vie moderne IV: La Modernité," in Baudelaire, *Œuvres complètes,* 2:695; trans. in Baudelaire, *The Painter of Modern Life and Other Essays,* 12. See also Jauß's comment on Baudelaire's "fashion's paradigm," in "Tradition, Innova-tion, and Aesthetic Experience," 383.

54. Benjamin, "Über den Begriff der Geschichte," 702; trans. as "Theses on the Philosophy of History," 254 (translation slightly modified).

55. Benjamin, *Das Passagen-Werk,* 578; trans. L. Hafrey and R. Sieburth as "N [Re the Theory of Knowledge, Theory of Progress]," in *Benjamin: Philosophy, History, Aesthetics,* ed. Gary Smith (Chicago: University of Chicago Press, 1989), 51 (translation modified).

56. Benjamin, *Das Passagen-Werk,* 118; see Barbara Vinken, "Eternity: A Frill on the Dress," *Fashion Theory* 1, no. 1 (March 1997), 59–67.

57. Walter Benjamin, "Das Paris des Second Empire bei Baudelaire," in Benjamin, *Gesammelte Schriften,* 1.2:548; trans. Harry Zohn in Benjamin, *Charles Baudelaire: A Lyric Poet in the Era of High Capitalism* (London: NLB, 1973), 45–46.

58. Benjamin, "Über den Begriff der Geschichte," 702–703; trans. as "Theses on the Philosophy of History," 254 (translation slightly modified).

59. See Habermas, *The Philosophical Discourse of Modernity,* 13.

60. Adorno's description of the *Arcades Project* in a letter from Oxford, 20 May 1935; reprinted in Theodor W. Adorno, *Über Walter Benjamin,* rev. ed. (Frankfurt a.M.: Suhrkamp, 1990), 118; trans. N. Walker in Theodor W. Adorno and Walter Benjamin, *The Complete Correspondence, 1928–1940* (Cambridge: Polity, 1999), 84.

61. Benjamin, "Über den Begriff der Geschichte," 704; trans. as "Theses on the Philosophy of History," 255 (translation modified).

62. Ibid., 693; trans., 245 (translation modified).

63. Theodor Adorno, letter dated "Hornberg i. Schwarzwald, 2 August 1935," in Benjamin, *Briefe* 2:675; trans. in *The Correspondence of Walter Benjamin, 1910–1940,* 497–498 (translation modified).

64. See Benjamin, *Das Passagen-Werk,* 457.

65. Louis Auguste Blanqui, *L'Éternité par les astres: Hypothèse astronomique* (Paris: Germer Baillière, 1872), 74–75. See Benjamin French's précis "Paris, Capitale du XIXème siècle," in *Das Passagen-Werk,* 76, and the reprise of the quote in the sheaf on Baudelaire, 458.

66. See Walter Benjamin's manuscript sheaf "D [boredom, eternal return]" in *Das Passagen-Werk,* 174–175.

67. Jauß, "Tradition, Innovation, and Aesthetic Experience," 382.

68. Karl Marx, *Der 18. Brumaire des Louis Napoleon,* in Karl Marx and Friedrich Engels, *Werke,* vol. 8 (Berlin: Dietz, 1988), 115; trans. as *The Eighteenth Brumaire of Louis Bonaparte,* in Marx and Engels, *Collected Works,* vol. 11 (London: Lawrence & Wishart, 1979), 103–104.

69. Benjamin, "Zentralpark," 677; trans. as "Central Park," 46.

70. Walter Benjamin, "Erste Notizen. Pariser Passagen I" (First Notes: Parisian Arcades I), in *Das Passagen-Werk,* 1026–1027.

71. Max Raphael, *Proudhon Marx Picasso. Trois études sur la sociologie d'art* (Paris: Excelsior, 1933); trans. I. Marcuse as *Proudhon Marx Picasso: Three Essays in Marxist Aesthetics* (London: Lawrence & Wishart, 1980).

72. Pablo Picasso, *Autoportrait,* winter 1901 (no. VI.35 as catalogued by Daix and Boudaille) and *Autoportrait avec palette,* autumn 1906 (Daix and Boudaille, no. XVI.28); see Raphael, *Proudhon Marx Picasso,* 213–214; trans., 131.

73. Raphael, *Proudhon Marx Picasso,* 214; trans. 131.

74. Ibid. Marx and Engels had stated in the *Communist Manifesto* of 1858: "In bourgeois society the past reigns over the present, in communist society the present reigns over the past." Karl Marx and Friedrich Engels, *Manifesto of the Communist Party,* in Marx and Engels, *Collected Works,* vol. 6 (London: Lawrence & Wishart, 1976), 36.

75. Friedrich Engels, letter dated "Manchester, 14 July 1858," in Marx and Engels, *Collected Works,* vol. 40 (London: Lawrence & Wishart, 1983), 327.

76. Friedrich Engels, *Dialectics of Nature,* in Marx and Engels, *Collected Works,* vol. 25 (London: Lawrence & Wishart, 1987), 549.

77. Friedrich Engels, *Anti-Dühring,* in Marx and Engels, *Collected Works,* 25:42–43; see also Engels's letter of 1891 to Carl Schmidt, in Karl Marx and Friedrich Engels, *Werke,* vol. 38 (Berlin: Dietz, 1968), 204.

78. Engels, *Anti-Dühring,* 61.

79. Georg Wilhelm Friedrich Hegel, "Wissenschaft der Logik I: Die objective Logik" (1812/1813), in Hegel, *Gesammelte Werke,* vol. 11 (Hamburg: Meiner, 1978), 218; see also his rewriting of 1832 as "Wissenschaft der Logik I: Die Lehre vom Sein," in *Gesammelte Werke,* vol. 21 (Hamburg: Meiner, 1985), 367; trans. W. H. Johnston and L. G. Struthers as *Science of Logic,* vol. 1 (London: Allen & Unwin, 1929), 388 (translation slightly modified).

80. Hegel, "Die Lehre vom Sein," 369; see "Die objektive Logik," 219–220; trans. in *Science of Logic,* 1:390 (translation slightly modified).

81. Hegel, "Die Lehre vom Sein," 367; see "Die objektive Logik," 219; trans. in *Science of Logic,* 1:389 (translation slightly modified).

82. Friedrich Engels, "The Development of Socialism from Utopia to Science," in Marx and Engels, *Collected Works,* 25:270.

83. Georg Lukács, "The Changing Function of Historical Materialism" (lecture given at the opening of the opening of the Research Institute of Historical Materialism in Budapest, June 1919), trans. R. Livingstone in Lukács, *History and Class Consciousness* (London: Merlin, 1971), 249 (translation slightly modified).

84. See Hegel, *Science of Logic,* 1:390.

85. Lukács, "The Changing Function of Historical Materialism," 250.

86. Ibid.

87. Ibid., 247.

88. On the connection between Benjamin and Lukács (a discussion that, as one comes to expect, omits fashion), see Bernd Witte, "Benjamin and Lukács: Historical Notes on the Relationship between Their Political and Aesthetic Theories," *New German Critique,* no. 5 (spring 1975), 3–26.

89. See Walter Benjamin, "Monadologie," in *Ursprung des Deutschen Trauerspiels;* in *Gesammelte Schriften* 1.1:227–228; trans. J. Osborne as *The Origin of German Tragic Drama* (London: NLB, 1977), 47–48.

90. Benjamin, "Pariser Passagen I," 1028.

91. Benjamin, *Das Passagen-Werk,* 460.

92. Walter Benjamin, MS no. 1126 (verso) in the Theodor W. Adorno Archive in Frankfurt a.M.; in Benjamin, *Das Passagen-Werk,* 1215.

93. Walter Benjamin, MS no. 1137; in ibid., 1213.

94. Benjamin, *Das Passagen-Werk,* 112.

95. Ibid. The "she-tiger" is the female equivalent to the dandy in sartorial obsession; yet, unlike him, she is also distinguished by openly displayed eroticism (often threatening to the male sex), outbursts of jealousy, etc.—see George Sand or the heroines of Balzac, Maupassant, etc.

96. Marguerite de Ponty, "La Mode," *La Dernière Mode,* no. 7 (6 December 1874), [2]; in Stéphane Mallarmé, *Œuvres complètes* (Paris: Gallimard, 1945), 812.

97. Benjamin, *Das Passagen-Werk,* 112.

98. Perhaps this phrase should appear rather in its feminine form, as *agent provocatrice!*
    The profession of agent or conspirator was the most rapidly growing, next to that of the purveyor of luxury goods (e.g., the couturier), between 1860 and 1890. "The *agents provocateurs* who infiltrated the crowds during the Second Empire were known as 'whiteshirts'"; Daniel Halévy, *Decadence de la liberté* (Paris: Grasset, 1931), 152 n. 1. See Benjamin, *Das Passagen-Werk,* 745.

99. Benjamin, *Das Passagen-Werk,* 1006.

100. Ibid., 211; see also the précis "Paris, die Hauptstadt des XIX. Jahrhunderts," in ibid., 46. Benjamin quoted from Jules Michelet, "Avenir! Avenir!" *Europe* 19, no. 73 (15 January 1929), 6, where the motto (dated 4 April 1839) reads: "to dream = to create / *velle videmur* / Each age dreams the following, creates it *in dreaming.*"

101. According to Marx, the monopolies dominated in the period of high capitalism in the eighteenth and nineteenth centuries, while the early capitalist period (beginning in the fifteenth century) was marked by individuals competing with each other—the capitalism of competition.

102. Raphael, *Proudhon Marx Picasso,* 146; trans., 88.

103. Jules Michelet (1798–1874) has been regarded, somewhat dismissively, as the great Romantic among nineteenth-century historians. In the wake of more recent French historiography—especially in the Annales group—Michelet has been reevaluated as someone who opened up levels of understanding that had been closed to positivist historical perception. Michelet broke new ground with his analyses of history as a "collective mentality" and his investigations of changes in philosophy of life and emotions, as well as in ecological realities and especially the conditions of material culture—in which fashion was seen as one dominant factor.

 See, e.g., Roland Barthes, "Modernité de Michelet," in *Œuvres complètes,* 3 vols. (Paris: Seuil, 1993–1995), 3:41–43; this essay was written in 1974, twenty years after Barthes's first study on the historian. See also the recent issue on Michelet of *Europe* 76, no. 829 (May 1998).

104. Chamfort [Nicolas Sébastien-Roche], "Maxime générale, no. 160," in *Maximes, pensées, caractères et anecdotes* (Paris: Garnier-Flammarion, 1968), 82. The *Maximes* were begun in 1779/1780 and first published in 1795. The label "the moralist of the revolt" was bestowed by Albert Camus, *L'Homme révolté* (Paris: Gallimard, 1951), 134.

105. Worth/Paquin sketchbooks, vol. 3, no. E.201-1957, in the Victoria and Albert Museum, London.

106. See Jules Michelet, *Cours au Collège de France,* vol. 2 (Paris: Gallimard, 1995), and Michelle Perrot, "Michelet, professeur de France," *Libération,* 28 September 1995, X/XI.

107. Entry from 3 March 1864; in Jules and Edmond de Goncourt, *Journal: Mémoires de la vie littéraire,* vol. 2, *1864–1874* (Paris: Fasquelle & Flammarion, 1956), 25.

108. Worth/Paquin sketchbooks, vol. 3, no. E.197-1957.

109. Ibid., vol. 4, no. E.252-1957.

110. Hegel, *Aesthetics,* 2:746–747; see Mallarmé on the relation of fashion and architecture in section 2.4.2 above.

111. Benjamin, "Pariser Passagen I," 1036.

112. Ibid., 1037.

113. Next to Simmel's writings, the books by Max von Boehn, *Die Mode im 19. Jahrhundert,* vols. 1–4 (Munich: Bruckmann, 1905–1919), were the most cited in Benjamin's notes on fashion—often without indicating the source. Although only vol. 2 is listed in the bibliography, a comparison of quotations like "B 2a, 10" of *Das Passagenwerk,* 177, with Boehn (4:148) shows that Benjamin indeed consulted the whole set of books.

114. Walter Benjamin, "Lebensläufe," in *Gesammelte Schriften,* 6:215–216.

115. I am indebted to Dr. W. Schultze from the library of the Humboldt-Universität zu Berlin for information on Simmel's and Benjamin's possible academic encounter. In the winter semester of 1912/1913 Simmel offered three lecture series: "Principles of Logic," "Philosophy of the Last 100 Years (from Fichte to Nietzsche and Bergson)," and, most significantly, "Philosophical Privatissimum for Advanced Students." The last was held at Simmel's house in the tradition of a group tutorial (some twenty select postgraduates), in which a variety of subjects were addressed (see Hans Simmel's "Auszüge aus den Lebenserinnerungen," in *Ästhetik und Soziologie um die Jahrhundertwende. Georg Simmel,* ed. Hannes Böhringer and Karlfried Gründer [Frankfurt a.M.: Klostermann, 1976], 255, 263). Given that Benjamin was still in his first year of study, his admission to such an advanced seminar appears unlikely. In the winter semester 1913/1914, Simmel gave two series of lectures: "General History of Philosophy" and "Philosophy of Art." Unfortunately, Benjamin neglected to enter these or any other lectures or seminars he attended during his years in Berlin into his *Studienbuch.* Therefore, the claim of direct communication of ideas between the two theoreticians on fashion must remain speculative. In this light, Fredric Jameson's assertion that "Benjamin attended Simmel's seminar in 1912"—see "The Theoretical Hesitation: Benjamin's Sociological Predecessor," *Critical Inquiry,* 25, no. 2 (winter 1999), 269—must be taken *cum grano salis.*

116. See the testimony of Simmel's son Hans regarding his father's discursive style and related disinterest in "discussions" in "Auszüge," 254–255.

117. See also Jameson's essay, whose analytical focus is not fashion but Simmel's observation of urban life in modernity; "The Theoretical Hesitation," 269, 273–277.

118. See Walter Benjamin, letter to Adorno, dated 1 May 1935; in Benjamin, *Das Passagen-Werk*, 1111–1112; trans. in Adorno and Benjamin, *The Complete Correspondence*, 80.

119. Walter Benjamin, letter to Gershom Scholem from Paris, date 20 May 1935; in Benjamin, *Briefe*, 2:653; trans. in *The Correspondence of Walter Benjamin, 1910–1940*, 481 (translation slightly modified).

120. Ibid., 654–655; trans., 482 (translation modified).

121. For a discussion of the changes within the political structure between notes and the précis, see, e.g., Kittsteiner, "Walter Benjamin's Historicism," 179–215, and Helmut Salzinger, "Kunstkritik als Klassenkampf" (Art Criticism as Class Conflict), in *Swinging Benjamin*, 58–93.

122. The editor Rolf Tiedemann has numbered the manuscripts "according to their contents"; in Benjamin, *Das Passagen-Werk*, 1206.

123. Walter Benjamin, MS no. 1109; in Benjamin, *Das Passagen-Werk*, 1208–1209.

124. Walter Benjamin, MS no. 1142; in Benjamin, *Das Passagen-Werk*, 1207.

125. See Alfred Delvau, *Les Dessous de Paris* (Paris: Poulet-Malassis & de Broise, 1860), including a chapter on the flâneur, titled "Les Trottoirs parisiens"; Delvau, *Les Heures parisiennes* (Paris: Librairie Centrale, 1866); and Delvau, *Les Lions du jour: Physiognomies parisiennes* (Paris: Dentu, 1867), on Daguerre, Nadar, *La Dame aux camélias,* etc.; Jakob von Falke, *Die Geschichte des modernen Geschmacks* (A History of Modern Taste) (Leipzig: Weigel, 1866), a guide to the Viennese Museum of Art and Industry with notes on the revival of classical taste in France, male fashion, etc.; more significantly, though it is not in the bibliography of the *Arcades Project,* Benjamin might have read Falke's *Kunstindustrie der Gegenwart* (Contemporary Industrial Arts) (Leipzig: Duandt & Händel, 1868), a guide to the Parisian World's Fair of 1867, in which Falke discussed the "ori-

entalization" in contemporary fashion and also devoted a chapter to the controversial Museum for the History of Labor at that fair.

126. See Gautier's description of the crinoline in section 1.2.3 above.

127. "The sceptre of shores of rose / stagnant on evenings of gold, it's / this white closed flight you pose / against the fire of a bracelet." Stéphane Mallarmé, "Autre Éventail (de Mademoiselle Mallarmé)," in Mallarmé, *Œuvres complètes,* 58; trans. C. F. MacIntyre in Mallarmé, *Selected Poems* (Berkeley: University of California Press, 1957), 69. The poem was first published in 1884; it is one of the "Trois poëmes de Stéphane Mallarmé" that were set to music by Claude Debussy in 1913.

128. Walter Benjamin, MS no. 1138 (verso); in Benjamin, *Das Passagen-Werk,* 1212–1213.

129. See "this female sovereign [*la mode*] (which is herself all the world!)" in section 4.8.2 above.

130. Walter Benjamin, MS no. 1137; in Benjamin, *Das Passagen-Werk,* 1213. "Odradek" is a fantastic creature tormenting a family man in Franz Kafka's story "Die Sorgen des Hausvaters" (written in 1917); it was first published in a volume of the complete writing (*Gesammelte Schriften,* 2 vols. [New York: Schocken, 1935], 155–156), which also included a piece on fashion's transient beauty, titled "Kleider" (written between 1903 and 1905).

131. See Edmond and Jules de Goncourt, *La Femme au XVIIIe siècle* (Paris: Firmin-Didot, 1862), and also a more recent edition with a new preface by Elisabeth Badinter (Paris: Champs Flammarion, 1982).

132. Walter Benjamin, MS no. 1126 (recto); in Benjamin, *Das Passagen-Werk,* 1213.

133. Ibid. (verso); in Benjamin, *Das Passagen-Werk,* 1214.

134. Karl Marx, letter Engels in Manchester, dated [London] 22 June 1867; in Karl Marx and Friedrich Engels, *Collected Works,* vol. 42 (London: Lawrence & Wishart, 1987), 384–385; see also Engels's letter of 16 June 1867 (382).

135. "Give us with red velvet / And this floral gown | And black satin / So / What rejoices our senses | And what distresses the body / Can be read from clothes." Benjamin, *Ursprung des*

*Deutschen Trauerspiels,* in *Gesammelte Schriften* 1.1:304; trans. as *The Origin of German Tragic Drama,* 125 (translation slightly modified). The original verses come from August Adolph von Haugwitz, "Maria Stuarda," in *Prodomos Poeticus* (Dresden, 1684).

136. Ibid.; trans., 125–126 (translation slightly modified).

137. Benjamin, *Das Passagen-Werk,* 161; the metaphor of the lining also appears on 1006 and 1054, where Benjamin added a reference to the dandy.

138. Walter Benjamin, MS no. 1126 (verso); in Benjamin, *Das Passagen-Werk,* 1214.

139. Walter Benjamin, MS no. 1127; in Benjamin, *Das Passagen-Werk,* 1215–1216.

140. Benjamin, "Paris, die Haupstadt des XIX. Jahrhunderts," 46–47; this précis was sent to New York at the end of May 1935; trans. E. Jephcott as "Paris, Capital of the Nineteenth Century," in Benjamin, *Reflections: Essays, Aphorisms, Autobiographical Writings* (New York: Schocken, 1986), 148.

141. Ibid., 50; trans., 151–152.

142. Ibid., 51; see Marx, *Das Kapital,* vol. 1, 85; trans. as *The Capital,* 81.

143. Marx, *Das Kapital,* vol.1, 86; trans. as *The Capital,* 82–83.

144.* Ibid.; trans., 83 (translation modified).

145. Benjamin, "Paris, die Haupstadt des XIX. Jahrhunderts," trans. as "Paris, Capital of the Nineteenth Century," 153.

146. Benjamin, *Das Passagen-Werk,* 1243; here I am citing an earlier version—sent on 31 May 1935 to Adorno, with the request "not to show it to anybody under any circumstances and to send it back to me as soon as possible" (1237)—because it contains some passages on fashion that are missing from the typescript in the Institut für Sozialforschung.

147. Walter Benjamin, "Pariser Passagen II," in *Das Passagen-Werk,* 1054–1055; repeated in the manuscript sheaf on fashion (ibid., 111).

148. Benjamin, "Pariser Passagen I," 997.

149. Walter Benjamin, "Über einige Motive bei Baudelaire," in Benjamin, *Gesammelte Schriften,* 1.2:643; trans. Harry Zohn as "On Some Motifs in Baudelaire," in Benjamin, *Illuminations,* 181 (translation not used).

150. Georg Simmel, *Die Philosophie des Geldes,* in Simmel, *Gesamtausgabe,* vol. 6 (Frankfurt a.M.: Suhrkamp, 1989), 639; trans. T. Bottomore and D. Frisby as *The Philosophy of Money,* 2d ed. (London: Routledge, 1990), 461.

151. Benjamin, "Paris, die Haupstadt des XIX. Jahrhundert," 55; trans. as "Paris, Capital of the Nineteenth Century," 158.

152. Theodor W. Adorno, letter dated 2 August 1935, in Benjamin, *Briefe* 2:672; trans. in *The Correspondence of Walter Benjamin, 1910–1940,* 495 (translation slightly modified).

153. Ibid.

154. Ibid.; see Marx, *Das Kapital,* vol. 1, 87–90; trans. as *The Capital,* 83–87.

155. Adorno, letter of 2 August 1935, in Benjamin, *Briefe,* 2:675; trans. in *The Correspondence of Walter Benjamin, 1910–1940,* 497–498 (translation slightly modified).

156. In ibid., 680; trans., 501 (translation slightly modified). Frau Hessel was married to Benjamin's co-translator of Proust, Franz Hessel. Under her maiden name, Helen Grund, she published—a few months before Adorno wrote his letter in 1935—a book titled *Vom Wesen der Mode* (On the Nature of Fashion) (produced in a limited edition of 2,000 copies by the German College of Master Printers for the German College of Fashion in Munich). In his *Arcades Project* Benjamin would often cite from this imaginative account of the couture industry.

157. Benjamin, *Briefe,* 2:679; trans. in *The Correspondence of Walter Benjamin, 1910–1940,* 501.

158. Max Raphael had based his "Marxist" art history (see, e.g., *Proudhon Marx Picasso,* 125) also on the *Introduction to the Critique of Political Economy,* which had been discovered among

Marx's papers in 1902 and appeared the following year in the German weekly *Die Neue Zeit* (21, no. 23 [1903], 710–718; no. 24, 741–745; and no. 25, 772–781).

159. This interpretation follows Hegel's in *The Science of Logic,* that each rule is based on the negation (of another rule); see Karl Marx, *Einleitung [zur Kritik der politischen Ökonomie],* in Marx and Engels, *Werke,* vol. 13 (Berlin: Dietz, 1971), 622; trans. as *Introduction,* in Marx and Engels, *Collected Works,* vol. 28 (London: Lawrence & Wishart, 1986), 28.

160. Ibid., 622–623; trans., 28.

161. Ibid., 623; trans., 29.

162. Benjamin, *Das Passagen-Werk,* 1243. The intricacy of the role Benjamin sees fashion performing is heightened by his choice of words. Fashion is seen as "matchmaker" or "procurer," adding a sexual dimension, which is of course integral to fashion's appeal and success.

163. Benjamin, "Pariser Passagen I," 1038.

## 5 The Imagination of Fashion in Modernity

1. "—No thanks, I know what time it is. Have you been shut up in this cage for long? What I need is the address of your tailor." André Breton and Philippe Soupault, "Barrières," in *Les Champs magnétiques* (Paris: Au sans pareil, 1920); in André Breton, *Œuvres complètes,* 2 vols. (Paris: Gallimard, 1988–1992), 1:74; trans. D. Gascoyne in Breton and Soupault, *The Magnetic Fields* (London: Atlas, 1985), 55.

2. The term "simulacrum" has been discussed by Gilles Deleuze in "Platon et le simulacre," part of the appendixes to his *Logiques du sens* (Paris: Minuit, 1969); trans. M. Lester (with C. Stivale) in Deleuze, *The Logic of Sense* (London: Athlone, 1990). Deleuze wrote: "In very general terms, the motive of the theory of Ideas must be sought in a will to select and to chose. It is a question of 'making a difference,' of distinguishing the 'thing' itself from its images, the original from its copy, the model from the simulacrum. But are all these expressions equivalent? The Platonic project comes to light only when we turn back to the method of division" (347; trans., 253). He continued: "The characteristic of division is to surmount the duality of myth and dialectic"—cf. section 5.3 above, "*Mythe et mode*"—"and to reunite in itself dialectical and mythical power"

(348–349; trans., 255). Later in his argument, Deleuze made the connection between the power of the myth and that of the simulacrum, rendering it integral to modernity as he echoed Baudelaire's dictum of 1860: "Modernity is defined by the power of the simulacrum. It behooves philosophy not to be modern at any cost, no more than to be nontemporal, but to extract from modernity something that Nietzsche designated as untimely, which pertains to modernity, but which must also be turned against it—in favour, I hope, of a time to come" (360–361; trans., 265).

See also the opening two chapters of Jean Baudrillard, *Simulacra et simulation* (Paris: Gallée, 1981); trans. S. F. Glaser as *Simulacra and Simulation* (Ann Arbor: University of Michigan Press, 1994).

3. Obviously, the classical and humanist ideals apply mainly to a certain dominant part of Western society, but corresponding ideals exist elsewhere as well.

4. We might appreciate the aesthetic value of former fashion as "costume," but hardly view them as options to be worn in the present. Yet it is the past that otherwise elevates other works of art, giving them an "eternal" presence, as both Kant and Hegel have postulated in their aesthetics.

5. Roland Barthes, *Système de la mode* (Paris: Seuil, 1967), 18; trans. M. Ward and R. Howard as *The Fashion System* (London: Cape, 1985), 8. "Signification" is to be understood in this context not purely as a linguistic term, but as denoting various interpretations (sociological, philosophical) that render the object significant.

6. Ibid.; the last expression in the quote, "[la] temporalité floue," can be seen as a pun intended by Barthes, since *flou* is an established term in haute couture encompassing the garments that are loose and not "constructed" (i.e., not tailored), such as chiffon blouses, dresses, underskirts, silk gowns, etc. The distinction between *l'atelier flou* and *l'atelier tailleur* still exist in the majority of *maisons*.

7. Ibid., 20; trans., 10.

8. Ibid., 22; trans., 12.

9. Ibid., 24; trans., 14.

10. Breton for one would have objected to any juxtaposition of Proust and surrealism, yet the coherence within French literary tradition was too strong for the well-read surrealists not to have succumbed to a certain degree.

11. Walter Benjamin, letter to Gershom Scholem, dated Berlin, 14 February 1929; in Benjamin, *Briefe,* ed. G. Scholem and T. W. Adorno, 2 vols. (Frankfurt a.M.: Suhrkamp, 1978), 1:489; trans. M. R. and E. M. Jacobsen in *The Correspondence of Walter Benjamin, 1910–1940,* ed. G. Scholem and T. W. Adorno (Chicago: University of Chicago Press, 1994), 347 (translation not used).

12. See ibid., 390, 393; trans., 274, 277. See also the gloss "Traumkitsch," in Walter Benjamin, *Gesammelte Schriften,* 7 vols. (Frankfurt a.M.: Suhrkamp, 1974–1989), 2.2:620–622, 2.3:1425–1427.

13. Walter Benjamin, "Der Sürrealismus: Die letzte Momentaufnahme der europäischen Intelligenz," originally published in the weekly *Die Literarische Welt* 5, no. 5 (1 February 1929), 3–4; no. 6 (8 February 1929), 4; and no. 7 (15 February 1929), 7–8; in Benjamin, *Gesammelte Schriften* 2.1:295–310, with notes in 2.3:1018–1044. The adjective *letzte* can be translated not only "last" but also "latest," which would eschew (a perhaps historically motivated, pessimistic) finality and equate the artistic movement with style and fashion. E. Jephcott's translation of this essay, "Surrealism: The Last Snapshot of the European Intelligentsia," can be found in Benjamin, *Reflections: Essays, Aphorisms, Autobiographical Writings* (New York: Schocken, 1986), 177–192.

14. Benjamin, "Der Sürrealismus," 299; trans. as "Surrealism," 181.

15. Walter Benjamin, "Die Gewalt des Surrealismus" (Surrealism's violence), in Benjamin, *Gesammelte Schriften,* 2.3:1031; this text contains the unpublished notes to the 1929 essay. In "Der Sürrealismus" Benjamin would discuss the revolutionary potential of surrealism partly through an analysis of Pierre Naville's *La Révolution et les intellectuels* (Paris: Gallimard, 1926), see 2.1:303 and passim.

Hal Foster has discussed the relation between the Benjaminian concept of the "dated" and surrealism's idea of the uncanny, as represented by the commodity (see Foster, *Compulsive Beauty* [Cambridge, Mass.: MIT Press, 1993], 129, 157–158, and passim. Foster, however, puts the emphasis not on the element of fashion but on the term *veraltet,* which is interpreted in a way unconnected to the original quotation (as he himself admits; see 159). Thus *Mode* is assigned to "mode of production" rather than to sartorial fashion, and the meaning that Benjamin intended in the phrase "die Kleider von vor fünf Jahren" is lost.

16. Max Ernst, "Au delà de la peinture," *Cahiers d'Art* 11, nos. 6–7 (1936), 165. Ernst here paraphrases Lautréamont's famous evocation from "Les Chants de Maldoror" (chap. 1, sixth chant); in Comte de Lautréamont *Œuvres complètes* (Paris: Gallimard, 1973), 327.

17. Walter Benjamin, *Das Passagen-Werk,* ed. Rolf Tiedemann, in *Gesammelte Schriften,* 5.1:112.

18. Ibid., 112–113.

19. Grandville, *Un Autre Monde* (Paris: Fournier, 1844). Three decades after its publication Mallarmé, in the guise of Marguerite de Ponty, would write: "Brilliant imagination, isn't it? that calls to mind the metamorphoses in which women's faces are combined with the bodies of insects in the old [!] albums by Grandville." Marguerite de Ponty, "La Mode," *La Dernière Mode,* no. 4 (18 October 1874), 3; in Stéphane Mallarmé, *Œuvres complètes* (Paris: Gallimard, 1945), 764. "Grandville" is the pseudonym of Jean-Ignace-Isidore Gérard (1803–1847).

20. Grandville, *Un Autre Monde,* 178.

21. Ibid., 179.

22. Ibid., 183–184.

23. "Aspasia" had been a widely employed *nom de plume(au)* for the "elevated" class of nineteenth-century Parisian prostitutes. In *De la prostitution dans la ville de Paris* (Paris: Baillière & fils, 1836), 132–133, A.-J.-B. Parent-Duchâtelet assembles the result of his research into pseudonyms, conducted between 1828 and 1831 in the French capital. He itemizes those names that he encountered most frequently, finding the "inferior class" headed by "Piece of meat" and "Doughnut," while the list for the "elevated class" begins "Palmire, Aspasia, . . ." The dadaist (Dr.) Walter Serner edited and wrote the foreword of this work's German translation (Berlin: Potthof, 1914)—significantly, one of his earliest literary activities.

24. Examples of this trend in corsets and crinolines can be found in Benjamin's "sourcebook": Max von Boehn, *Die Mode im 19. Jahrhundert,* 4 vols. (Munich: Bruckmann, 1905–1919), 3:52 and passim.

25. The arbiter for this taste had been Mme Récammier, celebrated in paintings by David, Gérard, and de Jeune; see again Max von Boehn, *Die Mode im 19. Jahrhundert,* 1:107 and passim.

26. Grandville, *Un Autre Monde,* 281–282.

27. Benjamin, *Das Passagen-Werk,* 267.

28. See Lautréamont, *Les Chants de Maldoror* (chant 6, verse 6): "The system of scales, modes, and their harmonic succession is not dependent on natural invariable laws but is, on the contrary, the consequence of aesthetic principles that have varied with the progressive development of mankind and will continue to vary." In Lautréamont, *Œuvres complètes,* 328; trans. P. Knight as *Maldoror* (Harmondsworth: Penguin, 1978), 228.

At the Courtauld Institute of Art in London the History of Dress Department led by Aileen Ribiero takes the opposite position, with scholarship that views clothes essentially in their historico-stylistic context. A piece of clothing helps "date" the painting that depicts it. Although this tactic may be valuable for placing a work of art at a certain point in time, it makes clothes nothing but costumes within a linear historical progression—and thus goes against the fundamental characteristics of fashion.

See also the recent issue on methodology in *Fashion Theory* 2, no. 4 (winter 1998).

29. Benjamin, *Das Passagen-Werk,* 998.

30. Ibid.

31. See ibid., 580; trans. L. Hafrey and R. Sieburth as "N[Re the Theory of Knowledge, Theory of Progress]," in *Benjamin: Philosophy, History, Aesthetics,* ed. Gary Smith (Chicago: University of Chicago Press, 1989), 52.

32. Ibid., 571–572; trans., 44–45.

33. See ibid., 579–580; trans., 52.

34. Walter Benjamin, letter to Alfred Cohn, dated Berlin, 12 December 1927; in "Nachträge" (Addenda), in *Gesammelte Schriften* 7.2:853. On *Le Paysan* as "the best book on Paris," see Benjamin, *Das Passagen-Werk,* 1207.

35. Louis Aragon, "Introduction à 1930," *La Révolution Surréaliste* 5, no. 12 (15 December 1929), 57–58; see also my conclusion, below.

36. Ibid., 57; this epigraph was taken from an essay by Xavier Forneret, a quondam Vaché and the original "homme vêtu en noir." See André Breton, *Anthologie de l'humour noir,* in Breton, *Œuvres complètes,* 2:949 and passim, and his foreword to Xavier Forneret, *Œuvres* (Paris: Slatkine, 1980).

37. See Louis Aragon, *Les Beaux quartiers,* new ed. (Paris: Le club de meilleur livre, 1959), 315–403.

38. See afterword to ibid. [405].

39. As Louis Aragon himself remembered in *Le Paysan de Paris* (Paris: Gallimard, 1926), 73.

40. Louis Aragon, *Anicet ou le panorama, roman* (Paris: Gallimard, 1920), 26; see Walter Benjamin, "Kaiserpanorama," in "Berliner Kindheit um Neunzehnhundert," in Benjamin, *Gesammelte Schriften* 4.1:239–240.

41. Aragon, *Anicet,* 27–28. For one critic, this quote emphasized that "much is left to be said about the significance of clothing in Aragon's apprehension of the real and surreal"; Jacqueline Lévi-Valensi, *Aragon romancier: D'Anicet à Aurélien* (Paris: SEDES, 1984), 60.

42. Aragon, *Anicet,* 28.

43. Breton and Soupault, *Les Champs magnétiques,* 91; trans. as *The Magnetic Fields,* 80 (translation slightly modified).

44. Breton, *Œuvres complètes,* 1:1166.

45. Breton and Soupault, *Les Champs magnétiques,* 92; trans. as *The Magnetic Fields,* 81 (translation slightly modified).

46. Roland Barthes, "Histoire et sociologie du vêtement," *Annales Economies, Sociétés, Civilisations* 12, no. 3 (June/September 1957), 430–441; in Roland Barthes, *Œuvres complètes,* 3 vols. (Paris: Seuil, 1993–1995), 1:741–752.

47. Ibid., 746; see also Ferdinand Saussure's disciple Charles Bally, who in 1909 had already considered "fashion itself a form of language [*langage*]," in *Traité de stylistique française,* 5th ed., 2 vols. (Geneva: Georg, 1970), 1:11–12.

48. See Barthes's later *Système de la mode,* 28.

49. Ibid.

50. Roland Barthes, "Les Maladies du costume de théâtre," *Théâtre Populaire,* no. 12 (March/April 1955); in Barthes, *Œuvres complètes,* 1:1205–1211; and "L'Activité structuraliste," *Lettres Nouvelles,* 11, no. 13 (February 1963); in *Œuvres complètes,* 1:1328–1333. Introducing Barthes to Anglo-American readers, the *Partisan Review* republished these two essays together, as "The Structuralist Activity" and "The Diseases of the Costume," *Partisan Review* 34, no. 1 (winter 1967), 82–97.

51. Barthes, "Histoire et sociologie du vêtement," 748.

52. J. C. Flügel, *The Psychology of Clothes* (London: Hogarth, 1930), 110, 113, and passim; see above, note 47 to chapter 1, for a critique of Flügel's postulate.

53. See Philippe Perrot, *Les Dessus et dessous de la bourgeoisie* (Brussels: Complexe, 1984), 69–109—trans. R. Bienvenu as *Fashioning the Bourgeosie: A History of Clothing in the Nineteenth Century* (Princeton: Princeton University Press, 1994), 36–57—for an account of how the outfit of the "lion" (or dandy), after having been worn and discarded, found its way to the room of the laborer, via different *bons marchés* and *chiffonniers.* Although the *drap* might have been much too fine for everyday use, the dandy's suit did not look out of place when adopted by the worker to become his Sunday best.

54. Jean Hugo, *Le Regard de la mémoire* (Paris: Actes Sud/Labor, 1983), 178–179.

55. Barthes, "Histoire et sociologie du vêtement," 748.

56. [Jules-A.] Barbey d'Aurevilly, *Du dandysme et de George Brummell* (first published privately 1844 in Caen); in Barbey d'Aurevilly, *Œuvres romanesques complètes,* vol. 2 (Paris: Gallimard, 1966), 673–674; trans. D. Ainslie as *Of Dandyism and of George Brummell* (London: Dent, 1897), 18–20 (this translation is far from being the best available; however, it contains more empathy and charm than any effort from the twentieth century).

Numerous texts have been written on dandyism and its history, most notably the collection by Émilien Carassus, *Le Mythe du dandy* (Paris: Colin, 1971), and the books by Jacques Boulenger, *Sous Louis-Philippe: Les Dandys* (Paris: Ollendorf, 1907); Elizabeth Creed, *Le Dandysme de Jules Barbey d'Aurevilly* (Paris: Droz, 1983); and Ellen Moers, *The Dandy: Brummell to Beerbohm* (London: Secker & Warburg, 1960). Rather than greatly extending the present text by attempting a cultural history of dandyism, I have chosen to make select references to the dandy at certain points in my argument—describing Baudelaire's clothing, the *habit noir,* Vaché's elegance, etc.

57. Barbey d'Aurevilly, *Du dandysme,* note on 673–674; trans. as *Of Dandyism,* 18–19.

58. Ibid., 675; trans., 23 (translation amended).

59. On the notion of disinterestedness see, e.g., Jerome Stolnitz, "On the Origins of 'Aesthetic Disinterestedness,'" *Journal of Aesthetics and Art Criticism* 20, no. 2 (winter 1961), 131–143. Stolnitz's point of reference is of course Immanuel Kant, *The Critique of Judgement,* trans. J. Creed Meredith (Oxford: Clarendon, 1952), 41–50, 61–80.

60. See, e.g., the surrealists' conversations (almost comical by today's standard) on sexual morality, which hover uneasily between pseudo-scientific research and confessional soul-searching; many were published in *La Révolution Surréaliste* and collected in José Pierre, ed., *Recherches sur la sexualité* (Paris: Gallimard, 1990); trans. M. Imrie as *Investigating Sex: Surrealist Research, 1928–1932* (London: Verso, 1992).

61. Aragon, *Anicet,* 94.

62. Alain and Odette Virmaux, *Cravan, Vaché, Rigaut* (Mortemart: Rougerie, 1982), 116.

63. Jacques Vaché, "Lettres de Jacques Vaché," *Littérature,* no. 7 (September 1919), 13; trans. P. Lenti in Vaché, *War Letters* (London: Atlas, 1993), 51; this letter was written during the late summer of 1918.

64. See Barbey d'Aurevilly, *Du dandysme,* 672 and passim; trans. as *Of Dandyism,* 11–13.

65. Jacques Vaché, *Quarante-trois lettres de guerre à Jeanne Derrien* (Paris: Place, 1991), [letter 4]; the letter was written between August and September 1916.

66. See, e.g., Francis Picabia, "Extrait de Jésus-Christ Rastaquouère," *391,* no. 13 (July 1920), 4; or "Jésus-Christ Rastaquouère," *391,* no. 14 (November 1920), 3.

67. Aragon, *Anicet,* 79, 82.

68. Aragon, *Anicet,* 82–83. "Concerning the masks, the first, Ange Miracle, is Jean Cocteau"; Aragon, quoted in Roger Garaudy, *L'Itinéraire d'Aragon* (Paris: Gallimard, 1961), 107. It was a flattering portrait of the upwardly mobile Cocteau, who, despite his professed interest in male fashion, had none of the true dandy's grace or distinction.

69. Louis Aragon, *Lautréamont et nous* (Pin-Balma: Sables, 1992), 71; the text had been published originally in *Les Lettres Françaises,* 1 and 8 June 1967.

70. "What I admire most is Dada's simplicity. The skeleton of the machines is dada or superior to those of the pithecanthropi"; Tzara, quoted by André Breton in "Quelles sont nos garanties?" (What are our guarantees?), in Breton, *Œuvres complètes,* 1:47.

71. Aragon, *Anicet,* 83–84.

72. Tzara's aptly titled poem "Haute Couture" is a prime example of this technique of cutting up; it was first published in *391,* no. 8 (February 1919), [upside down and untitled on page 6], and reprinted in Tristan Tzara, *Œuvres complètes,* 6 vols. (Paris: Flammarion, 1975–1985), 2:271–272.

73. One might think that such subversion could be effected in the ironic treatment of fundamental items such as Chanel's knitted costumes or, much later, Dior's "New Look" dresses. Under the "guidance" of designers such as Karl Lagerfeld and John Galliano, both these couture houses have taken it on themselves to undermine and parody their structure and tradition. Yet in our "post"-modern condition, this irony is but a pale commodified reflection of dada's original critique.

74. In principle, such "alterations" would be open to women as well. But as one can see from the photographic documents of Dada groups in 1921 or 1922, female members such as Mick Soupault or Celine Arnault just appear "dressed up" when shown in unusual poses, handling strange objects. They seem masked, not ironical. Some years later, the female surrealists wearing Schiaparelli—"ironic" haute couture, allegedly—including Eileen Agar and Leonore Fini, again look too subjective, too singular to be part of a sartorial structure that could be undermined. Their difficulty, to be sure, also reflects the patriarchal air within these circles: men stood for structure, while women represented adornment. It is telling indeed that the most effective subversion was achieved by women when they *discarded* their clothes.

75. In an interview on the occasion of the reprinting of his seminal essay "L'Habit noir" (written ca. 1888), Gustave Geffroy said in 1923: "To conclude our documentation, I would like to add that Stéphane Mallarmé, indulging these debuts of mine, showed himself very delighted with the symbolic quality that the *habit noir* and the top hat possess." *Monsieur* 4, no. 37 (January 1923), [6].

76. Barthes, "Histoire et sociologie du vêtement," 436; "praxis"—left in its German spelling in the French text—has to be seen here as social practice in the Marxist sense, as the entire societal process of changing reality.

77. Tristan Tzara, "Manifeste Dada 1918," *Dada,* no. 3 (December 1918), [2]; in Tzara, *Œuvres complètes,* 1:362. Aragon would later comment, "These two lines contained at the same time what united us with Tzara in 1919 and what would divide us in 1921" (*Lautréamont et nous,* 65).

78. Pierre Reverdy, "199 C$^{s.}$" *Dada,* nos. 4–5 (May 1919), [16].

79. Michel Sanouillet, ed., *Francis Picabia et "391,"* vol. 2 (Paris: Losfeld, 1966), 106.

80. Aragon, *Anicet,* 28. *Cocodès* could be a play on the colloquial *coco,* meaning communist—thus a *cocodès* could be a "pinko."

81. Louis Aragon, "Une Vague de rêves," *Commerce* [no. 2] (autumn 1924), 93–122. Aragon also published at his own cost in Berlin in 1923 a booklet of some thirty pages, elaborately titled *Les Plaisirs de la capitale—Paris la nuit—ses bas fonds, ses jardins secrets—Par l'auteur du Libertinage, de la Bible dépouillée de ses longeurs du Mauvais Plaisant, etc.* (The joys of the capital—Paris by night—Its crowds, its secret gardens—by the author of *Libertinage,* the Bible stripped of

the lengthy passages by a person with a warped sense of humor, etc.). Not actually a *flânerie* through either capital, the text is rather a surrealist chamber piece (somewhat anticipating "Une Vague de rêves") about a Faustian encounter between the narrator and his demon.

82. Louis Aragon, "La Femme française," in *La Libertinage* (Paris: Gallimard, 1924), 215; trans. J. Levy in Aragon, *The Libertine* (London: Calder, 1993), 161.

83. Aragon, *Anicet,* 25.

84. Aragon, "Une Vague de rêves," 113; Barclay was, next to Charvet, the most sophisticated and luxurious purveyor of men's shirts and haberdashery in Paris at that time.
　　The terms *cravate, fantôme,* and *assassin* can be understood as referring to a particular novel from the Fantômas crime series by Pierre Souvestre and Marcel Allain (whom Aragon mentions, 119), which was greatly admired by the surrealists: *Fantômas—La Cravate de chanvre* (Paris: Fayard, 1913). Pierre Reverdy borrowed the title for his 1922 collection of poetry, republished in *Plupart du temps* (Paris: Gallimard, 1945).
　　See also Benjamin's following observation in the arcade: "And the 'Fabrique de cravate au 2me'—is there a tie on sale that is fit for strangling someone?" *Das Passagen-Werk,* 1345 (and 1045).

85. Aragon, *Le Paysan de Paris,* 231; trans. S. Watson Taylor as *Paris Peasant* (London: Cape, 1971), 203 (translation slightly modified).

86. Ibid., 233; trans., 204.

87. Ibid., 237; trans., 208 (translation slightly modified); Garaudy in *L'Itinéraire d'Aragon,* 138, views "Le Songe de paysan" as an attempt to describe reality while remaining resolutely surreal.

88. Barthes, "Histoire et sociologie du vêtement," 436.

89. Roger Caillois, "Paris, mythe moderne," *La Nouvelle Revue Française* 25, no. 284 (1 May 1937), 692.

90. Aragon himself would deny this patrilineage vehemently later on ("Shit!"); see *Lautréamont et nous,* 75.

91. Maxime Alexandre, *Mémoires d'un surréaliste* (Paris: La Jeune parque, 1968), 168–169.

92. Let us ignore for the moment that the phallic neckwear has psychological connotations that are more obvious than those of any other male accessory or garment—see, e.g., Sigmund Freud, *The Interpretation of Dreams* in *The Standard Edition of the Complete Psychological Works of Sigmund Freud*, trans. James Strachey, vol. 5 (London: Hogarth, 1953), 356; or Stephan Hollós, "Schlangen und Krawattensymbolik" (The Symbolism of Snakes and Neckties), *Internationale Zeitschrift für Psychoanalyse* 9 (1923), 73.

93. Edmond and Jules de Goncourt, *Journal: Mémoires de la vie littéraire*, vol. 4, *1891–1896* (Paris: Fasquelle & Flammarion, 1956), 115; trans. R. Baldick as *The Goncourt Journal* (Oxford: Oxford University Press, 1962), 366.

94. Alexandre, *Mémoires d'un surréaliste*, 170.

95. Ibid.; Montesquiou prominently displayed above his cabinet "a somewhat homosexual photograph of Larochefoucault, the gymnast at the Mollier circus, taken in tights displaying to advantage his handsome ephebian figure" (E. and J. de Goncourt, *Journal*, 4:115; trans. as *The Goncourt Journal*, 366). If Breton had carried the analogy further in this direction, he could have easily found a corresponding feature in Aragon's taste. After all, Alexandre describes his "astonishment" when he was told of the "rather unorthodox gymnastic experiments" (*Mémoires d'un surréaliste*, 76) that Aragon undertook together with fellow dandy-poet Pierre Drieu la Rochelle.

   Of note is also Aragon's camp and dandyesque coming-out live on French television in the 1970s—at a time when he preferred to praise the new suit by Yves Saint Laurent rather than discuss poetry or politics (according to the late Stephen Spender, conversation with author). This might indicate that he did not entirely shed his interest in dandyism and fashion after the 1920s, but deferred it for reasons of political integrity.

96. André Breton, "Les Vases communicants I," in Breton, *Œuvres complètes* 2:128; trans. M. A. Caws and G. T. Harris as *Communicating Vessels* (Lincoln: University of Nebraska Press, 1990), 36.

97. "Finally, according to literary criticism, the dandy of 1913 had become extremely elegant, his apparel was never understudied nor without premeditation, he professed equal interest in the most elevated and the most minute of subjects . . . but without ever letting on that he regarded with any interest the things that occupied him so greatly." Marcel Boulenger, *Cours de vie parisienne* (Paris: Ollendorf, 1913), 215.

98. Aragon also had gone to college with Hilsum; "A certain taste for the quid pro quo guided them." Mireille Hilsum, "René Hilsum, un éditeur des années vingt," *Bulletin de Bibliophile,* no. 4 (1983), 464.

99. Henri Pastoureau, "Des influences dans la poésie présurréaliste d'André Breton," in *André Breton: Essais recueillis par Marc Eigeldinger* (Neuchâtel: Éditions de la Baconnière, 1970), 80. See the preface by Breton for Pastoureau, *Le Corps trop grand pour un cercueil: Poêmes* (Paris: Éditions Surréalistes, 1936).

100. Marguerite Bonnet identifies five in her commentary; in Breton, *Œuvres complètes,* 1:1068–1069.

101. André Breton, letter dated 22 June 1914; quoted in Marguerite Bonnet, *André Breton: Naissance de l'aventure surréaliste,* rev. ed. (Paris: Corti, 1988), 32.

102. Marguerite de Ponty, "La Mode—Bijoux ('Paris, le 1$^{er}$ août 1874')," *La Dernière Mode,* no. 1 (6 September 1874), 3; in Mallarmé, *Œuvres complètes,* 711, 714.

103. See Mme. de P[onty] on memory, mnemotechnique, and lace in *La Dernière Mode,* discussed in section 2.4.2 above.

104. André Breton, "Rêves," *La Révolution surréaliste* 1, no. 1 (1 December 1924), 3; see also the preface by Jacques Boiffard, Paul Éluard, and Roger Vitrac to this inaugural "review column of novelties, of fashion, etc.," which promised: "Fashion will be treated according to the gravitation of white letters on nocturnal bodies" (2).

On "the railings of the balcony," see Breton's later comment on his collage-poem "Le Corset mystère," discussed in section 5.8.2.

105. André Breton, *Le Surréalisme et la peinture: Nouvelle édition revue et corrigé 1918–1964* (Paris: Gallimard, 1965), 366. The quotation appears toward the end of his 1961 essay on Gustave Moreau. Breton judged the painting thus: "A pretty lesson in libertine taste, which, however, makes too little of a mysterious element: the attraction contained in precious stones (similar to those that appear in the second verse of 'Bijoux')"—a reference to Baudelaire's poem of that title in *Les Épaves;* see Charles Baudelaire, *Œuvres complètes,* 2 vols. (Paris: Gallimard, 1975–1976), 1:158–159. Yet another indication of the thematic tradition that informed the poetry of the surrealists.

106. André Breton, "Rieuse," in *Œuvres complètes,* 1:6.

107. "Your collar is fraying, embellished by the scroll of a vine. / It seems, looking at your hands, that they are embroidering / The leaves with a leafy-colored silk, among which you also could disappear. . . . I feel how distant you are and that your eyes, / The azure, your jewels of darkness and the stars of dawn / Will disappear, imprisoned by the tiresome floral pattern / That will soon appear on your extravagant dress." André Breton, "D'or vert," in Breton, *Œuvres complètes,* 1:7.

108. Breton's dedication was much more respectful than was the ironic, "mechanical" accolade given by Max Ernst in his print of 1919, titled "adieu mon beaux pays de MARIE LAURENCIN."

109. "A shawl that does awful injustice to your sensitive shoulder / Condemns us to gossip." André Breton, "L'an suave," in Breton, *Œuvres complètes,* 1:7.

110. The poem dedicated to the painter is "Crépuscule" (1905–1907), which Apollinaire included in his collection *Alcools;* on the significance of Laurencin as a muse, see the commentary in Breton, *Œuvres complètes,* 1:1076.

111. "The lady had a dress / Of violet-colored silk / And her gold-embroidered tunic / Was made up of two panels / Fastened at the shoulder." Guillaume Apollinaire, "1909," in *Alcools* (1913; reprint, Paris: Gallimard, 1927), 148; trans. O. Bernard in Apollinaire, *Selected Poems* (London: Anvil, 1965), 93.

112. "Boil lace. 'Have you / By any chance taken the cuffs?' / Not bothered by success, / Sighs Fanchette." André Breton, "Lingères," in Breton, *Œuvres complètes,* 1:40.

113. See, e.g., Walter Serner's "Manschetten," a number of poems allegedly composed on starched cuffs while sitting at a café table, which were reprinted in the dada magazine *Der Zeltweg* (November 1919), 9–10.

114. See Marguerite Bonnet, "Chronologie," in Breton, *Œuvres complètes,* 1:xxviii. Christian Dior is described as having had a similar childhood experience of seeing his mother's employees work with lace; the memory would later influence his own choice of work. See also George Sebbag's psychoanalytical interpretation of lace, Breton, and motherhood, in Vaché, *Quarante-trois lettres de guerre à Jeanne Derrien,* xv.

The young Tristan Tzara had been equally enchanted by women working with fabric (an attraction that is related to that of nineteenth-century poets for the *grisettes:* the poor, but well turned-out young milliner assistants or seamstresses). Among his earliest poetry, written around 1912 to 1915, while still in Romania, the piece "Chante, chante encore" (Sing, sing again) began: "Today I have met a girl on the street where I live / Salesgirl in a department store or seamstress / . . . I was poor but I bought her a swatch of precious fabric." Another poem started with the lines: "I don't mind whether you are a seamstress or not / Romance in the provinces is fashionable in literary schools." Tzara, *Œuvres complètes,* 1:66, 69.

115. Bonnet, "Chronologie," xxxiii.

116. Paul Valéry, letter dated February 1916, in Breton, *Œuvres complètes,* 1:1078. A different version of "Décembre" is dedicated to Apollinaire; see ibid., 1081–1082.

117. "Shirts clotted on the chair. A silk hat confers reflections of my pursuit. Man . . . A mirror avenges you and, vanquished, treats me like a discarded suit. The moment returns to cast its patina upon the flesh." André Breton, "Âge," in ibid., 9; trans. J.-P. Cauvin and M. A. Caws in Breton, *Poems of André Breton* (Austin: University of Texas Press, 1982), 5 (translation modified).

118. André Breton, "La Confession dédaigneuse," *La Vie Moderne* (winter 1923), a text then published as the first part of *Les Pas perdus* (Paris: Nouvelle Revue française, 1924); in *Œuvres complètes,* 1:198–199; trans. in parts adopted from Breton, *War Letters,* 16.

119. Ibid., 199.

120. See Michel Carassou, *Jacques Vaché et le groupe de Nantes* (Paris: Place, 1986).

121. My personal favorite is the description of the British lieutenant who, when the sun came out, left his foxhole wearing "a quite extravagant SUMMER attire: a cachou-colored silk shirt, short trousers (impeccably pressed!), black stockings also made from silk, and PUMPS." Vaché, *Quarante-trois lettres de guerre à Jeanne Derrien,* [letter 37; 29 July 1917].

122. Louis Aragon, *Les Collages* (Paris: Hermann, 1965), 53 n. 1.

123. See Jeanne Derrien's recollection in Vaché, *Quarante-trois lettres de guerre à Jeanne Derrien,* xxvi.

124. André Breton, "Jacques Vaché: Les Pas perdus," in Breton, *Œuvres complètes,* 1:228; trans. M. Polizzotti in Breton, *The Lost Steps* (Lincoln: University of Nebraska Press, 1996), 41. Here, Breton must have first encountered the combined metaphor of the funnel—top hat that would become significant some six years later. I return to locomotives and top hats at the end of this chapter.

125. "Way | Fondness strews you with brocaded / taffeta plans / except where the sheen of gold found its delight. / Let July, mad / witness, ate least count the sin / of the old novel for little girls that we read! | With little girls we / courted / dampens (Years, window blinds on the brink of oblivion), / failing / to nurse at the sweet torrent, / —Further pleasure what chosen deed initiates you?— / a future, dazzling Batavian Court. | Labelling balm vain love, have we guaranteed / by our coldness / a foundation, more than hours but, months? The girls / Are making batiste: Forever!—Anyway the smell / annihilates / this jealous spring, | Dear young ladies." André Breton, "Façon," in Breton, *Œuvres complètes,* 1:5; trans. B. Zavatsky and Z. Rogow in Breton, *Earthlight* (Los Angeles: Sun & Moon Press, 1993), 23.

126. André Breton, "Lingères," in Breton, *Œuvres complètes,* 1:40.

127. André Breton, letter to Théodore Fraenkel from November 1916; in Breton, *Œuvres complètes,* 1:1073.

128. Marcel Proust, *À l'ombre des jeunes filles en fleurs,* part 2 of *À la recherche du temps perdu* (Paris: Gallimard, 1988), 254; trans. C. K. Scott Moncrieff and T. Kilmartin as *Within a Budding Grove,* part 2 of *Remembrance of Things Past* (London: Chatto & Windus, 1981), 961.

129. "The message is a swatch of fabric"; Pierre Unik, "Place Vendôme," *La Révolution Surréaliste* 3, nos. 9–10 (1 October 1927), 24.

130. Paul Poiret, *En habillant l'époque* (Paris: Grasset, 1930), 22.

131. See Bonnet's analysis in Breton, *Œuvres complètes,* 1:1071–1072.

132. Letter from the end of June to the beginning of July 1916; in ibid., 1072. Coty is one of the most prestigious perfume houses in France; founded in 1904, it excels through the artistry of its packaging and promotion. After bottle designs by the glassmakers Baccarat, it was René Lalique who revolutionized from 1910 onward for Coty the form in which perfume was promoted (the

company was also the first to use advertising on private taxis); François Coti created a total of twenty-one original scents up to 1930. The boulevard des Capucines crosses north of the place Vendôme; in the 1910s some of the most prestigious artisans and designers had their workshops there.

133. Aragon, *Lautréamont et nous,* 27–28.

134. Breton, *Œuvres complètes,* 1:1072.

135. Pastoureau, "Des influences dans la poésie présurréaliste d'André Breton," 52.

136. In the very first issue of *La Dernière Mode,* Ponty enthused: "Nothing is simpler: it is now proven that a stroll along the rue de la Paix, repeated for several afternoons, is enough to teach us about 'all the things done best in the world,' to use this rather banal saying in its proper meaning." Marguerite de Ponty, "La Mode," *La Dernière Mode,* no. 1 (6 September 1876), 2; in Mallarmé, *Œuvres complètes,* 712–713.

137. Aragon, *Anicet,* 91.

138. Jacques Vaché, letter to Breton, dated 29 April 1917, in *Littérature,* no. 5 (July 1919), 4; trans. in Vaché, *War Letters,* 35.

139. Jacques Vaché, letter to Breton, dated 18 August 1917, in *Littérature,* no. 6 (August 1919), 13; trans. in Vaché, *War Letters,* 46–47 (translation slightly modified and amended).

140. Ibid.; trans., 13.

141. "Black Forest* | Out / Tender pod etc. melon / Madame de Saint-Gobain finds it tedious alone / A cutlet is withering | Contours of destiny / Where without shutters this white gable / Waterfalls / Sled-men are favored | It's blowing hard / *que salubre est le vent* the wind of dairies | The author of the Inn of the Guardian Angel / Died after all last year / Appropriately | From Tübingen come to meet me / Young Kepler and young Hegel / And the goodly comrade | *Rimbaud talking." André Breton, "Forêt-Noire," in *Œuvres complètes,* 1:12; trans. K. White in Breton, *Selected Poems* (London: Cape, 1969), 11.

142. Pastoureau, "Des influences dans la poésie présurréaliste d'André Breton," 60.

143. The significant passage in the biography reads: "One day [Verlaine] learned of his friend's new residence; he immediately rushed to see him. . . . In order to create a pleasant surprise for his erstwhile companion, whom he thought to find unchanged in manners and habits, Verlaine had chosen the most unfortunate of costumes, an outfit that made him look like a brigand. But Rimbaud, dressed moderately and bourgeois, in tune with his status as a private tutor, received him badly, full of venom even—absolutely furious that he dared to call on him here in Germany, in such a compromising way, particularly after the Belgian drama. However, Rimbaud yielded after a while to Verlaine's bizarre insistence, in order to have at least some peace and quiet at the doctor's. But already he plotted the revenge that he would execute some hours later in the Black Forest. 'Le Bateau ivre' had become much more reasonable and decent than 'Sagesse.' Verlaine intended to relive the heroic peregrinations; Rimbaud insisted on well-ordered circumstances. Conflict. Brawl. And Verlaine was left half-dead in said forest." Paterne Berrichon [i.e., Pierre Dufour, Rimbaud's brother-in-law], *La Vie de Jean-Arthur Rimbaud* (Paris: Mercure de France, 1897), 17–18.

In a later introduction to three previously unpublished letters by Rimbaud to Ernest Delahaye, Berrichon describes Verlaine's apparel: "he presented himself to Rimbaud in a rather Romantic outfit"; *La Nouvelle Revue Française* 6, no. 67 (1 July 1914), 50. Was it thus a conflict of bourgeoisie versus bohemia, or rather of *modernité* versus Romantic tradition?

144. Pastoureau, "Des influences dans la poésie présurréaliste d'André Breton," 61. He quotes from Arthur Rimbaud, "Délires II: Alchimie du verbe," in *Une saison en enfer;* in Rimbaud, *Œuvres complètes* (Paris: Gallimard, 1954), 236; trans. N. Cameron in Rimbaud, *A Season in Hell, and Other Poems* (London: Anvil, 1994), 176–177.

145. Verlaine's return to the fold of the Catholic Church and his resulting urge to convert Rimbaud must have exacerbated the conflict.

146. Such irony also follows Guillaume Apollinaire's credo: "*L'Esprit moderne* does not look toward transforming the ridiculous; it retains a role for it that is not without saving grace." "L'Esprit nouveau et les poètes" (lecture given at the conference at the Théâtre du Vieux-Colombier in Paris, 26 November 1917), in Apollinaire, *Œuvres complètes,* 4 vols. (Paris: Balland/Lecat, 1965–1966), 3:905.

147. Jacques Vaché, letter to Breton, dated 29 April 1917; in *Littérature,* no. 5 (July 1919), 5; trans. in Vaché, *War Letters,* 36.

148. Jacques Vaché, letter to Breton, dated 5 July [1916]; in *Littérature,* no. 5 (July 1919), 1–2; trans. in Vaché, *War Letters,* 31 (translation slightly modified). Vaché's ideal had its precedent in Baudelaire's "héroïsme de la vie moderne"; see Charles Baudelaire, "Salon de 1845," in Baudelaire, *Œuvres complètes,* 2:407.

149. Jacques Rivière imagines Rimbaud as a schoolboy in Charlesville: "I see him in the midst of his comrades, dressed without elegance but very neatly indeed, in a comfortable jacket and a little white collar—one of those who bear a homely smell at college." Rivière, "Rimbaud (1ère partie)," *La Nouvelle Revue Française* 6, no. 67 (1 July 1914), 21. The desperate attempt to exchange the "homely smell" for a taste of adventure would eventually lead Rimbaud into situations with which he could not cope.

See also Rimbaud's "ingenious system" of changing shirts, in "Arthur Rimbaud vu par Jules Mary," *Littérature,* no. 8 (October, 1919), 24.

150. The ability of sustaining distance and subversion for an extended period of time never was tested in the cases of Rimbaud, Vaché, and many other true dandies, simply because they chose to remove themselves (violently) from this possible "embarrassment" in/of life.

151. "The Mysterious Corset | My dear lady readers, / because we've seen some in all colours / Splendid maps, high-lighted, Venice / The furniture in my room used to be fastened solidly to the walls and I'd have myself strapped into it to write: I've found my sea legs / we're members of a kind of emotional Touring Club / A CASTLE INSTEAD OF A HEAD / it's the Charity Bazaar too / Entertaining games for all ages; / Poetry games, etc. / I hold Paris like—if I may unveil the future to you—your open hand / her elegant figure." André Breton, "Le Corset mystère," in Breton, *Œuvres complètes,* 1:16; trans. in Breton, *Earthlight,* 31.

152. Breton, *Œuvres complètes,* 1:1098.

153. See *Littérature,* no. 4 (June 1919), 7—*Mont de piété* was to appear finally in October 1919.

154. See Werner Spies et al., *Max Ernst: Werke 1906–1925* (Houston: Menil; Cologne: DuMont, 1975), 156 [catalogue raisonné no. 309]. Cologne was practically though not physically very distant, given the extremely limited exchanges between artists of the two countries so soon after the Great War.

155. Benjamin describes "the corset as the arcade/passage [*Passage*] of the torso"; see *Das Passagen-Werk,* 614.

156. See *Bulletin Dada,* no. 6 (February 1920), [2].

157. André Breton, letter dated 27 April 1919; in Bonnet, *André Breton,* 158 n. 192.

158. See Tristan Tzara's retrospective comment on the methods of dada in *Anthologie de la nouvelle poésie française,* rev. ed. (Paris: Kra, 1930), 423.

159. "White Acetylene / You as well!—My beautiful whiskies—My horrible mixture . . . / seeping yellow—pharmaceutical office—My green / chartreuse liquor—Citrin—Swayed rose of Carthame— / Smoke! / Smoke! / Smoke! / Black sickening angostura bitter and the uncertainty of cordials— / I am a mosaist / [ . . . ]." Jacques Vaché, letter to Breton, dated 26 November 1918, with the following marked "nota bene": "Everywhere the law opposes deliberate homicide— (and that's for moral reasons . . . no doubt?). (Harry James)"; facsimile in Carassou, *Jacques Vaché et le groupe de Nantes,* 253.

160. Bonnet, in Breton, *Œuvres complètes,* 1:1227.

161. Some five years later Breton would resume the fabrication of collage-poems for *Poisson soluble.* Once again, however, the cutups were not deemed suitable for the final published version; thus they remained in manuscript. See Breton, *Œuvres complètes,* 1:562–567, 571–583, 585–590, and the note by Bonnet, 1365–1377.

162. Breton, "La Confession dédaigneuse," 198–199.

163. Vaché, *Quarante-trois lettres de guerre à Jeanne Derrien* [letter no. 18, dated Friday, 20 April 1917].

164. Marguerite de Ponty, "Conseils sur l'education," *La Dernière Mode,* no. 7 (6 December 1874), 10; in Mallarmé, *Œuvres complètes,* 828; see section 2.4.2 above. On Vaché's use of lace to dress his puppets, see Vaché, *Quarante-trois lettres de guerre à Jeanne Derrien* [letter no. 19, dated Wednesday, 25 April 1917]; on Brummell's "sort of lace," see section 5.4.

165. Stéphane Mallarmé composed a sonnet in 1887 whose first verse commenced on an ironic as well as prophetic note: "Lace passes into nothingness, / With the ultimate Gamble in doubt, / in blasphemy revealing just / Eternal absence of any bed." Mallarmé, Œuvres complètes, 74; trans. P. Terry and M. Z. Shroder in Mallarmé, Selected Poetry and Prose (New York: New Directions, 1982), 58.

166. André Breton, "Jacques Vaché," in Anthologie de l'humour noir; in Breton, Œuvres complètes, 2:1128 (my emphasis); trans. in Vaché, War Letters, 23 (translation modified).

167. Barthes, Système de la mode, 246 n. 2; trans. as The Fashion System, 242 n. 11.

168. The psychological dimension of Vaché's attempt to "live fashion" is explored by Sebbag's introduction to Vaché, Quarante-trois lettres de guerre à Jeanne Derrien, xv. As a result, speculation about Vaché's sexuality (see also Carassou, Jacques Vaché et le groupe de Nantes, 217–218) could prove interesting, especially in relation to his close friendship with Breton, who—according to Derrien (xxvi)—first displayed a distinctly misogynist and later an openly homophobic attitude. Aragon wrote: "Who can say what happened between these two men? A mystery!" (Anicet, 91; see section 5.8.1 above).

169. Georg Wilhelm Friedrich Hegel, Vorlesungen über die Ästhetik II, in Werke, vol. 14 (Frankfurt a.M.: Suhrkamp, 1986), 406; trans. T. M. Knox as Hegel, Aesthetics: Lectures on Fine Arts, 2 vols. (Oxford: Clarendon, 1975), 2:745.

170. Carassus, Le Mythe du dandy, 108.

171. See Marc Eigeldinger, Lumières du mythe (Paris: Presses Universitaires de France, 1983), 175–220; Philippe Lavergne, André Breton et le mythe (Paris: Corti, 1985), 75–91; Caillois, "Paris, mythe moderne," 682–683.

172. André Breton, "Récit de trois rêves," Littérature, n.s., no. 1 (1 March 1922), 6–7, republished as "Cinq rêves," in Clair de terre; in Breton, Œuvres complètes, 1:151; trans. in Breton, Earthlight, 39–40 (translation slightly modified).

This dream has a prophetic quality itself, as Roger Lefébure came to act as an advocate for (the habitually monocled, as we will see) Tzara, in the litigation he brought against his former friend Éluard in the aftermath of the disastrous performance "Soirée du cœur à barbe" in July 1923; see Michel Sanouillet, Dada à Paris (Paris: Pauvert, 1965), 385–386.

173. See Sanouillet, *Francis Picabia et "391,"* 2:43, 93.

174. Pharamousse, "New York = Paris = Zurich = Barcelone," *391,* no. 8 (January–February 1919), 8.

175. Francis Picabia, *Le Philhaou-Thibaou* (a special "illustrated supplement" of *391*), 10 July 1921, 6.

176. The only one in the group who could have afforded Poiret's clothing was the English heiress Nancy Cunard, who had a liaison with Aragon in 1920/1921; Éluard's wife Nusch worked occasionally as a fashion model in the 1920s, and at one stage turned out for Poiret.

177. Man Ray's photographic chronicles of dada and surrealism had in turn been helped along by Tzara's enthusiasm; see Man Ray, *Self-Portrait* (1963; reprint, New York: Graphic Society, 1988), 100–115.

178. Tristan Tzara, "D'un certain automatisme du goût," *Minotaure,* nos. 3–4 (Skira, 1933), 81–94; in Tzara, *Œuvres complètes,* 4:321–331.

179. See, e.g., the 1911 analysis of a young woman's dream in Freud, *The Interpretation of Dreams,* 360–362; and also Max Ernst's collage-painting of 1920, *C'est le chapeau qui fait l'homme* (The Hat Maketh the Man), where erectile tubular structures are capped by (or even composed of) various models of *female* headgear, cut out from a catalogue for the hat factory by Ernst's father-in-law. The intricate relations of these ironic gestures toward Freud can hardly be surpassed.

180. See Jacques Gaucheron, "Esquisse pour un portrait," *Europe* 53, nos. 555–556 (July–August 1975), 33–34.

181. Quoted in Giuseppe Scaraffia, *Dizionario del dandy* (Rome: Laterza, 1981), 91, 94. Proust provides descriptions of the different ways to sport an eyeglass in *Du côté de chez Swann III* (*À la recherche du temps perdu,* part 1 [Paris: Gallimard, 1987], 321–322); see also Robert Saint-Loup's monocled elegance in *À l'ombre des jeunes filles en fleurs II* (*À la recherche du temps perdu,* part 2, 88–89). However, these examples, perfect as they are, belong to the nineteenth century and their analysis therefore reveals little about a modern mythology.

182. Quoted from unpublished memoirs by Karl Schodder, in Walter Serner, "Der Abreiser" (The Departee), in Serner, *Gesammelte Werke,* 2d ed., 10 vols. (Munich: Goldmann, 1989–1990), 10:236.

183. Walter Serner, "Der Schluck um die Achse-manifest" (The Sip around the Axis-Manifesto), *Der Zeltweg,* November 1919, [18]; see "Das Hirngeschwür," in Serner, *Gesammelte Werke,* 2:60.

184. See Sanouillet, *Dada à Paris,* 384–385; on the resulting lawsuit see note 172 above.

185. Stéphane Mallarmé, letter dated Sunday, 5 October [1890]; in Mallarmé, *Correspondance Mallarmé-Whistler: Histoire de la grande amitié de leurs dernières années,* ed. C. P. Barbier (Paris: Nizet, 1964), 68. The quotation from the review is on 68. On Mallarmé's acting as Whistler's ally in Paris, see Jean-Michel Nectoux, *Mallarmé: Un Clair Regard dans les ténèbres: Peinture, musique, poésie* (Paris: Biro, 1998), 84.

186. Cover of *Littérature,* n.s., no. 9 (1 February–1 March 1923).

187. See the photo of Hausmann from ca. 1920, assuming the pose of an athlete on the roof of his Berlin apartment, or the double portrait (collage) of him and fellow anarchist Johannes Baader dating from the same time; in Hanne Bergius, *Das Lachen Dadas* (Giessen: Anabas, 1989), 34, 158. August Sander in 1929 portrayed Hausmann again in an artificial pose, showing off his torso against white sailor trousers and the reflection of the ubiquitous monocle in his left eye (August Sander-Archive, Cologne).

See also Tristan Tzara, Hans Arp, and Walter Serner with their simultaneous poem of ca. 1916, which featured the line: "the athletes' mothers stick the monocles in the armpits of their dead sons and sing *it's a long way jusqu'au bout*"; in Tzara, *Œuvres complètes,* 1:498.

188. Tristan Tzara, "Dada à Weimar," in "L'Allemagne: Un film à épisodes"; in Tzara, *Œuvres complètes,* 1:603. Hausmann was, in fact, born in Vienna.

189. Jacques Vaché, letter to Breton, dated X. 11 October 1916/3 P.M., in *Littérature,* no. 5 (July 1919), 2–3; trans. in Vaché, *War Letters,* 32.

190. Jacques Vaché, letter to Fraenkel, dated X. 29 April 1917, in ibid., 6; trans. in Vaché, *War Letters,* 39.

191. Jacques Vaché, letter to Breton, dated 18 August 1917, in *Littérature,* no. 6 (August 1919), 14; trans. in Vaché, *War Letters,* 46–47 (translation modified). Note the reference to the locomotive.

192. Ibid.; trans., 47 (translation modified).

193. Ibid., 15; trans., 49 (translation modified).

194. Jean Sarment, *Cavalcadour* (Paris: Simoën, 1977), 538; see Sarment's initial, fictionalized account of Vaché in *Jean-Jacques de Nantes* (Paris: Plon, 1922), 112: "He dressed with great care and with deliberate dandyism. He wore his monocle in the left eye and dedicated himself to English style [*au genre anglais*]."

195. Breton, "Jacques Vaché," in 1127; trans. partly adopted from Vaché, *War Letters,* 22.

196. "Voir des papillons noirs" (to see black butterflies) is a French expression for being melancholy or depressed. With similar vocabulary, Breton and Soupault evoke a possible reminiscence to Vaché and to a mutual attraction to fashion in *Les Champs magnétiques:* "a butterfly of the sphinx variety. They wrap their icy utterances in silver-paper . . . and would not exchange places with fashion-plates" (56); trans. as *The Magnetic Fields,* 28 (translation slightly modified).

197. Jacques-Émile Blanche, quoted in Victor Castre, "Trois héros surréalistes [Rigaut, Vaché, Crevel]," *La Gazette des Lettres,* no. 39 (June 1947), 6; Blanche, "Sur Jacques Rigaut," *Les Nouvelles Littéraires,* 11 January 1930, 5.

198. Pierre Drieu la Rochelle, "La Valise vide," *La Nouvelle Revue Française* 10, no. 119 (1 August 1923), 166; the protagonist Gonzague in this story is a portrait of Rigaut.

199. See Elisabeth Lenk, *Der springende Narziß: André Bretons poetischer Materialismus* (Jumping Narcissus: The Poetic Materialism of André Breton) (Munich: Rogner & Bernhard, 1971), 22.

200. Arthur Cravan, *J'étais cigare* (Paris: Losfeld, 1971), 122.

201. See the account in André Salmon, *Souvenirs sans fin: 2ᵉ époque (1908–1920)* (Paris: Gallimard, 1956), 216. Another of Salmon's fictionalized memoirs is titled *Le Monocle à deux coups*

(Paris: Pauvert, 1968), see esp. chap. 4, "Ce monocle" (178–182), which describes his withdrawal symptoms when he is deprived of the eyeglass.

202. Louis Aragon, "Oscar Wilde—La Maison de la courtisane," review in "Livres choisis," *Littérature*, no. 8 (October 1919), 28.

203. Sanouillet, *Dada à Paris*, 163.

204. Ibid., 141.

205. Tristan Tzara, "Pile ou face [a pantomime in three acts]," in Tzara, *Œuvres complètes*, 1:525.

206. "Les Auteurs des Mémoires de Bilboquet," in *Paris-Viveur* (Paris: Taride, 1854), 26; this book, part of the series *Les Petits Paris*, is likely to have been written by two feuilletonists, Taxile Delord and Clément Caraguel.

207. The monocle was not so much a separate invention in itself, but a concentration of the lorgnette and quizzer into one glass circle without the handle—to which could be added the advantage of a magnifying glass; see D. C. Davidson, *Spectacles, Lorgnettes, and Monocles* (Aylesbury: Shire, 1989), 7–10, and Richard Corson, *Fashion in Eyeglasses* (London: Owen, 1967), 114, 221–225.

208. The typical nineteenth-century posture involved reclining into a soft chair or upholstered sofa in the salon (see, e.g., Sigfried Giedion, *Mechanization Takes Command: A Contribution to Anonymous History* [New York: Oxford University Press, 1948], 396 and passim; thus the upright and stiff posture of the head and neck while balancing the eyeglass seems an even starker contrast.

209. Even "intellectual" labor, such as writing literature, becomes extremely difficult with a monocle, as bowing the head over a piece of paper almost instantly forces the eyeglass from its designated place.

210. *DADAphone*, special issue of *Dada*, no. 7 (March 1920), 1–3.

211. After the confrontation of "Lâchez tout," Péret sided with Breton in declaring: "I left the dada glasses behind and got up to leave"; Benjamin Péret, "À travers mes yeux," *Littérature,* n.s., no. 5 (1 October 1922), 13.

212. Jimmy Ernst, *Nicht gerade ein Stilleben* (Cologne: Kiepenheuer & Witsch, 1985), 56.

213. Francis Picabia, "Post-scriptum aux Mariés de la Tour Eiffel," *Le Pilhaou-Thibaou,* 10 July 1921, 14. Jean Lorrain was the prolific nineteenth-century poet and monocle-wearing author of *Modernités* (Paris: Giraud, 1885), 9–12, 110–111; see Louis Aragon's poem "Moderne" in *La Grande gaïté* (Paris: Gallimard, 1929), 26: "Whorehouse for whorehouse / I myself prefer the Metro / It is more fun / And also it's warmer," which recalls Lorrain's refrain: "Modernity, Modernity / Through the cries, the booing / The shamelessness of whores / Sparkles in eternity."

214. Picabia, "Post-scriptum," 14.

215. Francis Picabia [?], *Cannibale,* no. 2 (25 May 1920), 15.

216. André Breton, *Poisson soluble II,* in *Œuvres complètes,* 1:522; this automatic writing was filled with "bijoux" and metaphors of material elegance. See Julien Gracq, "Spectre du 'Poisson soluble,'" in *André Breton: Essais et témoignages,* ed. Marc Eigeldinger (Neuchâtel: Baconnière, 1950), 216–217.

217. Aragon, "Une Vague de rêves," 114.

218. Man Ray's photograph is featured on the cover of *La Révolution surréaliste,* no. 1 (1 December 1924).

219. René Crevel, review published in *Les Nouvelles Littéraires,* 23 February 1924; quoted in Tzara, *Œuvres complètes,* 1:685. The scarf mentioned was a gift from the painter Sonia Delaunay-Terk, who also designed Crevel's abstract waistcoats.

220. [Breton], "Avant le Congrès de Paris," *Comœdia,* 3 January 1922, 1. For a complete chronological and critical account of the congress, see Sanouillet, *Dada à Paris,* 319–347, and also Georges Hugnet, *L'Aventure Dada (1916–1922)* (Paris: Galerie de l'Institut, 1957), 93.

221. André Breton, "Caractères de l'évolution moderne," in Breton, *Œuvres complètes,* 1:297; this talk was given at the Ateneo in Barcelona on 17 November 1922, to coincide with an exhibition of works by Picabia.

222. Tristan Tzara, quoted in Roger Vitrac, "Tristan Tzara Vaché cultiver ses vices," *Le Journal du Peuple,* 14 April 1923, 3; in Tzara, *Œuvres complètes,* 1:624.

223. [Breton], "Avant le Congrès de Paris," 1.

224. See *Dictionnaire de la langue française* (Paris: Larousse, 1992), s.v. "locomotive"; the word is a composite nominalization, from the Latin *locus* and *movere*—to move from a spot. In 1804, Richard Trevithik invented (for the Welsh mining industry) the first engine that ran on rails; George Stephenson's celebrated *Rocket* first ran in 1829.

225. The "top hat" (i.e., a cylindrical structure covered in black silk) is documented as having appeared first in 1797, created by the London haberdasher John Hetherington. Yet according to the anonymous, but fervently patriotic, author of "La Centenaire du chapeau" (*La Mode pratique,* no. 6 [6 February 1897], 66–67), a painting by Charles Vernet of 1796, titled *Incroyable,* "is proof that it existed in France before John Hetherington's 'adventure.'"

226. An untitled text, composed by Breton and signed by him, Fernand Léger, Robert Delaunay, Georges Auric, Amédée Ozenfant, and Roger Vitrac (the sixth member of the committee, the linguist Jean Paulhan, seems to have been absent); published in *Comœdia,* 7 February 1922; quoted in Sanouillet, *Dada à Paris,* 329.

227. Published in *Comœdia,* 8 February 1922; quoted in Tzara, *Œuvres complètes,* 1:590.

228. Ibid., 589.

229. Maxime du Camp, "Les Chants modernes," *Revue de Paris* 24 (February 1855), 337; the collection itself was published in Paris in March 1855 by Michel Lévy. Walter Benjamin in 1937 links the metaphor of the locomotive with modernist poems: "At the beginning there were the Saint-Simonians with their industrial poetry. They are followed by the realism of du Camp who sees the locomotive as the saint of the future. Finally there is a Ludwig Pfau: 'is it quite unnecessary to become an angel,' he wrote, 'since a locomotive is worth more than the nicest pair of wings.' This image of technology comes from the *Gartenlaube* [a *Reader's Digest*–type weekly for the German

bourgeois]. This may cause one to ask whether the *Gemütlichkeit* which the nineteenth-century bourgeoisie enjoyed does not arise from the hollow comfort of never having to experience how the productive forces had to develop under their hands." Benjamin, "Eduard Fuchs, der Sammler und der Historiker," in *Gesammelte Schriften* 2.2:475; trans. K. Tarnowski as "Eduard Fuchs: Collector and Historian," *New German Critique,* no. 5 (spring 1975), 34.

230. See Maxime du Camp, "La Locomotive," in *Les Chants modernes,* new ed. (Paris: Librairie Nouvelle/Bourdilliat, 1860), 197–203.

231. Ix., "Chronique de Paris," *La Dernière Mode,* no. 1 (6 September 1874), 5; in Mallarmé, *Œuvres complètes,* 719 (see also section 2.4.2 above). Ix.'s reflection is immediately followed by a "Menu d'un déjeuner au bord de la mer," and Mallarmé's readers thus travel together with his poetic imagination.

232. Tristan Tzara, "Atrocités d'Arthur & trompette & scaphandrier," *Der Zeltweg,* November 1919, [22]; see chap. 5 of *L'Antitête,* in Tzara, *Œuvres complètes,* 2:273.

233. Tristan Tzara, *L'Antitête* (XLIII), in Tzara, *Œuvres complètes,* 2:320.

234. Ix., "Chronique de Paris," *La Dernière Mode,* no. 5 (1 November 1874), [4]; in Mallarmé, *Œuvres complètes,* 784.

235. "Not gusts of wind that hold the streets / Always without the slightest reason / Subject to dark flights of hats; / But a dancing girl arisen." Stéphane Mallarmé, "Billet à Whistler," in Mallarmé, *Œuvres complètes,* 65; trans. H. Wenfield in Mallarmé, *Collected Poems,* (Berkeley: University of California Press, 1994), 62.
    Note Mallarmé's praise for the symbolism of the black suit and top hat to Geffroy (section 5.6, with n. 75, above). Geffroy wrote ca. 1888: "This century of the locomotive . . . cannot include . . . a population braided and adorned in iridescent colors. One has to clothe oneself in harmony with the machines and products of contemporary industry" ("L'Habit noir," [4]).

236. Max Morise, "Les Yeux enchantés," *La Révolution Surréaliste,* no. 1, (1 December 1924), 27.
    See also Rigaut's wordplay about woman and car (and top hat): "I count the woman in cylinders," or "Young, poor, mediocre man, twenty-one years of age, clean hands, would like to marry woman, twenty-four cylinders, healthy, erotomaniac, or able to speak Vietnamese." Jacques Rigaut, *Écrits* (Paris: Gallimard, 1970), 83, 26.

237. The word *gibus* was first recorded in the French language in 1834 (in the same year as *locomotive*), and together with the term *chapeau-claque*—more obviously referring to the ability of many hats to fold—it was used to describe the top hat until both were replaced in the late 1880s by the expression *chapeau haut-de-forme.*

238. Eugène Delacroix, *La Liberté guidant le peuple, ou "le 28 Juillet"* (1830; in Paris, Musée du Louvre); see Perrot, *Les Dessus et les dessous de la bourgeoisie,* 66 n. 9: "The top hat can be considered also as the reincarnation of revolutionary hairdos."

239. Jacques Boulenger, *Monsieur ou le professeur de snobisme* (Paris: Crès, 1901), 48.

240. Stéphane Mallarmé, "Sur le chapeau haut de forme," *Le Figaro,* 19 January 1897, [1]; in Mallarmé, *Œuvres complètes,* 881.

241. Henri Mondor, *Vie de Mallarmé* (Paris: Gallimard, 1941), 534; see also Mallarmé's ironic reference to "the atmospheric column" that is continued by the top hat (665).

242. Breton, "Jacques Vaché: Les Pas perdus," 228; trans. in Breton, *The Lost Steps,* 41—see section 5.8.1 of this chapter.

243. In English and German the industrial association is indicated by vernacular words: "stovepipe" and *Angströhre* (literally, "fear pipe").

244. André Breton, "Giorgio de Chirico—12 Tavola in Fototipia," review in "Livres choisis," *Littérature* 2, no. 11 (January 1920), 28.

245. "A top hat rests upon / A table bearing fruit / Near an apple the gloves lie dead / A lady wrings her neck / Beside a man who gulps himself." Guillaume Apollinaire, "Les Collines," verse 37, in *Calligrammes;* in Apollinaire, *Œuvres complètes,* 3:168; trans. A. Hyde Greet as "The Hills," in Apollinaire, *Calligrammes: Poems of Peace and War (1913–1916)* (Berkeley: University of California Press, 1980), 45. The poem was written in 1917.

246. The subtitle of the painting, *Cézanne's Hat,* refers to Georges Braques's acquired habit of sporting a bowler in reference to the forefather of cubism. However, Picasso's cubist style transforms the dome-shaped bowler hat into an elongated topper.

247. Richard Huelsenbeck, "Die Arbeiten von Hans Arp," *Dada,* no. 3 [German version] (1918), [9].

248. Sanouillet, *Dada à Paris,* 326. He quotes from Guillaume Apollinaire, "La Jolie russe," in *Calligrammes,* in Apollinaire, *Œuvres complètes,* 3:228–229.

Bonnet questions this assessment in *André Breton,* 221–222 n. 117. Her criticism is based on the assumption that the locomotive equals modernity, while the top hat represents the ancient. However, in light of Breton's own view on the prophetic powers of Lautréamont and Apollinaire, objects such as the umbrella, the sewing machine, and, of course, the top hat cannot be assigned exclusively to the past.

249. Caillois, "Paris, mythe moderne," 697; see Farid Chenoune, *Des modes et des hommes* (Paris: Flammarion, 1993), 109.

For Breton a similarly attired figure held "the possibility of going wherever I want to [*le clé des champs*—literally, 'the key to the fields']: this man was myself" (*Œuvres complètes,* 1:399); this attire was in turn copied by Caillois in a photograph of the 1970s, in which he is dressed as Fantômas holding a huge key (frontispiece to Roger Caillois, *Apprentissages de Paris* [Paris: Fata Morgana, 1984]).

250. Sanouillet, *Dada à Paris,* 176; in regard to the stiffness of the paper (or rather celluloid) collars that many Dadaists still used to complement their evening wear, Sanouillet remarks (not quite seriously): "After all, Raymond Duncan [the American Grecophile brother of the dancer Isadora] was more dadaist than the dadaists; did he not have the courage to wear an antique toga, visible symbol of his beliefs, while they still wore high wing-collars?" (158). However, any fanciful adherence to antiquity is contrary to dada, while the ironic adaptation and subversion of bourgeois past symbols is not.

251. "Unveiled Optimism | for . . . the ennui of money / a night of the highest order / a nitrogen cylinder covered by a top hat . . . / the cheapest and most resistant / for sale / everywhere / always." Tristan Tzara, "L'Optimisme dévoilé," in Tzara, *Œuvres complètes,* 1:226. The poem, written in 1919, was first published in *Mecano,* no. 3 (1922), under the title "Dada pour tous: L'Optimisme dévoilé."

252. Published in *La Tribune de Genève,* no. 19 (23 January 1920); quotation from Serner, "Das Hirngeschwür," 105; see also Sanouillet's slightly different quote (in *Dada à Paris,* 163) from "Du

Dadaïsme intégral" in the Swiss paper *L'Œuvre,* 16 February 1920; that article was not signed but was probably also submitted by Serner.

253. Tristan Tzara, "Manifeste Dada 1918," in Tzara, *Œuvres complètes,* 1:362.

254. See the reproduction of the cover study in Sanouillet, *Dada à Paris,* [593].

255. The "Connerie des Lilas" of the original is a wordplay on *con* (idiot, stupid jerk) and the *Closerie de Lilas,* the term for particular gardens or small parks used in nineteenth-century Paris for dancing and other entertainment.

256. Francis Picabia, "[Sentences]," *La Pomme de Pins,* 25 February 1922, [1]—a "numéro unique" published on occasion of the Congrès de Paris.

257. Jacques Vaché, letter to Breton, dated 18 November 1917; in *Littérature,* no. 6 (August 1919), 14; see section 5.9.1 above.

258. Stanislaw Ignaz Witkiewicz, *Szalona lokomotywa,* in *Dramaty,* vol. 2 (Warsaw: Panstwowy Instytut Wydanicy, 1962), 593–624; this "piece without thesis in two acts and epilogue" was written in 1923; the original was lost and it had to be retranslated (by K. Puzyna) from a French version that had been commissioned for a performance in Paris in the 1920s.

    See also Émile Zola's fourth part of the Rougon-Macquart cycle, in which the drama of a railway accident, involving the famed locomotive *La Lison,* is describes in realistic detail; *La Bête humaine,* vol. 4 of *Les Rougon-Macquart* (Paris: Gallimard, 1966), 1244–1275.

259. Osip Mandelstam, "The Egyptian Stamp," trans. C. Brown in *The Prose of Osip Mandelstam* (Princeton: Princeton University Press, 1965), 168; for the Russian original, see Mandelstam, *Collected Works,* vol. 2 (New York: Inter-Language Literary Associates, 1966), 59.

260. Aragon, *Anicet,* 152.

261. André Breton, "Clairement," *Littérature,* no. 4 [new series] (1 September 1922), 1, in Breton, *Œuvres complètes,* 1:264.

262. Breton and Soupault, "La Glace sans tain," in *Les Champs magnétiques,* in Breton, *Œuvres complètes,* 1:57; trans. in Breton and Soupault, *The Magnetic Fields,* 28.

263. Jacques Baron, "Autour de *Littérature,*" preface to reprint, in *Littérature* (Paris: Place, 1978), vii–viii.

264. Aragon, *Le Paysan de Paris,* 73; trans. as *Paris Peasant,* 71 (translation slightly modified).

265. The criticism of fashion and its snobbery never turned into a social revolt whose origin Mandelstam fictionalized in the "complaint" of the locomotive about the top hat as ballast left over from the unjust society of the previous century.

266. André Breton, "Second Manifeste du surréalisme," in Breton, *Œuvres complètes,* 1:779; trans. R. Seaver and H. R. Lane in Breton, *Manifestoes of Surrealism* (Ann Arbor: University of Michigan Press, 1972), 122. The practice described is essentially *dadaist,* of course; see the article on Tzara in *Anthologie de la nouvelle poésie française,* 423.

267. The text was first published by Kra in Paris in 1924; the complete passage to which Janet refers reads: "Everybody knows that the head of turkeys is a seven- or eight-faced prism just like the top hat is a prism with seven or eight reflective surfaces. / The top hat swayed on the sea barrier like an enormous mussel that sings on a rock. . . . / The turkey felt lost when he did not manage to move the passerby. The child saw the top hat and, because he was hungry, he took to emptying it of its contents; inside it was a beautiful jellyfish with a parrot beak." Breton, *Poisson soluble,* in *Œuvres complètes,* 1:386.

268. See, e.g., Yolande Papetti, Françoise Valier, Bernard de Freminville, and Serge Tisseron, *La Passion des étoffes chez un neuro-psychiatre: Gaëtan Gatian de Clérambault (1872–1934)* (Paris: Solin, 1990), and the film by Yvon Marciano, *Le Cri de soie* (CH/F/B, 1996).

269. On the psychology of the top hat, see, e.g., Flügel, *The Psychology of Clothes,* 37–38, 71, 209 (on the male costume).

270. André Breton, *L'Amour fou* (Paris: Gallimard, 1937); in Breton, *Œuvres complètes,* 2:680; trans. M. A. Caws as Breton, *Mad Love* (Lincoln: University of Nebraska Press, 1987), 10. His credo appears in the last sentence of *Nadja,* completed in 1928.

271. "Send me the photo of the forest of oak and cork trees / which grows over 400 locomotives abandoned / by the French industry." Blaise Cendrars, *Le Panorama ou les aventures de mes sept*

*oncles* (Paris: Sirène, 1918); in Cendrars, *Édition complète des œuvres,* vol. 1 (Paris: Denoël, 1963), 47; see Bonnet in Breton, *Œuvres complètes,* 2:1708.

272. Georges Auric, letter to Picabia from May 1921; quoted in Sanouillet, *Francis Picabia et "391,"* 2:137.

273. "Without even a glance at the locomotive in the grip of / great barometric roots / who bemoans in the virgin forest all its / deadly boilers." André Breton, "Facteur cheval," in *Le Revolver à cheveux blancs* (Paris: Cahiers libres, 1932); in Breton, *Œuvres complètes,* 2:90. The same book contains lines that are reminiscent of an early age of city life: "I am at the window far away in a city filled with horrors / Outside men with top hats follow each other at regular intervals" ("Non-lieu," 67).

274. André Breton, "Max Ernst" (preface in the catalogue of Ernst's exhibition at René Hilsum's bookstore Au sans pareil, 3 May–3 June 1921); in Breton, *Œuvres complètes,* 1:246. Breton alludes here to the celebrated film by Auguste and Louis Lumière that focuses on the front of a train as it arrives at the Gare La Ciotat in 1894.

See also René Magritte's painting *La Durée poignardée* (Time Transfixed, 1938), which shows a locomotive emerging from a bourgeois fireplace.

275. André Breton, "L'Année des chapeaux rouges," *Littérature,* n.s., no. 3 (1 May 1922), 9; this was the earliest text included in *Poisson soluble.*

276. André Breton, *Poisson soluble,* 351; this part was written between March and May of 1924.

277. Benjamin Péret, "La Nature dévore le progrès et le dépasse," *Minotaure,* no. 10 (winter 1937), 20, 21; on the machine and nature, see Tristan Tzara, "Sur un ride du Soleil" (1922): "the world / a hat with flowers / the world . . . a small locomotive with flowery eyes" (*De nos oiseaux,* in Tzara, *Œuvres complètes,* 1:238–239).

278. Guillermo de Torre, "Poème dadaïste: *Roues* (Madrid, 1920)," *Le Pilhaou-Thibaou,* 10 July 1921, 5.

279. Marcel Noll, quoted in Breton, *Œuvres complètes,* 1:1727. In Breton's questionnaire "What Is Surrealism?" the last answer read: "It is the violet that keeps Tristan Tzara's cantharide-green hats" (in ibid., 2:540).

280. Péret, "La Nature dévore le progrès et le dépasse," 21.

## Conclusion

1. Louis Aragon, "Introduction à 1930," *La Révolution Surréaliste* 5, no. 12 (12 December 1925), 58, 63; one of the two elements Aragon lists subsequently as examples of a "dated" modernity is—could it be otherwise?—the locomotive.

2. Charles Baudelaire, "Le Peintre de la vie moderne IV: La Modernité," in Baudelaire, *Œuvres complètes,* 2 vols. (Paris: Gallimard, 1975–1976), 2:694; trans. J. Mayne in Baudelaire, *The Painter of Modern Life and Other Essays* (London: Phaidon, 1995), 12; see section 1.2.1 above.

# Selected Bibliography

Abel, Hermant. *La Vie à Paris*. 3 vols. Paris: Flammarion, 1917–1919.

*Absolut modern sein: Culture technique in Frankreich 1889–1937*. Berlin: NGBK/Elefanten Press, 1986.

Ades, Dawn. *Dada and Surrealism Reviewed*. London: Arts Council, 1978.

Adler, Max. *Georg Simmels Bedeutung für die Geistesgeschiche*. Vienna: Anzengruber, 1919.

Adorno, Theodor Wiesengrund. *Aesthetic Theory*. Ed. Gretel Adorno and Rolf Tiedemann. Trans. C. Lenhardt. London: Routledge & Kegan Paul, 1984.

Adorno, Theodor Wiesengrund. *Über Walter Benjamin: Aufsätze, Artikel, Briefe*. Rev. ed. Frankfurt a.M.: Suhrkamp, 1990.

Adorno, Theodor Wiesengrund, and Walter Benjamin. *Briefwechsel 1928–1940*. Frankfurt a.M.: Suhrkamp, 1994.

Alexandre, Maxime. *Mémoires d'un surréaliste.* Paris: La Jeune Parque, 1968.

*Anthologie de la nouvelle poésie française.* New ed. Paris: Kra, 1928.

Aragon, Louis. *Anicet ou le panorama, roman.* Paris: Gallimard, 1921.

Aragon, Louis. *Lautréamont et nous.* 1967. Reprint, Pin-Balma: Sables, 1992.

Aragon, Louis. *The Libertine.* Trans. J. Levy. London: Calder, 1993.

Aragon, Louis. *Paris Peasant.* Trans. S. Watson Taylor. London: Cape, 1971.

Aragon, Louis. *Une Vague de rêves.* 1924. Reprint, Paris: Seghers, 1990.

Atget, Eugène. *The Work of Atget.* Vol. 4, *The New Century.* New York: Museum of Modern Art; Munich: Prestel, 1984.

Avenel, Vicomte George d'. *Le Méchanisme de la vie moderne.* 5 vols. Paris: Colin, 1896–1905.

Banville, Théodore de. *Œuvres.* 7 vols. Paris: Lemerre, 1889–1892.

Barbey d'Aurevilly, Jules A. *Œuvres romanesques complètes.* 2 vols. Paris: Gallimard, 1964–1966.

Barbey d'Aurevilly, Jules A. *Premiers articles (1834–1852).* Paris: Les Belles Lettres, 1973.

Barthes, Roland. *Œuvres complètes.* 3 vols. Paris: Seuil, 1993–1995.

Baudelaire, Charles. *Correspondance.* 2 vols. Paris: Gallimard, 1973.

Baudelaire, Charles. *Œuvres complètes.* 2 vols. Paris: Gallimard, 1975–1976.

Baudrillard, Jean. *Symbolic Exchange and Death.* Trans. I. H. Granti. London: Sage, 1993.

Baumann, Zygmunt. *Modernity and Ambivalence.* Cambridge: Polity, 1991.

Bellet, Roger, ed. *Paris au XIXe siècle: Aspects d'un mythe littéraire.* Lyons: Presses Universitaires de Lyon, 1984.

Benjamin, Walter. *The Correspondence of Walter Benjamin, 1910–1940.* Ed. G. Scholem and T. W. Adorno. Trans. M. R. and E. M. Jacobson. Chicago: University of Chicago Press, 1994.

Benjamin, Walter. *Gesammelte Schriften.* 7 vols. Frankfurt a.M.: Suhrkamp, 1974–1989.

Bergius, Hanne. *Das Lachen Dadas.* Gießen: Anabas, 1989.

Bergson, Henri. *Œuvres.* Paris: Presses Universitaires de France, 1959.

Berl, Emmanuel. *Essais.* Paris: Julliard, 1985.

Berman, Marshall. *All That Is Solid Melts into Air: The Experience of Modernity.* New York: Simon & Schuster, 1982.

Bibesco, Princesse Marthe. *Noblesse de robe.* Paris: Grasset, 1928.

Blanche, Jacques-Émile. *Mes modèles. Souvenirs littéraires.* Paris: Stock, 1929.

Boehn, Max von. *Modes and Manners of the Nineteenth Century, as Represented in the Pictures and Engravings of the Time.* Trans. M. Edwardes. 4 vols. London: Dent & Sons, 1927.

Bohrer, Karl Heinz, ed. *Mythos und Moderne: Begriff und Bild einer Rekonstruktion.* Frankfurt a.M.: Suhrkamp, 1983.

Böhringer, Hannes, and Karlfried Gründer, eds. *Ästhetik und Soziologie um die Jahrhundertwende: Georg Simmel.* Frankfurt a.M.: Klostermann, 1976.

Bolz, Norbert W., and Richard Faber, eds. *Antike und Moderne: Zu Walter Benjamins "Passagen."* Würzburg: Königshausen & Neumann, 1986.

Bolz, Norbert W., and Bernd Witte, eds. *Passagen. Walter Benjamins Urgeschichte des XIX. Jahrhunderts.* Munich: Fink, 1984.

Bonnet, Marguerite. *André Breton: Naissance de l'aventure surréaliste.* Rev. ed. Paris: Corti, 1988.

Borie, Jean. *Archéologie de la modernité.* Paris: Grasset & Fasquelle, 1999.

Boulenger, Jacques. *Sous Louis-Philippe: Les dandys.* Paris: Ollendorf, 1907.

Bourdieu, Pierre. *Sociology in Question.* Trans. R. Nice. London: Sage, 1993.

Bovenschen, Silvia, ed. *Die Listen der Mode.* Frankfurt a.M.: Suhrkamp, 1986.

Boym, Svetlana. *Death in Quotation Marks: Cultural Myths of the Modern Poet.* Cambridge, Mass.: Harvard University Press, 1991.

Breton, André. *Œuvres complètes.* 2 vols. Paris: Gallimard, 1988–1992.

Brin, Irene. *Usi e costumi 1920–1940.* Palermo: Sellerio, 1981.

Buchloh, Benjamin H. D., Serge Guilbaut, and David Solkin, eds. *Modernism and Modernity: The Vancouver Conference Papers.* Halifax, N.S.: Press of the Nova Scotia College of Art and Design, 1983.

Buck-Morss, Susan. *The Dialectics of Seeing: Walter Benjamin and the Arcades Project.* Cambridge, Mass.: MIT Press, 1989.

Bulthaupt, Peter, ed. *Materialien zu Benjamins Thesen "Über den Begriff der Geschichte."* Frankfurt a.M.: Suhrkamp, 1975.

Busch, Werner. *Das sentimentalistische Bild: Die Krise der Kunst im 18. Jahrhundert und die Geburt der Moderne.* Munich: Beck, 1993.

Calinescu, Matei. *Faces of Modernity: Avant-garde, Decadence, Kitsch.* Bloomington: Indiana University Press, 1977.

Carassou, Michel. *Jacques Vaché et le Groupe de Nantes.* Paris: Place, 1986.

Carassus, Émilien. *Le Mythe du dandy.* Paris: Colin, 1971.

Chapon, François. *Mystère et splendeurs de Jacques Doucet 1853–1929*. Paris: Lattès, 1984.

Chenoune, Farid. *Des modes et des hommes.* Paris: Flammarion, 1993.

Coleman, Elizabeth Ann. *The Opulent Era: Fashions of Worth, Doucet, and Pingat.* London: Thames & Hudson; New York: Brooklyn Museum, 1989.

Compagnon, Antoine. *The Five Paradoxes of Modernity.* Trans. F. Philip. New York: Columbia University Press, 1994.

Creed, Elizabeth. *Le Dandysme de Jules Barbey d'Aurevilly.* Paris: Droz, 1938.

Dahme, Heinz-Jürgen, and Otthein Rammstedt, eds. *Georg Simmel und die Moderne: Neue Interpretationen und Materialien.* Frankfurt a.M.: Suhrkamp, 1984.

*De la mode et des lettres.* Paris: Musée de la Mode et du Costume/Palais Galliera, 1984.

Deleuze, Gilles. *The Fold: Leibniz and the Baroque.* Trans. T. Conley. London: Athlone, 1993.

Deleuze, Gilles. *The Logic of Sense.* Trans. M. Lester with C. Stivale. London: Athlone, 1990.

Delord, Taxile. *Physiologie de la parisienne.* Paris: Aubert/Lavigne, 1873.

Delvau, Alfred. *Les Dessous de Paris.* Paris: Poulet-Malassis & de Broise, 1860.

de Man, Paul. *Blindness and Insight: Essays in the Rhetoric of Contemporary Criticism.* New York: Oxford University Press, 1971.

Eigeldinger, Marc. *Lumières du mythe.* Paris: Presses Universitaires de France, 1983.

Einstein, Carl, and Paul Westheim, eds. *Europa Almanach.* Potsdam: Kiepenheuer, 1925.

Eisenstadt, S. N., ed. *Patterns of Modernity.* Vol. 1, *The West.* London: Pinter, 1987.

Engels, Friedrich. *Anti-Dühring* (1876–1878, 1880). In vol. 25 of Karl Marx and Friedrich Engels, *Collected Works.* London: Lawrence & Wishart, 1983.

Engels, Friedrich. *Dialectics of Nature* (1873–1883). In vol. 25 of Karl Marx and Friedrich Engels, *Collected Works*. London: Lawrence & Wishart, 1983.

Falke, Jacob von. *Die Geschichte des modernen Geschmacks*. Leipzig: Weigel, 1866.

Fargue, Léon-Paul. *De la mode*. Paris: Éditions littéraires de France, 1945.

Fausch, Deborah, et al., eds. *Architecture: In Fashion*. New York: Princeton Architectural Press, 1994.

Fietkau, Wolfgang. *Schwanengesang auf 1848: Ein Rendez-vous am Louvre. Baudelaire, Marx, Proudhon und Victor Hugo*. Reinbek bei Hamburg: Rowohlt, 1978.

Fontainas, André. *De Stéphane Mallarmé à Paul Valéry: Notes d'un témoin 1894–1922*. Paris: Bernard, 1928.

Fortassier, Rose. *Les Écrivains français et la mode: De Balzac à nos jours*. Paris: Presses Universitaires de France, 1988.

Foster, Hal. *Compulsive Beauty*. Cambridge, Mass.: MIT Press, 1993.

Frisby, David. *Fragments of Modernity: Theories of Modernity in the Work of Simmel, Kracauer, and Benjamin*. Cambridge: Polity, 1985.

Frisby, David. *Sociological Impressionism: A Reassessment of Georg Simmel's Social Theory*. 2d ed. London: Routledge, 1992.

Froidevaux, Gérald. *Baudelaire: Représentation et modernité*. Paris: Corti, 1989.

Gassen, Kurt, and Michael Landmann, eds. *Buch des Dankes an Georg Simmel*. Berlin: Duncker & Humblot, 1958.

Gauthier, Xavière. *Surréalisme et sexualité*. Paris: Gallimard, 1971.

Gautier, Théophile. *De la mode*. Paris: Poulet-Malassis & de Broise, 1858.

Geffroy, Gustave. *Constantin Guys: L'Historien du Second Empire*. 1904. Reprint, Paris: Crès, 1920.

Geffroy, Gustave. *Images du jour et de la nuit*. 1897. Reprint, Paris: Grasset, 1924.

Giddens, Anthony. *Capitalism and Modern Social Theory: An Analysis of the Writings of Marx, Durkheim, and Max Weber*. London: Cambridge University Press, 1971.

Giddens, Anthony. *Modernity and Self-Identity*. Cambridge: Polity, 1991.

Giedion, Sigfried. *Mechanization Takes Command: A Contribution to Anonymous History*. New York: Oxford University Press, 1948.

Gomez, Carillo Enrique. *Psychologie de la mode*. Paris: Garnier, 1910.

Goncourt, Edmond de, and Jules de Goncourt. *Journal: Mémoires de la vie littéraire*. 4 vols. Paris: Fasquelle & Flammarion, 1956.

Gourmont, Rémy de. *Decadence and Other Essays on the Culture of Ideas*. Trans. W. A. Bradley. London: Grant Richards, 1922.

Gourmont, Rémy de. *Promenades philosophiques*. Paris: Mercure de France, 1905.

Grandville [Jean-Ignace-Isidore Gérard]. *Un Autre Monde*. Paris: Fournier, 1844.

Grumbach, Didier. *Histoires de la mode*. Paris: Seuil, 1993.

Grund, Helen. *Vom Wesen der Mode*. Munich: Meisterschule für Deutschlands Buchdrucker, 1935.

Guégan, Stéphane, ed. *Théophile Gautier: La Critique en liberté*. Les Dossiers du Musée d'Orsay, no. 62. Paris: Réunion des musées nationaux, 1997.

Habermas, Jürgen. *The Philosophical Discourse of Modernity*. Trans. F. Lawrence. Cambridge, Mass.: MIT Press, 1987.

Harvey, John. *Men in Black*. London: Reaktion, 1995.

Hegel, Georg Wilhelm Friedrich. *Aesthetics: Lectures on Fine Art*. Trans. T. M. Knox. Oxford: Clarendon, 1988.

Hobsbawn, Eric J. *The Age of Capital: 1848–1875*. London: Weidenfeld & Nicolson, 1975.

Hobsbawn, Eric. *On History.* London: Weidenfeld & Nicolson, 1997.

Hollander, Anne. *Seeing through Clothes*. New York: Viking, 1978.

Hollander, Anne. *Sex and Suits: The Evolution of Modern Dress*. New York: Kodansha Int., 1994.

Huelsenbeck, Richard. *Dada siegt; eine Bilanz des Dadaismus*. Berlin: Malik, 1920.

Hugnet, Georges. *L'Aventure Dada (1916–1922)*. Paris: Galerie de l'Institut, 1957.

Jameson, Fredric. *The Political Unconscious: Narrative as a Socially Symbolic Act*. London: Methuen, 1981.

Jauß, Hans Robert. *Literaturgeschichte als Provokation*. Frankfurt a.M.: Suhrkamp, 1970.

Johnson, Barbara. *A World of Difference*. Baltimore: Johns Hopkins University Press, 1987.

Kaern, Michael, Bernard S. Phillips, and Robert S. Cohen, eds. *Georg Simmel and Contemporary Sociology.* Dordrecht: Kluwer, 1990.

Kant, Immanuel. *The Critique of Judgment*. Trans. J. C. Meredith. Oxford: Clarendon, 1952.

Kempf, Roger. *Dandies: Baudelaire et Cie.* Paris: Seuil, 1977.

Koella, Rudolf. *Constantin Guys*. Exhib. Cat. Winterthur: Kunstmuseum, 1989.

Koselleck, Reinhart. *Critique and Crisis: Enlightenment and the Pathogenesis of Modern Society.* Oxford: Berg, 1988.

Koselleck, Reinhart. *Futures Past: On the Semantics of Historical Time.* Trans. K. Tribe. Cambridge, Mass.: MIT Press, 1985.

Kracauer, Siegfried. *The Mass Ornament: Weimar Essays.* Trans. and ed. T. Y. Levin. Cambridge, Mass.: Harvard University Press, 1995.

Kracauer, Siegfried. *Offenbach and the Paris of His Time.* Trans. G. David and E. Mosbacher. London: Constable, 1937.

Lartigue, Jacques Henri. *Diary of a Century.* Ed. R. Avedon. Trans. C. van Splunteren. New York: Penguin, 1970.

Lecercle, Jean-Pierre. *Mallarmé et la mode.* Paris: Séguier, 1989.

Lefebvre, Henri. *Introduction to Modernity: Twelve Preludes, September 1959–May 1961.* Trans. J. Moore. London: Verso, 1995.

Léger, François. *La Pensée de Georg Simmel: Contribution à l'histoire des idées en Allemagne au début du XXe siècle.* Paris: Kimé, 1989.

Lehnert, Gertrud, ed. *Mode, Weiblichkeit und Modernität.* Dortmund: Ebersbach, 1998.

Lemoine-Luccioni, Eugénie. *La Robe: Essai psychanalytique sur le vêtement.* Paris: Seuil, 1983.

Lenk, Elisabeth. *Der springende Narziß: André Bretons poetischer Materialismus.* Munich: Rogner & Bernhard, 1971.

Leroy-Beaulieu, Paul. *Le Travail des femmes au XIXe siècle.* Paris: Charpentier, 1873.

Levine, Donald N. *The Flight from Ambiguity.* Chicago: University of Chicago Press, 1985.

Lichtblau, Klaus. *Kulturkrise und Soziologie um die Jahrhundertwende: Zur Genealogie der Kultursoziologie in Deutschland.* Frankfurt a.M.: Suhrkamp, 1996.

Lilly, Reginald, ed. *The Ancients and Moderns.* Bloomington: Indiana University Press, 1996.

Lindner, Burkhardt, and W. Martin Lüdke, eds. *Materialien zur ästhetische Theorie: Theodor W. Adornos Konstruktion der Moderne*. Frankfurt a.M.: Suhrkamp, 1980.

Lipovetsky, Gilles. *The Empire of Fashion: Dressing Modern Democracy*. Trans. C. Porter. Princeton: Princeton University Press, 1994.

Loos, Adolf. *Spoken into the Void: Collected Essays, 1897–1900*. Trans. J. O. Newman and J. H. Smith. Cambridge, Mass.: MIT Press, 1982.

Löwith, Karl. *Permanence and Change: Lectures on the Philosophy of History*. Cape Town: Haum, 1969.

Lukács, Georg. *History and Class Consciousness: Studies in Marxist Dialectics*. Trans. R. Livingstone. London: Merlin, 1971.

Maigron, Louis. *Le Romantisme et la mode: D'après des documents inédits*. Paris: Champion, 1911.

Mallarmé, Stéphane. *Correspondance*. 11 vols. Paris: Gallimard, 1965–1985.

Mallarmé, Stéphane. *Le "livre" de Mallarmé*. Ed. Jacques Scherer. New ed. Paris: Gallimard, 1977.

Mallarmé, Stéphane. *Œuvres complètes*. Paris: Gallimard, 1945.

Martin-Fugier, Anne. *La Vie élégante ou la formation du Tout-Paris: 1815–1848*. Paris: Fayard, 1990.

Marx, Karl. *The Capital,* vol. 1 (1890). Vol. 35 of Karl Marx and Friedrich Engels, *Collected Works*. London: Lawrence & Wishart, 1996.

Marx, Karl. *The Eighteenth Brumaire of Louis Bonaparte* (1852). In vol. 11 of Karl Marx and Friedrich Engels, *Collected Works*. London: Lawrence & Wishart, 1979.

Marx, Karl, and Friedrich Engels. *The Communist Manifesto*. In vol. 6 of Marx and Engels, *Collected Works*. London: Lawrence & Wishart, 1976.

*Max Ernst: Das Rendezvous der Freunde.* Exhib. cat. Cologne: Museum Ludwig, 1991.

Mayer, Hans. *Der Zeitgenosse Walter Benjamin.* Frankfurt a.M.: Jüdischer Verlag, 1992.

McCormick, Peter J. *Modernity, Aesthetics, and the Bounds of Art.* Ithaca: Cornell University Press, 1990.

Menninghaus, Winfried. *Schwellenkunde: Walter Benjamins Passage des Mythos.* Frankfurt a.M.: Suhrkamp, 1986.

Michelet, Jules. *Cours au Collège de France.* 2 vols. Paris: Gallimard, 1995.

*La Mode, l'invention.* Change, 4. Paris: Seuil, 1969.

Mondor, Henri. *Vie de Mallarmé.* Paris: Gallimard, 1941.

Müller, Horst. *Lebensphilosophie und Religion bei Georg Simmel.* Berlin: Duncker & Humblot, 1960.

Naville, Pierre. *La Révolution et les intellectuels.* New ed. Paris: Gallimard, 1975.

Nectoux, Jean-Michel. *Mallarmé: Un Clair Regard dans les ténèbres: Peinture, musique, poésie.* Paris: Biro, 1998.

Newmark, Kevin, ed. *Phantom Proxies: Symbolism and the Rhetoric of History.* Special issue of *Yale French Studies,* no. 74 (1988).

Oehler, Dolf. *Pariser Bilder I (1830–1848): Antibourgeoise Ästhetik bei Baudelaire, Daumier und Heine.* Frankfurt a.M.: Suhrkamp, 1979.

Papetti, Yolande, Françoise Valier, Bernard de Freminville, and Serge Tisseron. *La Passion des étoffes chez un neuro-psychiatre: Gaëtan Gatian de Clérambault (1872–1934).* Paris: Solin, 1990.

Perrault, Charles. *Parallèle des anciens et des modernes. En ce qui regarde les arts et les sciences.* Intros. H.-R. Jauß and M. Imdahl. Munich: Eidos, 1964.

Perrot, Philippe. *Fashioning the Bourgeoisie: A History of Clothing in the Nineteenth Century.* Trans. R. Bienvenu. Princeton: Princeton University Press, 1994.

Perrot, Philippe. *Le Luxe: Une Richesse entre faste et confort, XVIIIe–XIXe siècles.* Paris: Seuil, 1995.

Peyré, Yves, ed. *Mallarmé 1842–1898: Un Destin d'écriture.* Paris: Gallimard/Réunion des Musées Nationaux, 1998.

Pichois, Claude. *Littérature et progrès: Vitesse et vision du monde.* Neuchâtel: La Baconnière, 1973.

Pippin, Robert B. *Modernism as a Philosophical Problem.* 2d ed. Oxford: Blackwell, 1999.

Poschardt, Ulf. *Anpassen.* Munich: Rogner & Bernhard, 1998.

Rammstedt, Otthein, ed. *Simmel und die frühen Soziologen. Nähe und Distanz zu Durkheim, Tönnies und Max Weber.* Frankfurt a.M.: Suhrkamp, 1988.

Raphael, Max. *Proudhon Marx Picasso: Three Essays in Marxist Asthetics.* Trans. I. Marcuse. London: Lawrence & Wishart, 1980.

Raphael, Max. *Theorie des geistigen Schaffens auf marxistischer Grundlage.* Frankfurt a.M.: Fischer, 1974.

Ray, Man. *Self Portrait.* Reprint, New York: Graphic Society, 1988.

Rigaut, Jacques. *Écrits.* Paris: Gallimard, 1970.

Roubaud, Jacques. *Au pays des mannequins.* Paris: Éditions de France, 1928.

Salzinger, Helmut. *Swinging Benjamin.* Rev. ed. Hamburg: Kellner, 1990.

Sanouillet, Michel. *Dada à Paris.* Paris: Pauvert, 1965.

Sanouillet, Michel, ed. *Francis Picabia et "391."* 2 vols. Paris: Belfond/Losfeld, 1960, 1966.

Sayer, Derek. *Capitalism and Modernity: An Excursus on Marx and Weber.* London: Routledge, 1991.

Schmidt, Alfred. *History and Structure: An Essay on Hegelian-Marxist and Structuralist Theories on History.* Trans. J. Herf. Cambridge, Mass.: MIT Press, 1981.

*The Second Empire: Art in France under Napoleon III.* Exhib. cat. Philadelphia: Philadelphia Museum of Art, 1978.

Simmel, Georg. *Gesamtausgabe.* Ed. O. Rammstedt. 16 vols. to date. Frankfurt a.M.: Suhrkamp, 1989–.

Smith, Gary, ed. *On Walter Benjamin: Critical Essays and Recollections.* Cambridge, Mass.: MIT Press, 1988.

Snell, Robert. *Théophile Gautier.* Oxford: Clarendon, 1982.

Sombart, Werner. *Liebe, Luxus und Kapitalismus: Über die Enstehung der modernen Welt aus dem Geist der Verschwendung.* 2d ed. Berlin: Wagenbach, 1992.

Steele, Valerie. *Paris Fashion: A Cultural History.* New York: Oxford University Press, 1988.

Stern, Radu. *Gegen den Strich/À contre-courant. Kleider von Künstlern/Vêtements d'artistes 1900–1940.* Berne: Benteli, 1992.

Tarde, Gabriel. *Les Lois de l'imitation.* Paris: Alcan, 1890.

Tzara, Tristan. *Œuvres complètes.* 6 vols. Paris: Flammarion, 1975–1985.

Vaché, Jacques. *Quarante-trois lettres de guerre à Jeanne Derrien.* Ed. Georges Sebbag. Paris: Place, 1991.

Vaché, Jacques. *Soixante-dix-neuf lettres de guerre.* Ed. Georges Sebbag. Paris: Place, 1989.

Varnier, Henriette, with Guy P. Palmade. *La Mode et ses métiers: Frivolités et luttes des classes 1830–1870.* Paris: Colin, 1960.

Vinken, Barbara. *Mode nach der Mode: Kleid und Geist am Ende des 20. Jahrhunderts.* Frankfurt a.M.: Fischer, 1993.

Virmaux, Alain, and Odette Virmaux. *Cravan, Vaché, Rigaut.* Mortemart: Rougerie, 1982.

Weber, Max. *The Protestant Ethic and the Spirit of Capitalism.* Trans. T. Parsons. London: Allen & Unwin, 1976.

Weidmann, Heiner. *Flanerie, Sammlung, Spiel: Die Erinnerung des 19. Jahrhunderts bei Walter Benjamin.* Munich: Fink, 1992.

Wellmer, Albrecht. *Endgames: The Irreconcilable Nature of Modernity.* Trans. D. Midgley. Cambridge, Mass.: MIT Press, 1998.

Wigley, Mark. *White Walls, Designer Dresses: The Fashioning of Modern Architecture.* Cambridge, Mass.: MIT Press, 1996.

Williams, Rosalind H. *Dream Worlds: Mass Consumption in Late Nineteenth-Century France.* Berkeley: University of California Press, 1982.

Wilson, Elizabeth. *Adorned in Dreams: Fashion and Modernity.* Berkeley: University of California Press, 1987.

Wißmann, H., ed. *Walter Benjamin et Paris.* Paris: Cerf, 1986.

# Index